Get the eBooks FREE!

(PDF, ePub, Kindle, and liveBook all included)

We believe that once you buy a book from us, you should be able to read it in any format we have available. To get electronic versions of this book at no additional cost to you, purchase and then register this book at the Manning website.

Go to https://www.manning.com/freebook and follow the instructions to complete your pBook registration.

That's it!
Thanks from Manning!

Real-World Cryptography

Real-World Cryptography

DAVID WONG

MANNING

SHELTER ISLAND

For online information and ordering of this and other Manning books, please visit
www.manning.com. The publisher offers discounts on this book when ordered in quantity.
For more information, please contact

Special Sales Department
Manning Publications Co.
20 Baldwin Road
PO Box 761
Shelter Island, NY 11964
Email: orders@manning.com

Manning Publications Co.
20 Baldwin Road
PO Box 761
Shelter Island, NY 11964

Development editor: Marina Michaels
Technical development editor: Sam Zaydel
Review editor: Mihaela Batinic
Production editor: Andy Marinkovich
Copy editor: Frances Buran
Proofreader: Keri Hales
Technical proofreader: Michal Rutka
Typesetter: Dennis Dalinnik
Cover designer: Marija Tudor

ISBN: 9781617296710
Printed in the United States of America

To my parents, Anne Cerclet and Henry Wong, who nurtured curiosity in me.
To my wife, Felicia Lupu, who supported me throughout this journey.

contents

preface

As you've picked up this book, you might be wondering, why another book on cryptography? Or even, why should I read this book? To answer this, you have to understand when it all started.

A book, years in the making

Today, if you want to learn about almost anything, you Google it, or Bing it, or Baidu it—you get the idea. Yet, for cryptography, and depending on what you're looking for, resources can be quite lacking. This is something I ran into a long time ago and which has been a continuous source of frustration since then.

Back when I was in school, I had to implement a differential power analysis attack for a class. This attack was a breakthrough in cryptanalysis at that time, as it was the first side-channel attack to be published. A differential power analysis attack is something magical: by measuring the power consumption of a device while it encrypts or decrypts something, you're able to extract its secrets. I realized that great papers could convey great ideas, while putting little effort in clarity and intelligibility. I remember banging my head against the wall trying to figure out what the author was trying to say. Worse, I couldn't find good online resources that explained the paper. So I banged my head a wee more, and finally I got it. And then, I thought, maybe I could help others like me who will have to go through this ordeal.

Motivated, I drew some diagrams, animated them, and recorded myself going over them. That was my first YouTube video on cryptography: https://www.youtube.com/watch?v=gbqNCgVcXsM.

Years later, after I uploaded the video, I still receive praises from random people on the internet. Just yesterday, as I'm writing this preface, someone posted, "Thank you, really a great explanation that probably saved me hours of trying to understand that paper."

What a reward! This baby step in adventuring myself on the other side of the educational landscape was enough to make me want to do more. I started recording more of these videos, and then I started a blog to write about cryptography. You can check it out here: https://cryptologie.net.

Before starting this book, I had amassed nearly 500 articles explaining the many concepts that stand beyond this intro. This was all just practice. In the back of my mind, the idea of writing a book was slowly maturing years before Manning Publications would reach out to me with a book proposal.

The real-world cryptographer curriculum

I finished my bachelor's in theoretical mathematics and didn't know what was next for me. I had also been programming my whole life, and I wanted to reconcile the two. Naturally, I became curious about cryptography, which seemed to have the best of both worlds, and started reading the different books at my disposal. I quickly discovered my life's calling.

Some things were annoying, though: in particular, the long introductions that would start with history; I was only interested in the technicalities and always had been. I swore to myself, if I ever wrote a book about cryptography, I would not write a single line on Vigenère ciphers, Caesar ciphers, and other vestiges of history. And so, after obtaining a master of cryptography at the University of Bordeaux, I thought I was ready for the real world. Little did I know.

I believed that my degree was enough, but my education lacked a lot about the real-world protocols I was about to attack. I had spent a lot of time learning about the mathematics of elliptic curves but nothing about how these were used in cryptographic algorithms. I had learned about LFSRs, and ElGamal, and DES, and a series of other cryptographic primitives that I would never see again.

When I started working in the industry at Matasano, which then became NCC Group, my first gig was to audit OpenSSL, the most popular SSL/TLS implementation—the code that basically encrypted the whole internet. Oh boy, did it hurt my brain. I remember coming back home every day with a strong headache. What a trainwreck of a library and a protocol! I had no idea at the time that I would, years later, become a coauthor of TLS 1.3, the latest version of the protocol.

But, at that point, I was already thinking, "This is what I should have learned in school. The knowledge I'm gaining now is what would have been useful to prepare me for the real world!" After all, I was now a specialized security practitioner in cryptography. I was reviewing real-world cryptographic applications. I was doing the job that one would wish they had after finishing a cryptography degree. I implemented, verified, used, and advised on what cryptographic algorithms to use. This is the reason

I'm the first reader of the book I'm writing. This is what I would have written to my past self in order to prepare him for the real world.

Where most of the bugs are

My consulting job led me to audit many real-world cryptographic applications such as OpenSSL, the encrypted backup system of Google, the TLS 1.3 implementation of Cloudflare, the certificate authority protocol of Let's Encrypt, the sapling protocol of the Zcash cryptocurrency, the threshold proxy re-encryption scheme of NuCypher, and dozens of other real-world cryptographic applications that I unfortunately cannot mention publicly.

Early in my job, I was tasked to audit the custom protocol a well-known corporation had written to encrypt their communications. It turns out that it was using signatures on almost everything but the ephemeral keys, which completely broke the whole protocol as one could have easily replaced those—a rookie mistake from anyone with some experience with secure transport protocols, but something that was missed by people who thought they were experienced enough to roll their own crypto. I remember explaining the vulnerability at the end of the engagement and a room full of engineers turning silent for a good 30 seconds.

This story repeated itself many times during my career. There was a time when, while auditing a cryptocurrency for another client, I found a way to forge transactions from already existing ones, due to some ambiguity of what was being signed. Looking at TLS implementations for another client, I found some subtle ways to break an RSA implementation, which in turn, transformed into a white paper with one of the inventors of RSA, leading to a number of Common Vulnerabilities and Exposures (CVEs) reported to a dozen of open source projects. More recently, while reading about the newer Matrix chat protocol as part of writing my book, I realized that their authentication protocol was broken, leading to a break of their end-to-end encryption. There are so many details that can, unfortunately, collapse under you when making use of cryptography. At this point, I knew I had to write something about these. This is why my book contains many of these anecdotes.

As part of the job, I would review cryptography libraries and applications in a multitude of programming languages. I discovered bugs (for example, CVE-2016-3959 in Golang's standard library), I researched ways that libraries could fool you into misusing those (for example, my paper "How to Backdoor Diffie-Hellman"), and I advised on what libraries to use. Developers never knew what library to use, and I always found the answer to be tricky.

I went on to invent the Disco protocol (https://discocrypto.com; https://embeddeddisco.com) and wrote its fully-featured cryptographic library in less than 1,000 lines of code, and that, in several languages. Disco only relied on two cryptographic primitives: the permutation of SHA-3 and Curve25519. Yes, from only those two things implemented in 1,000 lines of code, a developer could do any type of authenticated key exchange, signatures, encryption, MACs, hashing, key derivation, and so on. This gave me a unique perspective as to what a good cryptography library was supposed to be.

I wanted my book to contain these kinds of practical insights. So naturally, the different chapters contain examples on how to apply "crypto" in different programming languages, using well-respected cryptographic libraries.

A need for a new book?

As I was giving one of my annual cryptography training sessions at Black Hat (a well-known security conference), one student came to me and asked if I could recommend a good book or online course on cryptography. I remember advising the student to read a book from Boneh and Shoup and to attend Cryptography I from Boneh on Coursera. (I also recommend both of these resources at the end of this book.)

The student told me, "Ah, I tried, it's too theoretical!" This answer stayed with me. I disagreed at first, but slowly realized that they were right. Most of the resources are pretty heavy in math, and most developers interacting with cryptography don't want to deal with math. What else was there for them?

The other two somewhat-respected resources at the time were *Applied Cryptography* and *Cryptography Engineering* (both books by Bruce Schneier). But these books were starting to be quite outdated. *Applied Cryptography* spent four chapters on block ciphers with a whole chapter on cipher modes of operation but none on authenticated encryption. The more recent *Cryptography Engineering* had a single mention of elliptic curve cryptography in a footnote. On the other hand, many of my videos or blog posts were becoming good primary references for some cryptographic concepts. I knew I could do something special.

Gradually, many of my students started becoming interested in cryptocurrencies, asking more and more questions on the subject. At the same time, I started to audit more and more cryptocurrency applications. I later moved to a job at Facebook to lead security for the Libra cryptocurrency (now known as Diem). Cryptocurrency was, at that time, one of the hottest fields to work in, mixing a multitude of extremely interesting cryptographic primitives that so far had seen little-to-no real-world use (zero knowledge proofs, aggregated signatures, threshold cryptography, multi-party computations, consensus protocols, cryptographic accumulators, verifiable random functions, verifiable delay functions, . . . the list goes on). And yet, no cryptography book included a chapter on cryptocurrencies. I was now in a unique position.

I knew I could write something that would tell students, developers, consultants, security engineers, and others what modern applied cryptography was all about. This was going to be a book with few formulas but filled with many diagrams. This was going to be a book with little history but filled with modern stories about cryptographic failures that I had witnessed for real. This was going to be a book with little about legacy algorithms but filled with cryptography that I've personally seen being used at scale: TLS, the Noise protocol framework, the Signal protocol, cryptocurrencies, HSMs, threshold cryptography, and so on. This was going to be a book with little theoretical cryptography but filled with what could become relevant: password-authentication key exchanges, zero-knowledge proofs, post-quantum cryptography, and so on.

When Manning Publications reached out to me in 2018, asking if I wanted to write a book on cryptography, I already knew the answer. I already knew what I wanted to write. I had just been waiting for someone to give me the opportunity and the excuse to spend my time writing the book I had in mind. Coincidentally, Manning has a series of "real-world" books, and so naturally, I suggested that my book extend it. What you have in front of you is the result of more than two years of hard work and much love. I hope you like it.

acknowledgments

Thank you to Marina Michaels for her continued help and insights and without whom this book probably wouldn't have come to completion.

Thank you to Frances Buran, Sam Zaydel, Michael Rosenberg, Pascal Knecht, Seth David Schoen, Eyal Ronen, Saralynn Chick, Robert Seacord, Eloi Manuel, Rob Wood, Hunter Monk, Jean-Christophe Forest, Liviu Bartha, Mattia Reggiani, Olivier Guerra, Andrey Labunov, Carl Littke, Yan Ivnitskiy, Keller Fuchs, Roman Zabicki, M K Saravanan, Sarah Zennou, Daniel Bourdrez, Jason Noll, Ilias Cherkaoui, Felipe De Lima, Raul Siles, Matteo Bocchi, John Woods, Kostas Chalkias, Yolan Romailler, Gerardo Di Giacomo, Gregory Nazario, Rob Stubbs, Ján Jančár, Gabe Pike, Kiran Tummala, Stephen Singam, Jeremy O'Donoghue, Jeremy Boone, Thomas Duboucher, Charles Guillemet, Ryan Sleevi, Lionel Rivière, Benjamin Larsen, Gabriel Giono, Daan Sprenkels, Andreas Krogen, Vadim Lyubashevsky, Samuel Neves, Steven (Dongze) Yue, Tony Patti, Graham Steel, Jean-Philippe Aumasson, Fabian Becker, Daniel Li, Jeff Lau, Filipe Casal, Curtis Light, Vincent Herbert, Donald Piret, Dan Cashman, Ricky Han, Tshaka Lekholoane, and all the livebook commenters for the many discussions and corrections, as well as technical and editorial feedback.

To all the reviewers: Adhir Ramjiawan, Al Pezewski, Al Rahimi, Alessandro Campeis, Bobby Lin, Chad Davis, David T Kerns, Domingo Salazar, Eddy Vluggen, Gábor László Hajba, Geert Van Laethem, Grzegorz Bernaś, Harald Kuhn, Hugo Durana, Jan Pieter Herweijer, Jeff Smith, Jim Karabatsos, Joel Kotarski, John Paraskevopoulos, Matt Van Winkle, Michal Rutka, Paul Grebenc, Richard Lebel, Ruslan Shevchenko, Sanjeev Jaiswal, Shawn P Bolan, Thomas Doylend, William Rudenmalm, your suggestions helped make this a better book.

about this book

It has now been more than two years since I've started writing *Real-World Cryptography*. I originally intended for it to be an introduction to all there is to know about the type of cryptography that is used in the real world. But, of course, that's an impossible task. No field can be summarized in a single book. For this reason, I had to strike a balance between how much detail I wanted to give the reader and how much area I wanted to cover. I hope you find yourself in the same box I ended up wiggling myself into. If you're looking for a practical book that teaches you the cryptography that companies and products implement and use, and if you're curious about how real-world cryptography works underneath the surface but aren't looking for a reference book with all the implementation details, then this book is for you.

Who should read this book

Here is a list of what I believe are the types of people (although please don't let anyone put you in a box) that would benefit from this book.

Students

If you're studying computer science, security, or cryptography and want to learn about cryptography as used in the real world (because you are either targeting a job in the industry or want to work on applied subjects in academia), then I believe this is the textbook for you. Why? Because, as I said in the preface, I was once such a student, and I wrote the book I wish I had then.

Security practitioners

Pentesters, security consultants, security engineers, security architects, and other security roles comprised most of the students I had when I taught applied cryptography. Due to this, this material has been refined by the many questions I received while I was trying to explain complicated cryptography concepts to non-cryptographers. As a security practitioner myself, this book is also shaped by the cryptography I've audited for large companies and the bugs that I learned about or found along the way.

Developers who use cryptography directly or indirectly

This work has also been shaped by the many discussions I've had with clients and coworkers, who were by and large neither security practitioners nor cryptographers. Today, it's becoming harder and harder to write code without touching cryptography, and as such, you need to have some understanding of what you're using. This book gives you that understanding using coding examples in different programming languages and more if you're curious.

Cryptographers curious about other fields

This book is an introduction to applied cryptography that's useful to people like me. I wrote this first to myself, remember. If I managed to do a good job, a theoretical cryptographer should be able to get a quick understanding of what the applied cryptography world looks like; another one working on symmetric encryption should be able to swiftly pick up on password-authenticated key exchanges by reading the relevant chapter; a third one working with protocols should be able to rapidly get a good understanding of quantum cryptography; and so on.

Engineering and product managers who want to understand more

This book also attempts to answer questions that I find to be more product-oriented: what are the tradeoffs and limitations of these approaches? What risk am I getting into? Would this path help me comply with regulations? Do I need to do this and that to work with a government?

Curious people who want to know what real-world crypto is about

You don't need to be any of the previous types I've listed to read this book. You just need to be curious about cryptography as used in the real world. Keep in mind, I don't teach the history of cryptography, and I don't teach the basics of computer science, so at the very least, you should have heard of cryptography before getting into a book like this one.

Assumed knowledge, the long version

What will you need in order to get the most out of this book? You should know that this book assumes that you have some basic understanding of how your laptop or the internet works, and at least, you should have heard of encryption. The book is about real-world cryptography, and so it will be hard to put things in context if you're not at ease with computers or if you've never heard of the word *encryption* before.

Assuming that you somewhat know what you're getting into, it'll be a real plus if you know what bits and bytes are and if you've seen or even used bitwise operations like XOR, shift left, and those kinds of things. Is it a deal breaker if you haven't? No, but it might mean that you will have to stop for a few minutes here and there to do some Googling before you can resume reading.

Actually, no matter how qualified you are, when reading this book, you'll probably have to stop from time to time in order to get more information from the internet. Either because I (shame on me) forgot to define a term before using it or because I wrongly assumed you would know about it. In any case, this should not be a huge deal as I try to ELY5 (explain like you're 5) as best as I can the different concepts that I introduce.

Finally, when I use the word *cryptography*, your brain is probably thinking about math. If, in addition to that thought, your face grimaced, then you'll be glad to know that you shouldn't worry too much about that. *Real-World Cryptography* is about teaching insights so that you gain an intuition about how it all works, and it attempts to avoid the mathy nitty-gritty when possible.

Of course, I'd be lying if I said that no math was involved in the making of this book. There's no teaching cryptography without math. So here's what I'll say: it helps if you have achieved a good level in mathematics, but if you haven't, it shouldn't prevent you from reading most of this book. Some chapters will be unfriendly to you unless you have a more advanced understanding of math, specifically the last chapters (14 and 15) on quantum cryptography and next-generation cryptography, but nothing is impossible, and you can get through those chapters with willpower and by Googling about matrix multiplications and other things you might not know about. If you decide to skip these, make sure you don't skip chapter 16, as it's the icing on top of the cake.

How this book is organized: A roadmap

Real-World Cryptography is split into two parts. The first part is meant to be read from the first page to the last and covers most of the ingredients of cryptography: the stuff you'll end up using like Lego to construct more complex systems and protocols.

- Chapter 1 is an introduction to real-world cryptography, giving you some idea of what you'll learn.
- Chapter 2 talks about hash functions, a fundamental algorithm of cryptography used to create unique identifiers from bytestrings.
- Chapter 3 talks about data authentication and how you can ensure that nobody modifies your messages.
- Chapter 4 talks about encryption, which allows two participants to hide their communications from observers.

- Chapter 5 introduces key exchanges, which allows you to negotiate a common secret with someone else interactively.
- Chapter 6 describes asymmetric encryption, which allows multiple people to encrypt messages to a single person.
- Chapter 7 talks about signatures, cryptographic equivalents of pen-and-paper signatures.
- Chapter 8 talks about randomness and how to manage your secrets.

The second part of this book contains the systems that are built out of these ingredients.

- Chapter 9 teaches you how encryption and authentication are used to secure connections between machines (via the SSL/TLS protocol).
- Chapter 10 describes end-to-end encryption, which is really about how people like you and I can trust one another.
- Chapter 11 shows how machines authenticate people and how people can help machines sync with one another.
- Chapter 12 introduces the nascent field of cryptocurrencies.
- Chapter 13 spotlights hardware cryptography, the devices that you can use to prevent your keys from being extracted.

There are two bonus chapters: chapter 14 on post-quantum cryptography and chapter 15 on next-generation cryptography. These two fields are starting to make their way into products and companies, either because they are getting more relevant or because they are becoming more practical and efficient. While I won't judge you if you skip these last two chapters, you do have to read through chapter 16 (final words) before placing this book back on a shelf. Chapter 16 summarizes the different challenges and the different lessons that a cryptography practitioner (meaning you, once you finish this book) has to keep in mind. As Spider-Man's Uncle Ben said, "With great power comes great responsibility."

About the code

This book contains many examples of source code both in numbered listings and in line with normal text. In both cases, source code is formatted in a `fixed-width font like this` to separate it from ordinary text. Sometimes code is also **in bold** to highlight code that has changed from previous steps in the chapter, such as when a new feature adds to an existing line of code.

In many cases, the original source code has been reformatted; we've added line breaks and reworked indentation to accommodate the available page space in the book. In rare cases, even this was not enough, and listings include line-continuation markers (➡). Additionally, comments in the source code have often been removed from the listings when the code is described in the text. Code annotations accompany many of the listings, highlighting important concepts.

liveBook discussion forum

Purchase of *Real-World Cryptography* includes free access to a private web forum run by Manning Publications where you can make comments about the book, ask technical questions, and receive help from the author and from other users. To access the forum, go to https://livebook.manning.com/book/real-world-cryptography/discussion. You can also learn more about Manning's forums and the rules of conduct at https://livebook.manning.com/discussion.

Manning's commitment to our readers is to provide a venue where a meaningful dialogue between individual readers and between readers and the author can take place. It is not a commitment to any specific amount of participation on the part of the author, whose contribution to the forum remains voluntary (and unpaid). We suggest you try asking the author some challenging questions lest his interest stray! The forum and the archives of previous discussions will be accessible from the publisher's website as long as the book is in print.

about the author

DAVID WONG is a senior cryptography engineer at O(1) Labs working on the Mina cryptocurrency. Prior to that, he was the security lead for the Diem (formally known as Libra) cryptocurrency at Novi, Facebook, and before that, a security consultant at the Cryptography Services practice of NCC Group. David is also the author of the book *Real-World Cryptography*.

During his career, David has taken part in several publicly funded open source audits, such as OpenSSL and Let's Encrypt. He has spoken at various conferences, including Black Hat and DEF CON, and has taught a recurring cryptography course at Black Hat. He has contributed to standards like TLS 1.3 and the Noise Protocol Framework. He has found vulnerabilities in many systems, including CVE-2016-3959 in the Golang standard library, CVE-2018-12404, CVE-2018-19608, CVE-2018-16868, CVE-2018-16869, and CVE-2018-16870 in various TLS libraries.

Among others, he is the author of the Disco protocol (www.discocrypto.com and www.embeddeddisco.com) and the Decentralized Application Security Project for smart contracts (www.dasp.co). His research includes cache attacks on RSA (http://cat.eyalro.net/), protocol based on QUIC (https://eprint.iacr.org/2019/028), timing attacks on ECDSA (https://eprint.iacr.org/2015/839), or backdoors in Diffie-Hellman (https://eprint.iacr.org/2016/644). You can see and read about him these days on his blog at www.cryptologie.net.

about the cover illustration

The figure on the cover of *Real-World Cryptography* is captioned "Indienne de quito," or Quito Indian. The illustration is taken from a collection of dress costumes from various countries by Jacques Grasset de Saint-Sauveur (1757–1810), titled *Costumes de Différents Pays*, published in France in 1797. Each illustration is finely drawn and colored by hand. The rich variety of Grasset de Saint-Sauveur's collection reminds us vividly of how culturally apart the world's towns and regions were just 200 years ago. Isolated from each other, people spoke different dialects and languages. In the streets or in the countryside, it was easy to identify where they lived and what their trade or station in life was just by their dress.

The way we dress has changed since then and the diversity by region, so rich at the time, has faded away. It is now hard to tell apart the inhabitants of different continents, let alone different towns, regions, or countries. Perhaps we have traded cultural diversity for a more varied personal life—certainly for a more varied and fast-paced technological life.

At a time when it is hard to tell one computer book from another, Manning celebrates the inventiveness and initiative of the computer business with book covers based on the rich diversity of regional life of two centuries ago, brought back to life by Grasset de Saint-Sauveur's pictures.

Part 1

Primitives:
The ingredients
of cryptography

Welcome to the real-world of cryptography! The book you're holding in your hands (if you chose to acquire a printed version) is split into two equal parts of eight chapters. By going through all of it, you will learn (almost) all there is to know about cryptography in the real world—the one you're standing in.

Note that the first part of the book was written to be read in order, although each chapter should tell you what the prerequisites are, so do not view this as a mandatory constraint. The first eight chapters take you through the basics—the building blocks of cryptography. Each chapter introduces a new ingredient and teaches you what it does, how it works, and how it can be used with other elements. This first part is all about giving you good abstractions and insights before we start making use of it all in the second part of the book.

Good luck!

Introduction

Greetings, traveler; sit tight. You're about to enter a world of wonder and mystery—the world of cryptography. *Cryptography* is the ancient discipline of securing situations that are troubled with malicious characters. This book includes the spells that we need to defend ourselves against the malice. Many have attempted to learn this craft, but few have survived the challenges that stand in the way of mastery. Exciting adventures await, indeed!

In this book, we'll uncover how cryptographic algorithms can secure our letters, identify our allies, and protect treasures from our enemies. Sailing through the cryptographic sea will not be the smoothest journey as cryptography is the foundation of all security and privacy in our world—the slightest mistake could be deadly.

> **NOTE** If you find yourself lost, remember to keep moving forward. It will all eventually make sense.

1.1   *Cryptography is about securing protocols*

Our journey starts with an introduction to cryptography, the science aiming to defend protocols against saboteurs. But first, what's a *protocol*? Simply put, it's a list of steps that one (or more people) must follow in order to achieve something. For example, imagine the following premise: you want to leave your magic sword unattended for a few hours so you can take a nap. One protocol to do this could be the following:

1 Deposit weapon on the ground
2 Take nap under a tree
3 Recover weapon from the ground

Of course, it's not a great protocol as anybody can steal your sword while you're napping . . . And so, cryptography is about taking into account the adversaries who are looking to take advantage of you.

In ancient times, when rulers and generals were busy betraying each other and planning coups, one of their biggest problems was finding a way to *share confidential information with those they trusted*. From here, the idea of cryptography was born. It took centuries and hard work before cryptography became the serious discipline it is today. Now, it's used all around us to provide the most basic services in the face of our chaotic and adverse world.

The story of this book is about the practice of cryptography. It takes you on an expedition throughout the computing world to cover cryptographic protocols in use today; it also shows you what parts they are made of and how everything fits together. While a typical cryptography book usually starts with the discovery of cryptography and takes you through its history, I think that it makes little sense for me to kick off things that way. I want to tell you about the practical. I want to tell you about what I've witnessed myself, reviewing cryptographic applications for large companies as a consultant, or the cryptography I've made use of myself as an engineer in the field.

There will be (almost) no scary math formulas. The purpose of this book is to demystify cryptography, survey what is considered useful nowadays, and provide intuition about how things around you are built. This book is intended for curious people, interested engineers, adventurous developers, and inquisitive researchers. Chapter 1, this chapter, initiates a tour of the world of cryptography. We will discover the different types of cryptography, which ones matter to us, and how the world agreed on using these.

1.2 Symmetric cryptography: What is symmetric encryption?

One of the fundamental concepts of cryptography is *symmetric encryption.* It is used in a majority of cryptographic algorithms in this book, and it is, thus, extremely important. I introduce this new concept here via our first protocol.

Let's imagine that Queen Alice needs to send a letter to Lord Bob, who lives a few castles away. She asks her loyal messenger to ride his trusty steed and battle his way through the dangerous lands ahead in order to deliver the precious message to Lord Bob. Yet, she is suspicious; even though her loyal messenger has served her for many years, she wishes the message in transit to remain secret from all passive observers, including the messenger! You see, the letter most likely contains some controversial gossip about the kingdoms on the way.

What Queen Alice needs is a protocol that mimics handing the message to Lord Bob herself with no middlemen. This is quite an impossible problem to solve in practice unless we introduce cryptography (or teleportation) into the equation. This is what we ended up doing ages ago by inventing a new type of cryptographic algorithm—called a *symmetric encryption algorithm* (also known as a *cipher*).

> **NOTE** By the way, a type of cryptographic algorithm is often referred to as a *primitive.* You can think of a primitive as the smallest, useful construction you can have in cryptography, and it is often used with other primitives in order to build a protocol. It is mostly a term and has no particularly important meaning, although it appears often enough in the literature that it is good to know about it.

Let's see how we can use an encryption primitive to hide Queen Alice's message from the messenger. Imagine for now that the primitive is a black box (we can't see what's inside or what it's doing internally) that provides two functions:

- ENCRYPT
- DECRYPT

The first function, ENCRYPT, works by taking a *secret key* (usually a large number) and a *message*. It then outputs a series of random-looking numbers, some noisy data if you will. We will call that output the encrypted message. I illustrate this in figure 1.1.

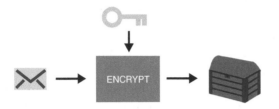

Figure 1.1   The ENCRYPT function takes a message and a secret key and outputs the encrypted message—a long series of numbers that look like random noise.

The second function, DECRYPT, is the inverse of the first one. It takes the same secret key and the random output of the first function (the encrypted message) and then it finds the original message. I illustrate this in figure 1.2.

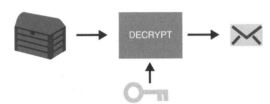

Figure 1.2   The DECRYPT function takes an encrypted message and a secret key and returns the original message.

To make use of this new primitive, Queen Alice and Lord Bob have to first meet in real life and decide on what secret key to use. Later, Queen Alice can use the provided ENCRYPT function to protect a message with the help of the secret key. She then passes the encrypted message to her messenger, who eventually delivers it to Lord Bob. Lord Bob then uses the DECRYPT function on the encrypted message with the same secret key to recover the original message. Figure 1.3 shows this process.

During this exchange, all the messenger had was something that looked random and that provided no meaningful insight into the content of the hidden message. Effectively, we augmented our insecure protocol into a secure one, thanks to the help of cryptography. The new protocol makes it possible for Queen Alice to deliver a confidential letter to Lord Bob without anyone (except Lord Bob) learning the content of it.

The process of using a secret key to render things to noise, making them indistinguishable from random, is a common way of securing a protocol in cryptography. You will see more of this as you learn more cryptographic algorithms in the next chapters.

By the way, symmetric encryption is part of a larger category of cryptography algorithms called *symmetric cryptography* or *secret key cryptography*. This is due to the same key being used by the different functions exposed by the cryptographic primitive. As you will see later, sometimes there's more than one key.

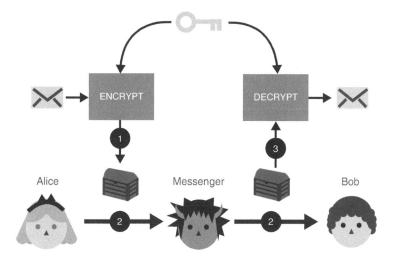

Figure 1.3 (1) Alice uses the ENCRYPT function with a secret key to transform her message into noise. (2) She then passes the encrypted message to her messenger, who will not learn anything about the underlying message. (3) Once Bob receives the encrypted message, he can recover the original content by using the DECRYPT function with the same secret key Alice used.

1.3   *Kerckhoff's principle: Only the key is kept secret*

To design a cryptographic algorithm (like our encryption primitive) is an easy task, but to design a *secure* cryptographic algorithm is not for the faint of heart. While we shy away from creating such algorithms in this book, we *do* learn how to recognize the good ones. This can be difficult as there is more choice than one can ask for the task. Hints can be found in the repeated failures of the history of cryptography, as well as the lessons that the community has learned from them. As we take a look at the past, we will grasp at what turns a cryptographic algorithm into a trusted-to-be-secure one.

Hundreds of years have passed and many queens and lords have been buried. Since then, paper has been abandoned as our primary means of communication in favor of better and more practical technologies. Today, we have access to powerful computers as well as the internet. More practical, sure, but this also means that our previous malicious messenger has become much more powerful. He is now everywhere: the Wi-Fi in the Starbucks cafe you're sitting in, the different servers making up the internet and forwarding your messages, and even in the machines running our algorithms. Our enemies are now able to observe many more messages as each request you make to a website might pass through the wrong wire and become altered or copied in a matter of nanoseconds without anyone noticing.

Before us, we can see that recent history contains many instances of encryption algorithms falling apart, being broken by secret state organizations or by independent researchers, and failing to protect their messages or accomplish their claims. Many lessons were learned, and we slowly came to understand how to produce good cryptography.

> **NOTE** A cryptographic algorithm can be considered *broken* in many ways. For an encryption algorithm, you can imagine several ways to attack the algorithm: the secret key can be leaked to the attacker, messages can be decrypted without the help of the key, some information about the message can be revealed just by looking at the encrypted message, and so on. Anything that would somehow weaken the assumptions we made about the algorithm could be considered a break.

A strong notion came out of the long process of trial and error that cryptography went through: to obtain confidence in the security claims made by a cryptographic primitive, the primitive has to be analyzed in the open by experts. Short of that, you are relying on *security through obscurity*, which hasn't worked well historically. This is why *cryptographers* (the people who build) usually use the help of *cryptanalysts* (the people who break) in order to analyze the security of a construction. (Although cryptographers are often cryptanalysts themselves and vice-versa.)

Let's take the Advanced Encryption Standard (AES) encryption algorithm as an example. AES was the product of an international competition organized by the National Institute of Standards and Technology (NIST).

> **NOTE** NIST is a United States agency whose role is to define standards and develop guidelines for use in government-related functions as well as other public or private organizations. Like AES, it has standardized many widely used cryptographic primitives.

The AES competition lasted several years, during which many volunteering cryptanalysts from around the world gathered to take a chance at breaking the various candidate constructions. After several years, once enough confidence was built by the process, a single competing encryption algorithm was nominated to become the Advanced

Encryption Standard itself. Nowadays, most people trust that AES to be a solid encryption algorithm, and it is widely used to encrypt almost anything. For example, you use it every day when you browse the web.

The idea to build cryptographic standards in the open is related to a concept often referred to as *Kerckhoffs' principle*, which can be understood as something like this: it would be foolish to rely on our enemies not to discover what algorithms we use because they most likely will. Instead, let's be open about them.

If the enemies of Queen Alice and Lord Bob knew exactly how they were encrypting messages, how is their encryption algorithm secure? The answer is the *secret key*! The secrecy of the key makes the protocol secure, not the secrecy of the algorithm itself. This is a common theme in this book: all the cryptographic algorithms that we will learn about and that are used in the real world are most often free to be studied and used. Only the secret keys used as input to these algorithms are kept secret. *Ars ipsi secreta magistro* (an art secret even for the master), said Jean Robert du Carlet in 1644. In the next section, I will talk about a totally different kind of cryptographic primitive. For now, let's use figure 1.4 to organize what we've learned so far.

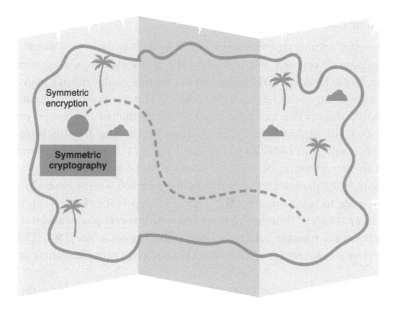

Figure 1.4   The cryptographic algorithms you have learned so far. AES is an instantiation of a symmetric encryption algorithm, which is a cryptographic primitive that is part of the broader class of symmetric cryptographic algorithms.

1.4 *Asymmetric cryptography: Two keys are better than one*

In our discussion about symmetric encryption, we said that Queen Alice and Lord Bob first met to decide on a symmetric key. This is a plausible scenario, and a lot of protocols actually do work like this. Nonetheless, this quickly becomes less practical in protocols with many participants: do we need our web browser to meet with Google, Facebook, Amazon, and the other billions of websites before securely connecting to those?

This problem, often referred to as *key distribution*, has been a hard one to solve for quite a long time, at least until the discovery in the late 1970s of another large and useful category of cryptographic algorithms called *asymmetric cryptography* or *public key cryptography*. Asymmetric cryptography generally makes use of different keys for different functions (as opposed to a single key used in symmetric cryptography) or provides different points of view to different participants. To illustrate what this means and how public key cryptography helps to set up trust between people, I'll introduce a number of asymmetric primitives in this section. Note that this is only a glance of what you'll learn in this book as I'll talk about each of these cryptographic primitives in more detail in subsequent chapters.

1.4.1 *Key exchanges or how to get a shared secret*

The first asymmetric cryptography primitive we'll look at is the *key exchange*. The first public key algorithm discovered and published was a key exchange algorithm named after its authors, Diffie-Hellman (DH). The DH key exchange algorithm's main purpose is to establish a common secret between two parties. This common secret can then be used for different purposes (for example, as a key to a symmetric encryption primitive).

In chapter 5, I will explain how Diffie-Hellman works, but for this introduction, let's use a simple analogy in order to understand what a key exchange provides. Like many algorithms in cryptography, a key exchange must start with the participants using a common set of parameters. In our analogy, we will simply have Queen Alice and Lord Bob agree to use a square (■). The next step is for them to choose their own random shape. Both of them go to their respective secret place, and out of sight, Queen Alice chooses a triangle (▲) and Lord Bob chooses a star (★). The objects they chose need to remain secret at all costs! These objects represent their *private keys* (see figure 1.5).

Once they chose their private keys, they both individually combine their secret shape with the common shape they initially agreed on using (the square). The combi-

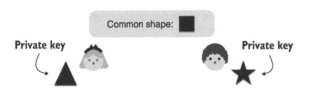

Figure 1.5 The first step of a DH (Diffie-Hellman) key exchange is to have both participants generate a private key. In our analogy, Queen Alice chooses a triangle as her private key, whereas Lord Bob chooses a star as his private key.

nations result in unique shapes representing their *public keys.* Queen Alice and Lord Bob can now exchange their public keys (hence the name *key exchange*) because public keys are considered public information. I illustrate this in figure 1.6.

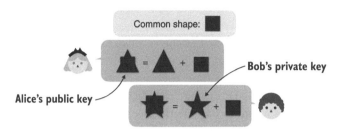

Figure 1.6   The second step of a DH key exchange where both participants exchange their public keys. Participants derive their public keys by combining their private keys with a common shape.

We are now starting to see why this algorithm is called a public key algorithm. It is because it requires a *key pair* comprised of a private key and a public key. The final step of the DH key exchange algorithm is quite simple: Queen Alice takes Lord Bob's public key and combines it with her private key. Lord Bob does the same with Queen Alice's public key and combines it with his own private key. The result should now be the same on each side; in our example, a shape combining a star, a square, and a triangle (see figure 1.7).

Figure 1.7   The final step of a DH key exchange where both participants produce the same shared secret. To do this, Queen Alice combines her private key with Lord Bob's public key, and Lord Bob combines his private key with Queen Alice's public key. The shared secret cannot be obtained from solely observing the public keys.

It is now up to the participants of the protocol to make use of this shared secret. You will see several examples of this in this book, but the most obvious scenario is to make use of it in an algorithm that requires a shared secret. For example, Queen Alice and Lord Bob could now use the shared secret as a key to encrypt further messages with a symmetric encryption primitive. To recap

1 Alice and Bob exchange their public keys, which masks their respective private keys.
2 With the other participant's public key and their respective private key, they can compute a shared secret.
3 An adversary who observes the exchange of public keys doesn't have enough information to compute the shared secret.

NOTE In our example, the last point is easily bypassable. Indeed, without the knowledge of any private keys, we can combine the public keys together to produce the shared secret. Fortunately, this is only a limitation of our analogy, but it works well enough for us to understand what a key exchange does.

In practice, a DH key exchange is quite insecure. Can you take a few seconds to figure out why?

Because Queen Alice accepts any public key she receives as being Lord Bob's public key, I could intercept the exchange and replace it with mine, which would allow me to impersonate Lord Bob to Queen Alice (and the same can be done to Lord Bob). We say that a *man-in-the-middle* (MITM) attacker can successfully attack the protocol. How do we fix this? We will see in later chapters that we either need to augment this protocol with another cryptographic primitive, or we need to be aware in advance of what Lord Bob's public key is. But then, aren't we back to square one?

Previously, Queen Alice and Lord Bob needed to know a shared secret; now Queen Alice and Lord Bob need to know their respective public keys. How do they get to know that? Is that a chicken-and-egg problem all over again? Well, kind of. As we will see, in practice, public key cryptography does not solve the problem of trust, but it simplifies its establishment (especially when the number of participants is large).

Let's stop here and move on to the next section as you will learn more about key exchanges in chapter 5. We still have a few more asymmetric cryptographic primitives to uncover (see figure 1.8) to finish our tour of real-world cryptography.

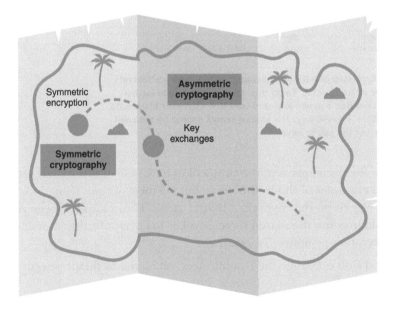

Figure 1.8 The cryptographic algorithms we have learned so far. Two large classes of cryptographic algorithms are symmetric cryptography (with symmetric encryption) and asymmetric cryptography (with key exchanges).

1.4.2 Asymmetric encryption, not like the symmetric one

The invention of the DH key exchange algorithm was quickly followed by the invention of the *RSA algorithm* named after Ron Rivest, Adi Shamir, and Leonard Adleman. RSA contains two different primitives: a public key encryption algorithm (or asymmetric encryption) and a (digital) signature scheme. Both primitives are part of the larger class of cryptographic algorithms called *asymmetric cryptography*. In this section, we will explain what these primitives do and how they can be useful.

The first one, asymmetric encryption, has a similar purpose to the symmetric encryption algorithm we talked about previously: it allows one to encrypt messages in order to obtain confidentiality. Yet, unlike symmetric encryption, which had the two participants encrypt and decrypt messages with the same symmetric key, asymmetric encryption is quite different:

- It works with two different keys: a public key and a private key.
- It provides an asymmetric point of view: anyone can encrypt with the public key, but only the owner of the private key can decrypt messages.

Let's now use a simple analogy to explain how one can use asymmetric encryption. We start with our friend Queen Alice again, who holds a private key (and its associated public key). Let's picture her public key as an open chest that she releases to the public for anyone to use (see figure 1.9).

Figure 1.9 To use asymmetric encryption, Queen Alice needs to first publish her public key (represented as an open box here). Now, anyone can use the public key to encrypt messages to her. And she should be able to decrypt them using the associated private key.

Now, you and I and everyone who wants can encrypt a message to her using her public key. In our analogy, imagine that you would insert your message into the open chest and then close it. Once the chest is closed, nobody but Queen Alice should be able to open it. The box effectively protects the secrecy of the message from observers. The closed box (or encrypted content) can then be sent to Queen Alice, and she can use her private key (only known to her, remember) to decrypt it (see figure 1.10).

Let's summarize in figure 1.11 the cryptographic primitives we have learned so far. We are only missing one more to finish our tour of real-world cryptography!

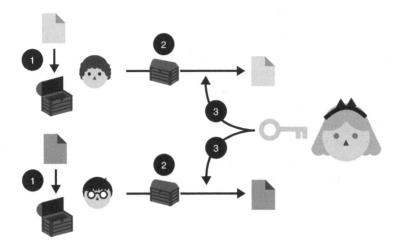

Figure 1.10   Asymmetric encryption: (1) anyone can use Queen Alice's public key to encrypt messages to her. (2) After receiving them, (3) she can decrypt the content using her associated private key. Nobody is able to observe the messages directed to Queen Alice while they are being sent to her.

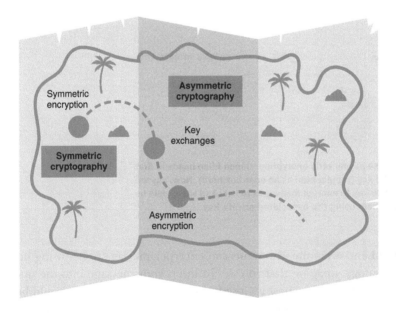

Figure 1.11   The cryptographic algorithms we have learned so far: two large classes of cryptographic algorithms are symmetric cryptography (with symmetric encryption) and asymmetric cryptography (with key exchanges and asymmetric encryption).

1.4.3 Digital signatures, just like your pen-and-paper signatures

We saw that RSA provides an asymmetric encryption algorithm, but as we mentioned earlier, it also provides a *digital signature* algorithm. The invention of this digital signature cryptographic primitive has been of immense help to set up trust between the Alices and Bobs of our world. It is similar to real signatures; you know, the one that you are required to sign on a contract when you're trying to rent an apartment, for example.

"What if they forge my signature?" you may ask, and indeed, real signatures don't provide much security in the real world. On the other hand, cryptographic signatures can be used in the same kind of way but provide a cryptographic certificate with your name on it. Your cryptographic signature is *unforgeable* and can easily be verified by others. Pretty useful compared to the archaic signatures you used to write on checks!

In figure 1.12, we can imagine a protocol where Queen Alice wants to show Lord David that she trusts Lord Bob. This is a typical example of how to establish trust in a multiparticipant setting and how asymmetric cryptography can help. By signing a piece of paper containing "I, Queen Alice, trust Lord Bob," Queen Alice can take a stance and notify Lord David that Lord Bob is to be trusted. If Lord David already trusts Queen Alice and her signature algorithm, then he can choose to trust Lord Bob in return.

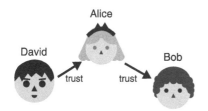

Figure 1.12 Lord David already trusts Queen Alice. Because Queen Alice trusts Lord Bob, can Lord David safely trust Lord Bob as well?

In more detail, Queen Alice can use the RSA signature scheme and her private key to sign the message, "I, Queen Alice, trust Lord Bob." This generates a signature that should look like random noise (see figure 1.13).

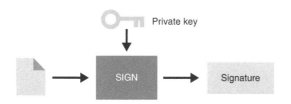

Figure 1.13 To sign a message, Queen Alice uses her private key and generates a signature.

Anyone can then *verify the signature* by combining:

- Alice's public key
- The message that was signed
- The signature

The result is either *true* (the signature is valid) or *false* (the signature is invalid) as figure 1.14 shows.

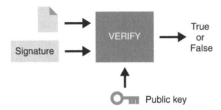

Figure 1.14   **To verify a signature from Queen Alice, one also needs the message signed and Queen Alice's public key. The result is either validating the signature or invalidating it.**

We have now learned about three different asymmetric primitives:

- Key exchange with Diffie-Hellman
- Asymmetric encryption
- Digital signatures with RSA

These three cryptographic algorithms are the most known and commonly used primitives in asymmetric cryptography. It might not be totally obvious how they can help to solve real-world problems, but rest assured, they are used every day by many applications to secure things around them. It is time to complete our picture with all the cryptographic algorithms we've learned about so far (see figure 1.15).

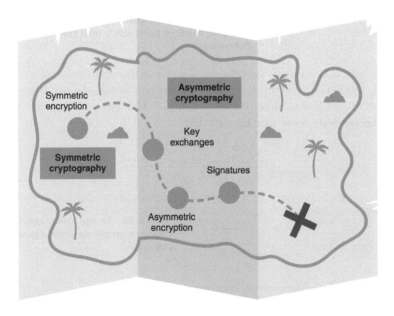

Figure 1.15   **The symmetric and asymmetric algorithms we have learned so far**

1.5   *Classifying and abstracting cryptography*

In the previous section, we surveyed two large classes of algorithms:

- *Symmetric cryptography (or secret key cryptography)*—A single secret is used. If several participants are aware of the secret, it is called a *shared* secret.
- *Asymmetric cryptography (or public key cryptography)*—Participants have an asymmetrical view of the secrets. For example, some will have knowledge of a public key, while some will have knowledge of both a public and private key.

Symmetric and asymmetric cryptography are not the only two categories of primitives in cryptography, and it's quite hard to classify the different subfields. But yet, as you will realize, a large part of our book is about (and makes use of) symmetric and asymmetric primitives. This is because a large part of what is useful in cryptography nowadays is contained in these subfields. Another way of dividing cryptography can be

- *Math-based constructions*—These rely on mathematical problems like factoring numbers. (The RSA algorithm for digital signatures and asymmetric encryption is an example of such a construction.)
- *Heuristic-based constructions*—These rely on observations and statistical analysis by cryptanalysts. (AES for symmetric encryption is an example of such a construction.)

There is also a speed component to this categorization as mathematic-based constructions are often much slower than heuristic-based constructions. To give you an idea, symmetric constructions are most often based on heuristics (what seems to be working), while most asymmetric constructions are based on mathematical problems (what is thought to be hard).

It is hard for us to rigorously categorize all of what cryptography has to offer. Indeed, every book or course on the subject gives different definitions and classifications. In the end, these distinctions are not too useful for us as we will see most of the cryptographic primitives as unique tools that make unique *security claims*. We can, in turn, use many of these tools as building blocks to create protocols. It is thus essential to understand how each of these tools work and what kind of security claims they provide in order to understand how they secure the protocols around us. For this reason, the first part of this book will go through the most useful cryptographic primitives and their security properties.

A lot of the concepts in the book can be quite complicated the first time around. But like everything, the more we read about them and the more we see them in context, the more natural they become, the more we can abstract them. The role of this book is to help you to create abstractions, to allow you to create a mental model of what these constructions do, and to understand how they can be combined together to produce secure protocols. I will often talk about the interface of constructions and give real-world examples of usage and composition.

The definition of cryptography used to be simple: Queen Alice and Lord Bob want to exchange secret messages. It isn't anymore. What cryptography is nowadays is quite complex to describe and has grown organically around discoveries, breakthroughs, and practical needs. At the end of the day, cryptography is what helps to augment a protocol in order to make it work in adversarial settings.

To understand exactly how cryptography can help, the set of goals that these protocols aim to achieve is what matters to us. That's the useful part. Most of the cryptographic primitives and protocols we'll learn about in this book provide one or two of the following properties:

- *Confidentiality*—It's about masking and protecting some information from the wrong eyes. For example, encryption masks the messages in transit.
- *Authentication*—It's about identifying who we are talking to. For example, this can be helpful in making sure that messages we receive indeed come from Queen Alice.

Of course, this is still a heavy simplification of what cryptography can provide. In most cases, the details are in the security claims of the primitives. Depending on how we use a cryptographic primitive in a protocol, it will achieve different security properties.

Throughout this book, we will learn new cryptographic primitives and how they can be combined to expose security properties like confidentiality and authentication. For now, appreciate the fact that cryptography is about providing insurances to a protocol in adversarial settings. While the "adversaries" are not clearly defined, we can imagine that they are the ones who attempt to break our protocol: a participant, an observer, a man in the middle. They reflect what a real-life adversary could be. Because eventually, cryptography is a practical field made to defend against bad actors in flesh and bones and bits.

1.6   *Theoretical cryptography vs. real-world cryptography*

In 1993, Bruce Schneier released *Applied Cryptography* (Wiley), a book targeting developers and engineers who want to build applications that involve cryptography. Circa 2012, Kenny Paterson and Nigel Smart started an annual conference called Real World Crypto that targets the same crowd. But what do applied cryptography and real-world cryptography refer to? Is there more than one type of cryptography?

To answer the questions, we have to start by defining *theoretical cryptography*, the cryptography that cryptographers and cryptanalysts work on. These crypto people are mostly from academia, working in universities, but sometimes from the industry or in specific departments of the government. They research everything and anything in cryptography. Results are shared internationally through publications and presentations in journals and conferences. Yet not everything they do is obviously useful or practical. Often, no "proof of concept" or code is released. It wouldn't make sense anyway, as no computer is powerful enough to run their research. Having said that, theoretical cryptography sometimes becomes so useful and practical that it makes its way to the other side.

The other side is the world of *applied cryptography* or *real-world cryptography*. It is the foundation of the security you find in all applications around you. Although it often seems like it's not there, almost transparent, it is there when you log into your bank account on the internet; it is with you when you message your friends; it helps protect you when you lose your phone. It is ubiquitous because, unfortunately, attackers are everywhere and actively try to observe and harm our systems. Practitioners are usually from the industry but will sometimes vet algorithms and design protocols with the help of the academic community. Results are often shared through conferences, blog posts, and open source software.

Real-world cryptography usually cares deeply about real-world considerations: what is the exact level of security provided by an algorithm? How long does it take to run the algorithm? What is the size of the inputs and outputs required by the primitive? Real-world cryptography is, as you might have guessed, the subject of this book. While theoretical cryptography is the subject of other books, we will still take a peek at what is brewing there in the last chapters of this book. Be prepared to be amazed as you might catch a glance of the real-world cryptography of tomorrow.

Now you might be wondering: how do developers and engineers choose what cryptography to use for their real-world applications?

1.7 From theoretical to practical: Choose your own adventure

Sitting on top are cryptanalysts who propose and solve hard mathematical problems [. . .] and at the bottom are software engineers who want to encrypt some data.

—Thai Duong ("So you want to roll your own crypto?," 2020)

In all the years I've spent studying and working with cryptography, I've never noticed a single pattern in which a cryptographic primitive ends up being used in real-world applications. Things are pretty chaotic. Before a theoretical primitive gets to be adopted, there's a long list of people who get to handle the primitive and shape it into something consumable and sometimes safer for the public at large. How can I even explain that to you?

Have you heard of *Choose Your Own Adventure*? It's an old book series where you got to pick how you want to step through the story. The principle was simple: you read the first section of the book; at the end of the section, the book lets you decide on the path forward by giving you different options. Each option was associated with a different section number that you could skip directly to if you so chose. So, I did the same here! Start by reading the next paragraph and follow the direction it gives you.

Where it all begins. Who are you? Are you Alice, a cryptographer? Are you David, working in the private industry and in need of a solution to your problems? Or are you Eve, working in a government branch and preoccupied by cryptography?

- You're Alice, go to step 1.
- You're David, go to step 2.
- You're Eve, go to step 3.

Step 1: Researchers gotta research. You're a researcher working in a university, or in the research team of a private company or a nonprofit, or in a government research organization like NIST or NSA. As such, your funding can come from different places and might incentivize you to research different things.

- You invent a new primitive, go to step 4.
- You invent a new construction, go to step 5.
- You start an open competition, go to step 6.

Step 2: The industry has a need. As part of your job, something comes up and you are in need of a new standard. For example, the Wi-Fi Alliance is a nonprofit funded by interested companies to produce the set of standards around the Wi-Fi protocol. Another example are banks that got together to produce the Payment Card Industry Data Security Standard (PCI-DSS), which enforces algorithms and protocols to use if you deal with credit card numbers.

- You decide to fund some much needed research, go to step 1.
- You decide to standardize a new primitive or protocol, go to step 5.
- You start an open competition, go to step 6.

Step 3: A government has a need. You're working for your country's government, and you need to push out some new crypto. For example, the NIST is tasked with publishing the *Federal Information Processing Standards* (FIPS), which mandates what cryptographic algorithms can be used by companies that deal with the US government. While many of these standards were success stories and people tend to have a lot of trust in standards being pushed by government agencies, there is (unfortunately) a lot to say about failures.

In 2013, following revelations from Edward Snowden, it was discovered that NSA had purposefully and successfully pushed for the inclusion of backdoor algorithms in standards (see "Dual EC: A Standardized Back Door" by Bernstein et al.), which included a hidden switch that allowed NSA, and only the NSA, to predict your secrets. These *backdoors* can be thought of as magic passwords that allow the government (and only it, supposedly) to subvert your encryption. Following this, the cryptographic community lost a lot of confidence in standards and suggestions coming from governmental bodies. Recently, in 2019, it was found that the Russian standard GOST had been a victim of the same treatment.

Cryptographers have long suspected that the agency planted vulnerabilities in a standard adopted in 2006 by the National Institute of Standards and Technology and later by the International Organization for Standardization, which has 163 countries as members. Classified N.S.A. memos appear to confirm that the fatal weakness, discovered by two Microsoft cryptographers in 2007, was engineered by the agency. The N.S.A. wrote the standard and aggressively pushed it on the international group, privately calling the effort "a challenge in finesse."

—*New York Times* ("N.S.A. Able to Foil Basic Safeguards
of Privacy on Web," 2013)

- You fund some research, go to step 1.
- You organize an open competition, go to step 6.
- You push for the standardization of a primitive or protocol that you're using, go to step 7.

Step 4: A new concept is proposed. As a researcher, you manage to do the impossible; you invent a new concept. Sure, someone already thought about encryption, but there are still new primitives being proposed every year in cryptography. Some of them will prove to be impossible to realize, and some will end up being solvable. Maybe you have an actual construction as part of your proposal, or maybe you'll have to wait to see if someone can come up with something that works.

- Your primitive gets implemented, go to step 5.
- Your primitive ends up being impossible to implement, go back to the beginning.

Step 5: A new construction or protocol is proposed. A cryptographer or a team of cryptographers proposes a new algorithm that instantiates a concept. For example, AES is an instantiation of an encryption scheme. (AES was initially proposed by Vincent Rijmen and Joan Daemen, who named their construction as a contraction of their names, Rijndael.) What's next?

- Someone builds on your construction, go to step 5.
- You partake in an open competition and win! Go to step 6.
- There's a lot of hype for your work; you're getting a standard! Go to step 7.
- You decide to patent your construction, go to step 8.
- You or someone else decides that it'll be fun to implement your construction. Go to step 9.

Step 6: An algorithm wins a competition. The process cryptographers love the most is an open competition! For example, AES was a competition that invited researchers from all over the world to compete. After dozens of submissions and rounds of analysis and help from cryptanalysts (which can take years), the list was reduced to a few candidates (in the case of AES, a single one), which then moved to become standardized.

- You got lucky, after many years of competition your construction won! Go to step 7.
- Unfortunately, you lost. Go back to the start.

Step 7: An algorithm or protocol is standardized. A standard is usually published by a government or by a standardization body. The aim is to make sure that everyone is on the same page so as to maximize interoperability. For example, NIST regularly publishes cryptographic standards. A well-known standardization body in cryptography is the

Internet Engineering Task Force (IETF), which is behind many standards on the internet (like TCP, UDP, TLS, and so on) and that you will hear about a lot in this book. Standards in the IETF are called *Request For Comment* (RFC) and can be written by pretty much anyone who wants to write a standard.

> *To reinforce that we do not vote, we have also adopted the tradition of "humming": When, for example, we have face-to-face meetings and the chair of the working group wants to get a "sense of the room", instead of a show of hands, sometimes the chair will ask for each side to hum on a particular question, either "for" or "against".*
>
> —RFC 7282 ("On Consensus and Humming in the IETF," 2014)

Sometimes, a company publishes a standard directly. For example, RSA Security LLC (funded by the creators of the RSA algorithm) released a series of 15 documents called the *Public Key Cryptography Standards* (PKCS) to legitimize algorithms and techniques the company used at that time. Nowadays, this is pretty rare, and a lot of companies go through the IETF to standardize their protocols or algorithms as an RFC instead of a custom document.

- Your algorithm or protocol gets implemented, go to step 9.
- Nobody cares about your standard, go back to the start.

Step 8: A patent expires. A patent in cryptography usually means that nobody will use the algorithm. Once the patent expires, it is not uncommon to see a renewed interest in the primitive. The most popular example is probably Schnorr signatures, which were the first contender to become the most popular signature scheme until Schnorr himself patented the algorithm in 1989. This led to the NIST standardizing a poorer algorithm called Digital Signature Algorithm (DSA), which became the go-to signature scheme at the time, but doesn't see much use nowadays. The patent over Schnorr signatures expired in 2008, and the algorithm has since started regaining popularity.

- It's been too long, your algorithm will be forever forgotten. Go back to the beginning.
- Your construction inspires many more constructions to get invented on top of it, go to step 5.
- Now people want to use your construction, but not before it's standardized for real. Go to step 7.
- Some developers are implementing your algorithm! Go to step 9.

Step 9: A construction or protocol gets implemented. Implementers have the hard task to not only decipher a paper or a standard (although standards are *supposed* to target implementers), but they also must make their implementations easy and safe to use. This is not always a simple task as many devastating bugs can arise in the way cryptography is used.

- Someone decides it is time for these implementations to be backed by a standard. It's embarrassing without one. Go to step 7.
- Hype is raining on your cryptographic library! Go to step 10.

Step 10: A developer uses a protocol or primitive in an application. A developer has a need, and your cryptographic library seems to solve it—easy peasy!

- The primitive solves the need, but it doesn't have a standard. Not great. Go to step 7.
- I wish this was written in my programming language. Go to step 9.
- I misused the library or the construction is broken. Game over.

You got it! There are many means for a primitive to go real-world. The best way involves many years of analysis, an implementor-friendly standard, and good libraries. A worse way involves a bad algorithm with a poor implementation. In figure 1.16, I illustrate the preferred path.

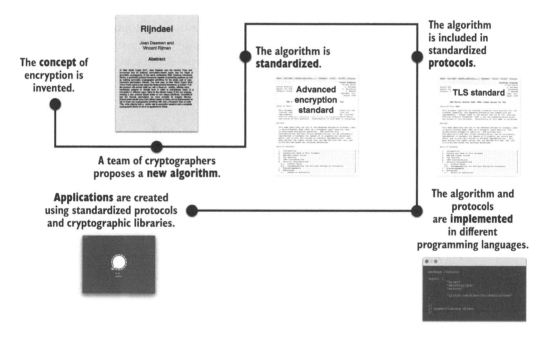

Figure 1.16 The ideal life cycle for a cryptographic algorithm starts when cryptographers instantiate a concept in a white paper. For example, AES is an instantiation of the concept of symmetric encryption (there are many more symmetric encryption algorithms out there). A construction can then be standardized: everybody agrees to implement it a certain way to maximize interoperability. Then support is created by implementing the standard in different languages.

1.8   *A word of warning*

> *Anyone, from the most clueless amateur to the best cryptographer, can create an algorithm that he himself can't break.*

> —Bruce Schneier ("Memo to the Amateur Cipher Designer," 1998)

I must warn you, the art of cryptography is difficult to master. It would be unwise to assume that you can build complex cryptographic protocols once you're done with this book. This journey should enlighten you, show you what is possible, and show you how things work, but it will not make you a master of cryptography.

This book is not the holy grail. Indeed, the last pages of this book take you through the most important lesson—do not go alone on a real adventure. Dragons can kill, and you need some support to accompany you in order to defeat them. In other words, cryptography is complicated, and this book alone does not permit you to abuse what you learn. To build complex systems, experts who have studied their trade for years are required. Instead, what you will learn is to recognize when cryptography should be used, or, if something seems fishy, what cryptographic primitives and protocols are available to solve the issues you're facing, and how all these cryptographic algorithms work under the surface. Now that you've been warned, go to the next chapter.

Summary

- A protocol is a step-by-step recipe where multiple participants attempt to achieve something like exchanging confidential messages.
- Cryptography is about augmenting protocols to secure them in adversarial settings. It often requires secrets.
- A cryptographic primitive is a type of cryptographic algorithm. For example, symmetric encryption is a cryptographic primitive, while AES is a specific symmetric encryption algorithm.
- One way to classify the different cryptographic primitives is to split them into two types: symmetric and asymmetric cryptography. Symmetric cryptography uses a single key (as you saw with symmetric encryption), while asymmetric cryptography makes use of different keys (as you saw with key exchanges, asymmetric encryption, and digital signatures).
- Cryptographic properties are hard to classify, but they often aim to provide one of these two properties: authentication or confidentiality. Authentication is about verifying the authenticity of something or someone, while confidentiality is about the privacy of data or identities.
- Real-world cryptography matters because it is ubiquitous in technological applications, while theoretical cryptography is often less useful in practice.
- Most of the cryptographic primitives contained in this book were agreed on after long standardization processes.
- Cryptography is complicated, and there are many dangers in implementing or using cryptographic primitives.

Hash functions

2

This chapter covers

- Hash functions and their security properties
- The widely adopted hash functions in use today
- Other types of hashing that exist

Attributing global unique identifiers to anything, that's the promise of the first cryptographic construction you'll learn about in this chapter—the *hash function*. Hash functions are everywhere in cryptography—everywhere! Informally, they take as input any data you'd like and produce a unique string of bytes in return. Given the same input, the hash function always reproduces the same string of bytes. This might seem like nothing, but this simple fabrication is extremely useful to build many other constructions in cryptography. In this chapter, you will learn everything there is to know about hash functions and why they are so versatile.

2.1 What is a hash function?

In front of you, a download button is taking a good chunk of the page. You can read the letters *DOWNLOAD*, and clicking this seems to redirect you to a different website containing a file. Below it, lies a long string of unintelligible letters:

```
f63e68ac0bf052ae923c03f5b12aedc6cca49874c1c9b0ccf3f39b662d1f487b
```

It is followed by what looks like an acronym of some sort: `sha256sum`. Sound familiar? You've probably downloaded something in your past life that was also accompanied with such an odd string (figure 2.1).

Figure 2.1   A web page linking to an external website containing a file. The external website cannot modify the content of the file because the first page provides a hash or digest of the file, which ensures the integrity over the downloaded file.

If you've ever wondered what was to be done with that long string:

1 Click the button to download the file
2 Use the SHA-256 algorithm to *hash* the downloaded file
3 Compare the output (the digest) with the long string displayed on the web page

This allows you to verify that you downloaded the right file.

NOTE   The output of a hash function is often called a *digest* or a *hash*. I use the two words interchangeably throughout this book. Others might call it a *check-sum* or a *sum*, which I avoid, as those terms are primarily used by noncryptographic hash functions and could lead to more confusion. Just keep that in mind when different codebases or documents use different terms.

To try hashing something, you can use the popular OpenSSL library. It offers a multipurpose command-line interface (CLI) that comes by default in a number of systems including macOS. For example, this can be done by opening the terminal and writing the following line:

```
$ openssl dgst -sha256 downloaded_file
f63e68ac0bf052ae923c03f5b12aedc6cca49874c1c9b0ccf3f39b662d1f487b
```

With the command, we used the SHA-256 hash function to transform the input (the downloaded file) into a unique identifier (the value echoed by the command). What do these extra steps provide? They provide *integrity and authenticity*. It tells you that what you downloaded is indeed the file you were meant to download.

All of this works, thanks to a security property of the hash function called *second preimage resistance*. This math-inspired term means that from the long output of the hash function, f63e..., you cannot find another file that will hash to the same output, f63e.... In practice, it means that this digest is closely tied to the file you're downloading and that no attacker should be able to fool you by giving you a different file.

The hexadecimal notation

By the way, the long output string f63e... represents binary data displayed in *hexadecimal* (a base-16 encoding, using numbers from 0 to 9 and letters from *a* to *f* to represent several bits of data). We could have displayed the binary data with 0s and 1s (base 2), but it would have taken more space. Instead, the hexadecimal encoding allows us to write 2 alphanumeric characters for every 8 bits (1 byte) encountered. It is somewhat readable by humans and takes less space. There are other ways to encode binary data for human consumption, but the two most widely used encodings are hexadecimal and base64. The larger the base, the less space it takes to display a binary string, but at some point, we run out of human-readable characters.

Note that this long digest is controlled by the owner(s) of the web page, and it could easily be replaced by anyone who can modify the web page. (If you are not convinced, take a moment to think about it.) This means that we need to trust the page that gave us the digest, its owners, and the mechanism used to retrieve the page (while we don't need to trust the page that gave us the file we downloaded). In this sense, *the hash function alone does not provide integrity*. The integrity and authenticity of the downloaded file comes from the digest combined with the trusted mechanism that gave us the digest (HTTPS in this case). We will talk about HTTPS in chapter 9, but for now, imagine that it magically allows you to communicate securely with a website.

Back to our hash function, which can be visualized as the black box in figure 2.2. Our black box takes a single input and gives out a single output.

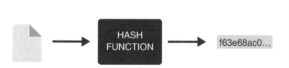

Figure 2.2 A hash function takes an arbitrary-length input (a file, a message, a video, and so on) and produces a fixed-length output (for example, 256 bits for SHA-256). Hashing the same input produces the same digest or hash.

The *input* of this function can be of any size. It can even be empty. The *output* is always of the same length and *deterministic*: it always produces the same result if given the same input. In our example, SHA-256 always provides an output of 256 bits (32 bytes), which is always encoded as 64 alphanumeric characters in hexadecimal. One major property of a hash function is that one cannot revert the algorithm, meaning that one shouldn't be able to find the input from just the output. We say that hash functions are *one-way*.

To illustrate how a hash function works in practice, we'll hash different inputs with the SHA-256 hash function using the same OpenSSL CLI. The following terminal session shows this.

Hashing the same input produces the same result.

```
$ echo -n "hello" | openssl dgst -sha256
2cf24dba5fb0a30e26e83b2ac5b9e29e1b161e5c1fa7425e73043362938b9824
$ echo -n "hello" | openssl dgst -sha256
2cf24dba5fb0a30e26e83b2ac5b9e29e1b161e5c1fa7425e73043362938b9824
$ echo -n "hella" | openssl dgst -sha256
70de66401b1399d79b843521ee726dcec1e9a8cb5708ec1520f1f3bb4b1dd984
$ echo -n "this is a very very very very very very
    very very very long sentence" | openssl dgst -sha256
1166e94d8c45fd8b269ae9451c51547dddec4fc09a91f15a9e27b14afee30006
```

A tiny change in the input completely changes the output.

The output is always of the same size, no matter the input size.

In the next section, we will see what are the exact security properties of hash functions.

2.2   *Security properties of a hash function*

Hash functions in applied cryptography are constructions that were commonly defined to provide three specific security properties. This definition has changed over time as we will see in the next sections. But for now, let's define the three strong foundations that make up a hash function. This is important as you need to understand where hash functions can be useful and where they will not work.

The first one is *pre-image resistance*. This property ensures that no one should be able to reverse the hash function in order to recover the input given an output. In figure 2.3, we illustrate this "one-wayness" by imagining that our hash function is like a blender, making it impossible to recover the ingredients from the produced smoothie.

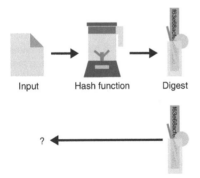

Input   Hash function   Digest

?

Figure 2.3   Given the digest produced by a hash function (represented as a blender here), it is impossible (or technically so hard we assume it will never happen) to reverse it and find the original input used. This security property is called *pre-image resistance*.

WARNING   Is this true if your input is small? Let's say that it's either *oui* or *non*, then it is easy for someone to hash all the possible 3-letter words and find out what the input was. What if your input space is small? Meaning that you always hash variants of the sentence, "I will be home on Monday at 3 a.m.," for example. Here, one who can predict this but does not know exactly the day of the week or the hour can still hash all possible sentences until it produces the correct output. As such, this first pre-image security property has an obvious caveat: *you can't hide something that is too small or that is predictable.*

The second property is *second pre-image resistance.* We already saw this security property when we wanted to protect the integrity of a file. The property says the following: if I give you an input and the digest it hashes to, you should not be able to find a different input that hashes to the same digest. Figure 2.4 illustrates this principle.

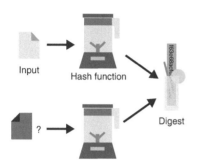

Figure 2.4 Considering an input and its associated digest, one should never be able to find a different input that hashes to the same output. This security property is called *second pre-image resistance*.

Note that *we do not control the first input.* This emphasis is important to understand the next security property for hash functions.

Finally, the third property is *collision resistance.* It guarantees that no one should be able to produce two different inputs that hash to the same output (as seen in figure 2.5). Here an attacker can choose the two inputs, unlike the previous property that fixes one of the inputs.

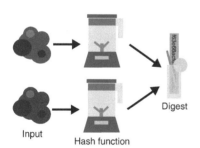

Figure 2.5 One should never be able to find two inputs (represented on the left as two random blobs of data) that hash to the same output value (on the right). This security property is called *collision resistance*.

People often confuse collision resistance and second pre-image resistance. Take a moment to understand the differences.

The random oracle

In addition, hash functions are usually designed so that their digests are *unpredictable and random*. This is useful because one cannot always prove a protocol to be

(continued)

secure, thanks to one of the security properties of a hash function we talked about (like collision resistance, for example). Many protocols are instead proven in the *random oracle model,* where a fictional and ideal participant called a random oracle is used. In this type of protocol, one can send any inputs as requests to that random oracle, which is said to return completely random outputs in response, and like a hash function, giving it the same input twice returns the same output twice.

Proofs in this model are sometimes controversial as we don't know for sure if we can replace these random oracles with real hash functions (in practice). Yet, many legitimate protocols are proven secure using this method, where hash functions are seen as more ideal than they probably are.

2.3   *Security considerations for hash functions*

So far, we saw three security properties of a hash function:

- Pre-image resistance
- Second pre-image resistance
- Collision resistance

These security properties are often meaningless on their own; it all depends on how you make use of the hash function. Nonetheless, it is important that we understand some limitations here before we look at some of the real-world hash functions.

First, these security properties assume that you are (reasonably) using the hash function. Imagine that I either hash the word *yes* or the word *no,* and I then publish the digest. If you have some idea of what I am doing, you can simply hash both of the words and compare the result with what I give you. Because there are no secrets involved, and because the hashing algorithm we used is public, you are free to do that. And indeed, one could think this would break the pre-image resistance of the hash function, but I'll argue that your input was not "random" enough. Furthermore, because a hash function accepts an arbitrary-length input and always produces an output of the same length, there are also an infinite number of inputs that hash to the same output. Again, you could say, "Well, isn't this breaking the second pre-image resistance?" Second pre-image resistance is merely saying that it is extremely hard to find another input, so hard we assume it's in practice impossible but not theoretically impossible.

Second, the size of the digest *does* matter. This is not a peculiarity of hash functions by any means. All cryptographic algorithms must care about the size of their parameters in practice. Let's imagine the following extreme example. We have a hash function that produces outputs of length 2 bits in a uniformly random fashion (meaning that it will output 00 25% of the time, 01 25% of the time, and so on). You're not going to have to do too much work to produce a collision: after hashing a few random input strings, you should be able to find two that hash to the same output. For this reason, there is a *minimum output size* that a hash function *must* produce in practice: 256 bits (or 32 bytes). With this large an output, collisions should be out of reach unless a breakthrough happens in computing.

How was this number obtained? In real-world cryptography, algorithms aim for a minimum of 128 bits of security. It means that an attacker who wants to break an algorithm (providing 128-bit security) has to perform around 2^{128} operations (for example, trying all the possible input strings of length 128 bits would take 2^{128} operations). For a hash function to provide all three security properties mentioned earlier, it needs to provide at least 128 bits of security against all three attacks. The easiest attack is usually to find collisions due to the *birthday bound*.

The birthday bound

The birthday bound takes its roots from probability theory in which the birthday problem reveals some unintuitive results. How many people do you need in a room so that with at least a 50% chance, two people share the same birthday (that's a collision). It turns out that 23 people taken at random are enough to reach these odds! Weird right?

This is called the *birthday paradox*. In practice, when we randomly generate strings from a space of 2^N possibilities, you can expect with a 50% chance that someone will find a collision after having generated approximately $2^{N/2}$ strings.

If our hash function generates random outputs of 256 bits, the space of all outputs is of size 2^{256}. This means that collisions can be found with good probability after generating 2^{128} digests (due to the birthday bound). This is the number we're aiming for, and this is why hash functions at a minimum must provide 256-bit outputs.

Certain constraints sometimes push developers to reduce the size of a digest by *truncating it* (removing some of its bytes). In theory, this is possible but can greatly reduce security. In order to achieve 128-bit security at a minimum, a digest must not be truncated under:

- 256 bits for collision resistance
- 128 bits for pre-image and second pre-image resistance

This means that depending on what property one relies on, the output of a hash function can be truncated to obtain a shorter digest.

2.4   *Hash functions in practice*

As we said earlier, in practice, hash functions are rarely used alone. They are most often combined with other elements to either create a cryptographic primitive or a cryptographic protocol. We will look at many examples of using hash functions to build more complex objects in this book, but this section describes a few different ways hash functions have been used in the real world.

2.4.1 *Commitments*

Imagine that you know that a stock in the market will increase in value and reach $50 in the coming month, but you really can't tell your friends about it (for some legal reason perhaps). You still want to be able to tell your friends that you knew about it after the fact because you're smug (don't deny it). What you can do is to commit to a sentence like, "Stock *X* will reach $50 next month." To do this, hash the sentence and give your friends the output. A month later, reveal the sentence. Your friends will be able to hash the sentence to observe that indeed, it is producing the same output.

This is what we call a *commitment scheme*. Commitments in cryptography generally try to achieve two properties:

- *Hiding*—A commitment must hide the underlying value.
- *Binding*—A commitment must hide a single value. In other words, if you commit to a value *x*, you shouldn't be able to later successfully reveal a different value *y*.

> **Exercise**
>
> Can you tell if a hash function provides hiding and binding if used as a commitment scheme?

2.4.2 *Subresource integrity*

It happens (often) that web pages import external JavaScript files. For example, a lot of websites use Content Delivery Networks (CDNs) to import JavaScript libraries or web-framework-related files in their pages. Such CDNs are placed in strategic locations in order to quickly deliver these files to visitors. Yet, if the CDN goes rogue and decides to serve malicious JavaScript files, this could be a real issue. To counter this, web pages can use a feature called *subresource integrity* that allows the inclusion of a digest in the import tag:

```
<script src="https://code.jquery.com/jquery-2.1.4.min.js"
    integrity="sha256-8WqyJLuWKRBVhxXIL1jBDD7SDxU936oZkCnxQbWwJVw="></script>
```

This is exactly the same scenario we talked about in the introduction of this chapter. Once the JavaScript file is retrieved, the browser hashes it (using SHA-256) and verifies that it corresponds to the digest that was hardcoded in the page. If it checks out, the JavaScript file gets executed as its integrity has been verified.

2.4.3 *BitTorrent*

Users (called *peers*) around the world use the BitTorrent protocol to share files directly among each other (what we also call *peer-to-peer*). To distribute a file, it is cut into chunks and each chunk is individually hashed. These hashes are then shared as a source of trust to represent the file to download.

BitTorrent has several mechanisms to allow a peer to obtain the different chunks of a file from different peers. In the end, the integrity of the entire file is verified by hashing each of the downloaded chunks and matching the output to its respectively known digests (before reassembling the file from the chunks). For example, the following "magnet link" represents the Ubuntu operating system, v19.04. It is a digest (represented in hexadecimal) obtained from hashing the metadata about the file as well as all the chunks' digests.

```
magnet:?xt=urn:btih:b7b0fbab74a85d4ac170662c645982a862826455
```

2.4.4 Tor

The Tor browser's goal is to give individuals the ability to browse the internet anonymously. Another feature is that one can create hidden web pages, whose physical locations are difficult to track. Connections to these pages are secured via a protocol that uses the web page's public key. (We will see more about how that works in chapter 9 when we talk about session encryption.) For example, Silk Road, which used to be the eBay of drugs until it got seized by the FBI, was accessible via `silkroad6ownowfk`
`.onion` in the Tor browser. This base32 string actually represented the hash of Silk Road's public key. Thus, by knowing the onion address, you can authenticate the public key of the hidden web page you're visiting and be sure that you're talking to the right page (and not an impersonator). If this is not clear, don't worry, I'll mention this again in chapter 9.

> **Exercise**
> By the way, there is no way this string represents 256 bits (32 bytes), right? How is this secure then, according to what you learned in section 2.3? Also, can you guess how the Dread Pirate Roberts (the pseudonym of Silk Road's webmaster) managed to obtain a hash that contains the name of the website?

In all examples in this section, a hash function provided *content integrity* or *authenticity* in situations where:

- Someone might tamper with the content being hashed.
- The hash is securely communicated to you.

We sometimes also say that we *authenticate* something or someone. It is important to understand that if the hash is not obtained securely, then anyone can replace it with the hash of something else! Thus, it does not provide integrity by itself. The next chapter on message authentication code will fix this by introducing *secrets*. Let's now look at what actual hash function algorithms you can use.

2.5   *Standardized hash functions*

We mentioned SHA-256 in our previous example, which is only one of the hash functions we can use. Before we go ahead and list the recommended hash functions of our time, let's first mention other algorithms that people use in real-world applications that are not considered cryptographic hash functions.

First, functions like CRC32 are *not* cryptographic hash functions but error-detecting code functions. While they helpfully detect some simple errors, they provide none of the previously mentioned security properties and are not to be confused with the hash functions we are talking about (even though they might share the name sometimes). Their output is usually referred to as a *checksum.*

Second, popular hash functions like MD5 and SHA-1 are considered broken nowadays. While they were both the standardized and widely accepted hash functions of the 1990s, MD5 and SHA-1 were shown to be broken in 2004 and 2016, respectively, when collisions were published by different research teams. These attacks were successful partly because of advances in computing, but mostly because flaws were found in the way the hash functions were designed.

> **Deprecation is hard**
> Both MD5 and SHA-1 were considered good hash functions until researchers demonstrated their lack of resistance from collisions. It remains that today, their pre-image and second pre-image resistance have not been affected by any attack. This does not matter for us as we want to only talk about secure algorithms in this book. Nonetheless, you will still see people using MD5 and SHA-1 in systems that only rely on the pre-image resistance of these algorithms and not on their collision resistance. These offenders often argue that they cannot upgrade the hash functions to more secure ones because of legacy and backward compatibility reasons. As the book is meant to last in time and be a beam of bright light for the future of real-world cryptography, this will be the last time I mention these hash functions.

The next two sections introduce SHA-2 and SHA-3, which are the two most widely used hash functions. Figure 2.6 introduces these functions.

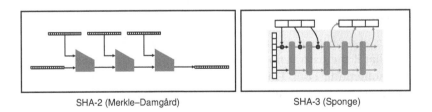

SHA-2 (Merkle–Damgård)   SHA-3 (Sponge)

Figure 2.6   SHA-2 and SHA-3, the two most widely adopted hash functions. SHA-2 is based on the Merkle–Damgård construction, while SHA-3 is based on the sponge construction.

2.5.1 The SHA-2 hash function

Now that we have seen what hash functions are and had a glimpse at their potential use cases, it remains to be seen which hash functions we can use in practice. In the next two sections, I introduce two widely accepted hash functions, and I also give high-level explanations of how they work from the inside. The high-level explanations should not provide deeper insights on how to use hash functions because the black box descriptions I gave should be enough. But nevertheless, it is interesting to see how these cryptographic primitives were designed by cryptographers in the first place.

The most widely adopted hash function is the *Secure Hash Algorithm 2* (SHA-2). SHA-2 was invented by NSA and standardized by NIST in 2001. It was meant to add itself to the aging Secure Hash Algorithm 1 (SHA-1) already standardized by NIST. SHA-2 provides 4 different versions, producing outputs of 224, 256, 384, or 512 bits. Their respective names omit the version of the algorithm: SHA-224, SHA-256, SHA-384, and SHA-512. In addition, two other versions, SHA-512/224 and SHA-512/256, provide 224-bit and 256-bit output, respectively, by truncating the result of SHA-512.

In the following terminal session, we call each variant of SHA-2 with the OpenSSL CLI. Observe that calling the different variants with the same input produces outputs of the specified lengths that are completely different.

```
$ echo -n "hello world" | openssl dgst -sha224
2f05477fc24bb4faefd86517156dafdecec45b8ad3cf2522a563582b
$ echo -n "hello world" | openssl dgst -sha256
b94d27b9934d3e08a52e52d7da7dabfac484efe37a5380ee9088f7ace2efcde9
$ echo -n "hello world" | openssl dgst -sha384
fdbd8e75a67f29f701a4e040385e2e23986303ea10239211af907fcbb83578b3
⮑ e417cb71ce646efd0819dd8c088de1bd
$ echo -n "hello world" | openssl dgst -sha512
309ecc489c12d6eb4cc40f50c902f2b4d0ed77ee511a7c7a9bcd3ca86d4cd86f
⮑ 989dd35bc5ff499670da34255b45b0cfd830e81f605dcf7dc5542e93ae9cd76f
```

Nowadays, people mostly use SHA-256, which provides the minimum 128 bits of security needed for our three security properties, while more paranoid applications make use of SHA-512. Now, let's look at a simplified explanation of how SHA-2 works.

The Exclusive OR operation

To understand what follows, you need to understand the *XOR* (exclusive OR) operation. XOR is a bitwise operation, meaning that it operates on bits. The following figure shows how this works. XOR is ubiquitous in cryptography, so make you sure you remember it.

XOR

$$1 \oplus 0 = 1$$
$$1 \oplus 1 = 0$$
$$0 \oplus 1 = 1$$
$$0 \oplus 0 = 0$$

(continued)
Exclusive OR or XOR (often denoted as ⊕) operates on 2 bits. It is similar to the OR operation except for the case where both operands are 1s.

It all starts with a special function called a *compression function*. A compression function takes two inputs of some size and produces one output of the size of one of the inputs. Put simply, it takes some data and returns less data. Figure 2.7 illustrates this.

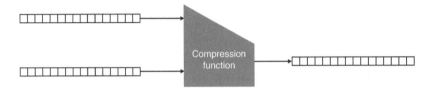

Figure 2.7   A compression function takes two different inputs of size *X* and *Y* (here both 16 bytes) and returns an output of size either *X* or *Y*.

While there are different ways of building a compression function, SHA-2 uses the *Davies–Meyer* method (see figure 2.8), which relies on a *block cipher* (a cipher that can encrypt a fixed-size block of data). I mentioned the AES block cipher in chapter 1, but you haven't yet learned about it. For now, accept the compression function as a black box until you read chapter 4 on authenticated encryption.

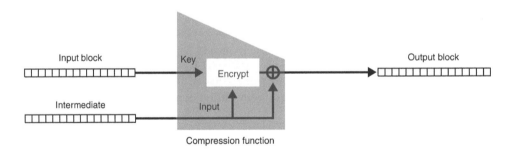

Figure 2.8   An illustration of a compression function built via the Davies–Meyer construction. The compression function's first input (the *input block*) is used as the key to a block cipher. The second input (the *intermediate value*) is used as input to be encrypted by the block cipher. It is then used again by XORing itself with the output of the block cipher.

SHA-2 is a *Merkle–Damgård* construction, which is an algorithm (invented by Ralph Merkle and Ivan Damgård independently) that hashes a message by iteratively calling such a compression function. Specifically, it works by going through the following two steps.

First, it applies a *padding* to the input we want to hash, then cuts the input into blocks that can fit into the compression function. Padding means to append specific bytes to the input in order to make its length a multiple of some block size. Cutting the padded input into chunks of the same block size allows us to fit these in the first argument of the compression function. For example, SHA-256 has a block size of 512 bit. Figure 2.9 illustrates this step.

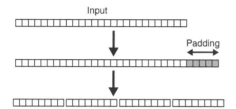

Figure 2.9 The first step of the Merkle–Damgård construction is to add some padding to the input message. After this step, the input length should be a multiple of the input size of the compression function in use (for example, 8 bytes). To do this, we add 5 bytes of padding at the end to make it 32 bytes. We then cut the messages into 4 blocks of 8 bytes.

Second, it iteratively applies the compression function to the message blocks, using the previous output of the compression function as second argument to the compression function. The final output is the *digest*. Figure 2.10 illustrates this step.

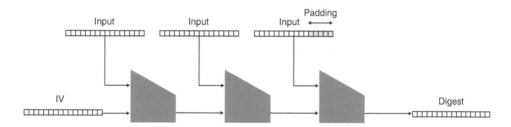

Figure 2.10 The Merkle–Damgård construction iteratively applies a compression function to each block of the input to be hashed and the output of the previous compression function. The final call to the compression function directly returns the digest.

And this is how SHA-2 works, by iteratively calling its compression function on fragments of the input until everything is processed into a final digest.

NOTE The Merkle–Damgård construction is proven collision resistant if the compression function itself is. Thus, the security of the *arbitrary-length input* hash function is reduced to the security of a *fixed-sized* compression function, which is easier to design and analyze. Therein lies the ingenuity of the Merkle–Damgård construction.

In the beginning, the second argument to the compression function is usually fixed and standardized to be a "nothing-up-my-sleeve" value. Specifically, SHA-256 uses the square roots of the first prime numbers to derive this value. A nothing-up-my-sleeve value is meant to convince the cryptographic community that it was not chosen to make the hash function weaker (for example, in order to create a backdoor). This is a popular concept in cryptography.

> **WARNING**   While SHA-2 is a perfectly fine hash function to use, it is not suitable for hashing secrets. This is because of a downside of the Merkle–Damgård construction, which makes SHA-2 vulnerable to an attack (called a *length-extension attack*) if used to hash secrets. We will talk about this in more detail in the next chapter.

2.5.2 *The SHA-3 hash function*

As I mentioned earlier, both the MD5 and SHA-1 hash functions were broken somewhat recently. These two functions made use of the same Merkle–Damgård construction I described in the previous section. Because of this, and the fact that SHA-2 is vulnerable to length-extension attacks, NIST decided in 2007 to organize an open competition for a new standard: *SHA-3*. This section introduces the newer standard and attempts to give a high-level explanation of its inner workings.

In 2007, 64 different candidates from different international research teams entered the SHA-3 contest. Five years later, Keccak, one of the submissions, was nominated as the winner and took the name SHA-3. In 2015, SHA-3 was standardized in the FIPS Publication 202 (https://nvlpubs.nist.gov/nistpubs/FIPS/NIST.FIPS.202.pdf).

SHA-3 observes the three previous security properties we talked about and provides as much security as the SHA-2 variants. In addition, it is not vulnerable to length-extension attacks and can be used to hash secrets. For this reason, it is now the recommended hash function to use. It offers the same variants as SHA-2, this time indicating the full name SHA-3 in their named variants: SHA-3-224, SHA-3-256, SHA-3-384, and SHA-3-512. Thus, similarly to SHA-2, SHA-3-256 provides 256 bits of output, for example. Let me now take a few pages to explain how SHA-3 works.

SHA-3 is a cryptographic algorithm built on top of a *permutation*. The easiest way to understand a permutation is to imagine the following: you have a set of elements on the left and the same set of elements on the right. Now trace arrows going from each element on the left to the right. Each element can only have one arrow starting from and terminating to it. You now have one permutation. Figure 2.11 illustrates this principle. By definition, any permutation is also *reversible*, meaning that from the output we can find the input.

SHA-3 is built with a *sponge construction*, a different construction from Merkle–Damgård that was invented as part of the SHA-3 competition. It is based on a particular permutation called *keccak-f* that takes an input and returns an output of the same size.

> **NOTE**   We won't explain how keccak-f was designed, but you will get an idea in chapter 4 about this because it substantially resembles the AES algorithm (with the exception that it doesn't have a key). This is no accident, as one of the inventors of AES was also one of the inventors of SHA-3.

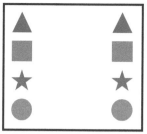 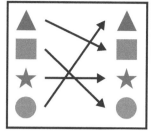 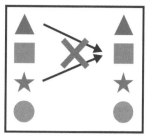

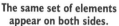

| The same set of elements appear on both sides. | Drawing arrows creates a permutation. | Each element must be connected to a single arrow. |

Figure 2.11 An example permutation acting on four different shapes. You can use the permutation described by the arrows in the middle picture to transform a given shape.

In the next few pages, I use an 8-bit permutation to illustrate how the sponge construction works. Because the permutation is set in stone, you can imagine that figure 2.12 is a good illustration of the mapping created by this permutation on all possible 8-bit inputs. Compared to our previous explanation of a permutation, you can also imagine that each possible 8-bit string is what we represented as different shapes (`000...` is a triangle, `100...` is a square, and so on).

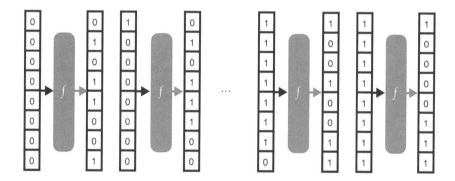

Figure 2.12 A sponge construction makes use of a specified permutation f. By operating on an input, our example permutation creates a mapping between all possible input of 8 bits and all possible output of 8 bits.

To use a permutation in our sponge construction, we also need to define an arbitrary division of the input and the output into a *rate* and a *capacity*. It's a bit weird but stick with it. Figure 2.13 illustrates this process.

Where we set the limit between the rate and the capacity is arbitrary. Different versions of SHA-3 use different parameters. We informally point out that the capacity is to be treated like a secret, and the larger it is, the more secure the sponge construction.

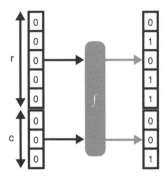

Figure 2.13   The permutation *f* randomizes an input of size 8 bits into an output of the same size. In a sponge construction, this permutation's input and output are divided into two parts: the rate (of size *r* and the capacity (of size *c*).

Now, like all good hash functions, we need to be able to hash something, right? Otherwise, it's a bit useless. To do that, we simply XOR ($\oplus$) the input with the rate of the permutation's input. In the beginning, this is just a bunch of 0s. As we pointed out earlier, the capacity is treated like a secret, so we won't XOR anything with it. Figure 2.14 illustrates this.

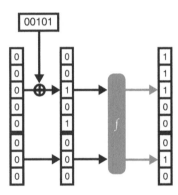

Figure 2.14   To absorb the 5 bits of input 00101, a sponge construction with a rate of 5 bits can simply XOR the 5 bits with the rate (which is initialized to 0s). The permutation then randomizes the state.

The output obtained should now look random (although we can trivially find what the input is as a permutation is reversible by definition). What if we want to ingest a larger input? Well, similarly to what we did with SHA-2, we would

1   Pad the input if necessary, then divide the input into blocks of the rate size.
2   Iteratively call the permutation while XORing each block with the input of a permutation and permuting the *state* (the intermediate value output by the last operation) after each block has been XORed.

I ignore the padding in the rest of these explanations for the sake of simplification, but padding is an important step of the process to distinguish between inputs like 0 and 00, for example. Figure 2.15 pictures these two steps.

So far so good, but we still haven't produced a digest. To do this, we can simply use the rate of the last state of the sponge (again, we are not touching the capacity). To

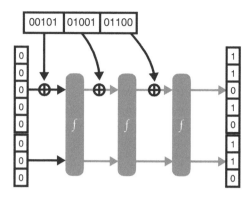

Figure 2.15 In order to absorb inputs larger than the rate size, a sponge construction iteratively XORs input blocks with the rate and permutates the result.

obtain a longer digest, we can continue to permute and read from the rate part of the state as figure 2.16 shows.

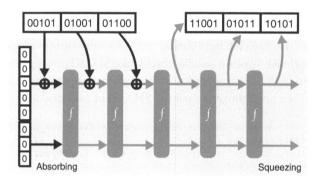

Figure 2.16 To obtain a digest with the sponge construction, one iteratively permutes the state and retrieves as much rate (the upper part of the state) as needed.

And this is how SHA-3 works. Because it is a *sponge construction*, ingesting the input is naturally called *absorbing* and creating the digest is called *squeezing*. The sponge is specified with a 1,600-bit permutation using different values for r and c, depending on the security advertised by the different versions of SHA-3.

SHA-3 is a random oracle

I talked about random oracles earlier: an ideal and fictional construction that returns perfectly random responses to queries and repeats itself if we query it with the same input twice. It turns out that the sponge construction behaves closely to a random oracle, as long as the permutation used by the construction looks random enough. How do we prove such security properties on the permutation? Our best approach is to try to break it, many times, until we gain strong confidence in its design (which is what happened during the SHA-3 competition). The fact that SHA-3 can be modeled as a random oracle instantly gives it the security properties we would expect from a hash function.

2.5.3   *SHAKE and cSHAKE: Two extendable output functions (XOF)*

I introduced the two major hash function standards: SHA-2 and SHA-3. These are well-defined hash functions that take arbitrary-length inputs and produce random-looking and fixed-length outputs. As you will see in later chapters, cryptographic protocols often necessitate this type of primitives but do not want to be constrained by the fixed sizes of a hash function's digest. For this reason, the SHA-3 standard introduced a more versatile primitive called an *extendable output function* or *XOF* (pronounced "zoff"). This section introduces the two standardized XOFs: SHAKE and cSHAKE.

SHAKE, specified in FIPS 202 along with SHA-3, can be seen as a hash function that returns an output of an arbitrary length. SHAKE is fundamentally the same construction as SHA-3, except that it is faster and permutes as much as you want it to permute in the squeezing phase. Producing outputs of different sizes is quite useful, not only to create a digest, but also to create random numbers, to derive keys, and so on. I will talk about the different applications of SHAKE again in this book; for now, imagine that SHAKE is like SHA-3 except that it provides an output of any length you might want.

This construction is so useful in cryptography that one year after SHA-3 was standardized, NIST published its Special Publication 800-185 containing a *customizable SHAKE* called *cSHAKE*. cSHAKE is pretty much exactly like SHAKE, except that it also takes a customization string. This customization string can be empty, or it can be any string you want. Let's first see an example of using cSHAKE in pseudocode:

```
cSHAKE(input="hello world", output_length=256, custom_string="my_hash")
-> 72444fde79690f0cac19e866d7e6505c
cSHAKE(input="hello world", output_length=256, custom_string="your_hash")
-> 688a49e8c2a1e1ab4e78f887c1c73957
```

As you can see, the two digests differ even though cSHAKE is as deterministic as SHAKE and SHA-3. This is because a different customization string was used. A *customization string* allows you to customize your XOF! This is useful in some protocols where, for example, different hash functions must be used in order to make a proof work. We call this *domain separation*.

As a golden rule in cryptography: if the same cryptographic primitive is used in different use cases, do not use it with the same key (if it takes a key) or/and apply domain separation. You will see more examples of domain separation as we survey cryptographic protocols in later chapters.

> **WARNING**   NIST tends to specify algorithms that take parameters in bits instead of bytes. In the example, a length of 256 bits was requested. Imagine if you had requested a length of 16 bytes and got 2 bytes instead, due to the program thinking you had requested 16 bits of output. This issue is sometimes called a *bit attack*.

As with everything in cryptography, the length of cryptographic strings like keys, parameters, and outputs is strongly tied to the security of the system. It is important that one does not request too short outputs from SHAKE or cSHAKE. *One can never go wrong by using an output of 256 bits* as it provides 128 bits of security against collision attacks. But real-world cryptography sometimes operates in constrained environments that could use shorter cryptographic values. This can be done if the security of the system is carefully analyzed. For example, if collision resistance does not matter in the protocol making use of the value, pre-image resistance only needs 128-bit long outputs from SHAKE or cSHAKE.

2.5.4 Avoid ambiguous hashing with TupleHash

In this chapter, I have talked about different types of cryptographic primitives and cryptographic algorithms. This included

- The SHA-2 hash function, which is vulnerable to length-extension attacks but still widely used when no secrets are hashed
- The SHA-3 hash function, which is the recommended hash function nowadays
- The SHAKE and cSHAKE XOFs, which are more versatile tools than hash functions because they offer a variable output length

I will talk about one more handy function, *TupleHash*, which is based on cSHAKE and specified in the same standard as cSHAKE. TupleHash is an interesting function that allows one to hash a *tuple* (a list of something). To explain what TupleHash is and why it is useful, let me tell you a story.

A few years ago I was tasked to review a cryptocurrency as part of my work. It included basic features one would expect from a cryptocurrency: accounts, payments, and so on. Transactions between users would contain metadata about who is sending how much to whom. It would also include a small fee to compensate the network for processing the transaction.

Alice, for example, can send transactions to the network, but to have them accepted, she needs to include proof that the transaction came from her. For this, she can hash the transaction and sign it (I gave a similar example in chapter 1). Anyone can hash the transaction and verify the signature on the hash to see that this is the transaction Alice meant to send. Figure 2.17 illustrates that a man-in-the-middle (MITM) attacker who intercepts the transaction before it reaches the network would not be

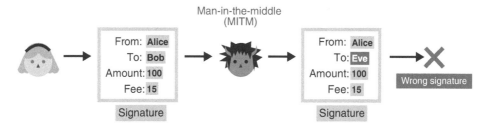

Figure 2.17 Alice sends a transaction as well as a signature over the hash of the transaction. If a MITM attacker attempts to tamper with the transaction, the hash will be different and, thus, the attached signature will be incorrect.

able to tamper with the transaction. This is because the hash would change, and the signature would then not verify the new transaction digest.

You will see in chapter 7 that such an attacker is, of course, unable to forge Alice's signature on a new digest. And thanks to the second pre-image resistance of the hash function used, the attacker cannot find a totally different transaction that would hash to the same digest either.

Is our MITM attacker harmless? We're not out of the woods yet. Unfortunately, for the cryptocurrency I was auditing, the transaction was hashed by simply concatenating each field:

```
$ echo -n "Alice""Bob""100""15" | openssl dgst -sha3-256
34d6b397c7f2e8a303fc8e39d283771c0397dad74cef08376e27483efc29bb02
```

What appeared as totally fine, actually completely broke the cryptocurrency's payment system. Doing this trivially allows an attacker to break the second pre-image resistance of the hash function. Take a few moments to think about how you could find a different transaction that hashes to the same digest, 34d6....

What happens if we move one digit from the *fee* field to the *amount* field? One can see that the following transaction hashes to the same digest Alice signed:

```
$ echo -n "Alice""Bob""1001""5" | openssl dgst -sha3-256
34d6b397c7f2e8a303fc8e39d283771c0397dad74cef08376e27483efc29bb02
```

And thus, a MITM attacker who would want Bob to receive a bit more money would be able to modify the transaction without invalidating the signature. As you've probably guessed, this is what TupleHash solves. It allows you to unambiguously hash a list of fields by using non-ambiguous encoding. What happens in reality is something close to the following (with the || string concatenation operation):

```
cSHAKE(input="5"||"Alice"||"3"||"Bob"||"3"||"100"||"2"||"10",
  ➥ output_length=256, custom_string="TupleHash"+"anything you want")
```

The input is this time constructed by prefixing each field of the transaction with its length. Take a minute to understand why this solves our issue. In general, one can use any hash function safely by always making sure to *serialize* the input before hashing it. Serializing the input means that there always exists a way to *deserialize* it (meaning to recover the original input). If one can deserialize the data, then there isn't any ambiguity on field delimitation.

2.6   *Hashing passwords*

You have seen several useful functions in this chapter that either are hash functions or extend hash functions. But before you can jump to the next chapter, I need to mention *password hashing*.

Imagine the following scenario: you have a website (which would make you a webmaster) and you want to have your users register and log in to the site, so you create two web pages for these two respective features. Suddenly, you wonder, how are you going to store their passwords? Do you store those in cleartext in a database? There seems to be nothing wrong with this at first, you think. It is not perfect though. People tend to reuse the same password everywhere and if (or when) you get breached and attackers manage to dump all of your users' passwords, it will be bad for your users, and it will be bad for the reputation of your platform. You think a little bit more, and you realize that an attacker who would be able to steal this database would then be able to log in as any user. Storing the passwords in cleartext is now less than ideal and you would like to have a better way to deal with this.

One solution could be to hash your passwords and only store the digests. When someone logs in to your website, the flow would be similar to the following:

1 You receive the user's password.

2 You hash the password they give you and get rid of the password.

3 You compare the digest with what you had stored previously; if it matches, the user is logged in.

The flow allows you to handle users' passwords for a limited time. Still, an attacker that gets into your servers can stealthily remain to log passwords from this flow until you detect its presence. We acknowledge that this is still not a perfect situation, but we still improved the site's security. In security, we also call this *defense in depth*, which is the act of layering imperfect defenses in hope that an attacker will not defeat all of those layers. This is what real-world cryptography is also about. But other problems exist with this solution:

- *If an attacker retrieves hashed passwords, a brute force attack or an exhaustive search (trying all possible passwords) can be undertaken.* This would test each attempt against the whole database. Ideally, we would want an attacker to only be able to attack one hashed password at a time.
- *Hash functions are supposed to be as fast.* Attackers can leverage this to brute force (many, many passwords per second). Ideally, we would have a mechanism to slow down such attacks.

The first issue has been commonly solved by using *salts*, which are random values that are public and different for each user. We use a salt along with the user's password when hashing it, which in some sense is like using a per-user customization string with cSHAKE: it effectively creates a different hash function for every user. Because each user uses a different hash function, an attacker cannot precompute large tables of passwords (called *rainbow tables*), hoping to test those against the whole database of stolen password hashes.

The second issue is solved with *password hashes*, which are designed to be slow. The current state-of-the-art choice for this is *Argon2*, the winner of the Password Hashing Competition (https://password-hashing.net) that ran from 2013 to 2015. At the time of this writing (2021), Argon2 is on track to be standardized as an RFC (https://datatracker .ietf.org/doc/draft-irtf-cfrg-argon2/). In practice, other nonstandard algorithms like

PBKDF2, bcrypt, and scrypt are also used. The problem is that these can be used with insecure parameters and are, thus, not straightforward to configure in practice.

In addition, only Argon2 and scrypt defend against heavy optimizations from attackers as other schemes are not memory hard. The term *memory hard* means that the algorithm can only be optimized through the optimization of memory access. In other words, optimizing the rest doesn't gain you much. As optimizing memory access is limited even with dedicated hardware (there's only so much cache you can put around a CPU), memory-hard functions are slow to run on any type of device. This is a desired property when you want to prevent attackers from getting a non-negligible speed advantage in evaluating a function.

Figure 2.18 reviews the different types of hash functions you saw in this chapter.

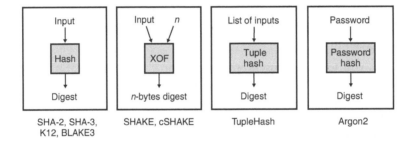

Figure 2.18   In this chapter, you saw four types of hash functions: (1) the normal kind that provide a unique random-looking identifier for arbitrary-length inputs; (2) extendable output functions that are similar but provide an arbitrary-length output; (3) tuple hash functions that unambiguously list hash values; and (4) password-hashing functions that can't be easily optimized in order to store passwords safely.

Summary

- A hash function provides collision resistance, pre-image resistance, and second pre-image resistance.
  - Pre-image resistance means that one shouldn't be able to find the input that produced a digest.
  - Second pre-image resistance means that from an input and its digest, one shouldn't be able to find a different input that hashes to the same digest.
  - Collision resistance means that one shouldn't be able to find two random inputs that hash to the same output.
- The most widely adopted hash function is SHA-2, while the recommended hash function is SHA-3 due to SHA-2's lack of resistance to length-extension attacks.
- SHAKE is an extendable output function (XOF) that acts like a hash function but provides an arbitrary-length digest.

- cSHAKE (for customizable SHAKE) allows one to easily create instances of SHAKE that behave like different XOFs. This is called domain separation.
- Objects should be serialized before being hashed in order to avoid breaking the second pre-image resistance of the hash function. Algorithms like TupleHash automatically take care of this.
- Hashing passwords make use of slower hash functions designed specifically for that purpose. Argon2 is the state-of-the-art choice.

3

Message authentication codes

This chapter covers

- Message authentication codes (MACs)
- The security properties and the pitfalls of MACs
- The widely adopted standards for MACs

Mix a hash function with a secret key and you obtain something called a *message authentication code* (MAC), a cryptographic primitive to protect the integrity of data. The addition of a secret key is the foundation behind any type of security: without keys there can be no confidentiality, and there can be no authentication. While hash functions can provide authentication or integrity for arbitrary data, they do that thanks to an additional trusted channel that cannot be tampered with. In this chapter, you will see how a MAC can be used to create such a trusted channel and what else it can do as well.

NOTE For this chapter, you'll need to have read chapter 2 on hash functions.

3.1 Stateless cookies, a motivating example for MACs

Let's picture the following scenario: you are a web page. You're bright, full of colors, and above all, you're proud of serving a community of loyal users. To interact with you, visitors must first log in by sending you their credentials, which you must then validate. If the credentials match the ones that were used when the user first signed up, then you have successfully *authenticated* the user.

Of course, a web browsing experience is composed not just of one, but of many requests. To avoid having the user re-authenticate with every request, you can make their browser store the user credentials and resend them automatically within each request. Browsers have a feature just for that—*cookies*! Cookies are not just for credentials. They can store anything you want the user to send you within each of their requests.

While this naive approach works well, usually you don't want to store sensitive information like user passwords in cleartext in the browser. Instead, a session cookie most often carries a random string, generated right after a user logs in. The web server stores the random string in a temporary database under a user's nickname. If the browser publishes the session cookie somehow, no information about the user's password is leaked (although it can be used to impersonate the user). The web server also has the possibility to kill the session by deleting the cookie on their side, which is nice.

There is nothing wrong with this approach, but in some cases, it might not scale well. If you have many servers, it could be annoying to have all the servers share the association between your users and the random strings. Instead, you could store more information on the browser side. Let's see how we can do this.

Naively, you can have the cookie contain a username instead of a random string, but this is obviously an issue, as I can now impersonate any user by manually modifying the username contained in the cookie. Perhaps the hash functions you learned about in chapter 2 can help us. Take a few minutes to think of a way hash functions can prevent a user from tampering with their own cookies.

A second naive approach could be to store not only a username, but a digest of that username as well in a cookie. You can use a hash function like SHA-3 to hash the username. I illustrate this in figure 3.1. Do you think this can work?

There's a big problem with this approach. Remember, the hash function is a public algorithm and can be recomputed on new data by a malicious user. If you do not trust

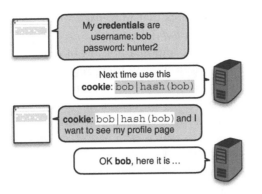

Figure 3.1   To authenticate the requests for a browser, a web server asks the browser to store a username and a hash of that username, sending this information in every subsequent request.

the origin of a hash, it does not provide data integrity! Indeed, figure 3.2 shows that if a malicious user modifies the username in their cookie, they can also simply recompute the digest part of the cookie.

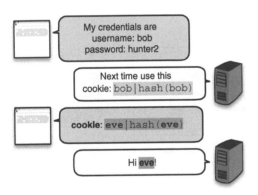

Figure 3.2   A malicious user can modify the information contained in their cookies. If a cookie contains a username and a hash, both can be modified to impersonate a different user.

Still, using a hash is not a foolish idea. What else can we do? Turns out that there is a similar primitive to the hash function, a MAC, that will do exactly what we need.

A *MAC* is a secret key algorithm that takes an input, like a hash function, but it also takes a secret key (who saw that coming?) It then produces a unique output called an *authentication tag*. This process is deterministic; given the same secret key and the same message, a MAC produces the same authentication tag. I illustrate this in figure 3.3.

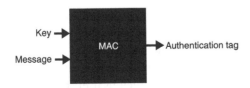

Figure 3.3   The interface of a message authentication code (MAC). The algorithm takes a secret key and a message, and deterministically produces a unique authentication tag. Without the key, it should be impossible to reproduce that authentication tag.

To make sure a user can't tamper with their cookie, let's now make use of this new primitive. When the user logs in for the first time, you produce an authentication tag from your secret key and their username and have them store their username and the authentication tag in a *cookie*. Because they don't know the secret key, they won't be able to forge a valid authentication tag for a different username.

To validate their cookie, you do the same: produce an authentication tag from your secret key and the username contained in the cookie and check if it matches the authentication tag contained in the cookie. If it matches, it must have come from you, as you were the only one who could have produced a valid authentication tag (under your secret key). I illustrate this in figure 3.4.

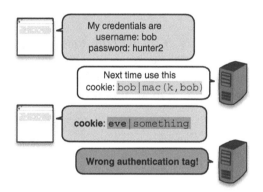

Figure 3.4 A malicious user tampers with his cookie but cannot forge a valid authentication tag for the new cookie. Subsequently, the web page cannot verify the authenticity and integrity of the cookie and, thus, discards the request.

A MAC is like a private hash function that only you can compute because you know the key. In a sense, you can personalize a hash function with a key. The relationship with hash functions doesn't stop there. You will see later in this chapter that MACs are often built from hash functions. Next, let's see a different example using real code.

3.2 An example in code

So far, you were the only one using a MAC. Let's increase the number of participants and use that as a motivation to write some code to see how MACs are used in practice. Imagine that you want to communicate with someone else, and you do not care about other people reading your messages. What you really care about, though, is the integrity of the messages: they must not be modified! A solution is to have both you and your correspondent use the same secret key with a MAC to protect the integrity of your communications.

For this example, we'll use one of the most popular MAC functions—*hash-based message authentication code* (HMAC)—with the Rust programming language. HMAC is a message authentication code that uses a hash function at its core. It is compatible with different hash functions, but it is mostly used in conjunction with SHA-2. As the following listing shows, the sending part simply takes a key and a message and returns an authentication tag.

Listing 3.1 Sending an authenticated message in Rust

```rust
use sha2::Sha256;
use hmac::{Hmac, Mac, NewMac};

fn send_message(key: &[u8], message: &[u8]) -> Vec<u8> {
    let mut mac = Hmac::<Sha256>::new(key.into());

    mac.update(message);

    mac.finalize().into_bytes().to_vec()
}
```

Instantiates HMAC with a secret key and the SHA-256 hash function

Buffers more input for HMAC

Returns the authentication tag

On the other side, the process is similar. After receiving both the message and the authentication tag, your friend can generate their own tag with the same secret key and then compare those. Similarly to encryption, both sides need to share the same secret key to make this work. The following listing shows how this works.

Listing 3.2 Receiving an authenticated message in Rust

```rust
use sha2::Sha256;
use hmac::{Hmac, Mac, NewMac};

fn receive_message(key: &[u8], message: &[u8],
  authentication_tag: &[u8]) -> bool {
    let mut mac = Hmac::<Sha256>::new(key);
    mac.update(message);

    mac.verify(&authentication_tag).is_ok()
}
```

The receiver needs to recreate the authentication tag from the same key and message.

Checks if the reproduced authentication tag matches the received one

---

Note that this protocol is not perfect: it allows replays. If a message and its authentication tag are replayed at a later point in time, they will still be authentic, but you'll have no way of detecting that it is an older message being resent to you. Later in this chapter, I'll tell you about a solution. Now that you know what a MAC can be used for, I'll talk about some of the "gotchas" of MACs in the next section.

3.3   *Security properties of a MAC*

MACs, like all cryptographic primitives, have their oddities and pitfalls. Before going any further, I will provide a few explanations on what security properties MACs provide and how to use them correctly. You will learn (in this order) that

- MACs are resistant against forgery of authentication tags.
- An authentication tag needs to be of a minimum length to be secure.
- Messages can be replayed if authenticated naively.
- Verifying an authentication tag is prone to bugs.

3.3.1 Forgery of authentication tag

The general security goal of a MAC is to prevent *authentication tag forgery* on a new message. This means that without knowledge of the secret key, k, one cannot compute the authentication tag $t = MAC(k, m)$ on messages m of their choice. This sounds fair, right? We can't compute a function if we're missing an argument.

  MACs provide much more assurance than that, however. Real-world applications often let attackers obtain authentication tags on some constrained messages. For example, this was the case in our introduction scenario, where a user could obtain almost arbitrary authentication tags by registering with an available nickname. Hence, MACs have to be secure even against these more powerful attackers. A MAC usually comes with a proof that even if an attacker can ask you to produce the authentication tags for a large number of arbitrary messages, the attacker should still not be able to forge an authentication tag on a never-seen-before message by themselves.

> **NOTE** One could wonder how proving such an extreme property is useful. If the attacker can directly request authentication tags on arbitrary messages, then what is there left to protect? But this is how security proofs work in cryptography: they take the most powerful attacker and show that even then, the attacker is hopeless. In practice, the attacker is usually less powerful and, thus, we have confidence that if a powerful attacker can't do something bad, a less powerful one has even less recourse.

As such, you should be protected against such forgeries *as long as the secret key used with the MAC stays secret*. This implies that the secret key has to be random enough (more on that in chapter 8) and large enough (usually 16 bytes). Furthermore, a MAC is vulnerable to the same type of ambiguous attack we saw in chapter 2. If you are trying to authenticate structures, make sure to serialize them before authenticating them with a MAC; otherwise, forgery might be trivial.

3.3.2 Lengths of authentication tag

Another possible attack against usage of MACs are *collisions*. Remember, finding a collision for a hash function means finding two different inputs X and Y such that $HASH(X) = HASH(Y)$. We can extend this definition to MACs by defining a collision when $MAC(k, X) = MAC(k, Y)$ for inputs X and Y.

  As we learned in chapter 2 with the birthday bound, collisions can be found with high probability if the output length of our algorithm is small. For example, with MACs, an attacker who has access to a service producing 64-bit authentication tags can find a collision with high probability by requesting a much lower number (2^{32}) of tags. Such a collision is rarely exploitable in practice, but there exist some scenarios where collision resistance matters. For this reason, we want an authentication tag size that would limit such attacks. In general, 128-bit authentication tags are used as they provide enough resistance.

[requesting 2^{64} authentication tags] would take 250,000 years in a continuous 1Gbps link, and without changing the secret key K during all this time.

—RFC 2104 ("HMAC: Keyed-Hashing for Message Authentication," 1997)

Using a 128-bit authentication tag might appear counterintuitive because we want 256-bit outputs for hash functions. But hash functions are public algorithms that one can compute *offline*, which allows an attacker to optimize and parallelize an attack heavily. With a keyed function like a MAC, an attacker cannot efficiently optimize the attack offline and is forced to directly request authentication tags from you, which usually makes the attack much slower. A 128-bit authentication tag requires $2^{64} online$ queries from the attacker in order to have a 50% chance to find collisions, which is deemed large enough. Nonetheless, one might still want to increase an authentication tag to 256-bit, which is possible as well.

3.3.3   *Replay attacks*

One thing I still haven't mentioned are *replay attacks*. Let's see a scenario that is vulnerable to such attacks. Imagine that Alice and Bob communicate in the open using an insecure connection. In order to protect the messages from tampering, they append each of their messages with an authentication tag. More specifically, they both use two different secret keys to protect different sides of the connection (as per best practice). I illustrate this in figure 3.5.

Figure 3.5   Two users sharing two keys, `k1` and `k2`, exchange messages along with authentication tags. These tags are computed from `k1` or `k2`, depending on the direction of the messages. A malicious observer replays one of the messages to the user.

In this scenario, nothing prevents a malicious observer from replaying one of the messages to its recipient. A protocol relying on a MAC must be aware of this and build protections against this. One way is to add an incrementing counter to the input of the MAC as shown in figure 3.6.

In practice, counters are often a fixed 64-bit length. This allows one to send 2^{64} messages before filling up the counter (and risking it to wrap around and repeat itself).

Wrong authentication tag

Figure 3.6 Two users sharing two keys, k1 and k2, exchange messages along with authentication tags. These tags are computed from k1 or k2, depending on the direction of the messages. A malicious observer replays one of the messages to the user. Because the victim has incremented his counter, the tag will be computed over 2, fine and you? and will not match the tag sent by the attacker. This allows the victim to successfully reject the replayed message.

Of course, if the shared secret is rotated frequently (meaning that after X messages, participants agree to use a new shared secret), then the size of the counter can be reduced and reset to 0 after a key rotation. (You should convince yourself that reusing the same counter with two different keys is OK.) Again, counters are *never variable-length* because of ambiguous attacks.

> **Exercise**
> Can you figure out how a variable-length counter could possibly allow an attacker to forge an authentication tag?

3.3.4 *Verifying authentication tags in constant time*

This last gotcha is dear to me as I found this vulnerability many times in applications I audited. When verifying an authentication tag, the comparison between the received authentication tag and the one you compute must be done in *constant time*. This means the comparison should always take the same time, assuming the received one is of the correct size. If the time it takes to compare the two authentication tags is not constant time, it is probably because it returns the moment the two tags differ. This usually gives enough information to enable attacks that can recreate byte by byte a valid authentication tag by measuring how long it takes for the verification to finish. I explain this in the following comic strip. We call these types of attacks *timing attacks*.

Fortunately for us, cryptographic libraries implementing MACs also provide convenient functions to verify an authentication tag in constant time. If you're wondering how this is done, listing 3.3 shows how Golang implements an authentication tag comparison in constant time code.

Listing 3.3 Constant time comparison in Golang

```
for i := 0; i < len(x); i++ {
    v |= x[i] ^ y[i]
}
```

The trick is that no branch is ever taken. How this works exactly is left as an exercise for the reader.

3.4   MAC in the real world

Now that I have introduced what MACs are and what security properties they provide, let's take a look at how people use them in real settings. The following sections address this.

3.4.1   Message authentication

MACs are used in many places to ensure that the communications between two machines or two users are not tampered with. This is necessary in both cases where communications are in cleartext and where communications are encrypted. I have already explained how this happens when communications are transmitted in cleartext, and in chapter 4, I will explain how this is done when communications are encrypted.

3.4.2   Deriving keys

One particularity of MACs is that they are often designed to produce bytes that look random (like hash functions). You can use this property to implement a single key to generate random numbers or to produce more keys. In chapter 8 on secrets and randomness, I will introduce the HMAC-based key derivation function (HKDF) that does exactly this by using HMAC, one of the MAC algorithms we will talk about in this chapter.

The pseudorandom function (PRF)

Imagine the set of all functions that take a variable-length input and produce a random output of a fixed size. If we could pick a function at random from this set and use it as a MAC (without a key), it would be swell. We would just have to agree on which function (kind of like agreeing on a key). Unfortunately, we can't have such a set as it is way too large, but we can emulate picking such a random function by designing something close enough: we call such constructions *pseudorandom functions (PRFs)*. HMAC and most practical MACs are such constructions. They are randomized by a key argument instead. Choosing a different key is like picking a random function.

Exercise

Caution: not all MACs are PRFs. Can you see why?

3.4.3   *Integrity of cookies*

To track your users' browser sessions, you can send them a random string (associated to their metadata) or send them the metadata directly, attached with an authentication tag so that they cannot modify it. This is what I explained in the introduction example.

3.4.4   *Hash tables*

Programming languages usually expose data structures called *hash tables* (also called hashmaps, dictionaries, associated arrays, and so on) that make use of noncryptographic hash functions. If a service exposes this data structure in such a way where the input of the noncryptographic hash function can be controlled by attackers, this can lead to *denial of service* (DoS) *attacks*, meaning that an attacker can render the service unusable. To avoid this, the noncryptographic hash function is usually randomized at the start of the program.

Many major applications use a MAC with a random key in place of the noncryptographic hash function. This is the case for many programming languages (like Rust, Python, and Ruby), or for major applications (like the Linux kernel). They all make use of *SipHash*, a poorly-named MAC optimized for short authentication tags, with a random key generated at the start of the program.

3.5   *Message authentication codes (MACs) in practice*

You learned that MACs are cryptographic algorithms that can be used between one or more parties in order to protect the integrity and the authenticity of information. As widely used MACs also exhibit good randomness, MACs are also often used to produce random numbers deterministically in different types of algorithms (for example, the time-based one-time password [TOTP] algorithm that you will learn in chapter 11). In this section, we will look at two standardized MAC algorithms that one can use nowadays—HMAC and KMAC.

3.5.1   *HMAC, a hash-based MAC*

The most widely used MAC is HMAC (for *hash-based MAC*), invented in 1996 by M. Bellare, R. Canetti, and H. Krawczyk, and specified in RFC 2104, FIPS Publication 198, and ANSI X9.71. HMAC, like its name indicates, is a way to use hash functions with a key. Using a hash function to build MACs is a popular concept as hash functions have widely available implementations, are fast in software, and also benefit from hardware support on most systems. Remember that I mentioned in chapter 2 that SHA-2 should not be used directly to hash secrets due to *length-extension attacks* (more on that at the end of this chapter). How does one figure out how to transform a hash function into a keyed function? This is what HMAC solves for us. Under the hood, HMAC follows these steps, which I illustrate visually in figure 3.7:

1   It first creates two keys from the main key: $k1 = k \oplus ipad$ and $k2 = k \oplus opad$, where *ipad* (inner padding) and *opad* (outer padding) are constants, and $\oplus$ is the symbol for the XOR operation.

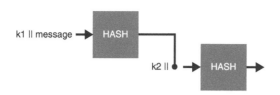

Figure 3.7 HMAC works by hashing the concatenation (| |) of a key, k1, and the input message, and then by hashing the concatenation of a key, k2, with the output of the first operation. k1 and k2 are both deterministically derived from a secret key, k.

2 It then concatenates a key, k1, with the message and hashes it.

3 The result is concatenated with a key, k2, and hashed one more time.

4 This produces the final authentication tag.

Because HMAC is customizable, the size of its authentication tag is dictated by the hash function used. For example, HMAC-SHA256 makes use of SHA-256 and produces an authentication tag of 256 bits, HMAC-SHA512 produces an authentication tag of 512 bits, and so on.

> **WARNING** While one can truncate the output of HMAC to reduce its size, an authentication tag should be at minimum 128 bits as we talked about earlier. This is not always respected, and some applications will go as low as 64 bits due to explicitly handling a limited amount of queries. There are tradeoffs with this approach, and once again, it is important to read the fine print before doing something nonstandard.

HMAC was constructed this way in order to facilitate proofs. In several papers, HMAC is proven to be secure against forgeries as long as the hash function underneath holds some good properties, which all cryptographically secure hash functions should. Due to this, we can use HMAC in combination with a large number of hash functions. Today, HMAC is mostly used with SHA-2.

3.5.2 *KMAC, a MAC based on cSHAKE*

As SHA-3 is not vulnerable to length-extension attacks (this was actually a requirement for the SHA-3 competition), it makes little sense to use SHA-3 with HMAC instead of something like SHA-3-256(key || message) that would work well in practice. This is exactly what *KMAC* does.

KMAC makes use of cSHAKE, the customizable version of the SHAKE extendable output function (XOF) that you saw in chapter 2. KMAC unambiguously encodes the MAC key, the input, and the requested output length (KMAC is some sort of extendable output MAC) and gives this to cSHAKE as an input to absorb (see figure 3.8). KMAC also uses "KMAC" as function name (to customize cSHAKE) and can, in addition, take a user-defined customization string.

Interestingly, because KMAC also absorbs the requested output length, several calls with different output lengths provide totally different results, which is rarely the case for XOFs in general. This makes KMAC quite a versatile function in practice.

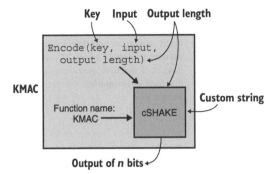

Figure 3.8   **KMAC is simply a wrapper around cSHAKE. To use a key, it encodes (in a unambiguous way) the key, the input, and the output length as the input to cSHAKE.**

3.6   *SHA-2 and length-extension attacks*

We have mentioned several times that one shouldn't hash secrets with SHA-2 as it is not resistant to *length-extension attacks*. In this section, we aim to provide a simple explanation of this attack.

Let's go back to our introduction scenario, to the step where we attempted to simply use SHA-2 in order to protect the integrity of the cookie. Remember that it was not good enough as the user can tamper with the cookie (for example, by adding an admin=true field) and recompute the hash over the cookie. Indeed, SHA-2 is a public function and nothing prevents the user from doing this. Figure 3.9 illustrates this.

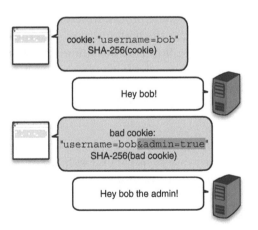

Figure 3.9   **A web page sends a cookie followed by a hash of that cookie to a user. The user is then required to send the cookie to authenticate themselves in every subsequent request. Unfortunately, a malicious user can tamper with the cookie and recompute the hash, breaking the integrity check. The cookie is then accepted as valid by the web page.**

The next best idea was to add a secret key to what we hash. This way, the user cannot recompute the digest as the secret key is required, much like a MAC. On receipt of the tampered cookie, the page computes SHA-256(key || tampered_cookie), where

|| represents the concatenation of the two values and obtains something that won't match what the malicious user probably sent. Figure 3.10 illustrates this approach.

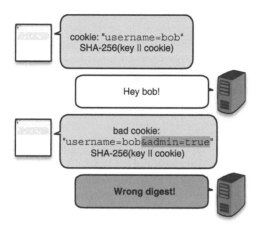

Figure 3.10 By using a key when computing the hash of the cookie, one could think that a malicious user who wants to tamper with their own cookie wouldn't be able to compute the correct digest over the new cookie. We will see later that this is not true for SHA-256.

Unfortunately, SHA-2 has an annoying peculiarity: from a digest over an input, one can compute the digest of an input and more. What does this mean? Let's take a look at figure 3.11, where one uses SHA-256 as `SHA-256(secret || input1)`.

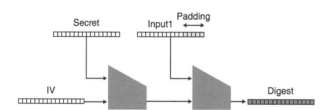

Figure 3.11 SHA-256 hashes a secret concatenated with a cookie (here named `input1`). Remember that SHA-256 works by using the Merkle–Damgård construction to iteratively call a compression function over blocks of the input, starting from an initialization vector (IV).

Figure 3.11 is highly simplified but imagine that `input1` is the string `user=bob`. Notice that the digest obtained is effectively the full intermediate state of the hash function at this point. Nothing prevents one from pretending that the `padding` section is part of the input, continuing the Merkle–Damgård dance. In figure 3.12, we illustrate this attack, where one would take the digest and compute the hash of `input1 || padding || input2`. In our example, `input2` is `&admin=true`.

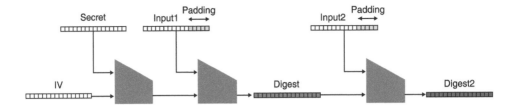

Figure 3.12   The output of the SHA-256 hash of a cookie (the middle digest) is used to extend the hash to more data, creating a hash (the right digest) of the secret concatenated with `input1`, the first padding bytes, and `input2`.

This vulnerability allows one to continue hashing from a given digest, like the operation was not finished. This breaks our previous protocol, as figure 3.13 illustrates.

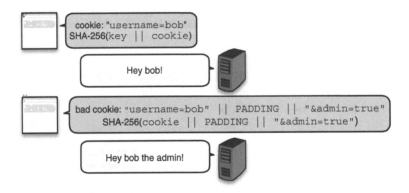

Figure 3.13   An attacker successfully uses a length-extension attack to tamper with their cookie and computes the correct hash using the previous hash.

The fact that the first padding now needs to be part of the input might prevent some protocols from being exploitable. Still, the smallest amount of change can reintroduce a vulnerability. For this reason one should *never* hash secrets with SHA-2. Of course, there are several other ways to do it correctly (for example, `SHA-256(k || message || k)` works), which is what HMAC provides. Thus, use HMAC if you want to use SHA-2 and use KMAC if you prefer SHA-3.

Summary

- Message authentication codes (MACs) are symmetric cryptographic algorithms that allow one or more parties who share the same key to verify the integrity and authenticity of messages.
    - To verify the authenticity of a message and its associated authentication tag, one can recompute the authentication tag of the message and a secret key,

and then match the two authentication tags. If they differ, the message has been tampered with.

– Always compare a received authentication tag with a computed one in constant time.

- While MACs protect the integrity of messages by default, they do not detect when messages are replayed.
- Standardized and well-accepted MACs are the HMAC and the KMAC standards.
- One can use HMAC with different hash functions. In practice, HMAC is often used with the SHA-2 hash function.
- Authentication tags should be of a minimum length of 128 bits to prevent collisions and forgery of authentication tags.
- Never use SHA-256 directly to build a MAC as it can be done incorrectly. Always use a function like HMAC to do this.

Authenticated encryption

Confidentiality is about hiding data from unwanted eyes and encryption is the way to achieve this. Encryption is what the science of cryptography was initially invented for; it's what preoccupied most of the early cryptographers. They would ask themselves, "How can we prevent observers from understanding our conversations?" While the science and its advances first bloomed behind closed doors, benefiting the governments and their militaries only, it is now opened throughout the world. Today, encryption is used everywhere to add privacy and security in the different aspects of our modern lives. In this chapter, we'll find out what encryption really is, what types of problems it solves, and how today's applications make heavy use of this cryptographic primitive.

NOTE For this chapter, you'll need to have read chapter 3 on message authentication codes.

4.1 What's a cipher?

It's like when you use slang to talk to your siblings about what you'll do after school so your mom doesn't know what you're up to.

—Natanael L. (2020, https://twitter.com/Natanael_L)

Let's imagine that our two characters, Alice and Bob, want to exchange some messages privately. In practice, they have many mediums at their disposal (the mail, phones, the internet, and so on), and each of these mediums are by default insecure. The mailman could open their letters; the telecommunication operators can spy on their calls and text messages; internet service providers or any servers on the network that are in between Alice and Bob can access the content of the packets being exchanged.

Without further ado, let's introduce Alice and Bob's savior: the *encryption algorithm* (also called a *cipher*). For now, let's picture this new algorithm as a black box that Alice can use to encrypt her messages to Bob. By *encrypting* a message, Alice transforms it into something that looks random. The encryption algorithm for this takes

- *A secret key*—It is crucial that this element is unpredictable, random, and well protected because the security of the encryption algorithm relies directly on the secrecy of the key. I will talk more about this in chapter 8 on secrets and randomness.
- *Some plaintext*—This is what you want to encrypt. It can be some text, an image, a video, or anything that can be translated into bits.

This encryption process produces a *ciphertext*, which is the encrypted content. Alice can safely use one of the mediums listed previously to send that ciphertext to Bob. The ciphertext will look random to anyone who does not know the secret key, and no information about the content of the message (the plaintext) will be leaked. Once Bob receives this ciphertext, he can use a *decryption algorithm* to revert the ciphertext into the original plaintext. Decryption takes

- *A secret key*—This is the same secret key that Alice used to create the ciphertext. Because the same key is used for both algorithms, we sometimes call the key a *symmetric key*. This is also why we also sometimes specify that we are using *symmetric encryption* and not just *encryption*.
- *Some ciphertext*—This is the encrypted message Bob receives from Alice.

The process then reveals the original plaintext. Figure 4.1 illustrates this flow.

Encryption allows Alice to transform her message into something that looks random and that can be safely transmitted to Bob. Decryption allows Bob to revert the encrypted message back to the original message. This new cryptographic primitive provides confidentiality (or secrecy or privacy) to their messages.

NOTE How do Alice and Bob agree to use the same symmetric key? For now, we'll assume that one of them had access to an algorithm that generates

1. Alice and Bob meet in real life to agree on a key.

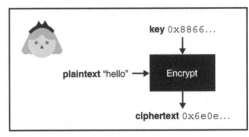

2. Alice can now use it to encrypt messages with an encryption algorithm and the symmetric key.

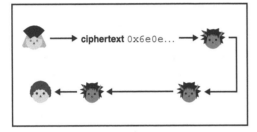

3. The ciphertext is sent to Bob. Observers on the way can't learn anything about the message.

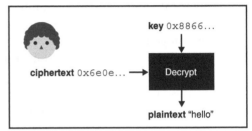

4. Finally Bob can decrypt the message with a decryption algorithm and the same symmetric key.

Figure 4.1   Alice (top right) encrypts the plaintext *hello* with the key `0x8866...` (an abbreviated hexadecimal). Then Alice sends the ciphertext to Bob. Bob (bottom right) decrypts the received ciphertext by using the same key and a decryption algorithm.

unpredictable keys, and that they met in person to exchange the key. In practice, how to bootstrap such protocols with shared secrets is often one of the great challenges companies need to solve. In this book, you will see many different solutions to this problem.

Notice that I have yet to introduce what the title of this chapter, "Authenticated encryption," refers to. I've only talked about encryption alone so far. While encryption alone is not secure (more about that later), I have to explain how it works before I can introduce the authenticated encryption primitive. So bear with me as I first go over the main standard for encryption: the *Advanced Encryption Standard* (AES).

4.2   *The Advanced Encryption Standard (AES) block cipher*

In 1997, NIST started an open competition for an *Advanced Encryption Standard* (AES), aimed at replacing the Data Encryption Standard (DES) algorithm, their previous standard for encryption that was starting to show signs of age. The competition lasted three years, during which time, 15 different designs were submitted by teams of cryptographers from different countries. At the end of the competition, only one submission, Rijndael, by Vincent Rijmen and Joan Daemen was nominated as the winner.

In 2001, NIST released AES as part of the FIPS (Federal Information Processing Standards) 197 publication. AES, the algorithm described in the FIPS standard, is still the main cipher used today. In this section, I explain how AES works.

4.2.1 *How much security does AES provide?*

AES offers three different versions: AES-128 takes a key of 128 bits (16 bytes), AES-192 takes a key of 192 bits (24 bytes), and AES-256 takes a key of 256 bits (32 bytes). The length of the key dictates the level of security—*the bigger, the stronger.* Nonetheless, most applications make use of AES-128 as it provides enough security (128 bits of security).

The term *bit security* is commonly used to indicate the security of cryptographic algorithms. For example, AES-128 specifies that the best attack we know of would take around 2^{128} operations. This number is gigantic, and it is the security level that most applications aim for.

> **Bit security is an upper bound**
> The fact that a 128-bit key provides 128 bits of security is specific to AES; it is not a golden rule. A 128-bit key used in some other algorithm could theoretically provide less than 128-bit security. While a 128-bit key can provide less than 128-bit security, it will never provide more (there's always the brute force attack). Trying all the possible keys would take at most 2^{128} operations, reducing the security to 128 bits at least.

How big is 2^{128}? Notice that the amount between two powers of 2 is doubled. For example 2^3 is twice as much as 2^2. If 2^{100} operations are pretty much impossible to reach, imagine achieving double that (2^{101}). To reach 2^{128}, you have doubled your initial amount 128 times! In plain English, 2^{128} is 340 undecillion 282 decillion 366 nonillion 920 octillion 938 septillion 463 sextillion 463 quintillion 374 quadrillion 607 trillion 431 billion 768 million 211 thousand 456. It is quite hard to imagine how big that number is, but you can assume that we will never be able to reach such a number in practice. We also didn't account for the amount of space required for any large and complex attack to work, which is equally as enormous in practice.

It is foreseeable that AES-128 will remain secure for a long time. That is unless advances in cryptanalysis find a yet undiscovered vulnerability that would reduce the number of operations needed to attack the algorithm.

4.2.2 *The interface of AES*

Looking at the interface of AES for encryption, we see the following:

- The algorithm takes a variable-length key as discussed previously.
- It also takes a plaintext of exactly 128 bits.
- It outputs a ciphertext of exactly 128 bits.

Because AES encrypts a fixed-size plaintext, we call it a *block cipher*. Some other ciphers can encrypt arbitrarily length plaintexts as you will see later in this chapter.

The decryption operation is exactly the reverse of this: it takes the same key, a ciphertext of 128 bits, and returns the original 128-bit plaintext. Effectively, decryption reverts the encryption. This is possible because the encryption and decryption operations are *deterministic*; they produce the same results no matter how many times you call them.

In technical terms, a block cipher with a key is a *permutation*: it maps all the possible plaintexts to all the possible ciphertexts (see the example in figure 4.2). Changing the key changes that mapping. A permutation is also reversible. From a ciphertext, you have a map back to its corresponding plaintext (otherwise, decryption wouldn't work).

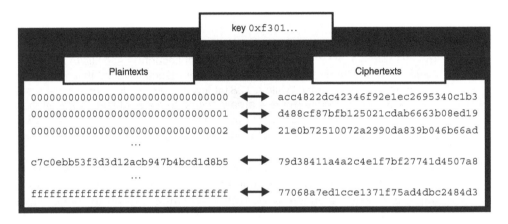

Figure 4.2   A cipher with a key can be seen as a permutation: it maps all the possible plaintexts to all the possible ciphertexts.

Of course, we do not have the room to list all the possible plaintexts and their associated ciphertexts. That would be 2^{128} mappings for a 128-bit block cipher. Instead, we design constructions like AES, which behave like permutations and are randomized by a key. We say that they are *pseudorandom permutations* (PRPs).

4.2.3   *The internals of AES*

Let's dig a bit deeper into the guts of AES to see what's inside. Note that AES sees the *state* of the plaintext during the encryption process as a 4-by-4 matrix of bytes (as you can see in figure 4.3).

This doesn't really matter in practice, but this is how AES is defined. Under the hood, AES works like many similar symmetric cryptographic primitives called *block ciphers*, which are ciphers that encrypt fixed-sized blocks. AES also has a *round function*

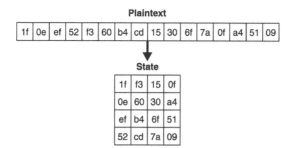

Plaintext

| 1f | 0e | ef | 52 | f3 | 60 | b4 | cd | 15 | 30 | 6f | 7a | 0f | a4 | 51 | 09 |

State

1f	f3	15	0f
0e	60	30	a4
ef	b4	6f	51
52	cd	7a	09

Figure 4.3 When entering the AES algorithm, a plaintext of 16 bytes gets transformed into a 4-by-4 matrix. This state is then encrypted and finally transformed into a 16-byte ciphertext.

that it iterates several times, starting on the original input (the plaintext). I illustrate this in figure 4.4.

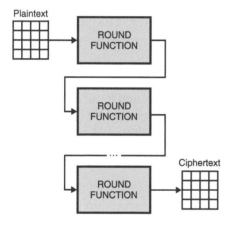

Plaintext

ROUND FUNCTION

ROUND FUNCTION

ROUND FUNCTION

Ciphertext

Figure 4.4 AES iterates a round function over a state in order to encrypt it. The round function takes several arguments including a secret key. (These are missing from the diagram for simplicity.)

Each call to the round function transforms the state further, eventually producing the ciphertext. Each round uses a different *round key*, which is derived from the main symmetric key (during what is called a *key schedule*). The combination of the key schedule and the rounds ensure that the slightest change in the bits of the key or the message renders a completely different encryption.

The round function consists of multiple operations that mix and transform the bytes of the state. The round function of AES specifically makes use of four different subfunctions. While we will shy away from explaining exactly how the subfunctions work (you can find this information in any book about AES), they are named SubBytes, ShiftRows, MixColumns, and AddRoundKey. The first three are easily reversible (you can find the input from the output of the operation), but the last one is not. It performs an exclusive OR (XOR) with the round key and the state and, thus, needs the knowledge of the round key to be reversed. I illustrate what goes into a round in figure 4.5.

The number of iterations of the round function in AES, which are usually practical on a reduced number of rounds, was chosen to thwart cryptanalysis. For example,

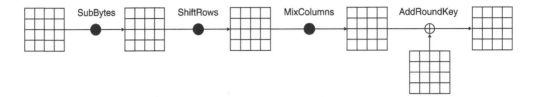

Figure 4.5   A typical round of AES. (The first and last rounds omit some operations.) Four different functions transform the state. Each function is reversible as decryption wouldn't work otherwise. The addition sign inside a circle (⊕) is the symbol for the XOR operation.

extremely efficient *total breaks* (attacks that recover the key) exist on three round variants of AES-128. By iterating many times, the cipher transforms plaintext into something that looks nothing like the original plaintext. The slightest change in the plaintext also returns a completely different ciphertext. This principle is called the *avalanche effect.*

> **NOTE** Real-world cryptographic algorithms are typically compared by the security, size, and speed they provide. We already talked about the security and size of AES; its security depends on the key size, and it can encrypt 128-bit blocks of data at a time. Speedwise, many CPU vendors have implemented AES in hardware. For example, AES New Instructions (AES-NI) is a set of instructions available in Intel and AMD CPUs, which can be used to efficiently implement encryption and decryption for AES. These special instructions make AES extremely fast in practice.

One question that you might still have is how do I encrypt more or less than 128 bits with AES? I'll answer this next.

4.3   *The encrypted penguin and the CBC mode of operation*

Now that we have introduced the AES block cipher and explained a bit about its internals, let's see how to use it in practice. The problem with a block cipher is that it can only encrypt a block by itself. To encrypt something that is not exactly 128 bits, we must use a *padding* as well as a *mode of operation.* So let's see what these two concepts are about.

Imagine that you want to encrypt a long message. Naively, you could divide the message into blocks of 16 bytes (the block size of AES). Then if the last block of plaintext is smaller than 16 bytes, you could append some more bytes at the end until the plaintext becomes 16 bytes long. This is what padding is about!

There are several ways to specify how to choose these *padding bytes*, but the most important aspect of padding is that it must be reversible. Once we decrypt ciphertext, we should be able to remove the padding to retrieve the original unpadded message. Simply adding random bytes, for example, wouldn't work because you wouldn't be able to discern if the random bytes were part of the original message or not.

The most popular padding mechanism is often referred to as *PKCS#7 padding*, which first appeared in the PKCS#7 standard published by RSA (a company) at the end of the 1990s. PKCS#7 padding specifies one rule: the value of each padding byte must be set to the length of the required padding. What if the plaintext is already 16 bytes? Then we add a full block of padding set to the value 16. I illustrate this visually in figure 4.6. To remove the padding, you can easily check the value of the last byte of plaintext and interpret it as the length of padding to remove.

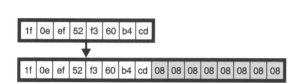

Figure 4.6   If the plaintext is not a multiple of the block size, it is padded with the length needed to reach a multiple of the block size. In the figure, the plaintext is 8 bytes, so we use 8 more bytes (containing the value 8) to pad the plaintext up to the 16 bytes required for AES.

Now, there's one big problem I need to talk about. So far, to encrypt a long message, you just divided it into blocks of 16 bytes (and perhaps you padded the last block). This naive way is called the *electronic codebook* (ECB) mode of operation. As you learned, encryption is deterministic, and so encrypting the same block of plaintext twice leads to the same ciphertext. This means that by encrypting each block individually, the resulting ciphertext might have repeating patterns.

This might seem fine, but allowing these repetitions lead to many problems. The most obvious one is that they leak information about the plaintext. The most famous illustration of this is the *ECB penguin*, pictured in figure 4.7.

Original penguin   ECB encrypted penguin

Figure 4.7   The famous ECB penguin is an encryption of an image of a penguin using the electronic codebook (ECB) mode of operation. As ECB does not hide repeating patterns, one can guess just by looking at the ciphertext what was originally encrypted. (Image taken from Wikipedia.)

To encrypt more than 128 bits of plaintext safely, better modes of operation exist that "randomize" the encryption. One of the most popular modes of operation for AES is *cipher block chaining* (CBC). CBC works for any deterministic block cipher (not just AES) by taking an additional value called an *initialization vector* (IV) to randomize the encryption. Because of this, the IV is the length of the block size (16 bytes for AES) and must be random and unpredictable.

To encrypt with the CBC mode of operation, start by generating a random IV of 16 bytes (chapter 8 tells you how to do this), then XOR the generated IV with the first 16 bytes of plaintext before encrypting those. This effectively randomizes the encryption. Indeed, if the same plaintext is encrypted twice but with different IVs, the mode of operation renders two different ciphertexts.

If there is more plaintext to encrypt, use the previous ciphertext (like we used the IV previously) to XOR it with the next block of plaintext before encrypting it. This randomizes the next block of encryption as well. Remember, the encryption of something is unpredictable and should be as good as the randomness we used to create our real IV. Figure 4.8 illustrates CBC encryption.

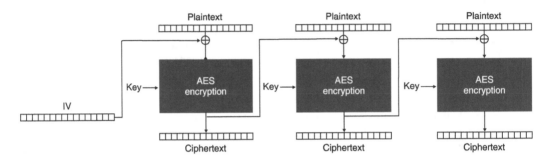

Figure 4.8   The CBC mode of operation with AES. To encrypt, we use a random initialization vector (IV) in addition to padded plaintext (split in multiple blocks of 16 bytes).

To decrypt with the CBC mode of operation, reverse the operations. As the IV is needed, it must be transmitted in clear text along with the ciphertext. Because the IV is supposed to be random, no information is leaked by observing the value. I illustrate CBC decryption in figure 4.9.

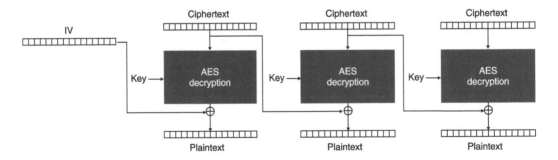

Figure 4.9   The CBC mode of operation with AES. To decrypt, the associated initialization vector (IV) is required.

Additional parameters like IVs are prevalent in cryptography. Yet, these are often poorly understood and are a great source of vulnerabilities. With the CBC mode of operation, an IV needs to be *unique* (it cannot repeat) as well as *unpredictable* (it really needs to be random). These requirements can fail for a number of reasons. Because developers are often confused by IVs, some cryptographic libraries have removed the possibility to specify an IV when encrypting with CBC and automatically generate one randomly.

> **WARNING** When an IV repeats or is predictable, the encryption becomes deterministic again, and a number of clever attacks become possible. This was the case with the famous BEAST attack (Browser Exploit Against SSL/TLS) on the TLS protocol. Note also that other algorithms might have different requirements for IVs. This is why it is always important to read the manual. Dangerous details lie in fine print.

Note that a mode of operation and a padding are still not enough to make a cipher usable. You're about to see why in the next section.

4.4 A lack of authenticity, hence AES-CBC-HMAC

So far, we have failed to address one fundamental flaw: the ciphertext as well as the IV in the case of CBC can still be modified by an attacker. Indeed, there's no integrity mechanism to prevent that! Changes in the ciphertext or IV might have unexpected changes in the decryption. For example, in AES-CBC (AES used with the CBC mode of operation), an attacker can flip specific bits of plaintext by flipping bits in its IV and ciphertext. I illustrate this attack in figure 4.10.

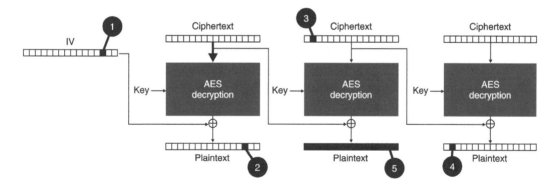

Figure 4.10 An attacker that intercepts an AES-CBC ciphertext can do the following: (1) Because the IV is public, flipping a bit (from 1 to 0, for example) of the IV also (2) flips a bit of the first block of plaintext. (3) Modifications of bits can happen on the ciphertext blocks as well. (4) Such changes impact the following block of decrypted plaintext. (5) Note that tampering with the ciphertext blocks has the direct effect of scrambling the decryption of that block.

Consequently, a cipher or a mode of operation must not be used as-is. They lack some sort of integrity protection to ensure that a ciphertext and its associated parameters (here the IV) cannot be modified without triggering some alarms.

To prevent modifications on the ciphertext, we can use the *message authentication codes* (MACs) that we saw in chapter 3. For AES-CBC, we usually use HMAC (for *hash-based MAC*) in combination with the SHA-256 hash function to provide integrity. We then apply the MAC after padding the plaintext and encrypting it over both the ciphertext and the IV; otherwise, an attacker can still modify the IV without being caught.

> **WARNING**   This construction is called *Encrypt-then-MAC*. The alternatives (like *MAC-then-Encrypt*) can sometimes lead to clever attacks (like the famous Vaudenay padding oracle attack) and are thus avoided in practice.

The created authentication tag can be transmitted along with the IV and the ciphertext. Usually, all are concatenated together as figure 4.11 illustrates. In addition, it is best practice to use different keys for AES-CBC and HMAC.

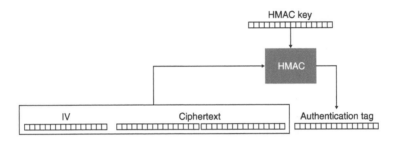

Figure 4.11   The AES-CBC-HMAC construction produces three arguments that are usually concatenated in the following order: the public IV, the ciphertext, and the authentication tag.

Prior to decryption, the tag needs to be verified (in constant time as you saw in chapter 3). The combination of all of these algorithms is referred to as *AES-CBC-HMAC* and was one of the most widely used authenticated encryption modes until we started to adopt more modern all-in-one constructions.

> **WARNING**   AES-CBC-HMAC is not the most developer-friendly construction. It is often poorly implemented and has some dangerous pitfalls when not used correctly (for example, the IV of each encryption *must* be unpredictable). I have spent a few pages introducing this algorithm as it is still widely used and still works, but I recommend against using it in favor of the more current constructions I introduce next.

4.5   *All-in-one constructions: Authenticated encryption*

The history of encryption is not pretty. Not only has it been poorly understood that encryption without authentication is dangerous, but misapplying authentication has also been a systemic mistake made by developers. For this reason, a lot of research has emerged seeking to standardize all-in-one constructions that simplify the use of encryption for developers. In the rest of this section, I introduce this new concept as well as two widely adopted standards: AES-GCM and ChaCha20-Poly1305.

4.5.1 What's authenticated encryption with associated data (AEAD)?

The most current way of encrypting data is to use an all-in-one construction called *authenticated encryption with associated data* (AEAD). The construction is extremely close to what AES-CBC-HMAC provides as it also offers confidentiality of your plaintexts while detecting any modifications that could have occurred on the ciphertexts. What's more, it provides a way to authenticate *associated data.*

The associated data argument is optional and can be empty or it can also contain metadata that is relevant to the encryption and decryption of the plaintext. This data will not be encrypted and is either implied or transmitted along with the ciphertext. In addition, the ciphertext's size is larger than the plaintext because it now contains an additional authentication tag (usually appended to the end of the ciphertext).

To decrypt the ciphertext, we are required to use the same implied or transmitted associated data. The result is either an error, indicating that the ciphertext was modified in transit, or the original plaintext. I illustrate this new primitive in figure 4.12.

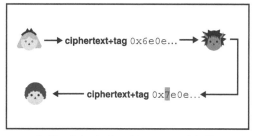

1. Alice and Bob meet in real life to agree on a key.

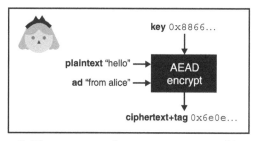

2. Alice can now use it to encrypt messages with an AEAD algorithm and the symmetric key. She can also add some optional associated data.

3. The ciphertext and tag are sent to Bob. An observer on the way intercepts them and modifies the ciphertext.

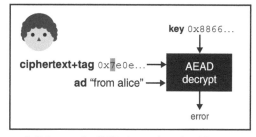

4. Bob uses the AEAD decryption algorithm on the modified ciphertext with the same key. The decryption fails.

Figure 4.12 Both Alice and Bob meet in person to agree on a shared key. Alice can then use an AEAD encryption algorithm with the key to encrypt her messages to Bob. She can optionally authenticate some associated data (ad); for example, the sender of the message. After receiving the ciphertext and the authentication tag, Bob can decrypt it using the same key and associated data. If the associated data is incorrect or the ciphertext was modified in transit, the decryption fails.

Let's see how to use a *cryptographic library* to encrypt and decrypt with an authenticated encryption primitive. For this, we'll use the JavaScript programming language and the Web Crypto API (an official interface supported by most browsers that provides low-level cryptographic functions) as the following listing shows.

Listing 4.1   Authenticated encryption with AES-GCM in JavaScript

```
let config = {                          Generates a 128-bit
    name: 'AES-GCM',                    key for 128 bits of
    length: 128                         security
};
let keyUsages = ['encrypt', 'decrypt'];
let key = await crypto.subtle.generateKey(config, false, keyUsages);

let iv = new Uint8Array(12);
await crypto.getRandomValues(iv);       Generates a 12-byte
                                        IV randomly

let te = new TextEncoder();
let ad = te.encode("some associated data");       Uses some associated
let plaintext = te.encode("hello world");         data to encrypt our
                                                  plaintext. Decryption
let param = {                                     must use the same IV
    name: 'AES-GCM',                              and associated data.
    iv: iv,
    additionalData: ad
};
let ciphertext = await crypto.subtle.encrypt(param, key, plaintext);

let result = await window.crypto.subtle.decrypt(      Decryption throws an
    param, key, ciphertext);                          exception if the IV,
new TextDecoder("utf-8").decode(result);              ciphertext, or associated
                                                      data are tampered with.
```

Note that Web Crypto API is a low-level API, and as such, does not help the developer to avoid mistakes. For example, it lets us specify an IV, which is a dangerous pattern. In this listing, I used AES-GCM, which is the most widely used AEAD. Next, let's talk more about this AES-GCM.

4.5.2   *The AES-GCM AEAD*

The most widely used AEAD is AES with the *Galois/Counter Mode* (also abbreviated AES-GCM). It was designed for high performance by taking advantage of hardware support for AES and by using a MAC (GMAC) that can be implemented efficiently.

AES-GCM has been included in NIST's Special Publication (SP 800-38D) since 2007, and it is the main cipher used in cryptographic protocols, including several versions of the TLS protocol that is used to secure connections to websites on the internet. Effectively, we can say that AES-GCM encrypts the web.

AES-GCM combines the Counter (CTR) mode of operation with the GMAC message authentication code. First, let's see how CTR mode works with AES. Figure 4.13 shows how AES is used with CTR mode.

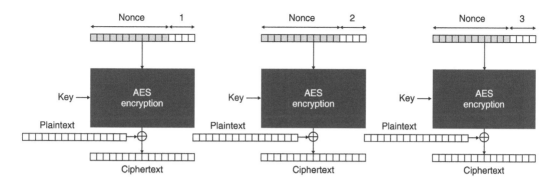

Figure 4.13 The AES-CTR algorithm combining the AES cipher with the Counter mode of operation (CTR mode). A unique nonce is concatenated with a counter and encrypted to produce a keystream. The keystream is then XORed with the actual bytes of the plaintext.

AES-CTR uses AES to encrypt a nonce concatenated with a number (starting at 1) instead of the plaintext. This additional argument, "a nonce for number once," serves the same purpose as an IV: it allows the mode of operation to randomize the AES encryption. The requirements are a bit different from the IV of CBC mode, however. A nonce needs to be unique but *not* unpredictable. Once this 16-byte block is encrypted, the result is called a *keystream*, and it is XORed with the actual plaintext to produce the encryption.

> **NOTE** Like IVs, nonces are a common term in cryptography, and they are found in different cryptographic primitives. Nonces can have different requirements, although the name often indicates that it should not repeat. But, as usual, what matters is what the manual says, not what the name of the argument implies. Indeed, the nonce of AES-GCM is sometimes referred to as an IV.

The nonce in AES-CTR is 96 bits (12 bytes) and takes most of the 16 bytes to be encrypted. The 32 bits (4 bytes) left serves as a counter, starting from 1 and incremented for each block encryption until it reaches its maximum value at $2^{4 \times 8} - 1 = 4{,}294{,}967{,}295$. This means that, at most, 4,294,967,295 blocks of 128 bits can be encrypted with the same nonce (so less than 69 GBs).

If the same nonce is used twice, the same keystream is created. By XORing the two ciphertexts together, the keystream is canceled and one can recover the XOR of the two plaintexts. This can be devastating, especially if you have some information about the content of one of the two plaintexts.

Figure 4.14 shows an interesting aspect of CTR mode: no padding is required. We say that it turns a block cipher (AES) into a stream cipher. It encrypts the plaintext byte by byte.

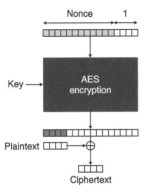

Figure 4.14 If the keystream of AES-CTR is longer than the plaintext, it is truncated to the length of the plaintext prior to XORing it with the plaintext. This permits AES-CTR to work without padding.

Stream ciphers

Stream ciphers are another category of ciphers. They are different than block ciphers because we can use them directly to encrypt a ciphertext by XORing it with a key-stream. No need for padding or a mode of operation, allowing the ciphertext to be of the same length as the plaintext.

In practice, there isn't much difference between these two categories of ciphers because block ciphers can easily be transformed into stream ciphers via the CTR mode of operation. But, in theory, block ciphers have the advantage as they can be useful when constructing other categories of primitives (similar to what you saw in chapter 2 with hash functions).

This is also a good moment to note that, by default, encryption doesn't (or badly) hides the length of what you are encrypting. Because of this, the use of compression before encryption can lead to attacks if an attacker can influence parts of what is being encrypted.

The second part of AES-GCM is *GMAC*. It is a MAC constructed from a keyed hash (called *GHASH*). In technical terms, GHASH is an almost XORed universal hash (AXU), which is also called a *difference unpredictable function* (DUF). The requirement of such a function is weaker than a hash. For example, an AXU does not need to be collision resistant. Thanks to this, GHASH can be significantly faster. Figure 4.15 illustrates the GHASH algorithm.

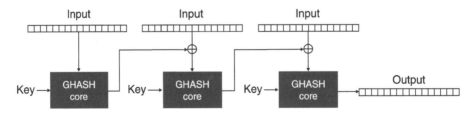

Figure 4.15 GHASH takes a key and absorbs the input block by block in a manner resembling CBC mode. It produces a digest of 16 bytes.

To hash something with GHASH, we break the input into blocks of 16 bytes and then hash them in a way similar to CBC mode. As this hash takes a key as input, it can theoretically be used as a MAC, but only once (otherwise, the algorithm breaks)—it's a *one-time MAC*. As this is not ideal for us, we use a technique (due to Wegman-Carter) to transform GHASH into a *many-time MAC*. I illustrate this in figure 4.16.

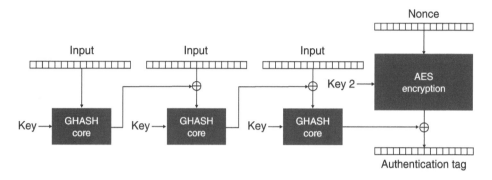

Figure 4.16 **GMAC uses GHASH with a key to hash the input, then encrypts it with a different key and AES-CTR to produce an authentication tag.**

GMAC is effectively the encryption of the GHASH output with AES-CTR (and a different key). Again, the nonce must be unique; otherwise, clever attackers can recover the authentication key used by GHASH, which would be catastrophic and would allow easy forgery of authentication tags.

Finally, AES-GCM can be seen as an intertwined combination of CTR mode and GMAC, similar to the Encrypt-then-MAC construction we previously discussed. I illustrate the whole algorithm in figure 4.17.

The counter starts at 1 for encryption, leaving the 0 counter for encrypting the authentication tag created by GHASH. GHASH, in turn, takes an independent key *H*, which is the encryption of the all-zero block with a key *K*. This way one does not need to carry two different keys as the key *K* suffices to derive the other one.

As I said previously, the 12-byte nonce of AES-GCM needs to be unique and, thus, to never repeat. Notice that it doesn't need to be random. Consequently, some people like to use it as a *counter*, starting it at 1 and incrementing it for each encryption. In this case, one must use a cryptographic library that lets the user choose the nonce. This allows one to encrypt $2^{12 \times 8} - 1$ messages before reaching the maximum value of the nonce. Suffice it to say, this is an impossible number of messages to reach in practice.

On the other hand, having a counter means that one needs to keep *state*. If a machine crashes at the wrong time, it is possible that nonce reuse could happen. For this reason, it is sometimes preferred to have a *random nonce*. Actually, some libraries will not let developers choose the nonce and will generate those at random. Doing

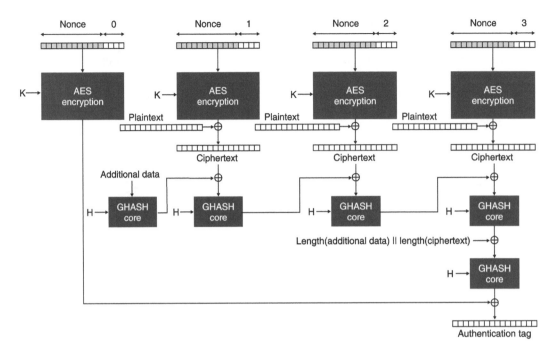

Figure 4.17   AES-GCM works by using AES-CTR with a symmetric key *K* to encrypt the plaintext and by using GMAC to authenticate the associated data and the ciphertext using an authentication key *H*.

this avoids repetition with probabilities so high that this shouldn't happen in practice. Yet, the more messages that are encrypted, the more nonces are used and the higher the chances of getting a collision. Because of the birthday bound we talked about in chapter 2, it is recommended not to encrypt more than $2^{96/3} \approx 2^{32}$ messages with the same key when generating nonces randomly.

Beyond birthday-bound security

2^{30} messages is quite a large number of messages. It might never be reached in many scenarios, but real-world cryptography often pushes the limit of what is considered reasonable. Some long-lived systems need to encrypt many, many messages per second, eventually reaching these limits. Visa, for example, processes 150 million transactions per day. If it needs to encrypt those with a unique key, it would reach the limit of 2^{30} messages in only a week. In these extreme cases, *rekeying* (changing the key used to encrypt) can be a solution. There also exists a research field called *beyond birthday-bound security* that aims to improve the maximum number of messages that can be encrypted with the same key.

4.5.3   *ChaCha20-Poly1305*

The second AEAD I will talk about is *ChaCha20-Poly1305*. It is the combination of two algorithms: the ChaCha20 stream cipher and the Poly1305 MAC. Both designed separately by Daniel J. Bernstein to be fast when used in software, contrary to AES, which is slow when hardware support is unavailable. In 2013, Google standardized the ChaCha20-Poly1305 AEAD in order to make use of it in Android mobile phones relying on low-end processors. Nowadays, it is widely adopted by internet protocols like OpenSSH, TLS, and Noise.

ChaCha20 is a modification of the Salsa20 stream cipher, which was originally designed by Daniel J. Bernstein around 2005. It was one of the nominated algorithms in the ESTREAM competition (https://www.ecrypt.eu.org/stream/). Like all stream ciphers, the algorithm produces a *keystream*, a series of random bytes of the length of the plaintext. It is then XORed with the plaintext to create the ciphertext. To decrypt, the same algorithm is used to produce the same keystream, which is XORed with the ciphertext to give back the plaintext. I illustrate both flows in figure 4.18.

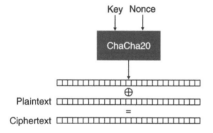

Figure 4.18   ChaCha20 works by taking a symmetric key and a unique nonce. It then generates a keystream that is XORed with the plaintext (or ciphertext) to produce the ciphertext (or plaintext). The encryption is length-preserving as the ciphertext and the plaintext are of the same length.

Under the hood, ChaCha20 generates a keystream by repeatedly calling a *block function* to produce many 64-byte blocks of keystream. The block function takes

- A 256-bit (32-byte) key like AES-256
- A 96-bit (12-byte) nonce like AES-GCM
- A 32-bit (4-byte) counter like AES-GCM

The process to encrypt is the same as with AES-CTR. (I illustrate this flow in figure 4.19.)

1 Run the block function, incrementing the counter every time, until enough keystream is produced
2 Truncate the keystream to the length of the plaintext
3 XOR the keystream with the plaintext

Due to the upper bound on the counter, you can use ChaCha20 to encrypt as many messages as with AES-GCM (as it is parameterized by a similar nonce). Because the output created by this block function is much larger, the size of a message that you can encrypt is also impacted. You can encrypt a message of size $2^{32} \times 64$ bytes ≈ 274 GB. If a nonce is reused to encrypt a plaintext, similar issues to AES-GCM arise. An observer

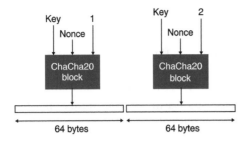

Figure 4.19   ChaCha20's keystream is created by calling an internal block function until enough bytes are produced. One block function call creates 64 bytes of random keystream.

can obtain the XOR of the two plaintexts by XORing the two ciphertexts and can also recover the authentication key for the nonce. These are serious issues that can lead to an attacker being able to forge messages!

The size of nonces and counters

The size of the nonces and the counters are (actually) not always the same everywhere (both for AES-GCM and ChaCha20-Poly1305), but they are the recommended values from the adopted standards. Still, some cryptographic libraries accept different sizes of nonce, and some applications increase the size of the counter (or the nonce) in order to allow encryption of larger messages (or more messages). Increasing the size of one component necessarily decreases the size of the other.

To prevent this, while allowing a large number of messages to be encrypted under a single key, other standards like XChaCha20-Poly1305 are available. These standards increase the size of the nonce while keeping the rest intact, which is important in cases where the nonce needs to be generated randomly instead of being a counter tracked in the system.

Inside the ChaCha20 block function, a state is formed. Figure 4.20 illustrates this state.

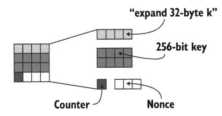

Figure 4.20   The state of the ChaCha20 block function. It is formed by 16 words (represented as squares) of 32 bits each. The first line stores a constant, the second and third lines store the 32-byte symmetric key, the following word stores a 4-byte counter, and the last 3 words store the 12-byte nonce.

This state is then transformed into 64 bytes of keystream by iterating a round function 20 times (hence the 20 in the name of the algorithm). This is similar to what was done with AES and its round function. The round function is itself calling a *Quarter Round* (QR) *function* 4 times per round, acting on different words of the internal state each time, depending if the round number is odd or even. Figure 4.21 shows this process.

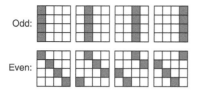

Odd:

Even:

Figure 4.21 A round in ChaCha20 affects all the words contained in a state. As the Quarter Round (QR) function only takes 4 arguments, it must be called at least 4 times on different words (grayed in the diagram) to modify all 16 words of the state.

The QR function takes four different arguments and updates them using only Add, Rotate, and XOR operations. We say that it is an *ARX* stream cipher. This makes ChaCha20 extremely easy to implement and fast in software.

Poly1305 is a MAC created via the Wegman-Carter technique, much like the GMAC we previously talked about. Figure 4.22 illustrates this cryptographic MAC.

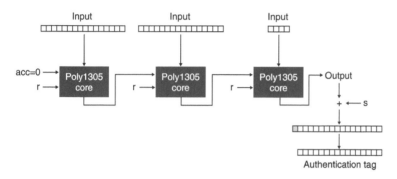

Figure 4.22 Poly1305's core function absorbs an input one block at a time by taking an additional accumulator set to 0 initially and an authentication key *r*. The output is fed as an accumulator to the next call of the core function. Eventually the output is added to a random value *s* to become the authentication tag.

In the figure, r can be seen as the authentication key of the scheme, like the authentication key H of GMAC. And s makes the MAC secure for multiple uses by encrypting the result, thus it must be unique for each usage.

The *Poly1305 core function* mixes the key with the accumulator (set to 0 in the beginning) and the message to authenticate. The operations are simple multiplications modulo a constant P.

> **NOTE** Obviously, a lot of details are missing from our description. I seldom mention how to encode data or how some arguments should be padded before being acted on. These are all implementation specificities that do not matter for us as we are trying to get an intuition of how these things work.

Eventually, we can use ChaCha20 and a counter set to 0 to generate a keystream and derive the 16-byte r and 16-byte s values we need for Poly1305. I illustrate the resulting AEAD cipher in figure 4.23.

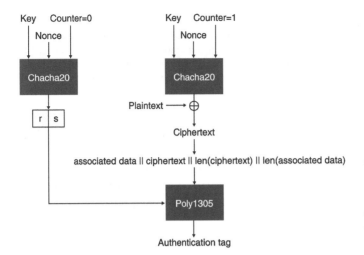

Figure 4.23 ChaCha20-Poly1305 works by using ChaCha20 to encrypt the plaintext and to derive the keys required by the Poly1305 MAC. Poly1305 is then used to authenticate the ciphertext as well as the associated data.

The normal ChaCha20 algorithm is first used to derive the authentication secrets r and s needed by Poly1305. The counter is then incremented, and ChaCha20 is used to encrypt the plaintext. After that, the associated data and the ciphertext (and their respective lengths) are passed to Poly1305 to create an authentication tag.

To decrypt, the exact same process is applied. ChaCha20 first verifies the authentication of the ciphertext and the associated data via the tag received. It then decrypts the ciphertext.

4.6   *Other kinds of symmetric encryption*

Let's pause for a moment and review the symmetric encryption algorithms you have learned so far:

- *Non-authenticated encryption*—AES with a mode of operation but without a MAC. This is insecure in practice as ciphertexts can be tampered with.
- *Authenticated encryption*—AES-GCM and ChaCha20-Poly1305 are the two most widely adopted ciphers.

The chapter could end here and it would be fine. Yet, real-world cryptography is not always about the agreed standards; it is also about *constraints* in size, in speed, in format, and so on. To that end, let me give you a brief overview of other types of symmetric encryption that can be useful when AES-GCM and ChaCha20-Poly1305 won't fit.

4.6.1   *Key wrapping*

One of the problems of nonce-based AEADs is that they all require a nonce, which takes additional space. Notice that when encrypting a key, you might not necessarily need randomization because what is encrypted is already random and will not repeat with high probabilities (or if it does repeat, it is not a big deal). One well-known standard for key wrapping is NIST's Special Publication 800-38F: "Recommendation for

Block Cipher Modes of Operation: Methods for Key Wrapping." These key wrapping algorithms do not take an additional nonce or IV and randomize their encryption based on what they are encrypting. Thanks to this, they do not have to store an additional nonce or IV next to the ciphertexts.

4.6.2 Nonce misuse-resistant authenticated encryption

In 2006, Phillip Rogaway published a new key wrapping algorithm called *synthetic initialization vector* (SIV). As part of the proposal, Rogaway notes that SIV is not only useful to encrypt keys, but also as a general AEAD scheme that is more tolerant to nonce repetitions. As you learned in this chapter, a repeating nonce in AES-GCM or ChaCha20-Poly1305 can have catastrophic consequences. It not only reveals the XOR of the two plaintexts, but it also allows an attacker to recover an authentication key and to forge valid encryption of messages.

The point of a nonce misuse-resistant algorithm is that encrypting two plaintexts with the same nonce only reveals if the two plaintexts are equal or not, and that's it. It's not great, but it's obviously not as bad as leaking an authentication key. The scheme has gathered a lot of interest and has since been standardized in RFC 8452: "AES-GCM-SIV: Nonce Misuse-Resistant Authenticated Encryption." The trick behind SIV is that the nonce used in the AEAD to encrypt is generated from the plaintext itself, which makes it highly unlikely that two different plaintexts would end up being encrypted under the same nonce.

4.6.3 Disk encryption

Encrypting the storage of a laptop or a mobile phone has some hefty constraints: it has to be fast (otherwise the user will notice) and you can only do it in place (saving space is important for a large number of devices). Because the encryption can't expand, AEADs that need a nonce and an authentication tag are not a good fit. Instead, unauthenticated encryption is used.

To protect against *bitflip attacks*, large blocks (think thousands of bytes) of data are encrypted in a way that a single bitflip would scramble the decryption of the whole block. This way, an attack has more of a chance of crashing the device than accomplishing its goal. These constructions are called *wide-block ciphers*, although this approach has also been dubbed *poor man's authentication*.

Linux systems and some Android devices have adopted this approach using Adiantum, a wide-block construction wrapping the ChaCha cipher and standardized by Google in 2019. Still, most devices use non-ideal solutions: both Microsoft and Apple make use of AES-XTS, which is unauthenticated and is not a wide-block cipher.

4.6.4 Database encryption

Encrypting data in a database is tricky. As the whole point is to prevent database breaches from leaking data, the key used to encrypt and decrypt the data must be stored away from the database server. Because clients don't have the data themselves, they are severely limited in the way they can query the data.

The simplest solution is called *transparent data encryption* (TDE) and simply encrypts selected columns. This works well in some scenarios, although one needs to be careful to authenticate associated data identifying the row and the column being encrypted; otherwise, encrypted content can be swapped. Still, one cannot search through encrypted data and so queries have to use the unencrypted columns.

Searchable encryption is the field of research that aims at solving this problem. A lot of different schemes have been proposed, but it seems like there is no silver bullet. Different schemes propose different levels of "searchability" as well as different degradations in security. Blind indexing, for example, simply allows you to search for exact matches, while order-preserving and order-revealing encryptions allow you to order results. The bottom line is, the security of these solutions are to be looked at carefully as they truly are tradeoffs.

Summary

- Encryption (or symmetric encryption) is a cryptographic primitive that can be used to protect the confidentiality of data. The security relies on a symmetric key that needs to remain secret.

- Symmetric encryption needs to be authenticated (after which we call it authenticated encrption) to be secure, as otherwise, ciphertexts can be tampered with.

- Authenticated encryption can be constructed from a symmetric encryption algorithm by using a message authentication code. But best practice is to use an authenticated encryption with associated data (AEAD) algorithm as they are all-in-one constructions that are harder to misuse.

- Two parties can use authenticated encryption to hide their communications, as long as they both have knowledge of the same symmetric key.

- AES-GCM and ChaCha20-Poly1305 are the two most widely adopted AEADs. Most applications nowadays use either one of these.

- Reusing nonces breaks the authentication of AES-GCM and ChaCha20-Poly1305. Schemes like AES-GCM-SIV are nonce misuse resistant, while encryption of keys can avoid that problem as nonces are not necessary.

- Real-world cryptography is about constraints, and AEADs cannot always fit every scenario. This is the case for database or disk encryption, for example, that require the development of new constructions.

Key exchanges

We are now entering the realm of *asymmetric cryptography* (also called *public key cryptography*) with our first asymmetric cryptographic primitive: the *key exchange*. A key exchange is, as the name hints, an exchange of keys. For example, Alice sends a key to Bob, and Bob sends a key to Alice. This allows the two peers to agree on a shared secret, which can then be used to encrypt communications with an authenticated encryption algorithm.

> **WARNING** As I hinted in the introduction of this book, there is much more math involved in asymmetric cryptography; therefore, the next chapters are going to be a tad more difficult for some readers. Don't get discouraged! What you will learn in this chapter will be helpful to understand many other primitives based on the same fundamentals.

NOTE For this chapter, you'll need to have read chapter 3 on message authentication codes and chapter 4 on authenticated encryption.

5.1   *What are key exchanges?*

Let's start by looking at a scenario where both Alice and Bob want to communicate privately but have never talked to each other before. This will motivate what key exchanges can unlock in the simplest of situations.

To encrypt communications, Alice can use the authenticated encryption primitive you learned about in chapter 4. For this, Bob needs to know the same symmetric key so Alice can generate one and send it over to Bob. After that, they can simply use the key to encrypt their communications. But what if an adversary is passively snooping in on their conversation? Now the adversary has the symmetric key and can decrypt all encrypted content that Alice and Bob are sending to each other! This is where using a key exchange can be interesting for Alice and Bob (and for ourselves in the future). By using a key exchange, they can obtain a symmetric key that a passive observer won't be able to reproduce.

A *key exchange* starts with both Alice and Bob generating some keys. To do this, they both use a key generation algorithm, which generates a *key pair*: a private key (or secret key) and a public key. Alice and Bob then send their respective public keys to each other. *Public* here means that adversaries can observe those without consequences. Alice then uses Bob's public key with her own private key to compute the shared secret. Bob can, similarly, use his private key with Alice's public key to obtain the same shared secret. I illustrate this in figure 5.1.

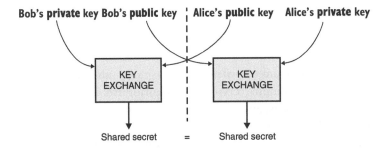

Figure 5.1   A key exchange provides the following interface: it takes your peer's public key and your private key to produce a shared secret. Your peer can obtain the same shared secret by using your public key and their private key.

Knowing how a key exchange works from a high level, we can now go back to our initial scenario and see how this helps. By starting their communication with a key exchange, Alice and Bob produce a shared secret to use as a key to an authenticated encryption primitive. Because any man-in-the-middle (MITM) adversaries observing the exchange cannot derive the same shared secret, they won't be able to decrypt communications. I illustrate this in figure 5.2.

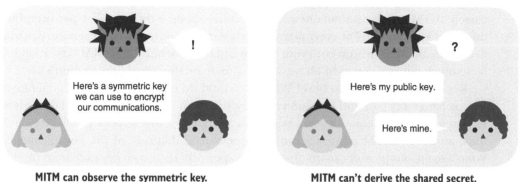

MITM can observe the symmetric key.   MITM can't derive the shared secret.

Figure 5.2 A key exchange between two participants allows them to agree on a secret key, while a man-in-the-middle (MITM) adversary can't derive the same secret key from passively observing the key exchange.

Note that the MITM here is passive; an *active* MITM would have no problem intercepting the key exchange and impersonating both sides. In this attack, Alice and Bob would effectively perform a key exchange with the MITM, both thinking that they agreed on a key with each other. The reason this is possible is that none of our characters have a way to verify who the public key they receive really belongs to. The key exchange is *unauthenticated*! I illustrate the attack in figure 5.3.

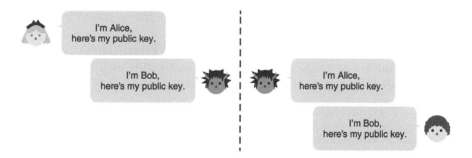

Figure 5.3 An unauthenticated key exchange is vulnerable to an active MITM attacker. Indeed, the attacker can simply impersonate both sides of the connection and perform two separate key exchanges.

Let's take a look at a different scenario to motivate *authenticated key exchanges*. Imagine that you want to run a service that gives you the time of day. Yet, you do not want this information to be modified by a MITM adversary. Your best bet is to authenticate your responses using the message authentication codes (MACs) you learned about in chapter 3. As MACs require a key, you could simply generate one and share it manually with all of your users. But then, any user is now in possession of the MAC key you're using with the others and might some day make use of it to perform the previously discussed MITM attack on someone else. You could set up a different key per user, but this is not ideal as well. For every new user that wants to connect to your service, you will need to manually provision both your service and the user with a new MAC key. It would be so much better if you didn't have anything to do on the server side, wouldn't it?

Key exchanges can help here! What you could do is have your service generate a key exchange key pair and provision any new user with the service's public key. This is known as an *authenticated key exchange*; your users know the server's public key, and thus, an active MITM adversary cannot impersonate that side of the key exchange. What a malicious person can do, though, is to perform their own key exchange (as the client side of the connection is not authenticated). By the way, when both sides are authenticated, we call that a *mutually authenticated key exchange*.

This scenario is extremely common, and the key exchange primitive allows it to scale well with an increase of users. But this scenario doesn't scale well if the number of services increase as well! The internet is a good example of this. We have many browsers trying to communicate securely with many websites. Imagine if you had to hardcode the public key of all the websites you might one day visit in your browser and what happens when more websites come online?

While key exchanges are useful, they do not scale well in all scenarios without their sister primitive—the *digital signature*. This is just a teaser though. In chapter 7, you will learn about that new cryptographic primitive and how it helps scaling trust in a system. Key exchanges are rarely used directly in practice, however. They are often just building blocks of a more complex protocol. That being said, they can still be useful on their own in certain situations (for example, as we saw previously against passive adversaries).

Let's now look at how you *would* use a key exchange cryptographic primitive in practice. libsodium is one of the most well known and widely used C/C++ libraries. The following listing shows how you would use libsodium in practice in order to perform a key exchange.

Listing 5.1   A key exchange in C

```
unsigned char client_pk[crypto_kx_PUBLICKEYBYTES];        Generates the
unsigned char client_sk[crypto_kx_SECRETKEYBYTES];        client's key pair
crypto_kx_keypair(client_pk, client_sk);

unsigned char server_pk[crypto_kx_PUBLICKEYBYTES];        We assume that we have some way
obtain(server_pk);                                        to obtain the server's public key.

unsigned char decrypt_key[crypto_kx_SESSIONKEYBYTES];     libsodium derives two symmetric
unsigned char encrypt_key[crypto_kx_SESSIONKEYBYTES];     keys instead of one per best
                                                          practice; each key is used to
                                                          encrypt a single direction.
```

```
if (crypto_kx_client_session_keys(decrypt_key, encrypt_key,
    client_pk, client_sk, server_pk) != 0) {
    abort_session();
}
```

> We perform a key exchange with our secret key and the server's public key.

> If the public key is malformed, the function returns an error.

libsodium hides a lot of details from the developer while also exposing safe-to-use interfaces. In this instance, libsodium makes use of the *X25519 key exchange algorithm*, which you will learn more about later in this chapter. In the rest of this chapter, you will learn about the different standards used for key exchanges, as well as how they work under the hood.

5.2 *The Diffie-Hellman (DH) key exchange*

In 1976, Whitfield Diffie and Martin E. Hellman wrote their seminal paper on the Diffie-Hellman (DH) key exchange algorithm entitled "New Direction in Cryptography." What a title! DH was the first key exchange algorithm invented and one of the first formalizations of a public key cryptographic algorithm. In this section, I lay out the math foundations of this algorithm, explain how it works, and finally, talk about the standards that specify how to use it in a cryptographic application.

5.2.1 *Group theory*

The DH key exchange is built on top of a field of mathematics called *group theory*, which is the base of most public key cryptography today. For this reason, I will spend some time in this chapter giving you the basics on group theory. I will do my best to provide good insights on how these algorithms work, but there's no way around it, there is going to be some math.

Let's start with the obvious question: what's a *group*? It's two things:

- A set of elements
- A special binary operation (like + or ×) defined on these elements

If the set and the operation manage to satisfy some properties, then we have a group. And, if we have a group, then we can do magical things . . . (more on that later). Note that DH works in a *multiplicative group*: a group where the multiplication is used as the defined binary operation. Due to this, the rest of the explanations use a multiplicative group as examples. I will also often omit the × symbol (for example, I will write $a \times b$ as *ab* instead).

I need to be a bit more specific here. For the set and its operation to be a group, they need the following properties. (As usual, I illustrate these properties in a more visual way in figure 5.4 to provide you with more material to grasp this new concept.)

- *Closure*—Operating on two elements results in another element of the same set. For example, for two elements of the group *a* and *b*, $a \times b$ results in another group element.

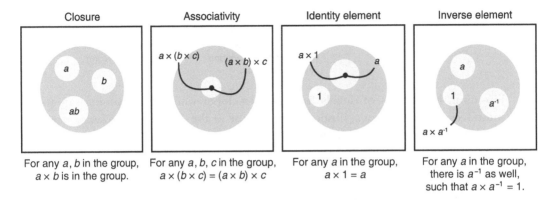

Figure 5.4   The four properties of a group: closure, associativity, identity element, and inverse element.

- *Associativity*—Operating on several elements at a time can be done in any order. For example, for three elements of the group *a*, *b*, and *c*, then $a(bc)$ and $(ab)c$ result in the same group element.
- *Identity element*—Operating with this element does not change the result of the other operand. For example, we can define the identity element as 1 in our multiplicative group. For any group element *a*, we have $a \times 1 = a$.
- *Inverse element*—Existing as an inverse to all group elements. For example, for any group element *a*, there's an inverse element a^{-1} (also written as $1/a$) such that $a \times a^{-1} = 1$ (also written as $a \times \frac{1}{a} = 1$).

I can imagine that my explanation of a group can be a bit abstract, so let's see what DH uses as a group in practice. First, DH uses a group comprised of the set of strictly positive integers: 1, 2, 3, 4, ···, $p - 1$, where *p* is a prime number and 1 is the identity element. Different standards specify different numbers for *p*, but intuitively, it has to be a large prime number for the group to be secure.

> **Prime numbers**
>
> A *prime number* is a number that can only be divided by 1 or by itself. The first prime numbers are 2, 3, 5, 7, 11, and so on. Prime numbers are everywhere in asymmetric cryptography! And, fortunately, we have efficient algorithms to find large ones. To speed things up, most cryptographic libraries will instead look for *pseudo-primes* (numbers that have a high probability of being primes). Interestingly, such optimizations were broken several times in the past; the most infamous occurrence was in 2017, when the ROCA vulnerability uncovered more than a million devices generating incorrect primes for their cryptographic applications.

Second, DH uses the *modular multiplication* as a special operation. Before I can explain what modular multiplication is, I need to explain what *modular arithmetic* is. Modular arithmetic, intuitively, is about numbers that "wrap around" past a certain number called a *modulus*. For example, if we set the modulus to be 5, we say that numbers past 5 go back to 1; for example, 6 becomes 1, 7 becomes 2, and so on. (We also note 5 as 0, but because it is not in our multiplicative group, we don't care too much about it.)

The mathematical way to express modular arithmetic is to take the *remainder* of a number and its *Euclidian division* with the modulus. Let's take, for example, the number 7 and write its Euclidian division with 5 as $7 = 5 \times 1 + 2$. Notice that the remainder is 2. Then we say that $7 = 2 \bmod 5$ (sometimes written as $7 \equiv 2 \pmod 5$). This equation can be read as 7 is congruent to 2 modulo 5. Similarly

- $8 = 1 \bmod 7$
- $54 = 2 \bmod 13$
- $170 = 0 \bmod 17$
- and so on

The classical way of picturing such a concept is with a clock. Figure 5.5 illustrates this concept.

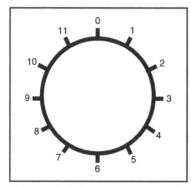
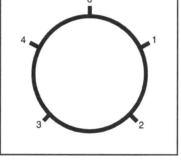

The normal clock **wraps around** at 12. 12 is 0, 13 is 1, 14 is 2, and so on.

Integers numbers **modulo 5**. 5 is 0, 6 is 1, and so on.

Figure 5.5 **The group of integers modulo the prime number 5 can be pictured as a clock that resets to 0 after the number 4. Thus 5 is represented as 0, 6 as 1, 7 as 2, 8 as 3, 9 as 4, 10 as 0, and so on.**

A modular multiplication is quite natural to define over such a set of numbers. Let's take the following multiplication as an example:

$$3 \times 2 = 6$$

With what you learned previously, you know that 6 is congruent to 1 modulo 5, and thus the equation can be rewritten as:

$$3 \times 2 = 1 \bmod 5$$

Quite straightforward, isn't it? Note that the previous equation tells us that 3 is the inverse of 2 and vice versa. We could also write the following:

$$3^{-1} = 2 \bmod 5$$

When the context is clear, the modulus part (mod 5 here) is often left out from equations. So don't be surprised if I sometimes omit it in this book.

NOTE It happens that when we use the positive numbers modulo a prime number, only the *zero* element lacks an inverse. (Indeed, can you find an element b such that $0 \times b = 1 \bmod 5$?) This is the reason why we do not include zero as one of our elements in the group.

OK, we now have a group, which includes the set of strictly positive integers $1, 2, \cdots, p-1$ for p a prime number, along with modular multiplication. The group we formed also happens to be two things:

- *Commutative*—The order of operations doesn't matter. For example, given two group elements a and b, then $ab = ba$. A group that has this property is often called an *Abelian group*.
- *A finite field*—A Galois group that has more properties, as well as an additional operation (in our example, we can also add numbers together).

Due to the last point, DH defined over this type of group is sometimes called *Finite Field Diffie-Hellman* (FFDH). If you understand what a group is (and make sure you do before reading any further), then a *subgroup* is just a group contained inside your original group. That is, it's a subset of the group elements. Operating on elements of the subgroup results in another subgroup element, and every subgroup element has an inverse in the subgroup, etc.

A *cyclic subgroup* is a subgroup that can be generated from a single *generator* (or *base*). A generator generates a cyclic subgroup by multiplying itself over and over. For example, the generator 4 defines a subgroup consisting of the numbers 1 and 4:

- $4 \bmod 5 = 4$
- $4 \times 4 \bmod 5 = 1$
- $4 \times 4 \times 4 \bmod 5 = 4$ (we start again from the beginning)
- $4 \times 4 \times 4 \times 4 \bmod 5 = 1$
- and so on

NOTE We can also write $4 \times 4 \times 4$ as 4^3.

It happens that when our modulus is prime, every element of our group is a generator of a subgroup. These different subgroups can have different sizes, which we call *orders*. I illustrate this in figure 5.6.

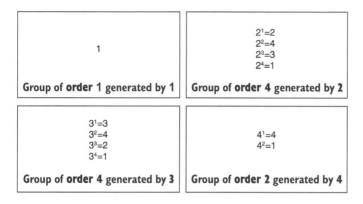

Figure 5.6 The different subgroups of the multiplicative group modulo 5. These all include the number 1 (called the *identity element*) and have different orders (number of elements).

All right, you now understand

- A group is a set of numbers with a binary operation that respects some properties (closure, associativity, identity element, inverse element).
- DH works in the Galois group (a group with commutativity), formed by the set of strictly positive numbers up to a prime number (not included) and the modular multiplication.
- In a DH group, every element is a generator of a subgroup.

Groups are the center of a huge amount of different cryptographic primitives. It is important to have good intuitions about group theory if you want to understand how other cryptographic primitives work.

5.2.2 The discrete logarithm problem: The basis of Diffie-Hellman

The security of the DH key exchange relies on the *discrete logarithm problem* in a group, a problem believed to be hard to solve. In this section, I briefly introduce this problem.

Imagine that I take a generator, let's say 3, and give you a random element among the ones it can generate, let's say $2 = 3^x \bmod 5$ for some x unknown to you. Asking you "what is x?" is the same as asking you to find the discrete logarithm of 2 in base 3. Thus, the discrete logarithm problem in our group is about finding out how many times we multiplied the generator with itself in order to produce a given group element. This is an important concept! Take a few minutes to think about it before continuing.

In our example group, you can quickly find that 3 is the answer (indeed, $3^3 = 2 \bmod 5$). But if we picked a much larger prime number than 5, things get much more complicated: it becomes hard to solve. This is the secret sauce behind Diffie-Hellman. You now know enough to understand how to generate a key pair in DH:

1 All the participants must agree on a large prime *p* and a generator *g*.
2 Each participant generates a random number *x*, which becomes their private key.
3 Each participant derives their public key as $g^x \bmod p$.

The fact that the discrete logarithm problem is *hard* means that no one should be able to recover the private key from the public key. I illustrate this in figure 5.7.

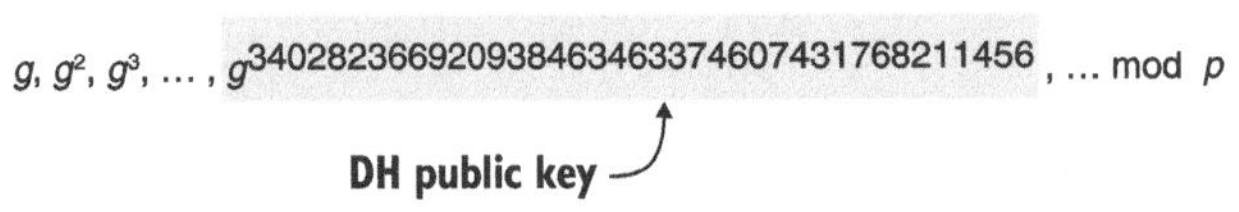

$$g, g^2, g^3, \ldots, g^{3402823669209384634633746074317682114.56}, \ldots \bmod p$$

DH public key

Figure 5.7   Choosing a private key in Diffie-Hellman is like choosing an index in a list of numbers produced by a generator g. The discrete logarithm problem is to find the index from the number alone.

While we do have algorithms to compute discrete logarithms, they are not efficient in practice. On the other hand, if I give you the solution *x* to the problem, you have extremely efficient algorithms at your disposal to check that, indeed, I provided you with the right solution: $g^x \bmod p$. If you are interested, the state-of-the-art technique to compute the modular exponentiation is called *square and multiply*. This computes the result efficiently by going through *x* bit by bit.

> **NOTE**   Like everything in cryptography, it is *not impossible* to find a solution by simply trying to guess. Yet, by choosing large enough parameters (here, a large prime number), it is possible to reduce the efficacy of such a search for a solution down to negligible odds. This means that even after hundreds of years of random tries, your odds of finding a solution should still be statistically close to zero.

Great. How do we use all of this math for our DH key exchange algorithm? Imagine that

- Alice has a private key *a* and a public key $A = g^a \bmod p$.
- Bob has a private key *b* and a public key $B = g^b \bmod p$.

With the knowledge of Bob's public key, Alice can compute the shared secret as $B^a \bmod p$. Bob can do a similar computation with Alice's public key and his own private key: $A^b \bmod p$. Naturally, we can see that these two calculations end up computing the same number:

$$B^a = (g^b)^a = g^{ab} = (g^a)^b = A^b \bmod p$$

And that's the magic of DH. From an outsider's point of view, just observing the public keys *A* and *B* does not help in any way to compute the result of the key exchange $g^{ab} \bmod p$. Next, you will learn about how real-world applications make use of this algorithm and the different standards that exist.

Computational and decisional Diffie-Hellman

By the way, in theoretical cryptography, the idea that observing g^a mod p and g^b mod p does not help you to compute g^{ab} mod p is called the *computational Diffie-Hellman assumption* (CDH). It is often confused with the stronger *decisional Diffie-Hellman assumption* (DDH), which intuitively states that given g^a mod p, g^b mod p, and z mod p, nobody should be able to confidently guess if the latter element is the result of a key exchange between the two public keys (g^{ab} mod p) or just a random element of the group. Both are useful theoretical assumptions that have been used to build many different algorithms in cryptography.

5.2.3 *The Diffie-Hellman standards*

Now that you have seen how DH works, you can understand that participants need to agree on a set of parameters, specifically on a prime number p and a generator g. In this section, you'll learn about how real-world applications choose these parameters and the different standards that exist.

First things first is the prime number p. As I stated earlier, the bigger, the better. Because DH is based on the discrete logarithm problem, its security is directly correlated to the best attacks known on the problem. Any advances in this area can weaken the algorithm. With time, we managed to obtain a pretty good idea of how fast (or slow) these advances are and how much is enough security. The currently known best practices are to use a prime number of 2,048 bits.

NOTE In general, https://keylength.com summarizes recommendations on parameter lengths for common cryptographic algorithms. The results are taken from authoritative documents produced by research groups or government bodies like the ANSSI (France), the NIST (US), and the BSI (Germany). While they do not always agree, they often converge towards similar orders of magnitude.

In the past, many libraries and software often generated and hardcoded their own parameters. Unfortunately, they were sometimes found to be either weak or, worse, completely broken. In 2016, someone found out that Socat, a popular command-line tool, had modified their default DH group with a broken one a year prior, raising the question whether this had been a mistake or an intentional backdoor. Using standardized DH groups might seem like a better idea, but DH is one of the unfortunate counterexamples. Only a few months after the Socat issue, Antonio Sanso, while reading RFC 5114, found that the standard had specified broken DH groups as well.

Due to all of these issues, newer protocols and libraries have converged towards either deprecating DH in favor of Elliptic Curve Diffie-Hellman (ECDH) or using the groups defined in the better standard, RFC 7919 (https://www.rfc-editor.org/info/rfc7919). For this reason, best practice nowadays is to use RFC 7919, which defines several groups of different sizes and security. For example, ffdhe2048 is the group defined by the 2,048-bit prime modulus:

p = 32317006071311007300153513477825163362488057133489075174588434139269
80683413621000279205636264016468545855635793533081692882902308057347262
52735547424612457410262025279165729728627063003252634282131457669314142
23654220941111348629991657478268034230553086349050635557712219187890332
72956969612974385624174123623722519734640269185579776797682301462539793
30580152268587307611975324364674758554607150438968449403661304976978128
54295958659597567051283852132784468522925504568272879113720098931873959
14337417583782600027803497319855206060753323412260325468408812003110590
7484281003994966956119696956248629032338072839127039

and with generator $g = 2$

> **NOTE** It is common to choose the number 2 for the generator as computers
> are quite efficient at multiplying with 2 using a simple left shift (<<) instruction.

The group size (or *order*) is also specified as $q = (p - 1)/2$. This implies that both private keys and public keys will be around 2,048 bits size-wise. In practice, these are quite large sizes for keys (compare that with symmetric keys, for example, that are usually 128-bit long). You will see in the next section that defining a group over the elliptic curves allow us to obtain much smaller keys for the same amount of security.

5.3   *The Elliptic Curve Diffie-Hellman (ECDH) key exchange*

It turns out that the DH algorithm, which we just discussed, can be implemented in different types of groups, not just the multiplicative groups modulo a prime number. It also turns out that a group can be made from elliptic curves, a type of curves studied in mathematics. The idea was proposed in 1985 by Neal Koblitz and Victor S. Miller, independently, and much later in 2000, it was adopted when cryptographic algorithms based on elliptic curves started seeing standardization.

The world of applied cryptography quickly adopted elliptic curve cryptography as it provided much smaller keys than the previous generation of public key cryptography. Compared to the recommended 2,048-bit parameters in DH, parameters of 256 bits were possible with the elliptic curve variant of the algorithm.

5.3.1   *What's an elliptic curve?*

Let's now explain how elliptic curves work. First and foremost, it is good to understand that elliptic curves are just curves! Meaning that they are defined by all the coordinates x and y that solves an equation. Specifically, this equation

$$y^2 + a_1 xy + a_3 y = x^3 + a_2 x^2 + a_4 x + a_6$$

for some a_1, a_2, a_3, a_4, and a_6. Note that for most practical curves today, this equation can be simplified as the *short Weierstrass equation*:

$$y^2 = x^3 + ax + b \text{ (where } 4a^3 + 27b^2 \neq 0)$$

While the simplification is not possible for two types of curves (called *binary curves* and *curves of characteristic 3*), these are used rarely enough that we will use the Weierstrass form in the rest of this chapter. Figure 5.8 shows an example of an elliptic curve with two points taken at random.

At some point in the history of elliptic curves, it was found that a *group* could be constructed over them. From there, implementing DH on top of these groups was straightforward. I will use this section to explain the intuition behind elliptic curve cryptography.

Groups over elliptic curves are often defined as *additive groups*. Unlike multiplicative groups defined in the previous section, the + sign is used instead.

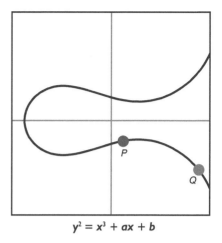

$$y^2 = x^3 + ax + b$$

Figure 5.8 One example of an elliptic curve defined by an equation.

NOTE Using an addition or a multiplication does not matter much in practice, it is just a matter of preference. While most of cryptography uses a multiplicative notation, the literature around elliptic curves has gravitated around an additive notation, and thus, this is what I will use when referring to elliptic curve groups in this book.

This time, I will define the operation before defining the elements of the group. Our *addition operation* is defined in the following way. Figure 5.9 illustrates this process.

1 Draw a line going through two points that you want to add. The line hits the curve at another point.

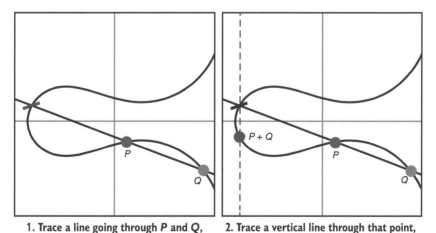

1. Trace a line going through *P* and *Q*, it hits the curve at another point.

2. Trace a vertical line through that point, it hits the curve at point *P+Q*.

Figure 5.9 An addition operation can be defined over points of an elliptic curve by using geometry.

2 Draw a vertical line from this newly found point. The vertical line hits the curve in yet another point.

3 This point is the result of adding the original two points together.

There are two special cases where this rule won't work. Let's define these as well:

- *How do we add a point to itself?* The answer is to draw the tangent to that point (instead of drawing a line between two points).

- *What happens if the line we draw in step 1 (or step 2) does not hit the curve at any other point?* Well, this is embarrassing, and we need this special case to work and produce a result. The solution is to define the result as a made-up point (something we make up). This newly invented point is called the *point at infinity* (that we usually write with a big letter *O*). Figure 5.10 illustrates these special cases.

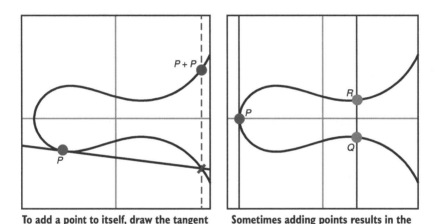

To add a point to itself, draw the tangent and follow the previous method.

Sometimes adding points results in the point at infinity: *P* + *P* = *O* and *R* + *Q* = *O*.

Figure 5.10 Building on figure 5.9, addition on an elliptic curve is also defined when adding a point to itself or when two points cancel each other to result in the point at infinity (O).

I know this point at infinity is some next-level weirdness, but don't worry too much about it. It is really just something we came up with in order to make the addition operation work. Oh, and by the way, it behaves like a zero, and it is our identity element:

$$O + O = O$$

and for any point *P* on the curve

$$P + O = P$$

All good. So far, we saw that to create a group on top of an elliptic curve, we need

- An elliptic curve equation that defines a set of valid points.
- A definition of what addition means in this set.
- An imaginary point called a point at infinity.

I know this is a lot of information to unpack, but we are missing one last thing. Elliptic curve cryptography makes use of the previously-discussed type of group defined over a *finite field*. In practice, what this means is that our coordinates are the numbers 1, 2, ···, $p - 1$ for some large prime number p. This should sound familiar! For this reason, when thinking of elliptic curve cryptography, you should think of a graph that looks much more like the one on the right in figure 5.11.

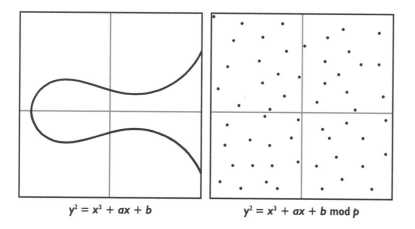

$y^2 = x^3 + ax + b$ $y^2 = x^3 + ax + b \bmod p$

Figure 5.11 Elliptic curve cryptography (ECC), in practice, is mostly specified with elliptic curves in coordinates modulo a large prime number p. This means that what we use in cryptography looks much more like the right graph than the left graph.

And that's it! We now have a group we can do cryptography on, the same way we had a group made with the numbers (excluding 0) modulo a prime number and a multiplication operation for Diffie-Hellman. How can we do Diffie-Hellman with this group defined on elliptic curves? Let's see how the *discrete logarithm* works now in this group.

Let's take a point G and add it to itself x times to produce another point P via the addition operation we defined. We can write that as $P = G + \cdots + G$ (x times) or use some mathematical syntactic sugar to write that as $P = [x]G$, which reads x times G. The *elliptic curve discrete logarithm problem* (ECDLP) is to find the number x from knowing just P and G.

NOTE We call $[x]G$ scalar multiplication as x is usually called a scalar in such groups.

5.3.2   *How does the Elliptic Curve Diffie-Hellman (ECDH) key exchange work?*

Now that we built a group on elliptic curves, we can instantiate the same Diffie-Hellman key exchange algorithm on it. To generate a key pair in ECDH:

1 All the participants agree on an elliptic curve equation, a finite field (most likely a prime number), and a generator G (usually called a *base point* in elliptic curve cryptography).

2 Each participant generates a random number x, which becomes their private key.

3 Each participant derives their public key as $[x]\,G$.

Because the elliptic curve discrete logarithm problem is hard, you guessed it, no one should be able to recover your private key just by looking at your public key. I illustrate this in figure 5.12.

$G, [2]G, [3]G, \ldots, [340282366920938463463374607431768211456]G, \ldots$

ECDH public key

Figure 5.12   Choosing a private key in ECDH is like choosing an index in a list of numbers produced by a generator (or base point) G. The Elliptic Curve Discrete Logarithm Problem (ECDLP) is to find the index from the number alone.

All of this might be a bit confusing as the operation we defined for our DH group was the multiplication, and for an elliptic curve, we now use addition. Again, these distinctions do not matter at all because they are equivalent. You can see a comparison in figure 5.13.

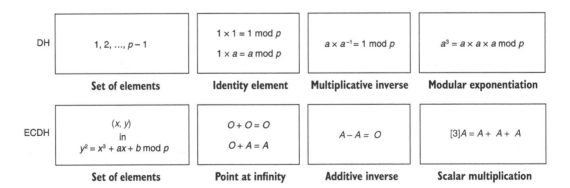

Figure 5.13   Some comparisons between the group used in Diffie-Hellman and the group used in Elliptic Curve Diffie-Hellman (ECDH).

You should now be convinced that the only thing that matters for cryptography is that we have a group defined with its operation, and that the discrete logarithm for this group is hard. For completion, figure 5.14 shows the difference between the discrete logarithm problem in the two types of groups we've seen.

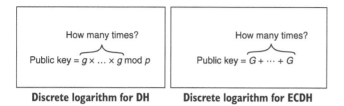

Discrete logarithm for DH   Discrete logarithm for ECDH

Figure 5.14 A comparison between the discrete logarithm problem modulo large primes and the discrete logarithm problem in elliptic curve cryptography (ECC). They both relate to the DH key exchange, as the problem is to find the private key from a public key.

A last note on the theory, the group we formed on top of elliptic curves differs with the group we formed with the strictly positive integers modulo a prime number. Due to some of these differences, the strongest attacks known against DH (known as *index calculus* or *number field sieve* attacks) do not work well on the elliptic curve groups. This is the main reason why parameters for ECDH can be much lower than the parameters for DH at the same level of security.

OK, we are done with the theory. Let's go back to defining ECDH. Imagine that

- Alice has a private key a and a public key $A = [a]\, G$.
- Bob has a private key b and a public key $B = [b]\, G$.

With the knowledge of Bob's public key, Alice can compute the shared secret as $[a]\, B$. Bob can do a similar computation with Alice's public key and his own private key: $[b]\, A$. Naturally, we can see that these two calculations end up computing the same number:

$$[a]\, B = [a]\, [b]\, G = [ab]\, G = [b]\, [a]\, G = [b]\, A$$

No passive adversary should be able to derive the shared point just from observing the public keys. Looks familiar, right? Next, let's talk about standards.

5.3.3 The standards for Elliptic Curve Diffie-Hellman

Elliptic curve cryptography has remained at its full strength since it was first presented in 1985. [. . .] The United States, the UK, Canada and certain other NATO nations have all adopted some form of elliptic curve cryptography for future systems to protect classified information throughout and between their governments.

—NSA ("The Case for Elliptic Curve Cryptography," 2005)

The standardization of ECDH has been pretty chaotic. Many standardization bodies have worked to specify a large number of different curves, which was then followed by many flame wars over which curve was more secure or more efficient. A large amount of research, mostly led by Daniel J. Bernstein, pointed out the fact that a number of curves standardized by NIST could potentially be part of a weaker class of curves only known to NSA.

> *I no longer trust the constants. I believe the NSA has manipulated them through their relationships with industry.*
>
> —Bruce Schneier ("The NSA Is Breaking Most Encryption on the Internet," 2013)

Nowadays, most of the curves in use come from a couple standards, and most applications have fixated on two curves: P-256 and Curve25519. In the rest of this section, I will go over these curves.

NIST FIPS 186-4, "Digital Signature Standard," initially published as a standard for signatures in 2000, contains an appendix specifying 15 curves for use in ECDH. One of these curves, P-256, is the most widely used curve on the internet. The curve was also specified in Standards for Efficient Cryptography (SEC) 2, v2, "Recommended Elliptic Curve Domain Parameters," published in 2010 under a different name, secp256r1. P-256 is defined with the short Weierstrass equation:

$$y^2 = x^3 + ax + b \bmod p$$

where $a = -3$ and

$b = 41058363725152142129326129780047268409114441015993725554835256314039$
467401291

and

$$p = 2^{256} - 2^{224} + 2^{192} + 2^{96} - 1$$

This defines a curve of prime order:

$n = 11579208921035624876269744694940757352999695522413576034242225906106$
8512044369

meaning that there are exactly n points on the curve (including the point at infinity). The base point is specified as

$G = (48439561293906451759052585252797914202762949526041747995844080717 0$
$82404635286, 36134250956749795798585127919587881956611106672985015071 87$
$7198253568414405109)$

The curve provides 128 bits of security. For applications that are using other cryptographic algorithms providing 256-bit security instead of 128 bits of security (for example, AES with a 256-bit key), P-521 is available in the same standard to match the level of security.

> ### Can we trust P-256?
>
> Interestingly, P-256 and other curves defined in FIPS 186-4 are said to be generated from a *seed*. For P-256, the seed is known to be the byte string
>
> 0xc49d360886e704936a6678e1139d26b7819f7e90
>
> I talked about this notion of "nothing-up-my-sleeve" numbers before—constants that aim to prove that there was no room for backdooring the design of the algorithm. Unfortunately, there isn't much explanation behind the P-256 seed other than the fact that it is specified along the curve's parameter.

RFC 7748, "Elliptic Curves for Security," which was published in 2016, specifies two curves: Curve25519 and Curve448. Curve25519 offers approximately 128 bits of security, while Curve448 offers around 224 bits of security for protocols that want to hedge against potential advances in the state of attacks against elliptic curves. I will only talk about Curve25519 here, which is a Montgomery curve defined by the equation:

$$y^2 = x^3 + 486662\ x^2 + x \bmod p, \text{ where } p = 2^{255} - 19$$

Curve25519 has an order

$$n = 2^{252} + 27742317777372353535851937790883648493$$

and the base point used is

$G = (9, 14781619447589544791020593568409986887264606134616475288964881837\\755586237401)$

The combination of ECDH with Curve25519 is often dubbed *X25519*.

5.4 *Small subgroup attacks and other security considerations*

Today, *I would advise you to use ECDH over DH* due to the size of the keys, the lack of known strong attacks, the quality of the available implementations, and the fact that elliptic curves are fixed and well standardized (as opposed to DH groups, which are all over the place). The latter point is quite important! Using DH means potentially using broken standards (like RFC 5114 mentioned previously), protocols that are too relaxed (many protocols, like older versions of TLS, don't mandate what DH groups to use), software that uses broken custom DH groups (the socat issue mentioned previously), and so on.

If you do have to use Diffie-Hellman, make sure to *stick to the standards*. The standards I mentioned previously make use of safe primes as modulus: primes of the form $p = 2q + 1$ where q is another prime number. The point is that groups of this form only have two subgroups: a small one of size 2 (generated by −1) and a large one of size q. (This is the best you can get, by the way; there exist no prime-order groups in DH.) The scarcity of small subgroups prevent a type of attack known as *small subgroup attack* (more on that later). Safe primes create secure groups because of two things:

- The order of a multiplicative group modulo a prime p is calculated as p − 1.
- The order of a group's subgroups are the factors of the group's order (this is the Lagrange theorem).

Hence, the order of our multiplicative group modulo a safe prime is $p − 1 = (2q + 1) − 1 = 2q$ that has factors 2 and q, which means that its subgroups can only be of order 2 or q. In such groups, small subgroup attacks are not possible because there are not enough small subgroups. A *small subgroup attack* is an attack on key exchanges in which an attacker sends several invalid public keys to leak bits of your private key gradually, and where the invalid public keys are generators of small subgroups.

For example, an attacker could choose −1 (the generator of a subgroup of size 2) as public key and send it to you. By doing your part of the key exchange, the resulting shared secret is an element of the small subgroup (−1 or 1). This is because you just raised the small subgroup generator (the attacker's public key) to the power of your private key. Depending on what you do with that shared secret, the attacker could guess what it is, and leak some information about your private key.

With our example of malicious public key, if your private key was even, the shared secret would be 1, and if your private key was odd, the shared secret would be −1. As a result, the attacker learned one bit of information: the least significant bit of your private key. Many subgroups of different sizes can lead to more opportunities for the attacker to learn more about your private key until the entire key is recovered. I illustrate this issue in figure 5.15.

While it is always a good idea to verify if the public key you receive is in the correct subgroup, not all implementations do that. In 2016, a group of researchers analyzed 20 different DH implementations and found that none were validating public keys (see "Measuring small subgroup attacks against Diffie-Hellman" from Valenta et al.) Make sure that the DH implementations you're using do! You can do this by raising the public key to the order of the subgroup, which should give you back the identity element if it is an element of that subgroup.

On the other hand, elliptic curves allow for groups of prime order. That is, they have no small subgroups (besides the subgroup of size 1 generated by the identity element), and thus, they are secure against small subgroup attacks. Well, not so fast . . . In 2000, Biehl, Meyer, and Muller found that small subgroup attacks are possible even in such prime-order elliptic curve groups due to an attack called *invalid curve attack*.

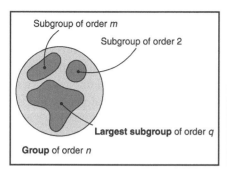
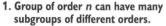
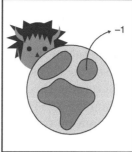
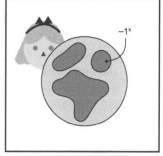

1. Group of order *n* can have many subgroups of different orders.

2. An attacker uses the generator of a subgroup as their public key.

3. The key exchange with Alice's private key *x* and the maliciously crafted public key results in a small subgroup element.

Figure 5.15 A small subgroup attack impacts DH groups that have many subgroups. By choosing generators of small subgroups as public keys, an attacker can leak bits of someone's private key little by little.

The idea behind invalid curve attacks is the following. First, the formulas to implement scalar multiplication for elliptic curves that use the short Weierstrass equation $y^2 = x^3 + ax + b$ (like NIST's P-256) are independent of the variable b. This means that an attacker can find different curves with the same equation except for the value b, and some of these curves will have many small subgroups. You probably know where this is going: the attacker chooses a point in another curve that exhibits small subgroups and sends it to a targeted server. The server goes on with the key exchange by performing a scalar multiplication with the given point, effectively doing a key exchange on a different curve. This trick ends up re-enabling the small subgroup attack, even on prime-order curves.

The obvious way to fix this is to, again, validate public keys. This can be done easily by checking if the public key is not the point at infinity and by plugging the received coordinates into the curve equation to see if it describes a point on the defined curve. Unfortunately, in 2015, Jager, Schwenk, and Somorovsky showed in "Practical Invalid Curve Attacks on TLS-ECDH" that several popular implementations did not perform these checks. If using ECDH, I would advise you to use the X25519 key exchange due to the quality of the design (which takes into account invalid curve attacks), the quality of available implementations, and the resistance against timing attacks by design.

Curve25519 has one caveat though—it is not a prime-order group. The curve has two subgroups: a small subgroup of size 8 and a large subgroup used for ECDH. On top of that, the original design did not prescribe validating received points, and libraries, in turn, did not implement these checks. This led to issues being found in different types of protocols that were making use of the primitive in more exotic ways. (One of these I found in the Matrix messaging protocol, which I talk about in chapter 11.)

Not verifying public keys can have unexpected behaviors with X25519. The reason is that the key exchange algorithm does not have *contributory behavior*: it does not allow both parties to contribute to the final result of the key exchange. Specifically, one of the participants can force the outcome of the key exchange to be all zeros by sending a point in the small subgroup as public key. RFC 7748 does mention this issue and proposes to check that the resulting shared secret is not the all zero output, yet lets the implementer decide to do the check or not! I would recommend making sure that your implementation performs the check, although it's unlikely that you're going to run into any issues unless you use X25519 in a nonstandard way.

Because many protocols rely on Curve25519, this has been an issue for more than just key exchanges. *Ristretto*, the internet draft soon-to-be RFC, is a construction that adds an extra layer of encoding to Curve25519, effectively simulating a curve of prime order (see https://tools.ietf.org/html/draft-hdevalence-cfrg-ristretto-01). The construction has been gaining traction as it simplifies the security assumptions made by other types of cryptographic primitives that want to benefit from Curve25519 but want a prime-order field.

Summary

- Unauthenticated key exchanges allow two parties to agree on a shared secret, while preventing any passive man-in-the-middle (MITM) attacker from being able to derive it as well.

- An authenticated key exchange prevents an active MITM from impersonating one side of the connection, while a mutually authenticated key exchange prevents an active MITM from impersonating both sides.

- One can perform an authenticated key exchange by knowing the other party's public key, but this doesn't always scale and signatures will unlock more complex scenarios (see chapter 7).

- Diffie-Hellman (DH) is the first key exchange algorithm invented and is still widely used.

- The recommended standard to use for DH is RFC 7919, which includes several parameters to choose from. The smallest option is the recommended 2,048-bit prime parameter.

- Elliptic Curve Diffie-Hellman (ECDH) has much smaller key sizes than DH. For 128 bits of security, DH needs 2,048-bit parameters, whereas ECDH needs 256-bit parameters.

- The most widely used curves for ECDH are P-256 and Curve25519. Both provide 128 bits of security. For 256-bit security, P-521 and Curve448 are available in the same standards.

- Make sure that implementations verify the validity of public keys you receive as invalid keys are the source of many bugs.

Asymmetric encryption and hybrid encryption

This chapter covers

- Asymmetric encryption to encrypt secrets to a public key
- Hybrid encryption to encrypt data to a public key
- The standards for asymmetric and hybrid encryption

In chapter 4, you learned about authenticated encryption, a cryptographic primitive used to encrypt data but limited by its symmetry (both sides of a connection had to share the same key). In this chapter, I'll lift this restriction by introducing asymmetric encryption, a primitive to encrypt to someone else's key without knowing the key. Without surprise, asymmetric encryption makes use of key pairs and encryption will use public keys instead of symmetric keys.

Halfway through this chapter, you will see that asymmetric encryption is limited by the size of the data it can encrypt and by the rate at which it can encrypt it. To remove this obstacle, I'll show you how to mix asymmetric encryption with authenticated encryption to form what we call *hybrid encryption*. Let's get started!

NOTE For this chapter, you'll need to have read chapter 4 on authenticated encryption and chapter 5 on key exchanges.

6.1   *What is asymmetric encryption?*

The first step in knowing how to encrypt a message is understanding *asymmetric encryption* (also called *public key encryption*). In this section, you will learn about this cryptographic primitive and its properties. Let's take a look at the following real-world scenario: *encrypted emails*.

You probably know that all the emails you send are sent "in the clear" for anyone sitting in between you and your recipient's email provider to read. That's not great. How do you fix this? You could use a cryptographic primitive like AES-GCM, which you learned about in chapter 4. To do that, you would need to set up a different shared symmetric secret for each person that wants to message you.

> **Exercise**
> Using the same shared secret with everyone would be very bad; can you see why?

But you can't expect to know in advance who'll want to message you, and generating and exchanging new symmetric keys will get tedious as more and more people want to encrypt messages to you. This is where asymmetric encryption helps by allowing anyone in possession of your public key to encrypt messages to you. Furthermore, you are the only one who can decrypt these messages using the associated private key that only you own. See figure 6.1 for an illustration of asymmetric encryption.

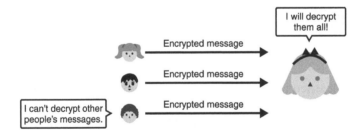

Figure 6.1   With asymmetric encryption, anyone can use Alice's public key to send her encrypted messages. Only Alice, who owns the associated private key, can decrypt these messages.

To set up asymmetric encryption, you first need to generate a key pair via some algorithm. As with any setup function for cryptographic algorithms, the key generation algorithm accepts a security parameter. This security parameter usually translates to "how big do you want your keys to be?" where bigger means more secure. Figure 6.2 illustrates this step.

The *key generation algorithm* generates a key pair comprised of two different parts: the public key part (as the name indicates) can be published and shared without

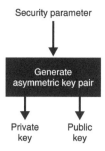

Figure 6.2   To use asymmetric encryption, you first need to generate a key pair. Depending on the security parameters you provide, you can generate keys of different security strengths.

much concerns, while the private key must remain secret. Similar to the key generation algorithms of other cryptographic primitives, a security parameter is required in order to decide on the bit security of the algorithm. Anyone can then use the public key part to encrypt messages, and you can use the private key part to decrypt as figure 6.3 illustrates. And similar to authenticated decryption, decryption can fail if presented with incoherent ciphertext.

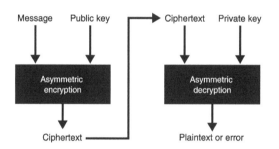

Figure 6.3   Asymmetric encryption allows one to encrypt a message (*plaintext*) using a recipient's public key. The recipient can then use a different algorithm to decrypt the encrypted message (*ciphertext*) using a private key that's related to the public key used previously.

Note that so far we haven't talked about authentication. Consider both sides of the wire:

- You are encrypting to a public key which you think is owned by Alice.
- Alice does not know for sure who sent this message.

For now, we will imagine that we obtained Alice's public key in a really secure way. In chapter 7, which covers digital signatures, you will learn how real-world protocols solve this bootstrapping issue in practice. You will also learn in chapter 7 how you can communicate to Alice who you really are, in a cryptographic way. Spoiler alert: you'll be signing your messages.

Let's move on to the next section where you'll learn about how asymmetric encryption is used in practice (and also why it's rarely used as-is in practice).

6.2   Asymmetric encryption in practice and hybrid encryption

You might be thinking asymmetric encryption is probably enough to start encrypting your emails. In reality, asymmetric encryption is quite limited due to the restricted length of messages it can encrypt. The speed of asymmetric encryption and decryption is also slow in comparison to symmetric encryption. This is due to asymmetric constructions implementing math operations, as opposed to symmetric primitives that often just manipulate bits.

In this section, you will learn about these limitations, what asymmetric encryption is actually used for in practice, and finally, how cryptography overcomes these impediments. This section is divided in two parts for the two main use cases of asymmetric encryption:

- *Key exchanges*—You will see that it is quite natural to perform a key exchange (or key agreement) with an asymmetric encryption primitive.
- *Hybrid encryption*—You will see that the use cases for asymmetric encryption are quite limited due to the maximum size of what you can encrypt. To encrypt larger messages, you will learn about a more useful primitive called *hybrid encryption*.

6.2.1   Key exchanges and key encapsulation

It turns out that asymmetric encryption can be used to perform a key exchange—the same kind as the ones we saw in chapter 5! In order to do this, you can start by generating a symmetric key and encrypt it with Alice's public key—what we also call *encapsulating a key*—as figure 6.4 demonstrates.

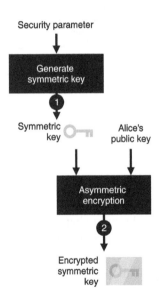

Figure 6.4   To use asymmetric encryption as a key exchange primitive, you (1) generate a symmetric key and then (2) encrypt it with Alice's public key.

You can then send the ciphertext to Alice, who will be able to decrypt it and learn the symmetric key. Subsequently, you will have both a shared secret! Figure 6.5 illustrates the complete flow.

Using asymmetric encryption to perform a key exchange is usually done with an algorithm called *RSA* (following the names of its inventors Rivest, Shamir, and Adleman)

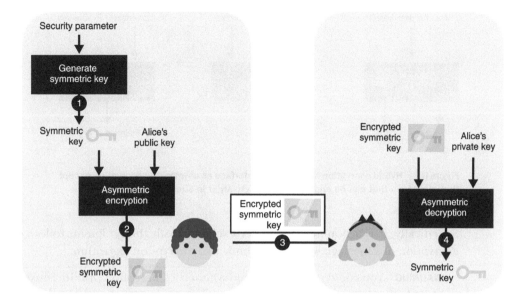

Figure 6.5   To use asymmetric encryption as a key exchange primitive, you can (1) generate a symmetric key and (2) encrypt it with Alice's public key. After (3) sending it to Alice, she can (4) decrypt it with her associated private key. At the end of the protocol, you both have the shared secret, while no one else is able to derive it from observing the encrypted symmetric key alone.

and used in many internet protocols. Today, RSA is often *not* the preferred way of doing a key exchange, and it is being used less and less in protocols in favor of Elliptic Curve Diffie-Hellman (ECDH). This is mostly due to historical reasons (many vulnerabilities have been discovered with RSA implementations and standards) and the attractiveness of the smaller parameter sizes offered by ECDH.

6.2.2   Hybrid encryption

In practice, asymmetric encryption can only encrypt messages up to a certain length. For example, the size of plaintext messages that can be encrypted by RSA are limited by the security parameters that were used during the generation of the key pair (and more specifically by the size of the modulus). Nowadays, with the security parameters used (4,096-bit modulus), the limit is approximately 500 ASCII characters—pretty small. Therefore, most applications make use of hybrid encryption, whose limitation is tied to the encryption limits of the authenticated encryption algorithm used.

Hybrid encryption has the same interface as asymmetric encryption in practice (see figure 6.6). People can encrypt messages with a public key, and the one who owns the associated private key can decrypt the encrypted messages. The real difference is in the size limitations of the messages that you can encrypt.

Under the cover, hybrid encryption is simply the combination of an *asymmetric* cryptographic primitive with a *symmetric* cryptographic primitive (hence the name).

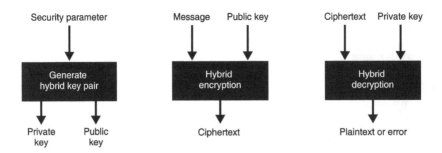

Figure 6.6 Hybrid encryption has the same interface as asymmetric encryption except that messages that can be encrypted are much larger in size.

Specifically, it is a non-interactive key exchange with the recipient, followed by the encryption of a message with an authenticated encryption algorithm.

> **WARNING** You could also use a simple symmetric encryption primitive instead of an authenticated encryption primitive, but symmetric encryption does not protect against someone tampering with your encrypted messages. This is why we never use symmetric encryption alone in practice (as seen in chapter 4).

Let's learn about how hybrid encryption works! If you want to encrypt a message to Alice, you first generate a symmetric key and encrypt your message with it and then use an authenticated encryption algorithm as figure 6.7 illustrates.

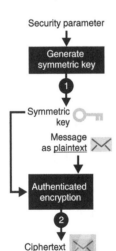

Figure 6.7 To encrypt a message to Alice using hybrid encryption with asymmetric encryption, you (1) generate a symmetric key for an authenticated encryption algorithm, then you (2) use the symmetric key to encrypt your message to Alice.

Once you have encrypted your message, Alice still cannot decrypt it without the knowledge of the symmetric key. How do we provide Alice with that symmetric key? Asymmetrically encrypt the symmetric key with Alice's public key as in figure 6.8.

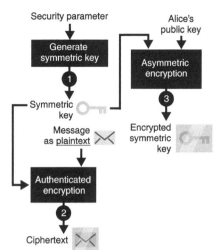

Figure 6.8   Building on figure 6.7, you (3) encrypt the symmetric key itself by using Alice's public key and an asymmetric encryption algorithm.

Finally, you can send both results to Alice. These include

- The asymmetrically encrypted symmetric key
- The symmetrically encrypted message

This is enough information for Alice to decrypt the message. I illustrate the full flow in figure 6.9.

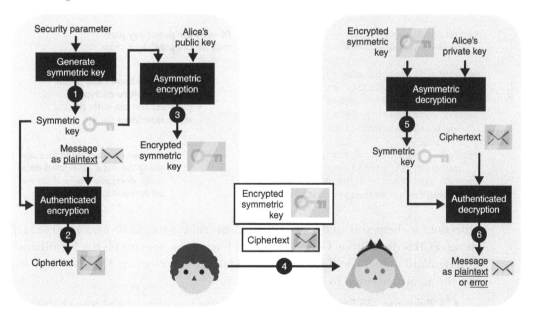

Figure 6.9   Building on figure 6.8, (4) after you send both the encrypted symmetric key and the encrypted message to Alice, (5) Alice decrypts the symmetric key using her private key. (6) She then uses the symmetric key to decrypt the encrypted message. (Note that steps 5 and 6 can both fail and return errors if the communications are tampered with by a MITM attacker at step 4.)

And this is how we can use the best of both worlds: mixing asymmetric encryption and symmetric encryption to encrypt large amounts of data to a public key. We often call the first asymmetric part of the algorithm a *key encapsulation mechanism* (KEM) and the second symmetric part a *data encapsulation mechanism* (DEM).

Before we move to the next section and learn about the different algorithms and standards that exist for both asymmetric encryption and hybrid encryption, let's see (in practice) how you can use a cryptographic library to perform hybrid encryption. To do this, I chose the Tink cryptography library. Tink was developed by a team of cryptographers at Google to support large teams inside and outside of the company. Because of the scale of the project, conscious design choices were made and sane functions were exposed in order to prevent developers from misusing cryptographic primitives. In addition, Tink is available in several programming languages (Java, C++, Obj-C, and Golang).

Listing 6.1   Hybrid encryption in Java

```java
import com.google.crypto.tink.HybridDecrypt;
import com.google.crypto.tink.HybridEncrypt;
import com.google.crypto.tink.hybrid.HybridKeyTemplates
  .ECIES_P256_HKDF_HMAC_SHA256_AES128_GCM;
import com.google.crypto.tink.KeysetHandle;

KeysetHandle privkey = KeysetHandle.generateNew(      Generates keys for a specific
    ECIES_P256_HKDF_HMAC_SHA256_AES128_GCM);          hybrid encryption scheme

KeysetHandle publicKeysetHandle =        Obtains the public key part
    privkey.getPublicKeysetHandle();     that we can publish or share

HybridEncrypt hybridEncrypt =
    publicKeysetHandle.getPrimitive(         Anyone who knows this public
        HybridEncrypt.class);                key can use it to encrypt
byte[] ciphertext = hybridEncrypt.encrypt(   plaintext and can authenticate
    plaintext, associatedData);              some associated data.

HybridDecrypt hybridDecrypt =                Decrypts an encrypted message
    privkey.getPrimitive(HybridDecrypt.class);   using the same associated data.
byte[] plaintext = hybridDecrypt.decrypt(    If the decryption fails, it throws
    ciphertext, associatedData);             an exception.
```

One note to help you understand the ECIES_P256_HKDF_HMAC_SHA256_AES128_GCM string: ECIES (for Elliptic Curve Integrated Encryption Scheme) is the hybrid encryption standard to use. You'll learn about this later in this chapter. The rest of the string lists the algorithms used to instantiate ECIES:

- P256 is the NIST standardized elliptic curve you learned about in chapter 5.
- HKDF is a key derivation function you will learn about in chapter 8.
- HMAC is the message authentication code you learned about in chapter 3.
- SHA-256 is the hash function you learned about in chapter 2.

- AES-128-GCM is the AES-GCM authenticated encryption algorithm using a 128-bit key you learned about in chapter 4.

See how everything is starting to fit together? In the next section, you will learn about RSA and ECIES, the two widely adopted standards for asymmetric encryption and hybrid encryption.

6.3 Asymmetric encryption with RSA: The bad and the less bad

It is time for us to look at the standards that define asymmetric encryption and hybrid encryption in practice. Historically, both of these primitives have not been spared by cryptanalysts, and many vulnerabilities and weaknesses have been found in both standards and implementations. This is why I will start this section with an introduction to the RSA asymmetric encryption algorithm and how not to use it. The rest of the chapter will go through the actual standards you can follow to use asymmetric and hybrid encryptions:

- *RSA-OAEP*—The main standard to perform asymmetric encryption with RSA
- *ECIES*—The main standard to perform hybrid encryption with Elliptic Curve Diffie-Hellman (ECDH)

6.3.1 Textbook RSA

In this section, you will learn about the RSA public key encryption algorithm and how it has been standardized throughout the years. This is useful to understand other secure schemes based on RSA.

Unfortunately, RSA has caught quite some bad rap since it was first published in 1977. One of the popular theories is that RSA is too easy to understand and implement, and thus, many people do it themselves, which leads to a lot of vulnerable implementations. It's an interesting idea, but it misses the whole story. While the concept of RSA (often called *textbook RSA*) is insecure if implemented naively, even standards have been found to be broken! But not so fast, to understand these issues, you will first need to learn how RSA works.

Remember the multiplicative group of numbers modulo a prime p? (We talked about it in chapter 5.) It is the set of strictly positive integers:

$$1, 2, 3, 4, \cdots, p-1$$

Let's imagine that one of these numbers is our message. For p large enough, let's say 4,096 bits, our message can contain around 500 characters tops.

NOTE For computers, a message is just a series of bytes, which can also be interpreted as a number.

We have seen that by exponentiating a number (let's say our message), we can generate other numbers that form a *subgroup*. I illustrate this in figure 6.10.

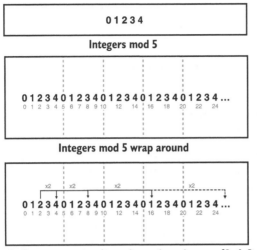

Let's take 2 as a generator, it produces the subgroup {2, 4, 3, 1}.

Figure 6.10   Integers modulo a prime (here 5) are divided in different subgroups. By picking an element as a generator (let's say the number 2) and exponentiating it, we can generate a subgroup. For RSA, the generator is the message.

This is useful for us when defining how to encrypt with RSA. To do this, we publish a public exponent e (for *encryption*) and a prime number p. (In reality p cannot be prime, but we'll ignore that for a moment.) To encrypt a message m, one computes

$$\text{ciphertext} = m^e \bmod p$$

For example, to encrypt the message $m = 2$ with $e = 2$ and $p = 5$, we compute

$$\text{ciphertext} = 2^2 \bmod 5 = 4$$

And this is the idea behind encryption with RSA!

NOTE Usually, a small number is chosen as the public exponent e so that encryption is fast. Historically, standards and implementations seem to have settled on the prime number 65,537 for the public exponent.

This is great! You now have a way for people to encrypt messages to you. But how do you decrypt those? Remember, if you continue to exponentiate a generator, you actually go back to the original number (see figure 6.11).

This should give you an idea of how to implement decryption: find out how much you need to exponentiate a ciphertext in order to recover the original generator (which is the message). Let's say that you know such a number, which we'll call the *private exponent d* (d for *decryption*). If you receive

$$\text{ciphertext} = \text{message}^e \bmod p$$

you should be able to raise it to the power d to recover the message:

$$\text{ciphertext}^d = (\text{message}^e)^d = \text{message}^{e \times d} = \text{message} \bmod p$$

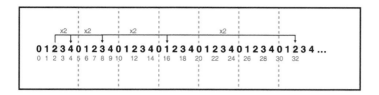

Figure 6.11 Let's say that our message is the number 2. By exponentiating it, we can obtain other numbers in our group. If we exponentiate it enough, we go back to our original message, 2. We say that the group is *cyclic*. This property can be used to recover a message after it has been raised to some power.

The actual mathematics behind finding this private exponent d is a bit tricky. Simply put, you compute the inverse of the public exponent modulo the order (number of elements) of the group:

$$d = e^{-1} \bmod \text{order}$$

We have an efficient algorithm to compute modular inverses (like the Extended Euclidean algorithm), and so this is not a problem. We do have another problem though! For a prime p, the order is simply $p - 1$, and thus, *it's easy for anyone to calculate the private exponent*. This is because every element in this equation besides d is public.

> ### Euler's theorem
> How did we obtain the previous equation to compute the private exponent d? Euler's theorem states that for m co-prime with p (meaning that they have no common factors):
>
> $$m^{order} = 1 \bmod p$$
>
> For *order*, the number of elements in the multiplicative group created by the integers modulo p. This implies, in turn, that for any integer *multiple*
>
> $$m^{1+multiple \times order} = m \times (m^{order})^{multiple} \bmod p = m \bmod p$$
>
> This tells us that the equation we are trying to solve
>
> $$m^{e \times d} = m \bmod p$$
>
> can be reduced to
>
> $$e \times d = 1 + multiple \times order$$
>
> which can be rewritten as
>
> $$e \times d = 1 \bmod order$$
>
> This, by definition, means that d is the inverse of e modulo *order*.

One way we could prevent others from computing the private exponent from the public exponent is to hide the order of our group. This is the brilliant idea behind RSA: if our modulus is not a prime anymore but a product of a prime $N = p \times q$ (where p and q are large primes known only to you), then the order of our multiplicative group is not easy to compute as long as we don't know p and q!

The order of an RSA group

You can calculate the order of the multiplicative group modulo a number N with Euler's totient function $\phi(N)$, which returns the count of numbers that are *co-prime* with N. For example, 5 and 6 are co-prime because the only positive integer that divides both of them is 1. On the other hand, 10 and 15 are not because 1 and 5 divide each of them. The order of a multiplicative group modulo an RSA modulus $N = p \times q$ is

$$\phi(N) = (p - 1) \times (q - 1)$$

which is too hard to calculate unless you know the factorization of N.

We're all good! To recapitulate, this is how RSA works:

- For key generation
  1. Generate two large prime numbers p and q.
  2. Choose a random public exponent e or a fixed one like $e = 65537$.
  3. Your public key is the public exponent e and the public modulus $N = p \times q$.
  4. Derive your private exponent $d = e^{-1} \mod (p - 1)(q - 1)$.
  5. Your private key is the private exponent d.
- For encryption, compute $\text{message}^e \mod N$.
- For decryption of the ciphertext, compute $\text{ciphertext}^d \mod N$.

Figure 6.12 reviews how RSA works in practice.

```
                    Exponentiate with e mod N  Exponentiate with d mod N
                          ┌──────────────┐  ┌──────────────┐
                          │              ▼  │              ▼
  0 1 2 3 4 ... 5490349040 ... 10398090934820 ... 5490349040 ...
```

Figure 6.12   RSA encryption works by exponentiating a number (our message) with the public exponent e modulo the public modulus N = p × q. RSA decryption works by exponentiating the encrypted number with the private exponent d modulo the public modulus N.

We say that RSA relies on the *factorization problem*. Without the knowledge of p and q, no one can compute the order; thus, no one but you can compute the private exponent from the public exponent. This is similar to how Diffie-Hellman was based on the discrete logarithm problem (see figure 6.13).

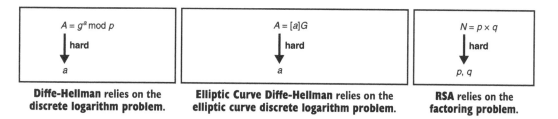

Diffe-Hellman relies on the discrete logarithm problem.

Elliptic Curve Diffe-Hellman relies on the elliptic curve discrete logarithm problem.

RSA relies on the factoring problem.

Figure 6.13　Diffie-Hellman (DH), Elliptic Curve Diffie-Hellman (ECDH), and RSA are asymmetric algorithms that rely on three distinct problems in mathematics that we believe to be hard. *Hard* meaning that we do not know efficient algorithms to solve them when instantiated with large numbers.

Thus, textbook RSA works modulo a composite number $N = p \times q$, where p and q are two large primes that need to remain secret. Now that you understand how RSA works, let's see how insecure it is in practice and what standards do to make it secure.

6.3.2　*Why not to use RSA PKCS#1 v1.5*

You learned about "textbook RSA," which is insecure by default for many reasons. Before you can learn about the secure version of RSA, let's see what you need to avoid.

There are many reasons why you cannot use textbook RSA directly. One example is that if you encrypt small messages (for example $m = 2$), then some malicious actor can encrypt all the small numbers between 0 and 100, for example, and quickly observe if any of their encrypted numbers match your ciphertext. If it does, they will know what you encrypted.

Standards fix this issue by making your messages too big to be brute-forced in such a way. Specifically, they maximize the size of a message (before encryption) with a *nondeterministic* padding. For example, the RSA PKCS#1 v1.5 standard defines a padding that adds a number of random bytes to the message. I illustrate this in figure 6.14.

The PKCS#1 standard is actually the first standard based on RSA, published as part of a series of Public Key Cryptography Standard (PKCS) documents written by the RSA company in the early 90s. While the PKCS#1 standard fixes some known issues, in 1998, Bleichenbacher found a practical attack on PKCS#1 v1.5 that allowed an attacker to decrypt messages encrypted with the padding specified by the standard. As it required a million messages, it is infamously called the *million message attack*. Mitigations were later found, but interestingly, over the years, the attack has been rediscovered again and again as researchers found that the mitigations were too hard to implement securely (if at all).

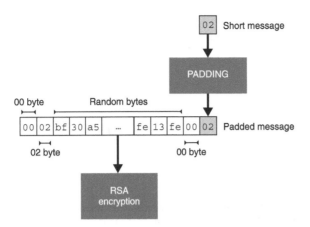

Figure 6.14   The RSA PKCS#1 v1.5 standard specifies a padding to apply to a message prior to encryption. The padding must be reversible (so that decryption can get rid of it) and must add enough random bytes to the message in order to avoid brute force attacks.

Adaptive chosen-ciphertext attacks

Bleichenbacher's million message attack is a type of attack called an *adaptive chosen ciphertext attack* (CCA2) in theoretical cryptography. CCA2 means that to perform this attack, an attacker can submit arbitrary RSA encrypted messages (*chosen ciphertext*), observe how it influences the decryption, and continue the attack based on previous observations (the *adaptive* part). CCA2 is often used to model attackers in cryptographic security proofs.

To understand why the attack was possible, you need to understand that RSA ciphertexts are *malleable*: you can tamper with an RSA ciphertext without invalidating its decryption. If I observe the ciphertext $c = m^e \bmod N$, then I can submit the following ciphertext:

$$3^e \times m^e = (3m)^e \bmod N$$

which will decrypt as

$$((3m)^e)^d = (3m)^{e \times d} = 3m \bmod N$$

I used the number 3 as an example here, but I can multiply the original message with whatever number I want. In practice, a message must be well-formed (due to the padding), and thus, tampering with a ciphertext should break the decryption. Nevertheless, it happens that sometimes, even after the malicious modification, the padding is accepted after decryption.

Bleichenbacher made use of this property in his million message attack on RSA PKCS#1 v1.5. His attack works by intercepting an encrypted message, modifying it, and sending it to the person in charge of decrypting it. By observing if that person can decrypt it (the padding remained valid), we obtain some information about the message range. Because the first two bytes are 0x0002, we know that the decryption is smaller than some value. By doing this iteratively, we can narrow that range down to the original message itself.

Even though the Bleichenbacher attack is well-known, there are still many systems in use today that implement RSA PKCS#1 v1.5 for encryption. As part of my work as a security consultant, I found many applications that were vulnerable to this attack—so be careful!

6.3.3   Asymmetric encryption with RSA-OAEP

In 1998, version 2.0 of the same PKCS#1 standard was released with a new padding scheme for RSA called *Optimal Asymmetric Encryption Padding* (OAEP). Unlike its predecessor, PKCS#1 v1.5, OAEP is not vulnerable to Bleichenbacher's attack and is, thus, a strong standard to use for RSA encryption nowadays. Let's see how OAEP works and prevents the previously discussed attacks.

First, let's mention that like most cryptographic algorithms, OAEP comes with a key generation algorithm. This takes a security parameter as figure 6.15 illustrates.

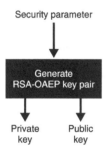

Figure 6.15   RSA-OAEP, like many public key algorithms, first needs to generate a key pair that can be used later in the other algorithms provided by the cryptographic primitive.

This algorithm takes a security parameter, which is a number of bits. As with Diffie-Hellman, operations happen in the set of numbers modulo a large number. When we talk about the security of an instantiation of RSA, we usually refer to the size of that large modulus. This is similar to Diffie-Hellman if you remember.

Currently, most guidelines (see https://keylength.com) estimate a modulus between 2,048 and 4,096 bits to provide 128-bit security. As these estimations are quite different, most applications seem to conservatively settle on 4,096-bit parameters.

> **NOTE** We saw that RSA's large modulus is not a prime but a product $N = p \times q$ of two large prime numbers p and q. For a 4,096-bit modulus, the key generation algorithm typically splits things in the middle and generates both p and q of size approximately 2,048 bits.

To encrypt, the algorithm first pads the message and mixes it with a random number generated per encryption. The result is then encrypted with RSA. To decrypt the ciphertext, the process is reversed as figure 6.16 shows.

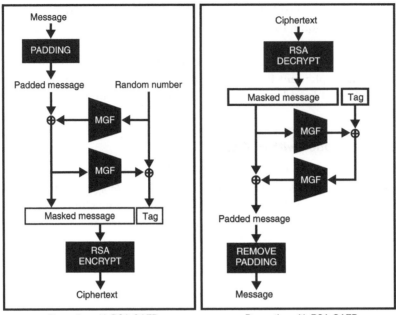

Encryption with RSA-OAEP   Decryption with RSA-OAEP

Figure 6.16   RSA-OAEP works by mixing the message with a random number prior to encryption. The mixing can be reverted after decryption. At the center of the algorithm, a mask generation function (MGF) is used to randomize and enlarge or reduce an input.

RSA-OAEP uses this mixing in order to make sure that if a few bits of what is encrypted with RSA leak, no information on the plaintext can be obtained. Indeed, to reverse the OAEP padding, you need to obtain (close to) all the bytes of the OAEP padded plaintext! In addition, Bleichenbacher's attack should not work anymore because the scheme makes it impossible to obtain well-formed plaintext by modifying a ciphertext.

> **NOTE** *Plaintext-awareness* is the property that makes it too difficult for an attacker to create a ciphertext that will successfully decrypt (of course without the help of encryption). Due to the plaintext-awareness provided by OAEP, Bleichenbacher's attack does not work on the scheme.

Inside of OAEP, *MGF* stands for *mask generation function*. In practice, an MGF is an extendable output function (XOF); you learned about XOFs in chapter 2. As MGFs were invented before XOFs, they are built using a hash function that hashes the input repeatedly with a counter (see figure 6.17). And this is how OAEP works!

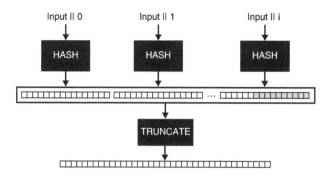

Figure 6.17 A mask generation function (MGF) is simply a function that takes an arbitrary length input and produces a random-looking arbitrary length output. It works by hashing an input and a counter, concatenating the digests together, and truncating the result to obtain the length desired.

Manger's padding oracle attack

Only three years after the release of the OAEP standard, James Manger found a timing attack similar to Bleichenbacher's million message attack (but much more practical) on OAEP if not implemented correctly. Fortunately, it is much simpler to securely implement OAEP compared to PKCS#1 v1.5, and vulnerabilities in this scheme's implementation are much more rare.

Furthermore, the design of OAEP is not perfect; better constructions have been proposed and standardized over the years. One example is RSA-KEM, which has stronger proofs of security and is much simpler to implement securely. You can observe how much more elegant the design is in figure 6.18.

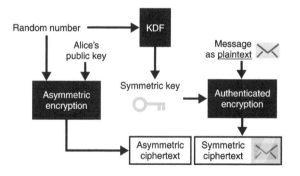

Figure 6.18 RSA-KEM is an encryption scheme that works by simply encrypting a random number under RSA. No padding is needed. We can pass the random number through a key derivation function (KDF) to obtain a symmetric key. We then use the symmetric key to encrypt a message via an authenticated encryption algorithm.

Note the key derivation function (KDF) in use here. It is another cryptographic primitive that can be replaced with an MGF or a XOF. I'll talk more about what KDFs are in chapter 8 on randomness and secrets.

Nowadays, most protocols and applications that use RSA either still implement the insecure PKCS#1 v1.5 or OAEP. On the other hand, more and more protocols are moving away from RSA encryption in favor of Elliptic Curve Diffie-Hellman (ECDH) for both key exchanges and hybrid encryption. This is understandable as ECDH provides shorter public keys and benefits, in general, from much better standards and much safer implementations.

6.4   *Hybrid encryption with ECIES*

While there exist many hybrid encryption schemes, the most widely adopted standard is *Elliptic Curve Integrated Encryption Scheme* (ECIES). The scheme has been specified to be used with ECDH and is included in many standards like ANSI X9.63, ISO/IEC 18033-2, IEEE 1363a, and SECG SEC 1. Unfortunately, every standard seems to implement a different variant, and different cryptographic libraries implement hybrid encryption differently, in part due to this.

For this reason, I rarely see two similar implementations of hybrid encryption in the wild. It is important to understand that while this is annoying, if all the participants of the protocol use the same implementation or document the details of the hybrid encryption scheme they have implemented, then there would be no issues.

ECIES works similarly to the hybrid encryption scheme explained in section 6.2. The difference is that we implement the KEM part with an ECDH key exchange instead of with an asymmetric encryption primitive. Let's explain this step by step.

First, if you want to encrypt a message to Alice, you use an (EC)DH-based key exchange with Alice's public key and a key pair that you generate for the occasion (this is called an *ephemeral key pair*). You can then use the obtained shared secret with an authenticated symmetric encryption algorithm like AES-GCM to encrypt a longer message to her. Figure 6.19 illustrates this.

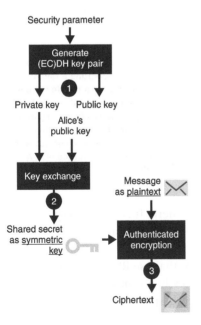

Figure 6.19 To encrypt a message to Alice using hybrid encryption with (EC)DH, you (1) generate an ephemeral (elliptic curve) DH key pair. Then (2) perform a key exchange with your ephemeral private key and Alice's public key. (3) Use the resulting shared secret as a symmetric key to an authenticated encryption algorithm to encrypt your message.

After this, you can send the ephemeral public key and the ciphertext to Alice. Alice can use your ephemeral public key to perform a key exchange with her own key pair. She can then use the result to decrypt the ciphertext and retrieve the original message. The result is either the original message or an error if the public key or the encrypted message are tampered with in transit. Figure 6.20 illustrates the full flow.

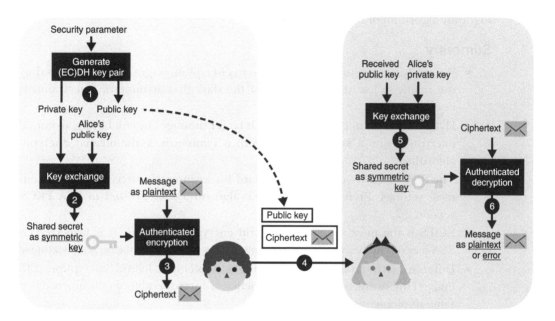

Figure 6.20 Building on figure 6.19, (4) after you send your ephemeral public key and your encrypted message to Alice, (5) Alice can perform a key exchange with her private key and your ephemeral public key. (6) She finally uses the resulting shared secret as a symmetric key to decrypt the encrypted message with the same authenticated encryption algorithm.

And this is pretty much how ECIES work. There also exists a variant of ECIES using Diffie-Hellman, called IES, that works pretty much the same way, but not many people seem to use it.

Removing bias in a key exchange output

Note that I simplified figure 6.20. Most authenticated encryption primitives expect an uniformly random symmetric key. Because the output of a key exchange is generally *not* uniformly random, we need to pass the shared secret through a KDF or a XOF (as seen in chapter 2) beforehand. You will learn more about this in chapter 8.

Not uniformly random here means that statistically, some of the bits of the key exchange result might be 0 more often than 1, or the opposite. The first bits might always be set to 0, for example.

Exercise

Do you see why you can't use the key exchange output right away?

And that's it for the different standards you can use. In the next chapter, you'll learn about signatures, which will be the last, and perhaps most important, public key cryptography algorithm of part 1.

Summary

- We rarely use asymmetric encryption to encrypt messages directly. This is due to the relatively low size limitations of the data that asymmetric encryption can encrypt.
- Hybrid encryption can encrypt much larger messages by combining asymmetric encryption (or a key exchange) with a symmetric authenticated encryption algorithm.
- The RSA PKCS#1 version 1.5 standard for asymmetric encryption is broken in most settings. Prefer the RSA-OAEP algorithm standardized in RSA PKCS#1 version 2.2.
- ECIES is the most widely used hybrid encryption scheme. It is preferred over RSA-based schemes due to its parameter sizes and its reliance on solid standards.
- Different cryptographic libraries might implement hybrid encryption differently. This is not a problem in practice if interoperable applications use the same implementations.

Signatures and zero-knowledge proofs

This chapter covers

- Zero-knowledge proofs and cryptographic signatures
- The existing standards for cryptographic signatures
- The subtle behaviors of signatures and avoiding their pitfalls

You're about to learn one of the most ubiquitous and powerful cryptographic primitives—digital signatures. To put it simply, digital signatures are similar to the real-life signatures that you're used to, the ones that you scribe on checks and contracts. Except, of course, that digital signatures are cryptographic and so they provide much more assurance than their pen-and-paper equivalents.

In the world of protocols, digital signatures unlock so many different possibilities that you'll run into them again and again in the second part of this book. In this chapter, I will introduce what this new primitive is, how it can be used in the real world, and what the modern digital signature standards are. Finally, I will talk about security considerations and the hazards of using digital signatures.

NOTE Signatures in cryptography are often referred to as *digital signatures* or *signature schemes*. In this book, I interchangeably use these terms.

For this chapter, you'll need to have read

- Chapter 2 on hash functions
- Chapter 5 on key exchanges
- Chapter 6 on asymmetric encryption

7.1   *What is a signature?*

I explained in chapter 1 that cryptographic signatures are pretty much like real-life signatures. For this reason, they are usually one of the most intuitive cryptographic primitives to understand:

- Only you can use your signature to sign arbitrary messages.
- Anybody can verify your signature on a message.

As we're in the realm of asymmetric cryptography, you can probably guess how this asymmetry is going to take place. A *signature scheme* typically consists of three different algorithms:

- A key pair generation algorithm that a signer uses to create a new private and public key (the public key can then be shared with anyone).
- A signing algorithm that takes a private key and a message to produce a signature.
- A verifying algorithm that takes a public key, a message, and a signature and returns a success or error message.

Sometimes the private key is also called the *signing key*, and the public key is called the *verifying key*. Makes sense, right? I recapitulate these three algorithms in figure 7.1.

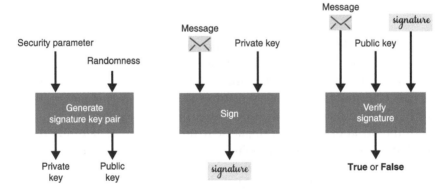

Figure 7.1   The interface of a digital signature. Like other public key cryptographic algorithms, you first need to generate a key pair via a key generation algorithm that takes a security parameter and some randomness. You can then use a signing algorithm with the private key to sign a message and a verifying algorithm with the public key to validate a signature over a message. You can't forge a signature that verifies a public key if you don't have access to its associated private key.

What are signatures good for? They are good for authenticating the origin of a message as well as the integrity of a message:

- *Origin*—If my signature is on it, it came from me.
- *Integrity*—If someone modifies the message, it voids the signature.

NOTE While these two properties are linked to authentication, they are often distinguished as two separate properties: *origin authentication* and *message authentication* (or integrity).

In a sense, signatures are similar to the message authentication codes (MACs) that you learned about in chapter 3. But unlike MACs, they allow us to authenticate messages asymmetrically: a participant can verify that a message hasn't been tampered without knowledge of the private or signing key. Next, I'll show you how these algorithms can be used in practice.

Exercise

As you saw in chapter 3, authentication tags produced by MACs must be verified in constant time to avoid timing attacks. Do you think we need to do the same for verifying signatures?

7.1.1 How to sign and verify signatures in practice

Let's look at a practical example. For this, I use pyca/cryptography (https://cryptography.io), a well-respected Python library. The following listing simply generates a key pair, signs a message using the private key part, and then verifies the signature using the public key part.

Listing 7.1 Signing and verifying signatures in Python

```
from cryptography.hazmat.primitives.asymmetric.ed25519 import (
    Ed25519PrivateKey                    ◁──┐ Uses the Ed25519 signing algorithm,
)                                            a popular signature scheme

private_key = Ed25519PrivateKey.generate()   First generates the private key and
public_key = private_key.public_key()        then generates the public key

message = b"example.com has the public key 0xab70..."   Using the private key, signs a
signature = private_key.sign(message)                    message and obtains a signature

try:
    public_key.verify(signature, message)    Using the public key,
    print("valid signature")                 verifies the signature
except InvalidSignature:                      over the message
    print("invalid signature")
```

As I said earlier, digital signatures unlock many use cases in the real world. Let's see an example in the next section.

7.1.2   *A prime use case for signatures: Authenticated key exchanges*

Chapters 5 and 6 introduced different ways to perform key exchanges between two participants. In the same chapters, you learned that these key exchanges are useful to negotiate a shared secret, which can then be used to secure communications with an authenticated encryption algorithm. Yet, key exchanges didn't fully solve the problem of setting up a secure connection between two participants as an active man-in-the-middle (MITM) attacker can trivially impersonate both sides of a key exchange. This is where signatures enter the ring.

Imagine that Alice and Bob are trying to set up a secure communication channel between themselves and that Bob is aware of Alice's verifying key. Knowing this, Alice can use her signing key to authenticate her side of the key exchange: she generates a key exchange key pair, signs the public key part with her signing key, then sends the key exchange public key along with the signature. Bob can verify that the signature is valid using the associated verifying key he already knows and then use the key exchange public key to perform a key exchange.

We call such a key exchange an *authenticated key exchange*. If the signature is invalid, Bob can tell someone is actively MITM'ing the key exchange. I illustrate authenticated key exchanges in figure 7.2.

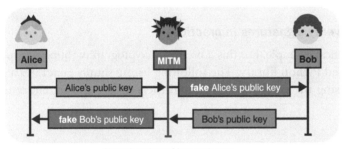

Unauthenticated key exchange

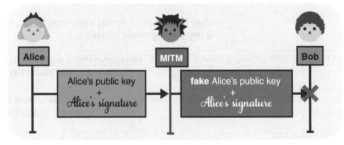

Authenticated key exchange

Figure 7.2   The first picture (top) represents an unauthenticated key exchange, which is insecure to an active MITM attacker who can trivially impersonate both sides of the exchange by swapping their public keys with their own. The second picture (bottom) represents the beginning of a key exchange, authenticated by Alice's signature over her public key. As Bob (who knows Alice's verifying key) is unable to verify the signature after the message was tampered by the MITM attacker, he aborts the key exchange.

Note that in this example, the key exchange is only authenticated on one side: while Alice cannot be impersonated, Bob can. If both sides are authenticated (Bob would sign his part of the key exchange), we call the key exchange a *mutually-authenticated key exchange*. Signing key exchanges might not appear super useful yet. It seems like we moved the problem of not knowing Alice's key exchange public key in advance to the problem of not knowing her verifying key in advance. The next section introduces a real-world use of authenticated key exchanges that will make much more sense.

7.1.3 A real-world usage: Public key infrastructures

Signatures become much more powerful if you assume that trust is *transitive*. By that, I mean that if you trust me and I trust Alice, then you can trust Alice. She's cool.

Transitivity of trust allows you to scale trust in systems in extreme ways. Imagine that you have confidence in some authority and their verifying key. Furthermore, imagine that this authority has signed messages indicating what the public key of Charles is, what the public key of David is, and so on. Then, you can choose to have faith in this mapping! Such a mapping is called a *public key infrastructure*. For example, if you attempt to do a key exchange with Charles and he claims that his public key is a large number that looks like 3848 . . . , you can verify that by checking if your "beloved" authority has signed some message that looks like "the public key of Charles is 3848 . . ."

One real-world application of this concept is the *web public key infrastructure* (web PKI). The web PKI is what your web browser uses to authenticate key exchanges it performs with the multitude of websites you visit every day. A simplified explanation of the web PKI (illustrated in figure 7.3) is as follows: when you download a browser, it comes with some verifying key baked into the program. This verifying key is linked to an authority whose responsibility is to sign thousands and thousands of websites' public keys so that you can trust these without knowing about them. What you're not seeing is that these websites have to prove to the authority that they truly own their domain name before they can obtain a signature on their public key. (In reality, your browser trusts many authorities to do this job, not just a single one.)

In this section, you learned about signatures from a high-level point of view. Let's dig deeper into how signatures really work. But for this, we first need to make a detour and take a look at something called a zero-knowledge proof (ZKP).

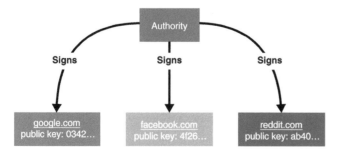

Figure 7.3 In the web PKI, browsers trust an authority to certify that some domains are linked to some public keys. When visiting a website securely, your browser can verify that the website's public key is indeed theirs (and not from some MITM) by verifying a signature from the authority.

7.2   Zero-knowledge proofs (ZKPs): The origin of signatures

The best way to understand how signatures work in cryptography is to understand where they come from. For this reason, let's take a moment to briefly introduce ZKPs and then I'll get back to signatures.

Imagine that Peggy wants to prove something to Victor. For example, she wants to prove that she knows the discrete logarithm to the base of some group element. In other words, she wants to prove that she knows x given $Y = g^x$ with g the generator of some group.

Of course, the simplest solution is for Peggy to simply send the value x (called the *witness*). This solution would be a simple *proof of knowledge*, and this would be OK, unless Peggy does not want Victor to learn it.

> **NOTE**   In theoretical terms, we say that the protocol to produce a proof is *complete* if Peggy can use it to prove to Victor that she knows the witness. If she can't use it to prove what she knows, then the scheme is useless, right?

In cryptography, we're mostly interested in proofs of knowledge that don't divulge the witness to the verifier. Such proofs are called *zero-knowledge proofs* (ZKPs).

7.2.1   Schnorr identification protocol: An interactive zero-knowledge proof

In the next pages, I will build a ZKP incrementally from broken protocols to show you how Alice can prove that she knows x without revealing x.

The typical way to approach this kind of problem in cryptography is to "hide" the value with some randomness (for example, by encrypting it). But we're doing more than just hiding: we also want to prove that it is there. To do that, we need an algebraic way to hide it. A simple solution is to simply add a randomly generated value k to the witness:

$$s = k + x$$

Peggy can then send the hidden witness s along with the random value k to Victor. At this point, Victor has no reason to trust that Peggy did, in fact, hide the witness in s. Indeed, if she doesn't know the witness x then s is probably just some random value. What Victor does know is that the witness x is hiding in the exponent of g because he knows $Y = g^x$.

To see if Peggy really knows the witness, Victor can check if what she gave him matches what he knows, and this has to be done in the exponent of g as well (as this is where the witness is). In other words, Victor checks that these two numbers are equal:

- g^s $(= g^{k+x})$
- $Y \times g^k$ $(= g^x \times g^k = g^{x+k})$

The idea is that only someone who knows the witness x could have constructed a "blinded" witness s that satisfies this equation. And as such, it's a proof of knowledge. I recapitulate this ZKP system in figure 7.4.

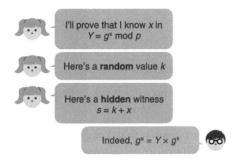

Figure 7.4 In order to prove to Victor that she knows a witness x, Peggy hides it (by adding it to a random value k) and sends the hidden witness s instead.

Not so fast. There's one problem with this scheme—it's obviously not secure! Indeed, because the equation hiding the witness x only has one unknown (x itself), Victor can simply reverse the equation to retrieve the witness:

$$x = s - k$$

To fix this, Peggy can hide the random value k itself! This time, she has to hide the random value in the exponent (instead of adding it to another random value) to make sure that Victor's equation still works:

$$R = g^k$$

This way, Victor does not learn the value k (this is the discrete logarithm problem covered in chapter 5) and, thus, cannot recover the witness x. Yet, he still has enough information to verify that Peggy knows x! Victor simply has to check that g^s $(= g^{k+x} = g^k \times g^x)$ is equal to $Y \times R$ $(= g^x \times g^k)$. I review this second attempt at a ZKP protocol in figure 7.5.

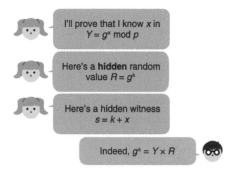

Figure 7.5   To make a knowledge proof *zero-knowledge*, the prover can hide the witness *x* with a random value *k* and then hide the random value itself.

There is one last issue with our scheme—Peggy can cheat. She can convince Victor that she knows x without knowing x! All she has to do is to reverse the step in which she computes her proof. She first generates a random value s and then calculates the value R based on s:

$$R = g^s \times Y^{-1}$$

Victor then computes $Y \times R = Y \times g^s \times Y^{-1}$, which indeed matches g^s. (Peggy's trick of using an inverse to compute a value is used in many attacks in cryptography.)

NOTE   In theoretical terms, we say that the scheme is "sound" if Peggy cannot cheat (if she doesn't know x, then she can't fool Victor).

To make the ZKP protocol sound, Victor must ensure that Peggy computes s from R and not the inverse. To do this, Victor makes the protocol *interactive*:

1 Peggy must commit to her random value k so that she cannot change it later.
2 After receiving Peggy's commitment, Victor introduces some of his own randomness in the protocol. He generates a random value c (called a *challenge*) and sends it to Peggy.
3 Peggy can then compute her hidden commit based on the random value k and the challenge c.

NOTE   You learned about commitment schemes in chapter 2 where we used a hash function to commit to a value that we can later reveal. But commitment schemes based on hash functions do not allow us to do interesting arithmetic on the hidden value. Instead, we can simply raise our generator to the value, g^k, which we're already doing.

Because Peggy cannot perform the last step without Victor's challenge c, and Victor won't send that to her without seeing a commitment on the random value k, Peggy is forced to compute s based on k. The obtained protocol, which I illustrate in figure 7.6, is often referred to as the *Schnorr identification protocol*.

So-called *interactive ZKP systems* that follow a three-movement pattern (commitment, challenge, and proof) are often referred to as *Sigma protocols* in the literature

Figure 7.6 The Schnorr identification protocol is an interactive ZKP that is *complete* (Peggy can prove she knows some witness), *sound* (Peggy cannot prove anything if she doesn't know the witness), and *zero-knowledge* (Victor learns nothing about the witness).

and are sometimes written as Σ protocols (due to the illustrative shape of the Greek letter). But what does that have to do with digital signatures?

NOTE The Schnorr identification protocol works in the *honest verifier zero-knowledge* (HVZK) *model*: if the verifier (Victor) acts dishonestly and does not choose a challenge randomly, they can learn something about the witness. Some stronger ZKP schemes are zero-knowledge even when the verifier is malicious.

7.2.2 *Signatures as non-interactive zero-knowledge proofs*

The problem with the previous interactive ZKP is that, well, it's *interactive*, and real-world protocols are, in general, not fond of interactivity. Interactive protocols add some non-negligible overhead as they require several messages (potentially over the network) and add unbounded delays, unless the two participants are online at the same time. Due to this, interactive ZKPs are mostly absent from the world of applied cryptography.

All of this discussion is not for nothing though! In 1986, Amos Fiat and Adi Shamir published a technique that allowed one to easily convert an interactive ZKP into a non-interactive ZKP. The trick they introduced (referred to as the *Fiat-Shamir heuristic* or *Fiat-Shamir transformation*) was to make the prover compute the challenge themselves, in a way they can't control.

Here's the trick—compute the challenge as a hash of all the messages sent and received as part of the protocol up to that point (which we call the *transcript*). If we assume that the hash function gives outputs that are indistinguishable from truly-random numbers (in other words, it looks random), then it can successfully simulate the role of the verifier.

Schnorr went a step further. He noticed that anything can be included in that hash! For example, what if we included a message in there? What we obtain is not only a proof that we know some witness x, but a commitment to a message that is cryptographically linked to the proof. In other words, if the proof is correct, then only someone with the knowledge of the witness (which becomes the signing key) could have committed that message.

That's a signature! Digital signatures are just non-interactive ZKPs. Applying the Fiat-Shamir transform to the Schnorr identification protocol, we obtain the *Schnorr signature scheme*, which I illustrate in figure 7.7.

Schnorr identification protocol   **Schnorr signature**

Figure 7.7   The left protocol is the Schnorr identification protocol previously discussed, which is an interactive protocol. The right protocol is a Schnorr signature, which is a non-interactive version of the left protocol (where the verifier message is replaced by a call to a hash function on the transcript).

To recapitulate, a Schnorr signature is essentially two values, R and s, where R is a commitment to some secret random value (which is often called a *nonce* as it needs to be unique per signature), and s is a value computed with the help of the commitment R, the private key (the witness x), and a message. Next, let's look at the modern standards for signature algorithms.

7.3   *The signature algorithms you should use (or not)*

Like other fields in cryptography, digital signatures have many standards, and it is sometimes hard to understand which one to use. This is why I'm here! Fortunately, the types of algorithms for signatures are similar to the ones for key exchanges: there are algorithms based on arithmetic modulo a large number like Diffie-Hellman (DH) and RSA, and there are algorithms based on elliptic curves like Elliptic Curve Diffie-Hellman (ECDH).

Be sure you understand the algorithms in chapter 5 and chapter 6 well enough as we're now going to build on those. Interestingly, the paper that introduced the DH key exchange also proposed the concept of digital signatures (without giving a solution):

In order to develop a system capable of replacing the current written contract with some purely electronic form of communication, we must discover a digital phenomenon with the same properties as a written signature. It must be easy for anyone to recognize the signature as authentic, but impossible for anyone other than the legitimate signer to produce it. We will call any such technique one-way authentication. Since any digital signal can be copied precisely, a true digital signature must be recognizable without being known.

—Diffie and Hellman ("New Directions in Cryptography," 1976)

A year later (in 1977), the first signature algorithm (called RSA) was introduced along with the RSA asymmetric encryption algorithm (which you learned about in chapter 6). RSA for signing is the first algorithm we'll learn about.

In 1991, NIST proposed the *Digital Signature Algorithm (DSA)* as an attempt to avoid the patents on Schnorr signatures. For this reason, DSA is a weird variant of Schnorr signatures, published without a proof of security (although no attacks have been found so far). The algorithm was adopted by many but was quickly replaced with an elliptic curve version called *ECDSA* (for Elliptic Curve Digital Signature Algorithm), the same way Elliptic Curve Diffie-Hellman (ECDH) replaced Diffie-Hellman (DH), thanks to its smaller keys (see chapter 5). ECDSA is the second signature algorithm I will talk about in this section.

After the patents on Schnorr signatures expired in 2008, Daniel J. Bernstein, the inventor of ChaCha20-Poly1305 (covered in chapter 4) and X25519 (covered in chapter 5), introduced a new signature scheme called *EdDSA* (for Edwards-curve Digital Signature Algorithm), based on Schnorr signatures. Since its invention, EdDSA has quickly gained adoption and is nowadays considered state-of-the-art in terms of a digital signature for real-world applications. EdDSA is the third and last signature algorithm I will talk about in this section.

7.3.1 *RSA PKCS#1 v1.5: A bad standard*

RSA signatures are currently used everywhere, even though they shouldn't be (as you will see in this section, they present many issues). This is due to the algorithm being the first signature scheme to be standardized as well as real-world applications being slow to move to newer and better algorithms. Because of this, you will most likely encounter RSA signatures in your journey, and I cannot avoid explaining how they work and which standards are the adopted ones. But let me say that if you understood how RSA encryption works in chapter 6, then this section should be straightforward because signing with RSA is the opposite of encrypting with RSA:

- To sign, you *encrypt* the message with the private key (instead of the public key), which produces a signature (a random element in the group).
- To verify a signature, you *decrypt* the signature with the public key (instead of the private key). If it gives you back the original message, then the signature is valid.

NOTE In reality, a message is often hashed before being signed as it'll take less space (RSA can only sign messages that are smaller than its modulus). The result is also interpreted as a large number so that it can be used in mathematical operations.

If your private key is the private exponent d, and your public key is the public exponent e and public modulus N, you can

- Sign a message by computing *signature = message^d* mod N
- Verify a signature by computing *signature^e* mod N and check that it is equal to the message

I illustrate this visually in figure 7.8.

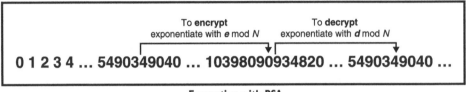

Encryption with RSA

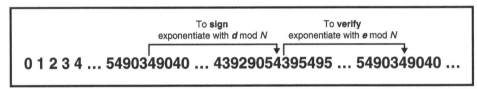

Signature with RSA

Figure 7.8   To sign with RSA, we simply do the inverse of the RSA encryption algorithm: we exponentiate the message with the private exponent, then to verify, we exponentiate the signature with the public exponent, which returns to the message.

This works because only the one knowing about the private exponent d can produce a signature over a message. And, as with RSA encryption, the security is tightly linked with the hardness of the factorization problem.

What about the standards to use RSA for signatures? Luckily, they follow the same pattern as does RSA encryption:

- *RSA for encryption was loosely standardized in the PKCS#1 v1.5 document.* The same document contained a specification for signing with RSA (without a security proof).
- *RSA was then standardized again in the PKCS#1 v2 document with a better construction (called RSA-OAEP).* The same happened for RSA signatures with RSA-PSS being standardized in the same document (with a security proof).

I talked about RSA PKCS#1 v1.5 in chapter 6 on asymmetric encryption. The signature scheme standardized in that document is pretty much the same as the encryption scheme. To sign, first hash the message with a hash function of your choice, then pad it according to PKCS#1 v1.5's padding for signatures (which is similar to the padding for encryption in the same standard). Next, encrypt the padded and hashed message with your private exponent. I illustrate this in figure 7.9.

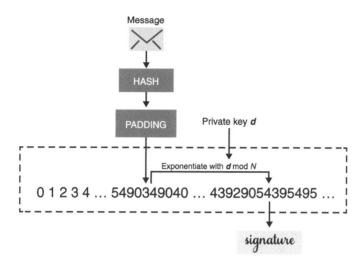

Figure 7.9   RSA PKCS#1 v1.5 for signatures. To sign, hash then pad the message with the PKCS#1 v1.5 padding scheme. The final step exponentiates the padded hashed message with the private key *d* modulo *N*. To verify, simply exponentiate the signature with the public exponent *e* modulo *N* and verify that it matches the padded and hashed message.

The many RSAs

By the way, don't get confused by the different terms surrounding RSA. There is RSA (the *asymmetric encryption primitive*) and RSA (the *signature primitive*). On top of that, there is also RSA (the company), founded by the inventors of RSA. When mentioning encryption with RSA, most people refer to the schemes RSA PKCS#1 v1.5 and RSA-OAEP. When mentioning signatures with RSA, most people refer to the schemes RSA PKCS#1 v1.5 and RSA-PSS.

I know this can be confusing, especially for the PKCS#1 v1.5 standard. While there are official names to distinguish the encryption from the signing algorithm in PKCS#1 v1.5 (RSAES-PKCS1-v1_5 for encryption and RSASSA-PKCS1-v1_5 for signature), I rarely see those used.

In chapter 6, I mentioned that there were damaging attacks on RSA PKCS#1 v1.5 for encryption; the same is unfortunately true for RSA PKCS#1 v1.5 signatures. In 1998, after Bleichenbacher found a devastating attack on RSA PKCS#1 v1.5 for encryption, he decided to take a look at the signature standard. Bleichenbacher came back in 2006 with a *signature forgery* attack on RSA PKCS#1 v1.5, one of the most catastrophic types of attack on signatures—attackers can forge signatures without knowledge of the private key! Unlike the first attack that broke the encryption algorithm directly, the second attack was an implementation attack. This meant that if the signature scheme was implemented correctly (according to the specification), the attack did not work.

An implementation flaw doesn't sound as bad as an algorithm flaw, that is, if it's easy to avoid and doesn't impact many implementations. Unfortunately, it was shown in 2019 that an embarrassing number of open source implementations of RSA PKCS#1 v1.5 for signatures actually fell for that trap and misimplemented the standard (see "Analyzing Semantic Correctness with Symbolic Execution: A Case Study on PKCS#1 v1.5 Signature Verification" by Chau et al.) The various implementation flaws ended up enabling different variants of Bleichenbacher's forgery attack.

Unfortunately, RSA PKCS#1 v1.5 for signatures is still widely used. Be aware of these issues if you really *have to* use this algorithm for backward compatibility reasons. Having said that, this does not mean that RSA for signatures is insecure. The story does not end here.

7.3.2   *RSA-PSS: A better standard*

RSA-PSS was standardized in the updated PKCS#1 v2.1 and included a proof of security (unlike the signature scheme standardized in the previous PKCS#1 v1.5). The newer specification works like this:

- Encode the message using the PSS encoding algorithm
- Sign the encoded message using RSA (as was done in the PKCS#1 v1.5 standard)

The PSS encoding is a bit more involved and similar to OAEP (Optimal Asymmetric Encryption Padding). I illustrate this in figure 7.10.

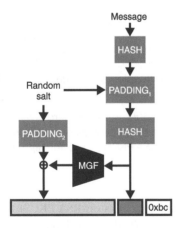

Figure 7.10   The RSA-PSS signature scheme encodes a message using a mask generation function (MGF) like the RSA-OAEP algorithm you learned about in chapter 6 before signing it in the usual RSA way.

Verifying a signature produced by RSA-PSS is just a matter of inverting the encoding once the signature has been raised to the public exponent modulo the public modulus.

> ### Provable security for PSS
>
> PSS (for *Probabilistic Signature Scheme*) is provably secure, meaning that no one should be able to forge a signature without knowledge of the private key. Instead of proving that if RSA is secure then RSA-PSS is secure, RSA-PSS proves the contrapositive: if someone can break RSA-PSS then that someone can also break RSA. That's a common way to prove things in cryptography. Of course, this only works if RSA is secure, which we assume in the proof.

If you remember, I also talked about a third algorithm in chapter 6 for RSA encryption (called RSA-KEM)—a simpler algorithm that is not used by anyone and yet is proven to be secure as well. Interestingly, RSA for signatures also mirror this part of the RSA encryption history and has a much simpler algorithm that pretty much nobody uses; it's called *Full Domain Hash* (FDH). FDH works by simply hashing a message and then signing it (by interpreting the digest as a number) using RSA.

Despite the fact that both RSA-PSS and FDH come with proofs of security and are much easier to implement correctly, today most protocols still make use of RSA PKCS#1 v1.5 for signatures. This is just another example of the slowness that typically takes place around deprecating cryptographic algorithms. As older implementations still have to work with newer implementations, it is difficult to remove or replace algorithms. Think of users that do not update applications, vendors that do not provide new versions of their softwares, hardware devices that cannot be updated, and so on. Next, let's take a look at a more modern algorithm.

7.3.3   *The Elliptic Curve Digital Signature Algorithm (ECDSA)*

In this section, let's look at the ECDSA, an elliptic curve variant of DSA that was itself invented only to circumvent patents in Schnorr signatures. The signature scheme is specified in many standards including ISO 14888-3, ANSI X9.62, NIST's FIPS 186-2, IEEE P1363, and so on. Not all standards are compatible, and applications that want to interoperate have to make sure that they use the same standard.

Unfortunately, ECDSA, like DSA, does not come with a proof of security, while Schnorr signatures did. Nonetheless, ECDSA has been widely adopted and is one of the most used signature schemes. In this section, I will explain how ECDSA works and how it can be used. As with all such schemes, the public key is pretty much always generated according to the same formula:

- The private key is a large number x generated randomly.
- The public key is obtained by viewing x as an index in a group created by a generator (called *base point* in elliptic curve cryptography).

More specifically, in ECDSA the public key is computed using $[x]G$, which is a scalar multiplication of the scalar x with the base point G.

> ### Additive or multiplicative notation?
>
> Notice that I use the *additive notation* (with the elliptic curve syntax of placing brackets around the scalar), but that I could have written *public_key* = G^x if I had wanted to use the *multiplicative notation*. These differences do not matter in practice. Most of the time, cryptographic protocols that do not care about the underlying nature of the group are written using the multiplicative notation, whereas protocols that are defined specifically in elliptic curve-based groups tend to be written using the additive notation.

To compute an ECDSA signature, you need the same inputs required by a Schnorr signature: a hash of the message you're signing ($H(m)$), your private key x, and a random number k that is unique per signature. An ECDSA signature is two integers, r and s, computed as follows:

- r is the x-coordinate of $[k]\ G$
- s equals $k^{-1}\ (H(m) + xr) \bmod p$

To verify an ECDSA signature, a verifier needs to use the same hashed message $H(m)$, the signer's public key, and the signature values r and s. The verifier then

1. Computes $[H(m)\ s^{-1}]G + [rs^{-1}]public\_key$
2. Validates that the x-coordinate of the point obtained is the same as the value r of the signature

You can certainly recognize that there are some similarities with Schnorr signatures. The random number k is sometimes called a *nonce* because it is a number that must only be used once, and is also sometimes called an *ephemeral key* because it must remain secret.

> **WARNING** I'll reiterate this: k must never be repeated nor be predictable! Without that, it is trivial to recover the private key.

In general, cryptographic libraries perform the generation of this nonce (the k value) behind the scenes, but sometimes they don't and let the caller provide it. This is, of course, a recipe for disaster. For example, in 2010, Sony's Playstation 3 was found using ECDSA with repeating nonces (which leaked their private keys).

> **WARNING** Even more subtle, if the nonce k is not picked uniformly and at random (specifically, if you can predict the first few bits), there still exist powerful attacks that can recover the private key in no time (so-called *lattice attacks*). In theory, we call these kinds of key retrieval attacks *total breaks* (because they break everything!). Such total breaks are quite rare in practice, which makes ECDSA an algorithm that can fail in spectacular ways.

Attempts at avoiding issues with nonces exist. For example, RFC 6979 specifies a *deterministic ECDSA* scheme that generates a nonce based on the message and the private key. This means that signing the same message twice involves the same nonce twice and, as such, produces the same signature twice (which is obviously not a problem).

The elliptic curves that tend to be used with ECDSA are pretty much the same curves that are popular with the Elliptic Curve Diffie-Hellman (ECDH) algorithm (see chapter 5) with one notable exception: *Secp256k1*. The Secp256k1 curve is defined in SEC 2: "Recommended Elliptic Curve Domain Parameters" (https://secg.org/sec2-v2.pdf), written by the Standards for Efficient Cryptography Group (SECG). It gained a lot of traction after Bitcoin decided to use it instead of the more popular NIST curves, due to the lack of trust in the NIST curves I mentioned in chapter 5.

Secp256k1 is a type of elliptic curve called a *Koblitz curve*. A Koblitz curve is just an elliptic curve with some constraints in its parameters that allow implementations to optimize some operations on the curve. The elliptic curve has the following equation:

$$y^2 = x^3 + ax + b$$

where $a = 0$ and $b = 7$ are constants, and x and y are defined over the numbers modulo the prime p:

$$p = 2^{192} - 2^{32} - 2^{12} - 2^8 - 2^7 - 2^6 - 2^3 - 1$$

This defines a group of prime order, like the NIST curves. Today, we have efficient formulas to compute the number of points on an elliptic curve. Here is the prime number that is the number of points in the Secp256k1 curve (including the point at infinity):

1157920892373161954235709850086879078528375642790749043826051631415181 61494337

And we use as a generator (or base point) the fixed-point G of coordinates

$x = 5506626302227734366957871889516853432625060345377759417550018736038 9116729240$

and

$y = 3267051002075881697808308513050704318447127338065924327593890433575 7337482424$

Nonetheless, today ECDSA is mostly used with the NIST curve P-256 (sometimes referred to as *Secp256r1*; note the difference). Next let's look at another widely popular signing scheme.

7.3.4 *The Edwards-curve Digital Signature Algorithm (EdDSA)*

Let me introduce the last signature algorithm of the chapter, the *Edwards-curve Digital Signature Algorithm* (EdDSA), published in 2011 by Daniel J. Bernstein in response to the lack of trust in NIST and other curves created by government agencies. The name

EdDSA seems to indicate that it is based on the DSA algorithm like ECDSA is, but this is deceptive. EdDSA is actually based on Schnorr signatures, which is possible due to the patent on Schnorr signatures expiring earlier in 2008.

One particularity of EdDSA is that the scheme does not require new randomness for every signing operation. EdDSA produces signatures *deterministically*. This has made the algorithm quite attractive, and it has since been adopted by many protocols and standards.

EdDSA is on track to be included in NIST's upcoming update for its FIPS 186-5 standard (still a draft as of early 2021). The current official standard is RFC 8032, which defines two curves of different security levels to be used with EdDSA. Both of the defined curves are *twisted Edwards curves* (a type of elliptic curve enabling interesting implementation optimizations):

- *Edwards25519 is based on Daniel J. Bernstein's Curve25519 (covered in chapter 5).* Its curve operations can be implemented faster than those of Curve25519, thanks to the optimizations enabled by the type of elliptic curve. As it was invented after Curve25519, the key exchange X25519 based on Curve25519 did not benefit from these speed improvements. As with Curve25519, Edwards25519 provides 128-bit security.
- *Edwards448 is based on Mike Hamburg's Ed448-Goldilocks curve.* It provides 224-bit security.

In practice, EdDSA is mostly instantiated with the Edwards25519 curve and the combo is called *Ed25519* (whereas EdDSA with Edwards448 is shortened as Ed448). Key generation with EdDSA is a bit different from other existing schemes. Instead of generating a signing key directly, EdDSA generates a secret key that is then used to derive the actual signing key and another key that we call the nonce key. That nonce key is important! It is the one used to deterministically generate the required per signature nonce.

> **NOTE** Depending on the cryptographic library you're using, you might be storing the secret key or the two derived keys: the signing key and the nonce key. Not that this matters, but if you don't know this, you might get confused if you run into Ed25519 secret keys being stored as 32 bytes or 64 bytes, depending on the implementation used.

To sign, EdDSA first deterministically generates the nonce by hashing the nonce key with the message to sign. After that, a process similar to Schnorr signatures follows:

1. Compute the nonce as *HASH*(*nonce key* || *message*)
2. Compute the commitment R as [*nonce*]G, where G is the base point of the group
3. Compute the challenge as *HASH*(*commitment* || *public key* || *message*)
4. Compute the proof S as *nonce + challenge × signing key*

The signature is (R, S). I illustrate the important parts of EdDSA in figure 7.11.

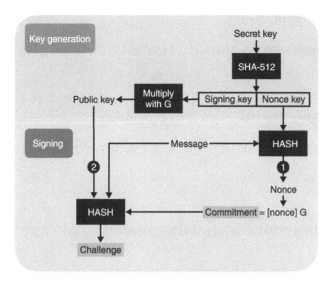

Figure 7.11 EdDSA key generation produces a secret key that is then used to derive two other keys. The first derived key is the actual signing key and can thus be used to derive the public key; the other derived key is the nonce key, used to deterministically derive the nonce during signing operations. EdDSA signatures are then like Schnorr signatures with the exception that (1) the nonce is generated deterministically from the nonce key and the message, and (2) the public key of the signer is included as part of the challenge.

Notice how the nonce (or ephemeral key) is derived deterministically and not probabilistically from the nonce key and the given message. This means that signing two different messages should involve two different nonces, ingeniously preventing the signer from reusing nonces and, in turn, leaking out the key (as can happen with ECDSA). Signing the same message twice produces the same nonce twice, which then produces the same signature twice as well. This is obviously not a problem. A signature can be verified by computing the following two equations:

$$[S]\,G$$

$$R + [HASH(R \,\|\, public\ key \,\|\, message)]\ public\ key$$

The signature is valid if the two values match. This is exactly how Schnorr signatures work, except that we are now in an elliptic curve group and I use the additive notation here.

The most widely used instantiation of EdDSA, Ed25519, is defined with the Edwards25519 curve and the SHA-512 as a hash function. The Edwards25519 curve is defined with all the points satisfying this equation:

$$-x^2 + y^2 = 1 + d \times x^2 \times y^2 \bmod p$$

where the value *d* is the large number

37095705934669439343138083508754565189542113879843219016388785533085940
283555

and the variables *x* and *y* are taken modulo *p* the large number $2^{255} - 19$ (the same prime used for Curve25519). The base point is *G* of coordinate

x = 15112221349535400772501151409588531511454012693041857206046113283949
847762202

and

y = 46316835694926478169428839400347516314130799386625622561578303360 3165
251855960

RFC 8032 actually defines three variants of EdDSA using the Edwards25519 curve. All three variants follow the same key generation algorithm but with different signing and verification algorithms:

- *Ed25519 (or pureEd25519)*—That's the algorithm that I explained previously.
- *Ed25519ctx*—This algorithm introduces a mandatory customization string and is rarely implemented, if even used, in practice. The only difference is that some user-chosen prefix is added to every call to the hash function.
- *Ed25519ph (or HashEd25519)*—This allows applications to prehash the message before signing it (hence the *ph* in the name). It also builds on Ed25519ctx, allowing the caller to include an optional custom string.

The addition of a *customization string* is quite common in cryptography as you saw with some hash functions in chapter 2 or will see with key derivation functions in chapter 8. It is a useful addition when a participant in a protocol uses the same key to sign messages in different contexts. For example, you can imagine an application that would allow you to sign transactions using your private key and also to sign private messages to people you talk to. If you mistakenly sign and send a message that looks like a transaction to your evil friend Eve, she could try to republish it as a valid transaction if there's no way to distinguish the two types of payload you're signing.

Ed25519ph was introduced solely to please callers that need to sign large messages. As you saw in chapter 2, hash functions often provide an "init-update-finalize" interface that allows you to continuously hash a stream of data without having to keep the whole input in memory.

You are now done with your tour of the signature schemes used in real-world applications. Next, let's look at how you can possibly shoot yourself in the foot when using these signature algorithms. But first, a recap:

- RSA PKCS#1 v1.5 is still widely in use but is hard to implement correctly and many implementations have been found to be broken.
- RSA-PSS has a proof of security, is easier to implement, but has seen poor adoption due to newer schemes based on elliptic curves.
- ECDSA is the main competition to RSA PKCS#1 v1.5 and is mostly used with NIST's curve P-256, except in the cryptocurrency world where Secp256k1 seems to dominate.
- Ed25519 is based on Schnorr signatures, has received wide adoption, and it is easier to implement compared to ECDSA; it does not require new randomness for every signing operation. This is the algorithm you should use if you can.

7.4 Subtle behaviors of signature schemes

There are a number of subtle properties that signature schemes might exhibit. While they might not matter in most protocols, not being aware of these "gotchas" can end up biting you when working on more complex and nonconventional protocols. The end of this chapter focuses on known issues with digital signatures.

7.4.1 Substitution attacks on signatures

> *A digital signature does not uniquely identify a key or a message.*
>
> —Andrew Ayer ("Duplicate Signature Key Selection
> Attack in Let's Encrypt," 2015)

Substitution attacks, also referred to as *duplicate signature key selection* (DSKS), are possible on both RSA PKCS#1 v1.5 and RSA-PSS. Two DSKS variants exist:

- *Key substitution attacks*—A different key pair or public key is used to validate a given signature over a given message.
- *Message key substitution attacks*—A different key pair or public key is used to validate a given signature over a *new* message.

One more time: the first attack fixes both the message and the signature; the second one only fixes the signature. I recapitulate this in figure 7.12.

Existential unforgeability under adaptive chosen message attack (EUF-CMA)

Substitution attacks are a syndrome of a gap between theoretical cryptography and applied cryptography. Signatures in cryptography are usually analyzed with the *EUF-CMA model*, which stands for existential unforgeability under adaptive chosen message attack. In this model, you generate a key pair, and then I request you to sign a number of arbitrary messages. While I observe the signatures you produce, I win if I can at some point in time produce a valid signature over a message I hadn't requested before. Unfortunately, this EUF-CMA model doesn't seem to encompass every edge case, and dangerous subtleties like the substitution ones are not taken into account.

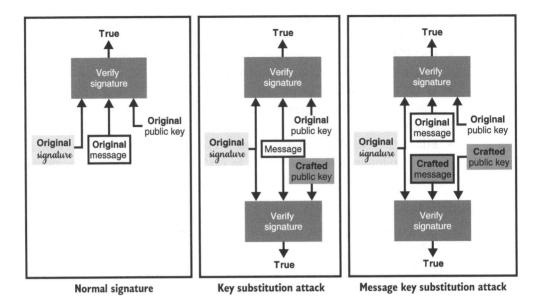

Figure 7.12 Signature algorithms like RSA are vulnerable to key substitution attacks, which are surprising and unexpected behaviors for most users of cryptography. A *key substitution* attack allows one to take a signature over a message and to craft a new key pair that validates the original signature. A variant called *message key substitution* allows an attacker to create a new key pair and a new message that validates under the original signature.

7.4.2 Signature malleability

> *In February 2014 MtGox, once the largest Bitcoin exchange, closed and filed for bankruptcy claiming that attackers used malleability attacks to drain its accounts.*
>
> —Christian Decker and Roger Wattenhofer
> ("Bitcoin Transaction Malleability and MtGox," 2014)

Most signature schemes are *malleable*: if you give me a valid signature, I can modify the signature so that it becomes a different, but still valid signature. I have no clue what the signing key was, yet I managed to create a new valid signature.

Non-malleability does not necessarily mean that signatures are unique: if I'm the signer, I can usually create different signatures for the same message and that's usually OK. Some constructions like verifiable random functions (which you'll see later in chapter 8) rely on signature uniqueness, and so they must deal with this or use signature schemes that have unique signatures (like the Boneh–Lynn–Shacham, or BLS, signatures).

What to do with all of this information? Rest assured, signature schemes are definitely not broken, and you probably shouldn't worry if your use of signatures is not too out-of-the-box. But if you're designing cryptographic protocols or if you're implementing a protocol that's more complicated than everyday cryptography, you might want to keep these subtle properties in the back of your mind.

The strong EUF-CMA

A newer security model called SUF-CMA (for strong EUF-CMA) attempts to include non-malleability (or resistance to malleability) in the security definition of signature schemes. Some recent standards like RFC 8032, which specifies Ed25519, include mitigations against malleability attacks. Because these mitigations are not always present or common, you should never rely on signatures being non-malleable in your protocols.

Summary

- Digital signatures are similar to pen-and-paper signatures but are backed with cryptography, making them unforgeable by anyone who does not control the signing (private) key.
- Digital signatures can be useful to authenticate origins (for example, one side of a key exchange) as well as providing transitive trust (if I trust Alice and she trusts Bob, I can trust Bob).
- Zero-knowledge proofs (ZKPs) allow a prover to prove the knowledge of a particular piece of information (called a witness), without revealing that something. Signatures can be seen as non-interactive ZKPs as they do not require the verifier to be online during the signing operation.
- You can use many standards to sign:
  - RSA PKCS#1 v1.5 is widely used today but not recommended as it is hard to implement correctly.
  - RSA-PSS is a better signature scheme as it is easier to implement and has a proof of security. Unfortunately, it is not popular nowadays due to elliptic curve variants that support shorter keys and are, thus, more attractive for network protocols.
  - The most popular signature schemes currently are based on elliptic curves: ECDSA and EdDSA. ECDSA is often used with NIST's curve P-256, and EdDSA is often used with the Edwards25519 curve (this combination is referred to as Ed25519).
- Some subtle properties can be dangerous if signatures are used in a nonconventional way:
  - Always avoid ambiguity as to who signed a message because some signature schemes are vulnerable to key substitution attacks. External actors can create a new key pair that would validate an already existing signature over a message or create a new key pair and a new message that would validate a given signature.
  - Do not rely on the uniqueness of signatures. First, in most signature schemes, the signer can create an arbitrary amount of signatures for the same message. Second, most signature schemes are *malleable*, meaning that external actors can take a signature and create another valid signature for the same message.

Randomness and secrets

8

This chapter covers

- What randomness is and why it's important
- Obtaining strong randomness and producing secrets
- The pitfalls of randomness

This is the last chapter of the first part of this book, and I have one last thing to tell you before we move on to the second part and learn about actual protocols used in the real world. It is something I've grossly neglected so far—randomness.

You must have noticed that in every cryptographic algorithm you've learned (with the exception of hash functions), you had to use randomness at some point: secret keys, nonces, IVs, prime numbers, challenges, and so on. As I was going through these different concepts, randomness always came from some magic black box. This is not atypical. In cryptography white papers, randomness is often represented by drawing an arrow with a dollar sign on top. But at some point, we need to ask ourselves the question, "Where does this randomness really come from?"

In this chapter, I will provide you with an answer as to what cryptography means when it mentions randomness. I will also give you pointers about the practical ways that exist to obtain randomness for real-world cryptographic applications.

> **NOTE** For this chapter, you'll need to have read chapter 2 on hash functions and chapter 3 on message authentication codes.

8.1 *What's randomness?*

Everyone understands the concept of randomness to some degree. Whether playing with dice or buying some lottery tickets, we've all been exposed to it. My first encounter with randomness was at a very young age, when I realized that a RAND button on my calculator would produce a different number every time I pressed it. This troubled me to no end. I had little knowledge about electronics, but I thought I could understand some of its limitations. When I added 4 and 5 together, surely some circuits would do the math and give me the result. But a random button? Where were the random numbers coming from? I couldn't wrap my head around it.

It took me some time to ask the right questions and to understand that calculators actually cheated! They would hardcode large lists of random numbers and go through those one by one. These lists would exhibit good randomness, meaning that if you looked at the random numbers you were getting, there'd be as many 1s as 9s, as many 1s as 2s, and so on. These lists would simulate a *uniform distribution*: the numbers were distributed in equal proportions (uniformly).

When random numbers are needed for security and cryptography purposes, then randomness must be *unpredictable*. Of course, at that time, nobody would have used those calculators' "randomness" for anything related to security. Instead, cryptographic applications extract randomness from observing hard-to-predict physical phenomena.

For example, it is hard to predict the outcome of a dice roll, even though throwing a die is a deterministic process; if you knew all the initial conditions (how you're throwing the die, the die itself, the air friction, the grip of the table, and so on), you should be able to predict the result. That being said, all of these factors impact the end result so much that a slight imprecision in the knowledge of the initial conditions would mess with our predictions. The extreme sensitivity of an outcome to its initial conditions is known as *chaos theory*, and it is the reason why things like the weather are hard to predict accurately past a certain number of days.

The following image is a picture that I snapped during one of my visits to the headquarters of Cloudflare in San Francisco. LavaRand is a wall of lava lamps, which are lamps that produce hard-to-predict shapes of wax. A camera is set in front of the wall to extract and convert the images to random bytes.

Applications usually rely on the operating system to provide usable randomness, which in turn, gather randomness using different tricks, depending on the type of device it is run on. Common sources of randomness (also called *entropy sources*) can be the timing of hardware interrupts (for example, your mouse movements), software interrupts, hard disk seek time, and so on.

Entropy

In information theory, the word *entropy* is used to judge how much randomness a string contains. The term was coined by Claude Shannon, who devised an entropy formula that would output larger and larger numbers as a string would exhibit more and more unpredictability (starting at 0 for completely predictable). The formula or the number itself is not that interesting for us, but in cryptography, you often hear "this string has low entropy" (meaning that it is predictable) or "this string has high entropy" (meaning that it is less predictable).

Observing interrupts and other events to produce randomness is not great; when a device boots, these events tend to be highly predictable, and they can also be maliciously influenced by external factors. Today, more and more devices have access to additional sensors and hardware aids that provide better sources of entropy. These hardware random number generators are often called *true random number generators* (TRNGs) as they make use of external unpredictable physical phenomena like thermal noise to extract randomness.

The noise obtained via all these different types of input is usually not "clean" and sometimes does not provide enough entropy (if at all). For example, the first bit obtained from some entropy source could be 0 more often than not, or successive bits could be (more likely than chance) equal. Due to this, *randomness extractors* must clean and gather several sources of noise together before it can be used for cryptographic applications. This can be done, for example, by applying a hash function to the different sources and XORing the digests together.

Is this all there is to randomness? Unfortunately not. Extracting randomness from noise is a process that can be slow. For some applications that might need lots of random numbers quickly, it can become a bottleneck. The next section describes how OSs and real-world applications boost the generation of random numbers.

8.2 Slow randomness? Use a pseudorandom number generator (PRNG)

Randomness is used everywhere. At this point, you should be convinced that this is true at least for cryptography, but surprisingly, cryptography is not the only place making heavy use of random numbers. For example, simple Unix programs like ls require randomness too! As a bug in a program can be devastating if exploited, binaries attempt to defend against low-level attacks using a multitude of tricks; one of them is *ASLR* (address space layout randomization), which randomizes the memory layout of a process every time it runs and, thus, requires random numbers. Another example is the network protocol TCP, which makes use of random numbers every time it creates a connection to produce an unpredictable sequence of numbers and thwarts attacks attempting to hijack connections. While all of this is beyond the scope of this book, it is good to have an idea of how much randomness ends up being used for security reasons in the real world.

I hinted in the last section that, unfortunately, obtaining unpredictable randomness is somewhat of a slow process. This is sometimes due to a source of entropy being slow to produce noise. As a result, OSs often optimize their production of random numbers by using *pseudorandom number generators* (PRNGs).

> **NOTE** In order to contrast with random number generators that are not designed to be secure (and that are useful in different types of applications, like video games), PRNGs are sometimes called CSPRNGs for *cryptographically secure* PRNGs. NIST, wanting to do things differently (as usual), often calls their PRNGs *deterministic random bit generators* (DRBGs).

A PRNG needs an initial secret, usually called a *seed*, that we can obtain from mixing different entropy sources together and can then produce lots of random numbers quickly. I illustrate a PRNG in figure 8.1.

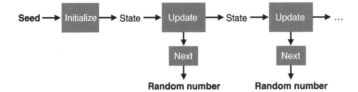

Figure 8.1   A pseudorandom number generator (PRNG) generates a sequence of random numbers based on a seed. Using the same seed makes the PRNG produce the same sequence of random numbers. It should be impossible to recover the state using knowledge of the random outputs (the function `next` is one way). It follows that it should also be impossible from observing the produced random numbers alone to predict future random numbers or to recover previously generated random numbers.

Cryptographically secure PRNGs usually tend to exhibit the following properties:

- *Deterministic*—Using the same seed twice produces the same sequence of random numbers. This is unlike the unpredictable randomness extraction I talked about previously: if you know a seed used by a PRNG, the PRNG should be completely predictable. This is why the construction is called *pseudo*random, and this is what allows a PRNG to be extremely fast.
- *Indistinguishable from random*—In practice, you should not be able to distinguish between a PRNG outputting a random number from a set of possible numbers and a little fairy impartially choosing a random number from the same set (assuming the fairy knows a magical way to pick a number such that every possible number can be picked with equal probability). Consequently, observing the random numbers generated alone shouldn't allow anyone to recover the internal state of the PRNG.

The last point is important! A PRNG simulates picking a number *uniformly at random*, meaning that each number from the set has an equal chance of being picked. For example, if your PRNG produces random numbers of 8 bytes, the set is all the possible strings of 8 bytes, and each 8-byte value should have equal probability of being the next value that can be obtained from your PRNG. This includes values that have already been produced by the PRNG at some point in the past.

In addition, many PRNGs exhibit additional security properties. A PRNG has *forward secrecy* if an attacker learning the state (by getting in your computer at some point in time, for example) doesn't allow the PRNG to retrieve previously generated random numbers. I illustrate this in figure 8.2.

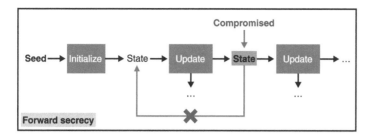

Figure 8.2   A PRNG has forward secrecy if compromise of a state does not allow recovering previously generated random numbers.

Obtaining the *state* of a PRNG means that you can determine all future pseudorandom numbers that it will generate. To prevent this, some PRNGs have mechanisms to "heal" themselves periodically (in case there was a compromise). This healing can be achieved by reinjecting (or re-seeding) new entropy after a PRNG was already seeded. This property is called *backward secrecy*. I illustrate this in figure 8.3.

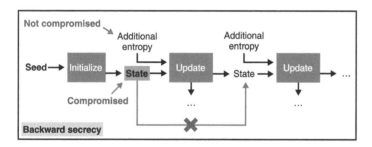

Figure 8.3   A PRNG has backward secrecy if compromise of a state does not allow predicting future random numbers generated by the PRNG. This is true only once new entropy is produced and injected in the update function after the compromise.

> **NOTE**   The terms *forward* and *backward secrecy* are often sources of confusion. If you read this section thinking shouldn't forward secrecy be backward secrecy and backward secrecy be forward secrecy instead, then you are not crazy. For this reason, backward secrecy is sometimes called *future secrecy* or even *post-compromise security* (PCS).

PRNGs can be extremely fast and are considered safe methods to generate large numbers of random values for cryptographic purposes if properly seeded. Using a predictable number or a number that is too small is obviously not a secure way to seed a PRNG. This effectively means that we have secure cryptographic ways for quickly stretching a secret of appropriate size to billions of other secret keys. Pretty cool, right? This is why most (if not all) cryptographic applications do not use random numbers directly extracted from noise, but instead use them to seed a PRNG in an initial step and then switch to generating random numbers from the PRNG when needed.

> **The Dual-EC backdoor**
>
> Today, PRNGs are mostly heuristic-based constructions. This is because constructions based on hard mathematical problems (like the discrete logarithm) are too slow to be practical. One notorious example is *Dual EC*, invented by NSA, which relies on elliptic curves. The Dual EC PRNG was pushed to various standards including some NIST publications around 2006, and not too long after, several researchers independently discovered a potential backdoor in the algorithm. This was later confirmed by the Snowden revelations in 2013, and a year later the algorithm was withdrawn from multiple standards.

To be secure, a PRNG must be seeded with an *unpredictable* secret. More accurately, we say that the PRNG takes a key of n bytes sampled uniformly at random. This means that we should pick the key randomly from the set of all possible n-byte strings, where each byte string has the same chance of being picked.

In this book, I talked about many cryptographic algorithms that produce outputs indistinguishable from random (from values that would be chosen uniformly at random). Intuitively, you should be thinking can we use these algorithms to generate random numbers then? And you would be right! Hash functions, XOFs, block ciphers, stream ciphers, and MACs can be used to produce random numbers. Hash functions and MACs are theoretically not defined as providing outputs that are indistinguishable from random, but in practice, they often are. Asymmetric algorithms like key exchange and signatures, on the other hand, are (almost all the time) not indistinguishable from random. For this reason, their output is often hashed before being used as random numbers.

Actually, because AES is hardware-supported on most machines, it is customary to see AES-CTR being used to produce random numbers. The symmetric key becomes the seed, and the ciphertexts become the random numbers (for the encryption of an infinite string of 0s, for example). In practice, there is a bit more complexity added to these constructions in order to provide forward and backward secrecy. Fortunately, you now understand enough to go to the next section, which provides an overview of obtaining randomness for real.

8.3   *Obtaining randomness in practice*

You've learned about the three ingredients that an OS needs to provide cryptographically secure random numbers to its programs:

- *Noise sources*—These are ways for the OS to obtain raw randomness from unpredictable physical phenomena like the temperature of the device or your mouse movements.

- *Cleaning and mixing*—Although raw randomness can be of poor quality (some bits might be biased), OSs clean up and mix a number of sources together in order to produce a good random number.
- *PRNGs*—Because the first two steps are slow, a single, uniformly random value can be used to seed a PRNG that can quickly produce random numbers.

In this section, I will explain how systems bundle the three concepts together to provide simplified interfaces to developers. These functions exposed by the OS usually allow you to generate a random number by issuing a system call. Behind these system calls is, indeed, a system bundling up noise sources, a mixing algorithm, and a PRNG (summarized in figure 8.4).

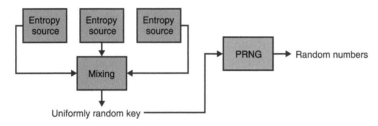

Figure 8.4   Generating random numbers on a system usually means that entropy was mixed together from different noise sources and used to seed a long-term PRNG.

Depending on the OS and on the hardware available, these three concepts might be implemented differently. In 2021, Linux uses a PRNG that's based on the ChaCha20 stream cipher, while macOS uses a PRNG that's based on the SHA-1 hash function. In addition, the random number generator interface exposed to developers will be different depending on the OS. On Windows, the `BCryptGenRandom` system call can be used to produce random numbers, while on other platforms, a special file (usually called /dev/urandom) is exposed and can be read to provide randomness. For example, on Linux or macOS, one can read 16 bytes from the terminal using the `dd` command-line tool:

```
$ dd if=/dev/urandom bs=16 count=1 2> /dev/null | xxd -p
40b1654b12320e2e0105f0b1d61e77b1
```

One problem with /dev/urandom is that it might not provide enough entropy (its numbers won't be random enough) if used too early after booting the device. OSs like Linux and FreeBSD offer a solution called `getrandom`, which is a system call that pretty much offers the same functionality as reading from /dev/urandom. In rare cases, where not enough entropy is available for initializing its PRNG, `getrandom` will block the continuation of the program and wait until properly seeded. For this reason,

I recommend that you use `getrandom` if it is available on your system. The following listing shows how one can securely use `getrandom` in C:

Listing 8.1 Getting random numbers in C

```
#include <sys/random.h>          Fills a buffer with random bytes
                                 (note that getrandom is limited
uint8_t secret[16];              to up to 256 bytes per call).
int len = getrandom(secret, sizeof(secret), 0);
                                                      The default flags (0)
if (len != sizeof(secret)) {                          is to not block, unless
    abort();                                          properly seeded.
                          It is possible that the function fails or returns
}                         less than the desired amount of random bytes.
                          If this is the case, the system is corrupt and
                          aborting might be the best thing to do.
```

With that example in mind, it is also good to point out that many programming languages have standard libraries and cryptographic libraries that provide better abstractions. It might be easy to forget that `getrandom` only returns up to 256 bytes per call, for example. For this reason, you should always attempt to generate random numbers through the standard library of the programming language you're using.

> **WARNING** Note that many programming languages expose functions and libraries that produce predictable random numbers. These are not suited for cryptographic use! Make sure that you use random libraries that generate *cryptographically strong* random numbers. Usually the name of the library helps (for example, you can probably guess which one you should use between the `math/rand` and `crypto/rand` packages in Golang), but nothing replaces reading the manual!

Listing 8.2 shows how to generate some random bytes using PHP 7. Any cryptographic algorithm can use these random bytes. For example, as a secret key to encrypt with an authenticated encryption algorithm. Every programming language does things differently, so make sure to consult your programming language's documentation in order to find the standard way to obtain random numbers for cryptographic purposes.

Listing 8.2 Getting random numbers in PHP

```
<?php
$bad_random_number = rand(0, 10);        Produces a random integer between 0
                                         and 10. While fast, rand does not produce
$secret_key = random_bytes(16);          cryptographically secure random numbers
?>                                       so it is not suitable for cryptographic
          random_bytes creates and fills a buffer    algorithms and protocols.
          with 16 random bytes. The result is suitable
          for cryptographic algorithms and protocols.
```

Now that you've learned how you can obtain cryptographically secure randomness in your programs, let's think about the security considerations you need to keep in mind when you generate randomness.

8.4   *Randomness generation and security considerations*

It is good to remember at this point that any useful protocol based on cryptography requires good randomness and that a broken PRNG could lead to the entire cryptographic protocol or algorithm being insecure. It should be clear to you that a MAC is only as secure as the key used with it or that the slightest ounce of predictability usually destroys signature schemes like ECDSA, and so on.

So far, this chapter makes it sound like generating randomness should be a simple part of applied cryptography, but in practice, it is not. Randomness has actually been the source of many, many bugs in real-world cryptography due to a multitude of issues: using a noncryptographic PRNG, badly seeding a PRNG (for example, using the current time, which is predictable), and so on.

One example includes programs using *userland PRNGs* as opposed to *kernel PRNGs*, which are behind system calls. Userland PRNGs usually add unnecessary friction and if misused can, in the worst of cases, break the entire system. This was notably the case with the PRNG offered by the OpenSSL library that was patched into some OSs in 2006, inadvertently affecting all SSL and SSH generated keys using the vulnerable PRNG.

> *Removing this code has the side effect of crippling the seeding process for the OpenSSL PRNG. Instead of mixing in random data for the initial seed, the only random value that was used was the current process ID. On the Linux platform, the default maximum process ID is 32,768, resulting in a very small number of seed values being used for all PRNG operations.*

> —H. D. Moore ("Debian OpenSSL Predictable PRNG Toys," 2008)

For this reason and others, I will mention later in this chapter that it is wise to avoid userland PRNG and to stick to randomness provided by the OS when available. In most situations, sticking to what the programming language's standard library or what a good cryptography library provides should be enough.

> *We cannot keep on adding 'best practice' after 'best practice' to what developers need to keep in the back of their heads when writing everyday code.*

> —Martin Boßlet ("OpenSSL PRNG Is Not (Really) Fork-safe," 2013)

Unfortunately, no amount of advice can really prepare you for the many pitfalls of acquiring good randomness. Because randomness is at the center of every cryptography algorithm, making tiny mistakes can lead to devastating outcomes. It is good to keep in mind the following edge cases should you run into them:

- *Forking processes*—When using a userland PRNG (some applications with extremely high performance requirements might have no other choice), it is important to keep in mind that a program that forks will produce a new child process that will have the same PRNG state as its parent. Consequently, both PRNGs will produce the same sequence of random numbers from there on. For this reason, if you really want to use a userland PRNG, you have to be careful to make forks use different seeds for their PRNGs.

- *Virtual machines (VMs)*—Cloning of PRNG state can also become a problem when using the OS PRNG. Think about VMs. If the entire state of a VM is saved and then started several times from this point on, every instance might produce the exact same sequence of random numbers. This is sometimes fixed by hypervisors and OSs, but it is good to look into what the hypervisor you're using is doing before running applications that request random numbers in VMs.

- *Early boot entropy*—While OSs should have no trouble gathering entropy in user-operated devices due to the noise produced by the user's interactions with the device, embedded devices and headless systems have more challenges to overcome in order to produce good entropy at boot time. History has shown that some devices tend to boot in a similar fashion and end up amassing the same initial noise from the system, leading to the same seed being used for their internal PRNGs and the same series of random numbers being generated.

There is a window of vulnerability—a boot-time entropy hole—during which Linux's urandom may be entirely predictable, at least for single-core systems. [. . .] When we disabled entropy sources that might be unavailable on a headless or embedded device, the Linux RNG produced the same predictable stream on every boot.

—Heninger et al. ("Mining Your Ps and Qs: Detection of
Widespread Weak Keys in Network Devices," 2012)

In these rare cases, where you really, really need to obtain random numbers early during boot, one can help the system by providing some initial entropy generated from another machine's well-seeded `getrandom` or /dev/urandom. Different OSs might provide this feature, and you should consult their manuals (as usual) if you find yourself in this situation.

If available, a TRNG provides an easy solution to the problem. For example, modern Intel CPUs embed a special hardware chip that extracts randomness from thermal noise. This randomness is available through an instruction called `RDRAND`.

The `RDRAND` controversy

Interestingly, Intel's `RDRAND` has been quite controversial due to the fear of backdoors. Most OSs that have integrated `RDRAND` as a source of entropy mix it with other sources of entropy in a way that is *contributory*. Contributory here means that one source of entropy cannot force the outcome of the randomness generation.

Exercise

Imagine for a minute that mixing different sources of entropy was done by simply XORing them together. Can you see how this might fail to be contributory?

Finally, let me mention that one solution to avoid the randomness pitfalls is to use algorithms that rely *less* on randomness. For example, you saw in chapter 7 that ECDSA requires you to generate a random nonce every time you sign, whereas EdDSA does not. Another example you saw in chapter 4 is AES-GCM-SIV, which does not catastrophically break down if you happen to reuse the same nonce twice, as opposed to AES-GCM, which will leak the authentication key and will then lose integrity of the ciphertexts.

8.5 Public randomness

So far, I've talked mostly about *private randomness*, the kind you might need for your private keys. Sometimes, privacy is not required and *public randomness* is needed. In this section, I briefly survey some ways to obtain such public randomness. I distinguish two scenarios:

- *One-to-many*—You want to produce randomness for others.
- *Many-to-many*—A set of participants want to produce randomness together.

First, let's imagine that you want to generate a stream of randomness in a way that many participants can verify it. In other words, the stream should be unpredictable but impossible to alter from your perspective. Now imagine that you have a signature scheme that provides unique signatures based on a key pair and a message. With such a signature scheme, there exists a construction called a *verifiable random function* (VRF) to obtain random numbers in a verifiable way (figure 8.5 illustrates this concept). The following shows how this works:

1 You generate a key pair and publish the verifying key. You also publish a public seed.

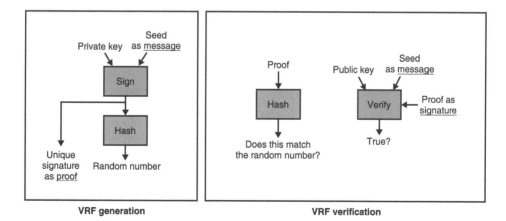

VRF generation   **VRF verification**

Figure 8.5 A verifiable random function (VRF) generates verifiable randomness via public key cryptography. To generate a random number, simply use a signature scheme which produces unique signatures (like BLS) to sign a seed, then hash the signature to produce the public random number. To validate the resulting randomness, make sure that the hash of the signature is indeed the random number and verify the signature over the seed.

2 To generate random numbers, you sign the public seed and hash the signature. The digest is your random number, and the signature is also published as proof.

3 To verify the random number, anyone can hash the signature to check if it matches the random number and verify that the signature is correct with the public seed and verifying key.

This construction can be extended to produce many random numbers by using the public seed like a counter. Because the signature is unique and the public seed is fixed, there is no way for the signer to generate a different random number.

> **Exercise**
>
> Signature schemes like BLS (mentioned in figure 8.5 and in chapter 7) produce unique signatures, but this is not true for ECDSA and EdDSA. Do you see why?

To solve this, the Internet Draft (a document that is meant to become an RFC) https://tools.ietf.org/html/draft-irtf-cfrg-vrf-08 specifies how to implement a VRF using ECDSA. In some scenarios (for example, a lottery game), several participants might want to randomly decide on a winner. We call them *decentralized randomness beacons* as their role is to produce the same verifiable randomness even if some participants decide not to take part in the protocol. A common solution is to use the previously discussed VRFs, not with a single key but with a *threshold distributed key*, a key that is split among many participants and that produces a unique valid signature for a given message only after a threshold of participants have signed the message. This might sound a bit confusing as this is the first time I've talked about distributed keys. Know that you will learn more about these later in this chapter.

One popular decentralized randomness beacon is called *drand* and is run in concert by several organizations and universities. It is available at https://leagueofentropy.com.

> *The main challenge in generating good randomness is that no party involved in the randomness generation process should be able to predict or bias the final output. A drand network is not controlled by anyone of its members. There is no single point of failure, and none of the drand server operators can bias the randomness generated by the network.*
>
> —https://drand.love ("How drand works," 2021)

Now that I've talked extensively about randomness and how programs obtain it nowadays, let's move the discussion towards the role of secrets in cryptography and how one can manage those.

8.6   *Key derivation with HKDF*

PRNGs are not the only constructions one can use to derive more secrets from one secret (in other words, to stretch a key). Deriving several secrets from one secret is actually such a frequent pattern in cryptography that this concept has its own name: *key derivation*. So let's see what this is about.

A *key derivation function* (KDF) is like a PRNG in many ways, except for a number of subtleties as noted in the following list. The differences are summarized in figure 8.6.

- *A KDF does not necessarily expect a uniformly random secret (as long as it has enough entropy).* This makes a KDF useful for deriving secrets from key exchange output, which produce high entropy but biased results (see chapter 5). The resulting secrets are, in turn, uniformly random, so you can use these in constructions that expect uniformly random keys.
- *A KDF is generally used in protocols that require participants to rederive the same keys several times.* In this sense, a KDF is expected to be deterministic, while PRNGs sometimes provide backward secrecy by frequently reseeding themselves with more entropy.
- *A KDF is usually not designed to produce a LOT of random numbers.* Instead, it is normally used to derive a limited number of keys.

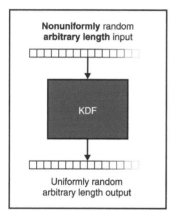
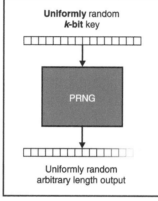

Figure 8.6 A key derivation function (KDF) and a PRNG are two similar constructions. The main differences are that a KDF does not expect a fully uniformly random secret as input (as long as it has enough entropy) and is usually not used to generate too much output.

The most popular KDF is the *HMAC-based key derivation function* (HKDF). You learned about HMAC (a MAC based on hash functions) in chapter 3. HKDF is a light KDF built on top of HMAC and defined in RFC 5869. For this reason, one can use HKDF with different hash functions, although, it is most commonly used with SHA-2. HKDF is specified as two different functions:

- *HKDF-Extract*—Removes biases from a secret input, producing a uniformly random secret.
- *HKDF-Expand*—Produces an arbitrary length and uniformly random output. Like PRNGs, *it expects a uniformly random secret as input* and is, thus, usually ran after HKDF-Extract.

Let's look at HKDF-Extract first, which I illustrate in figure 8.7. Technically, a hash function is enough to uniformize the randomness of an input byte string (remember, the output of a hash function is supposed to be indistinguishable from random), but HKDF goes further and accepts one additional input: a *salt*. As for password hashing, a salt

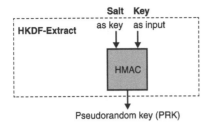

Figure 8.7   HKDF-Extract is the first function specified by HKDF. It takes an optional salt that is used as the key in HMAC and the input secret that might be nonuniformly random. Using different salts with the same input secret produces different outputs.

differentiates different usages of HKDF-Extract in the same protocol. While this salt is optional and set to an all-zero byte string if not used, it is recommended that you do use it. Furthermore, HKDF does not expect the salt to be a secret; it can be known to everyone, including adversaries. Instead of a hash function, HKDF-Extract uses a MAC (specifically HMAC), which coincidentally has an interface that accepts two arguments.

Let's now look at HKDF-Expand, which I illustrate in figure 8.8. If your input secret is already uniformly random, you can skip HKDF-Extract and use HKDF-Expand.

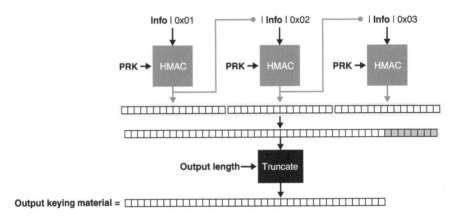

Figure 8.8   HKDF-Expand is the second function specified by HKDF. It takes an optional `info` byte string and an input secret that needs to be uniformly random. Using different `info` byte strings with the same input secret produces different outputs. The length of the output is controlled by a `length` argument.

Similar to HKDF-Extract, HKDF-Expand also accepts an additional and optional customization argument called `info`. While a salt is meant to provide some domain separation between calls within the same protocol for HKDF (or HKDF-Extract), `info` is meant to be used to differentiate your version of HKDF (or HKDF-Expand) from other protocols. You can also specify how much output you want, but keep in mind that HKDF is not a PRNG and is not designed to derive a large number of secrets. HKDF is limited by the size of the hash function you use; more precisely, if you use SHA-512 (which produces outputs of 512 bits) with HKDF, you are limited to 512 × 255 bits = 16,320 bytes of output for a given key and an `info` byte string.

Calling HKDF or HKDF-Expand several times with the same arguments, except for the output length, produces the same output truncated to the different length requested (see figure 8.9). This property is called *related outputs* and can, in rare scenarios, surprise protocol designers. It is good to keep this in mind.

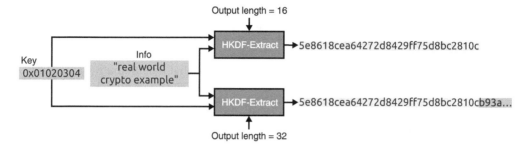

Figure 8.9   HKDF and HKDF-Expands provide related outputs, meaning that calling the function with different output lengths truncates the same result to the requested length.

Most cryptographic libraries combine HKDF-Extract and HKDF-Expand into a single call as figure 8.10 illustrates. As usual, make sure to read the manual (in this case, RFC 5869) before using HKDF.

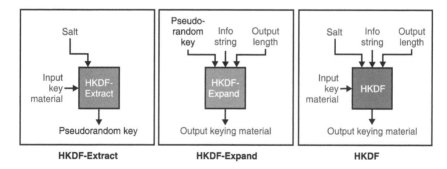

Figure 8.10   HKDF is usually found implemented as a single function call that combines both HKDF-Extract (to extract uniform randomness from an input key) and HKDF-Expand (to generate an arbitrary length output).

HKDF is not the only way to derive multiple secrets from one secret. A more naive approach is to use *hash functions*. As hash functions do not expect a uniformly random input and produce uniformly random outputs, they are fit for the task. Hash functions are not perfect, though, as their interface does not take into account *domain separation* (no customization string argument) and their output length is fixed. Best practice is to avoid hash functions when you can use a KDF instead. Nonetheless, some well-accepted algorithms do use hash functions for this purpose. For example, you learned in chapter 7 about the Ed25519 signature scheme that hashes a 256-bit key with SHA-512 to produce two 256-bit keys.

Do these functions really produce random outputs?

In theory, a hash function's properties do not say anything about the output being uniformly random; the properties only dictate that a hash function should be collision resistant, pre-image resistant, and second pre-image resistant. In the real world, though, we use hash functions all over the place to implement random oracles (as you learned in chapter 2), and thus, we assume that their outputs are uniformly random. This is the same with MACs, which are, in theory, not expected to produce uniformly random outputs (unlike PRFs as seen in chapter 3), but in practice, do for the most part. This is why HMAC is used in HKDF. In the rest of this book, I will assume that popular hash functions (like SHA-2 and SHA-3) and popular MACs (like HMAC and KMAC) produce random outputs.

The extended output functions (XOFs) we saw in chapter 2 (SHAKE and cSHAKE) can be used as a KDF as well! Remember, a XOF

- Does not expect a uniformly random input
- Can produce a practically infinitely large uniformly random output

In addition, KMAC (a MAC covered in chapter 3) does not have the related output issue I mentioned earlier. Indeed, KMAC's length argument randomizes the output of the algorithm, effectively acting like an additional customization string.

Finally, there exists an edge case for inputs that have low entropy. Think about passwords, for example, that can be relatively guessable compared to a 128-bit key. The password-based key derivation functions used to hash passwords (covered in chapter 2) can also be used to derive keys as well.

8.7   *Managing keys and secrets*

All right, all good, we know how to generate cryptographic random numbers, and we know how to derive secrets in different types of situations. But we're not out of the woods yet.

Now that we're using all of these cryptographic algorithms, we end up having to maintain a lot of secret keys. How do we store these keys? And how do we prevent these extremely sensitive secrets from being compromised? And what do we do if a secret becomes compromised? This problem is commonly known as *key management*.

Crypto is a tool for turning a whole swathe of problems into key management problems.

—Lea Kissner (2019, http://mng.bz/eMrJ)

While many systems choose to leave keys close to the application that makes use of them, this does not necessarily mean that applications have no recourse when bad things happen. To prepare against an eventual breach or a bug that would leak a key, most serious applications employ two defense-in-depth techniques:

- *Key rotation*—By associating an expiration date to a key (usually a public key) and by replacing your key with a new key periodically, you can "heal" from an eventual compromise. The shorter the expiration date and rotation frequency, the faster you can replace a key that might be known to an attacker.
- *Key revocation*—Key rotation is not always enough, and you might want to cancel a key as soon as you hear it has been compromised. For this reason, some systems allow you to ask if a key has been revoked before making use of it. (You will learn more about this in the next chapter on secure transport.)

Automation is often indispensable to successfully using these techniques as a well-oiled machine is much more apt to work correctly in times of crisis. Furthermore, you can also associate a particular role to a key in order to limit the consequences of a compromise. For example, you could differentiate two public keys in some fabricated application as public key 1, which is only for signing transactions, and public key 2, which is only for doing key exchanges. This allows a compromise of the private key associated with public key 2 to not impact transaction signing.

If one does not want to leave keys lying around on device storage media, hardware solutions exist that aim at preventing keys from being extracted. You will learn more about these in chapter 13 on hardware cryptography.

Finally, many ways exist for applications to delegate key management. This is often the case on mobile OSs that provide *key stores* or *key chains*, which will keep keys for you and will even perform cryptographic operations!

Applications living in the cloud can sometimes have access to cloud key management services. These services allow an application to delegate creation of secret keys and cryptographic operations and to avoid thinking about the many ways to attack those. Nonetheless, as with hardware solutions, if an application is compromised, it will still be able to do any type of request to the delegated service.

> **NOTE** There are no silver bullets, and you should still consider what you can do to detect and respond to a compromise.

Key management is a hard problem that is beyond the scope of this book, so I will not dwell on this topic too much. In the next section, I go over cryptographic techniques that attempt to avoid the key management problem.

8.8 *Decentralize trust with threshold cryptography*

Key management is a vast field of study that can be quite annoying to invest in as users do not always have the resources to implement best practices, nor the tools available in the space. Fortunately, cryptography has something to offer for those who want to lessen the burden of key management. The first one I'll talk about is *secret sharing* (or *secret splitting*). Secret splitting allows you to break a secret into multiple parts that can be shared among a set of participants. Here, a secret can be anything you want: a symmetric key, a signing private key, and so on.

Typically, a person called a *dealer* generates the secret, then splits it and shares the different parts among all participants before deleting the secret. The most famous secret splitting scheme was invented by Adi Shamir (one of the co-inventors of RSA) and is called *Shamir's Secret Sharing* (SSS). I illustrate this process in figure 8.11.

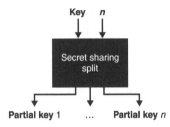

Figure 8.11   Given a key and a number of shares *n*, the Shamir's Secret Sharing scheme creates *n* partial keys of the same size as the original key.

When the time comes and the secret is needed to perform some cryptographic operation (encrypting, signing, and so on), all share owners need to return their private shares back to the dealer who is in charge of reconstructing the original secret. Such a scheme prevents attackers from targeting a single user as each share is useless by itself and, instead, forces attackers to compromise all the participants before they can exploit a key! I illustrate this in figure 8.12.

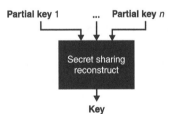

Figure 8.12   The Shamir's Secret Sharing scheme used to split a secret in *n* partial keys requires all of the *n* partial keys to reconstruct the original key.

The mathematics behind the scheme's algorithm are actually not too hard to understand! So let me spare a few paragraphs here to give you a simplified idea of the scheme.

Imagine a random straight line on a 2-dimensional space, and let's say that its equation—$y = ax + b$—is the secret. By having two participants hold two random points on the line, they can collaborate to recover the line equation. The scheme generalizes to polynomials of any degree and, thus, can be used to divide a secret into an arbitrary number of shares. This is illustrated in figure 8.13.

Secret splitting is a technique often adopted due to its simplicity. Yet, in order to be useful, key shares must be gathered into one place to recreate the key each and every time it is used in a cryptographic operation. This creates a window of opportunity in which the secret becomes vulnerable to robberies or accidental leaks, effectively getting

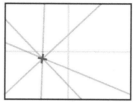

The **secret** is a random line. Pick two **random points** on the line as **partial keys**.

With **one point**, you can define an **infinite number of lines** passing through it.

The curve can be **reconstructed** only with the knowledge of the **two points**.

Figure 8.13 The idea behind the Shamir's Secret Sharing scheme is to see a polynomial defining a curve as the secret and random points on the curve as partial keys. To recover a polynomial of degree n that defines a curve, one needs to know $n + 1$ points on the curve. For example, $f(x) = 3x + 5$ is of degree 1, so you need any two points $(x, f(x))$ to recover the polynomial, and $f(x) = 5x^2 + 2x + 3$ is of degree 2, so you need any three points to recover the polynomial.

us back to a *single point of failure* model. To avoid this single point of failure issue, there exist several cryptographic techniques that can be useful in different scenarios.

For example, imagine a protocol that accepts a financial transaction only if it has been signed by Alice. This places a large burden on Alice, who might be afraid of getting targeted by attackers. In order to reduce the impact of an attack on Alice, we can, instead, change the protocol to accept (on the same transaction) a number n of signatures from n different public keys, including Alice's. An attacker would have to compromise all n signatures in order to forge a valid transaction! Such systems are called *multi-signature* (often shortened as *multi-sig*) and are widely adopted in the cryptocurrency space.

Naive multi-signature schemes, though, can add some annoying overhead. Indeed, the size of a transaction in our example grows linearly with the number of signatures required. To solve this, some signature schemes (like the BLS signature scheme) can compress several signatures down to a single one. This is called *signature aggregation*. Some multi-signature schemes go even further in the compression by allowing the n public keys to be aggregated into a single public key. This technique is called *distributed key generation* (DKG) and is part of a field of cryptography called *secure multi-party computation*, which I will cover in chapter 15.

DKG lets n participants collaboratively compute a public key without ever having the associated private key in the clear during the process (unlike SSS, there is no dealer). If participants want to sign a message, they can then collaboratively create a signature using each participant's private shares, which can be verified using the public key they previously created. Again, the private key never exists physically, preventing the single point of failure problem SSS has. Because you saw Schnorr signatures in chapter 7, figure 8.14 shows the intuition behind a simplified Schnorr DKG scheme.

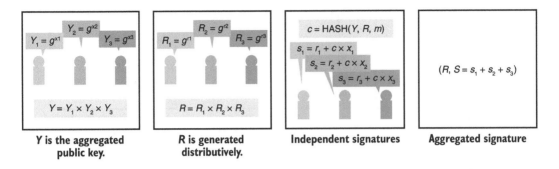

Figure 8.14   The Schnorr signature scheme can be decentralized into a distributed key generation scheme.

Finally, note that

- Each scheme I've mentioned can be made to work even when only a threshold *m* out of the *n* participants take part in the protocol. This is really important as most real-world systems must tolerate a number of malicious or inactive participants.
- These types of schemes can work with other asymmetric cryptographic algorithms. For example, using threshold encryption, a set of participants can collaborate to asymmetrically decrypt a message.

I review all these examples in figure 8.15.

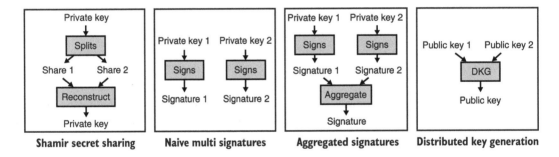

Figure 8.15   A recap of existing techniques to split the trust we have in one participant into several participants.

Threshold schemes are an important new paradigm in the key management world, and it is a good idea to follow their development. NIST currently has a threshold cryptography group, which organizes workshops and has the intent to standardize primitives and protocols in the long run.

Summary

- A number is taken uniformly and at random from a set if it was picked with equal probability compared to all the other numbers from that set.
- Entropy is a metric to indicate how much randomness a byte string has. High entropy refers to byte strings that are uniformly random, while low entropy refers to byte strings that are easy to guess or predict.
- Pseudorandom number generators (PRNGs) are algorithms that take a uniformly random seed and generate (in practice) a nearly infinite amount of randomness that can be used for cryptographic purposes (as cryptographic keys, for example) if the seed is large enough.
- To obtain random numbers, one should rely on a programming language's standard library or on its well-known cryptographic libraries. If these are not available, operating systems generally provide interfaces to obtain random numbers:
  - Windows offers the `BCryptGenRandom` system call.
  - Linux and FreeBSD offer the `getrandom` system call.
  - Other Unix-like operating systems usually have a special file called /dev/urandom that exhibites randomness.
- Key derivation functions (KDFs) are useful in scenarios where one wants to derive secrets from a biased but high entropy secret.
- HKDF (HMAC-based key derivation function) is the most widely used KDF and is based on HMAC.
- Key management is the field of keeping secrets, well, secret. It mostly consists of finding where to store secrets, proactively expiring and rotating secrets, figuring out what to do when secrets are compromised, and so on.
- To lessen the burden of key management, one can split the trust from one participant into multiple participants.

Part 2

Protocols: The recipes of cryptography

Y**ou** are now entering the second part of this book, which is going to make use of most of what you've learned in the first part. Think about it this way: if the cryptographic primitives you've learned about were the basic ingredients of cryptography, you're now about to learn some recipes. And there's a lot to cook! While Caesar might have only been interested in encrypting his communications, today cryptography is all over the place, and it's quite hard to keep track of it all.

In chapter 9, 10, and 11, I show you where you are most likely to run into cryptography and how cryptography is used to solve real-world problems; that is, how cryptography encrypts communications and how it authenticates participants in protocols. For the most part, that's what cryptography is about. Participants will be numerous or few, and made of bits or flesh. As you'll quickly realize, real-world cryptography is about tradeoffs and, based on the context, solutions will differ.

Chapter 12 and 13 take you into two quickly evolving fields of cryptography: cryptocurrencies and hardware cryptography. The former topic has been ignored by most books on cryptography. (I believe that this book, *Real-World Cryptography*, is the first cryptography book to include a chapter on cryptocurrencies.) The latter topic, hardware cryptography, is often overlooked too; cryptographers often assume that their primitives and protocols run in a trusted environment, which is less and less the case. Hardware cryptography is about pushing the boundaries of where cryptography can run and providing security assurances when attackers are getting closer and closer to you.

In chapters 14 and 15, I touch on the bleeding edge: what's not here yet but will be and what's sort of here. You'll learn about postquantum cryptography, which is a field of cryptography that might be useful, depending on if we, as a human species, invent scalable quantum computers. These quantum computers, based on novel paradigms coming from the realm of quantum physics, could revolutionize research and, perhaps, even break our crypto . . . You'll also learn about what I call "next-generation cryptography," cryptographic primitives that have rarely seen the light of day but that you will most likely see more frequently as these get studied, become more efficient, and get adopted by application designers. Finally, I conclude the book in chapter 16 with some final remarks on real-world cryptography and some words on ethics.

Secure transport

The heaviest use of cryptography today is most probably to encrypt communications. After all, cryptography was invented for this purpose. To do this, applications generally do not make use of cryptographic primitives like authenticated encryption directly, but instead use much more involved protocols that abstract the use of the cryptographic primitives. I call these protocols *secure transport protocols*, for lack of a better term.

In this chapter, you will learn about the most widely used secure transport protocol: the Transport Layer Security (TLS) protocol. I will also lightly cover other secure transport protocols and how they differ from TLS.

9.1 The SSL and TLS secure transport protocols

In order to understand why *transport protocols* (protocols used to encrypt communications between machines) are a thing, let's walk through a motivating scenario. When you enter, say, `http://example.com` in your web browser, your browser uses a number of protocols to connect to a web server and to retrieve the page you requested. One of those is the *Hypertext Transfer Protocol* (HTTP), which your browser uses to tell the web server on the other side which page it is interested in. HTTP uses a human-readable format. This means that you can look at the HTTP messages that are being sent and received over the wire and read them without the help of any other tool. But this is not enough for your browser to communicate to the web server.

HTTP messages are encapsulated into other types of messages, called *TCP frames*, which are defined in the Transmission Control Protocol (TCP). TCP is a binary protocol, and thus, it is not human-readable: you need a tool to understand the fields of a TCP frame. TCP messages are further encapsulated using the Internet Protocol (IP), and IP messages are further encapsulated using something else. This is known as the *Internet protocol suite*, and as it is the subject of many books, I won't go much further into this.

Back to our scenario, as there's a confidentiality issue that we need to talk about. Anyone sitting on the wire in between your browser and the web server of example.com has an interesting position: they can passively observe and read your requests as well as the server's responses. Worse, MITM attackers can also actively tamper and reorder messages. This is not great.

Imagine your credit card information leaking out every time you buy something on the internet, your passwords being stolen when you log into a website, your pictures and private messages pilfered as you send those to your friends, and so forth. This scared enough people that in the 1990s, the predecessor of TLS—the *Secure Sockets Layer* (SSL) *protocol*—was born. While SSL can be used in different kinds of situations, it was first built by and for web browsers. As such, it started being used in combination with HTTP, extending it into the *Hypertext Transfer Protocol Secure* (HTTPS). HTTPS now allowed browsers to secure their communications to the different websites they visited.

9.1.1   *From SSL to TLS*

Although SSL was not the only protocol that attempted to secure some of the web, it did attract most of the attention and, with time, has become the de facto standard. But this is not the whole story. Between the first version of SSL and what we currently use today, a lot has happened. All versions of SSL (the last being SSL v3.0) were broken due to a combination of bad design and bad cryptographic algorithms. (Many of the attacks have been summarized in RFC 7457.)

After SSL 3.0, the protocol was officially transferred to the Internet Engineering Task Force (IETF), the organization in charge of publishing *Request For Comments* (RFCs) standards. The name SSL was dropped in favor of TLS, and TLS 1.0 was released in 1999 as RFC 2246. The most recent version of TLS is TLS 1.3, specified in RFC 8446 and published in 2018. TLS 1.3, unlike its predecessor, stems from a solid collaboration between the industry and academia. Yet, today, the internet is still divided between many different versions of SSL and TLS as servers have been slow to update.

NOTE There's a lot of confusion around the two names SSL and TLS. The protocol is now called *TLS*, but many articles and even libraries still choose to use the term *SSL*.

TLS has become more than just the protocol securing the web; it is now used in many different scenarios and among many different types of applications and devices as a protocol to secure communications. Thus, what you will learn about TLS in this chapter is not only useful for the web, but also for any scenario where communications between two applications need to be secure.

9.1.2 Using TLS in practice

How do people use TLS? First let's define some terms. In TLS, the two participants that want to secure their communications are called a *client* and a *server*. It works the same way as with other network protocols like TCP or IP: the client is the one that initiates the connection, and the server is the one that waits for one to be initiated. A TLS client is typically built from

- *Some configuration*—A client is configured with the versions of SSL and TLS that it wants to support, cryptographic algorithms that it is willing to use to secure the connection, ways it can authenticate servers, and so on.

- *Some information about the server it wants to connect to*—It includes at least an IP address and a port, but for the web, it often includes a fully qualified domain name instead (like example.com).

Given these two arguments, a client can initiate a connection with a server to produce a secure *session*, a channel that both the client and the server can use to share encrypted messages with each other. In some cases, a secure session cannot successfully be created and fails midway. For example, if an attacker attempts to tamper with the connection or if the server's configuration is not compatible with the client's (more on that later), the client fails to establish a secure session.

A TLS server is often much simpler as it only takes a configuration, which is similar to the client's configuration. A server then waits for clients to connect to it in order to produce a secure session. In practice, using TLS on the client side can be as easy as the following listing demonstrates (that is, if you use a programming language like Golang).

Listing 9.1 A TLS client in Golang

```
import "crypto/tls"

func main() {
    destination := "google.com:443"
    TLSconfig := &tls.Config{}
    conn, err := tls.Dial("tcp", destination, TLSconfig)
    if err != nil {
        panic("failed to connect: " + err.Error())
```

The fully qualified domain name and the server's port (443 is the default port for HTTPS).

An empty config serves as the default configuration.

```
        }
    conn.Close()
}
```

How does the client know that the connection it established is really with google.com and not some impersonator? By default, Golang's TLS implementation uses your operating system's configuration to figure out how to authenticate TLS servers. (Later in this chapter, you will learn exactly how the authentication in TLS works.) Using TLS on the server side is pretty easy as well. The following listing shows how simple this is.

Listing 9.2   A TLS server in Golang

```
import (
    "crypto/tls"
    "net/http"
)

func hello(rw http.ResponseWriter, req *http.Request) {
    rw.Write([]byte("Hello, world\n"))
}

func main() {
    config := &tls.Config{                       A solid minimal
        MinVersion: tls.VersionTLS13,            configuration for
    }                                            a TLS 1.3 server

    http.HandleFunc("/", hello)     ◁——— Serves a simple page displaying "Hello, world".

    server := &http.Server{              An HTTPS server
        Addr:      ":8080",              starts on port
        TLSConfig: config,               8080.
    }

    cert := "cert.pem"                                Some .pem files
    key := "key.pem"                                  containing a certificate
    err := server.ListenAndServeTLS(cert, key)  ◁——  and a secret key (more
     if err != nil {                                  on this later)
        panic(err)
    }
}
```

Golang and its standard library do a lot for us here. Unfortunately, not all languages' standard libraries provide easy-to-use TLS implementations, if they provide a TLS implementation at all, and not all TLS libraries provide secure-by-default implementations! For this reason, configuring a TLS server is not always straightforward, depending on the library. In the next section, you will learn about the inner workings of TLS and its different subtleties.

NOTE   TLS is a protocol that works on top of TCP. To secure UDP connections, we can use DTLS (*D* is for *datagram*, the term for UDP messages), which is fairly similar to TLS. For this reason, I ignore DTLS in this chapter.

9.2 How does the TLS protocol work?

As I said earlier, today TLS is the de facto standard to secure communications between applications. In this section, you will learn more about how TLS works underneath the surface and how it is used in practice. You will find this section useful for learning how to use TLS properly and also for understanding how most (if not all) secure transport protocols work. You will also find out why it is hard (and strongly discouraged) to redesign or reimplement such protocols.

At a high level, TLS is split into two phases as noted in the following list. Figure 9.1 illustrates this idea.

- *A handshake phase*—A secure communication is negotiated and created between two participants.
- *A post-handshake phase*—Communications are encrypted between the two participants.

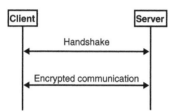

Figure 9.1   At a high level, secure transport protocols first create a secure connection during a handshake phase. After that, applications on both sides of the secure connection can communicate securely.

At this point, because you learned about hybrid encryption in chapter 6, you should have the following (correct) intuition about how these two steps works:

- *The handshake is, at its core, simply a key exchange.* The handshake ends up with the two participants agreeing on a set of symmetric keys.
- *The post-handshake phase is purely about encrypting messages between participants.* This phase uses an authenticated encryption algorithm and the set of keys produced at the end of the handshake.

Most transport security protocols work this way, and the interesting parts of these protocols always lie in the handshake phase. Next, let's take a look at the handshake phase.

9.2.1 The TLS handshake

As you've seen, TLS is (and most transport security protocols are) divided into two parts: a *handshake* and a *post-handshake* phase. In this section, you'll learn about the handshake first. The handshake itself has four aspects that I want to tell you about:

- *Negotiation*—TLS is highly configurable. Both a client and a server can be configured to negotiate a range of SSL and TLS versions as well as a menu of acceptable cryptographic algorithms. The negotiation phase of the handshake aims at finding common ground between the client's and the server's configurations in order to securely connect the two peers.

- *Key exchange*—The whole point of the handshake is to perform a key exchange between two participants. Which key exchange algorithm to use? This is one of the things decided as part of the client/server negotiation process.
- *Authentication*—As you learned in chapter 5 on key exchanges, it is trivial for MITM attackers to impersonate any side of a key exchange. Due to this, key exchanges must be authenticated. Your browser must have a way to ensure that it is talking to google.com, for example, and not your internet service provider (ISP).
- *Session resumption*—As browsers often connect to the same websites again and again, key exchanges can be costly and can slow down a user's experience. For this reason, mechanisms to fast-track secure sessions without redoing a key exchange are integrated into TLS.

This is a comprehensive list! As fast as greased lightning, let's start with the first item.

NEGOTIATION IN TLS: WHAT VERSION AND WHAT ALGORITHMS?

Most of the complexity in TLS comes from the negotiation of the different moving parts of the protocol. Infamously, this negotiation has also been the source of many issues in the history of TLS. Attacks like FREAK, LOGJAM, DROWN, and others took advantage of weaknesses present in older versions to break more recent versions of the protocol (sometimes even when the server did not support older versions!). While not all protocols have versioning or allow for different algorithms to be negotiated, SSL/TLS was designed for the web. As such, SSL/TLS needed a way to maintain backward compatibility with older clients and servers that could be slow to update.

This is what happens on the web today: your browser might be recent and up-to-date and made to support TLS version 1.3, but when visiting some old web page, chances are that the server behind it only supports TLS versions up to 1.2 or 1.1 (or worse). Vice-versa, many websites must support older browsers, which translates into supporting older versions of TLS (as some users are still stuck in the past).

Are older versions of SSL and TLS secure?

Most versions of SSL and TLS have security issues, except for TLS versions 1.2 and 1.3. Why not just support the latest version (1.3) and call it a day? The reason is that some companies support older clients that can't easily be updated. Due to these requirements, it is not uncommon to find libraries implementing mitigations to known attacks in order to securely support older versions. Unfortunately, these mitigations are often too complex to implement correctly.

For example, well-known attacks like Lucky13 and Bleichenbacher98 have been rediscovered again and again by security researchers in various TLS implementations that had previously attempted to fix the issues. Although it is possible to mitigate a number of attacks on older TLS versions, I would recommend against it, and I am not the only one telling you this. In March 2021, the IETF published RFC 8996: "Deprecating TLS 1.0 and TLS 1.1," effectively making the deprecation official.

Negotiation starts with the client sending a first request (called a *ClientHello*) to the server. The ClientHello contains a range of supported SSL and TLS versions, a suite of cryptographic algorithms that the client is willing to use, and some more information that could be relevant for the rest of the handshake or for the application. The suite of cryptographic algorithms include

- *One or more key exchange algorithms*—TLS 1.3 defines the following algorithms allowed for negotiations: ECDH with P-256, P-384, P-521, X25519, X448, and FFDH with the groups defined in RFC 7919. I talked about all of these in chapter 5. Previous versions of TLS also offered RSA key exchanges (covered in chapter 6), but they were removed in the last version.

- *Two (for different parts of the handshake) or more digital signature algorithms*—TLS 1.3 specifies RSA PKCS#1 version 1.5 and the newer RSA-PSS, as well as more recent elliptic curve algorithms like ECDSA and EdDSA. I talked about these in chapter 7. Note that digital signatures are specified with a hash function, which allows you to negotiate, for example, RSA-PSS with either SHA-256 or SHA-512.

- *One or more hash functions to be used with HMAC and HKDF*—TLS 1.3 specifies SHA-256 and SHA-384, two instances of the SHA-2 hash function. (You learned about SHA-2 in chapter 2.) This choice of hash function is unrelated to the one used by the digital signature algorithm. As a reminder, HMAC is the message authentication code you learned in chapter 3, and HKDF is the key derivation function we covered in chapter 8.

- *One or more authenticated encryption algorithms*—These can include AES-GCM with keys of 128 or 256 bits, ChaCha20-Poly1305, and AES-CCM. I talked about all of these in chapter 4.

The server then responds with a *ServerHello* message, which contains one of each type of cryptographic algorithm, cherry-picked from the client's selection. The following illustration depicts this response.

HELLO! I WANT TO CONNECT WITH TLS 1.3. I SUPPORT X448 AND X25519 FOR KEY EXCHANGES. AES-GCM AND CHACHA20-POLY1305 FOR AUTHENTICATED ENCRYPTION. ETC.

HELLO! FOR SURE. LET'S DO X25519 FOR KEY EXCHANGE, AES-GCM FOR AUTHENTICATED ENCRYPTION, ETC.

If the server is unable to find an algorithm it supports, it aborts the connection. Although in some cases, the server does not have to abort the connection and can ask the client to provide more information instead. To do this, the server replies with a message called a *HelloRetryRequest*, asking for the missing piece of information. The client can then resend its ClientHello, this time with the added requested information.

TLS AND FORWARD-SECURE KEY EXCHANGES

The key exchange is the most important part of the TLS handshake! Without it, there's obviously no symmetric key being negotiated. But for a key exchange to happen, the client and the server must first trade their respective public keys.

In TLS 1.2 and previous versions, the client and the server start a key exchange only after both participants agree on which key exchange algorithm to use. This happens during a negotiation phase. TLS 1.3 optimizes this flow by attempting to do both the negotiation and the key exchange at the same time: the client speculatively chooses a key exchange algorithm and sends a public key in the first message (the ClientHello). If the client fails to predict the server's choice of key exchange algorithm, then the client falls back to the outcome of the negotiation and sends a new ClientHello containing the correct public key. The following steps describe how this might look. I illustrate the difference in figure 9.2.

1 The client sends a TLS 1.3 ClientHello message announcing that it can do either an X25519 or an X448 key exchange. It also sends an X25519 public key.
2 The server does not support X25519 but does support X448. It sends a Hello-RetryRequest to the client announcing that it only supports X448.
3 The client sends the same ClientHello but with an X448 public key instead.
4 The handshake goes on.

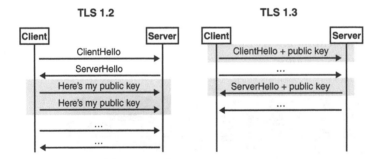

Figure 9.2   In TLS 1.2, the client waits for the server to choose which key exchange algorithm to use before sending a public key. In TLS 1.3, the client speculates on which key exchange algorithm(s) the server will settle on and preemptively sends a public key (or several) in the first message, potentially avoiding an extra round trip.

TLS 1.3 is full of such optimizations, which are important for the web. Indeed, many people worldwide have unstable or slow connections, and it is important to keep non-application communication to the bare minimum required. Furthermore, in TLS 1.3

(and unlike previous versions of TLS), all key exchanges are *ephemeral*. This means that for each new session, the client and the server both generate new key pairs, then get rid of them as soon as the key exchange is done. This provides *forward secrecy* to the key exchange: a compromise of the long-term keys of the client or the server, which won't allow an attacker to decrypt this session as long as the ephemeral private keys were safely deleted.

Imagine what would happen if, instead, a TLS server used a single private key for every key exchange it performs with its clients. By performing ephemeral key exchanges and getting rid of private keys as soon as a handshake ends, the server protects against such attackers. I illustrate this in figure 9.3.

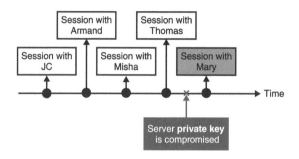

Figure 9.3   In TLS 1.3, each session starts with an ephemeral key exchange. If a server is compromised at some point in time, no previous sessions will be impacted.

Exercise

A compromise of the server's private key at some point in time would be devastating as MITM attackers would then be able to decrypt all previously recorded conversations. Do you understand how this can happen?

Once ephemeral public keys are traded, a key exchange is performed, and keys can be derived. TLS 1.3 derives different keys at different points in time to encrypt different phases with independent keys.

The first two messages, the ClientHello and the ServerHello, cannot be encrypted because no public keys were traded at this point. But after that, as soon as the key exchange happens, TLS 1.3 encrypts the rest of the handshake. (This is unlike previous versions of TLS that did not encrypt any of the handshake messages.)

To derive the different keys, TLS 1.3 uses HKDF with the hash function negotiated. HKDF-Extract is used on the output of the key exchange to remove any biases, while HKDF-Expand is used with different `info` parameters to derive the encryption keys. For example, `tls13 c hs traffic` (for "client handshake traffic") is used to derive symmetric keys for the client to encrypt to the server during the handshake, and `tls13 s ap traffic` (for "server application traffic") is used to derive symmetric keys for the server to encrypt to the client after the handshake. Remember though, *unauthenticated* key exchanges are insecure! Next, you'll see how TLS addresses this.

TLS AUTHENTICATION AND THE WEB PUBLIC KEY INFRASTRUCTURE

After some negotiations and after the key exchange has taken place, the handshake must go on. What happens next is the other most important part of TLS—*authentication.* You saw in chapter 5 on key exchanges that it is trivial to intercept a key exchange and impersonate one or both sides of the key exchange. In this section, I'll explain how your browser cryptographically validates that it is talking to the right website and not to an impersonator. But, first, let's take a step back. There is something I haven't told you yet. A TLS 1.3 handshake is actually split into three different stages (as figure 9.4 illustrates):

1   *Key exchange*—This phase contains the *ClientHello* and *ServerHello* messages that provide some negotiation and perform the key exchange. All messages including handshake messages after this phase are encrypted.

2   *Server parameters*—Messages in this phase contain additional negotiation data from the server. This is negotiation data that does not have to be contained in the first message of the server and that could benefit from being encrypted.

3   *Authentication*—This phase includes authentication information from both the server and the client.

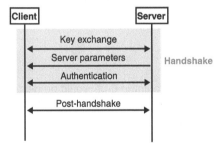

Figure 9.4   A TLS 1.3 handshake is divided into three phases: the key exchange phase, the server parameters phase, and (finally) the authentication phase.

On the web, authentication in TLS is usually one-sided. Only the browser verifies that google.com, for example, is indeed google.com, but google.com does not verify who you are (or at least not as part of TLS).

Mutually-authenticated TLS

Client authentication is often delegated to the application layer for the web, most often via a form asking you for your credentials. That being said, client authentication can also happen in TLS if requested by the server during the server parameters phase. When both sides of the connection are authenticated, we talk about *mutually-authenticated TLS* (sometimes abbreviated as mTLS).

Client authentication is done the same way as server authentication. This can happen at any point after the authentication of the server (for example, during the handshake or in the post-handshake phase).

Let's now answer the question, "When connecting to google.com, how does your browser verify that you are indeed handshaking with google.com?" The answer is by using the *web public key infrastructure (web PKI)*.

You learned about the concept of public key infrastructure in chapter 7 on digital signatures, but let me briefly reintroduce this concept as it is quite important in understanding how the web works. There are two sides to the web PKI. First, browsers must trust a set of root public keys that we call *certificate authorities* (CAs). Usually, browsers will either use a hardcoded set of trusted public keys or will rely on the operating system to provide them.

The web PKI

For the web, there exist hundreds of these CAs that are independently run by different companies and organizations across the world. It is quite a complex system to analyze, and these CAs can sometimes also sign the public keys of intermediate CAs that, in turn, also have the authority to sign the public keys of websites. For this reason, organizations like the *Certification Authority Browser Forum* (CA/Browser Forum) enforce rules and decide when new organizations can join the set of trusted public keys or when a CA can no longer be trusted and must be removed from that set.

Second, websites that want to use HTTPS must have a way to obtain a certification (a signature of their signing public key) from these CAs. In order to do this, a website owner (or a webmaster, as we used to say) must prove to a CA that they own a specific domain.

NOTE Obtaining a certificate for your own website used to involve a fee. This is no longer the case as CAs like Let's Encrypt provide certificates for free.

To prove that you own example.com, for example, a CA might ask you to host a file at example.com/some_path/file.txt that contains some random numbers generated for your request. The following comic strip shows this exchange.

After this, a CA can provide a signature over the website's public key. As the CA's signature is usually valid for a period of years, we say that it is over a long-term signing public key (as opposed to an ephemeral public key). More specifically, CAs do not actually sign public keys, but instead they sign *certificates* (more on this later). A certificate contains the long-term public key, along with some additional important metadata like the web page's domain name.

To prove to your browser that the server it is talking to is indeed google.com, the server sends a *certificate chain* as part of the TLS handshake. The chain comprises

- Its own leaf certificate, containing (among others) the domain name (google .com, for example), Google's long-term signing public key, as well as a CA's signature
- A chain of intermediate CA certificates from the one that signed Google's certificate to the root CA that signed the last intermediate CA

This is a bit wordy so I illustrated this in figure 9.5.

Figure 9.5   Web browsers only have to trust a relatively small set of root CAs in order to trust the whole web. These CAs are stored in what is called a *trust store*. In order for a website to be trusted by a browser, the website must have its leaf certificate signed by one of these CAs. Sometimes root CAs only sign intermediate CAs, which, in turn, sign other intermediate CAs or leaf certificates. This is what's known as the web PKI.

The certificate chain is sent in a certificate TLS message by the server and by the client as if the client has been asked to authenticate. Following this, the server can use its certified long-term key pair to sign all handshake messages that have been received and previously sent in what is called a *CertificateVerify* message. Figure 9.6 reviews this flow, where only the server authenticates itself.

The signature in the CertificateVerify message proves to the client what the server has so far seen. Without this signature, a MITM attacker could intercept the server's handshake messages and replace the ephemeral public key of the server contained in the ServerHello message, allowing the attacker to successfully impersonate the server. Take a few moments to understand why an attacker cannot replace the server's ephemeral public key in the presence of the CertificateVerify signature.

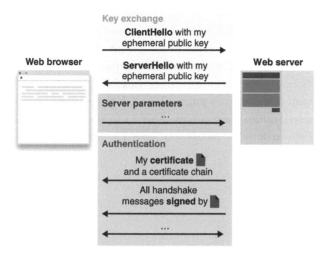

Figure 9.6 The authentication part of a handshake starts with the server sending a certificate chain to the client. The certificate chain starts with the leaf certificate (the certificate containing the website's public key and additional metadata like the domain name) and ends with a root certificate that is trusted by the browser. Each certificate contains a signature from the certificate above it in the chain.

Story time

A few years ago, I was hired to review a custom TLS protocol made by a large company. It turned out that their protocol had the server provide a signature that did not cover the ephemeral key. When I told them about the issue, the whole room went silent for a full minute. It was, of course, a substantial mistake: an attacker who could have intercepted the custom handshake and replaced the ephemeral key with its own would have successfully impersonated the server.

The lesson here is that it is important not to reinvent the wheel. Secure transport protocols are hard to get right, and if history has shown anything, they can fail in many unexpected ways. Instead, you should rely on mature protocols like TLS and make sure you use a popular implementation that has received a substantial amount of public attention.

Finally, in order to officially end the handshake, both sides of the connection must send a *Finished* message as part of the authentication phase. A Finished message contains an authentication tag produced by HMAC, instantiated with the negotiated hash function for the session. This allows both the client and the server to tell the other side, "These are all the messages I have sent and received in order during this handshake." If the handshake is intercepted and tampered with by MITM attackers, this integrity check allows the participants to detect and abort the connection. This is especially useful as some handshakes modes are *not* signed (more on this later).

Before heading to a different aspect of the handshake, let's look at X.509 certificates. They are an important detail of many cryptographic protocols.

AUTHENTICATION VIA X.509 CERTIFICATES

While certificates are optional in TLS 1.3 (you can always use plain keys), many applications and protocols, not just the web, make heavy use of them in order to certify additional metadata. Specifically, the X.509 certificate standard version 3 is used.

X.509 is a pretty old standard that was meant to be flexible enough to be used in a multitude of scenarios: from email to web pages. The X.509 standard uses a description language called *Abstract Syntax Notation One* (ASN.1) to specify information contained in a certificate. A data structure described in ASN.1 looks like this:

```
Certificate  ::=  SEQUENCE  {
    tbsCertificate        TBSCertificate,
    signatureAlgorithm    AlgorithmIdentifier,
    signatureValue        BIT STRING  }
```

You can literally read this as a structure that contains three fields:

- tbsCertificate—The to-be-signed certificate. This contains all the information that one wants to certify. For the web, this can contain a domain name (google.com, for example), a public key, an expiration date, and so on.
- signatureAlgorithm—The algorithm used to sign the certificate.
- signatureValue—The signature from a CA.

> **Exercise**
>
> The values signatureAlgorithm and signatureValue are not contained in the actual certificate, tbsCertificate. Do you know why?

You can easily check what's in an X.509 certificate by connecting to any website using HTTPS and then using your browser functionalities to observe the certificate chain sent by the server. See figure 9.7 for an example.

You might encounter X.509 certificates as .pem files, which is some base64-encoded content surrounded by some human-readable hint of what the base64-encoded data contains (here, a certificate). The following snippet represents the content of a certificate in a .pem format:

```
-----BEGIN CERTIFICATE-----
MIIJQzCCCCugAwIBAgIQC1QW6WUXJ9ICAAAAEbPdjANBgkqhkiG9w0BAQsFADBC
MQswCQYDVQQGEwJVUzEeMBwGA1UEChMVR29vZ2xlIFRydXN0IFNlcnZpY2VzMRMw
EQYDVQQDEwpHVFMgQ0EgMU8xMB4XDTE5MTAwMzE3MDk0NVoXDTE5MTIyNjE3MDk0
NVowZjELMAkGA1UEBhMCVVMxEzARBgNVBAgTCkNhbGlmb3JuaWExFjAUBgNVBAcT
[...]
vaoUqelfNJJvQjJbMQbSQEp9y8EIi4BnWGZjU6Q+q/3VZ7ybR3cOzhnaLGmqiwFv
4PNBdnVVfVbQ9CxRiplKVzZSnUvypgBLryYnl6kquh1AJS5gnJhzogrz98IiXCQZ
c7mkvTKgCNIR9fedIus+LPHCSD7zUQTgRoOmcB+kwY7jrFqKn6thTjwPnfB5aVNK
dl0nq4fcF8PN+ppgNFbwC2JxX08L1wEFk2LvDOQgKqHR1TRJ0U3A2gkuMtf6Q6au
3KBzGW6l/vt3coyyDkQKDmT61tjwy5k=
-----END CERTIFICATE-----
```

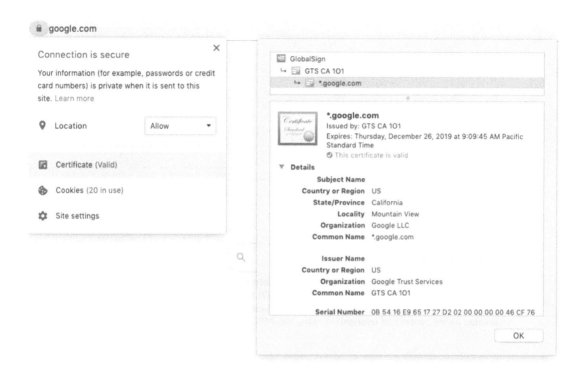

Figure 9.7 Using Chrome's Certificate Viewer, we can observe the certificate chain sent by Google's server. The root CA is Global Sign, which is trusted by your browser. Down the chain, an intermediate CA called GTS CA 101 is trusted due to its certificate containing a signature from Global Sign. In turn, Google's leaf certificate, valid for *.google.com (google.com, mail.google.com, and so on), contains a signature from GTS CA 101.

If you decode the base64 content surrounded by BEGIN CERTIFICATE and END CERTIF-ICATE, you end up with a *Distinguished Encoding Rules* (DER) encoded certificate. DER is a *deterministic* (only one way to encode) binary encoding used to translate X.509 certificates into bytes. All these encodings are often quite confusing to newcomers! I recap all of this in figure 9.8.

DER only encodes information as "here is an integer" or "this is a bytearray." Field names described in ASN.1 (like tbsCertificate) are lost after encoding. Decoding DER without the knowledge of the original ASN.1 description of what each field truly means is thus pointless. Handy command-line tools like OpenSSL allow you to decode and translate in human terms the content of a DER-encoded certificate. For example, if you download google.com's certificate, you can use the following code snippet to display its content in your terminal.

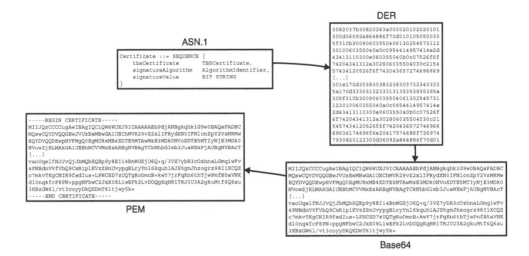

Figure 9.8   On the top left corner, an X.509 certificate is written using the ASN.1 notation. It is then transformed into bytes that can be signed via the DER encoding. As this is not text that can easily be copied around or recognized by humans, it is base64-encoded. The last touch wraps the base64 data with some handy contextual information using the PEM format.

```
$ openssl x509 -in google.pem -text
Certificate:
    Data:
        Version: 3 (0x2)
        Serial Number:
            0b:54:16:e9:65:17:27:d2:02:00:00:00:00:46:cf:76
        Signature Algorithm: sha256WithRSAEncryption
        Issuer: C = US, O = Google Trust Services, CN = GTS CA 1O1
        Validity
            Not Before: Oct  3 17:09:45 2019 GMT
            Not After : Dec 26 17:09:45 2019 GMT
        Subject: C = US, ST = California, L = Mountain View, O = Google LLC,
CN = *.google.com
        Subject Public Key Info:
            Public Key Algorithm: id-ecPublicKey
                Public-Key: (256 bit)
                pub:
                    04:74:25:79:7d:6f:77:e4:7e:af:fb:1a:eb:4d:41:
                    b5:27:10:4a:9e:b8:a2:8c:83:ee:d2:0f:12:7f:d1:
                    77:a7:0f:79:fe:4b:cb:b7:ed:c6:94:4a:b2:6d:40:
                    5c:31:68:18:b6:df:ba:35:e7:f3:7e:af:39:2d:5b:
                    43:2d:48:0a:54
                ASN1 OID: prime256v1
                NIST CURVE: P-256
[...]
```

Having said all of this, X.509 certificates are quite controversial. Validating X.509 certificates has been comically dubbed "the most dangerous code in the world" by a team of researchers in 2012. This is because DER encoding is a difficult protocol to parse correctly, and the complexity of X.509 certificates makes for many mistakes to be potentially devastating. For this reason, I don't recommend any modern application to use X.509 certificates unless it has to.

PRE-SHARED KEYS AND SESSION RESUMPTION IN TLS OR HOW TO AVOID KEY EXCHANGES

Key exchanges can be costly and are sometimes not needed. For example, you might have two machines that only connect to each other, and you might not want to have to deal with a public key infrastructure in order to secure their communications. TLS 1.3 offers a way to avoid this overhead with *pre-shared keys* (PSKs). A PSK is simply a secret that both the client and the server know, one that can be used to derive symmetric keys for the session.

In TLS 1.3, a PSK handshake works by having the client advertise in its ClientHello message that it supports a list of PSK identifiers. If the server recognizes one of the PSK IDs, it can say so in its response (the ServerHello message), and both can then avoid doing a key exchange (if they want to). By doing this, the authentication phase is skipped, making the Finished message at the end of the handshake important to prevent MITM attacks.

Client random and server random

An avid reader might have noticed that ephemeral public keys brought randomness to the session, and without them the symmetric session keys at the end of the hand-shake might end up always being the same. Using different symmetric keys for different sessions is extremely important as you do not want these sessions to be linked. Worse, because encrypted messages might be different between sessions, this could lead to nonce reuses and their catastrophic implications (see chapter 4).

To mitigate this, both the ClientHello and ServerHello messages have a `random` field, which is randomly generated for every new session (and often referred to as *client random* and *server random*). As these random values are used in the derivation of symmetric keys in TLS, it effectively randomizes the session symmetric keys for each new connection.

Another use case for PSKs is *session resumption*. Session resumption is about reusing secrets created from a previous session or connection. If you have already connected to google.com and have already verified their certificate chain, performed a key exchange, agreed on a shared secret, etc., why do this dance again a few minutes or hours later when you revisit? TLS 1.3 offers a way to generate a PSK after a handshake is successfully performed, which can be used in subsequent connections to avoid having to redo a full handshake.

If the server wants to offer this feature, it can send a New Session Ticket message at any time during the post-handshake phase. The server can create so-called *session tickets* in several ways. For example, the server can send an identifier, associated with the relevant information in a database. This is not the only way, but as this mechanism is quite complex and most of the time not necessary, I won't touch on more of it in this chapter. Next, let's see the easiest part of TLS—how communications eventually get encrypted.

9.2.2   *How TLS 1.3 encrypts application data*

Once a handshake takes place and symmetric keys derived, both the client and the server can send each other encrypted application data. This is not all: TLS also ensures that such messages cannot be replayed nor reordered! To do this, the nonce used by the authenticated encryption algorithm starts at a fixed value and is incremented for each new message. If a message is replayed or reordered, the nonce will be different from what is expected and decryption fails. When this happens, the connection is killed.

Hiding the plaintext's length

As you learned in chapter 4, encryption does not always hide the length of what is being encrypted. TLS 1.3 comes with *record padding* that you can configure to pad application data with a random number of zero bytes before encrypting it, effectively hiding the true length of the message. In spite of this, statistical attacks that remove the added noise may exist, and it is not straightforward to mitigate them. If you really require this security property, you should refer to the TLS 1.3 specification.

Starting with TLS 1.3, if a server decides to allow it, clients have the possibility to send encrypted data as part of their first series of messages, right after the ClientHello message. This means that browsers do not necessarily have to wait until the end of the handshake to start sending application data to the server. This mechanism is called *early data* or *0-RTT* (for zero round trip time). It can only be used with the combination of a PSK as it allows derivation of symmetric keys during the ClientHello message.

> **NOTE**   This feature was quite controversial during the development of the TLS 1.3 standard because a passive attacker can replay an observed ClientHello followed by the encrypted 0-RTT data. This is why 0-RTT must be used only with application data that can be replayed safely.

For the web, browsers treat every GET query as *idempotent*, meaning that GET queries should not change state on the server side and are only meant to retrieve data (unlike POST queries, for example). This is, of course, not always the case, and applications have been known to do whatever they want to do. For this reason, if you are confronted with the decision of using 0-RTT or not, it is simpler just to not use it.

9.3   *The state of the encrypted web today*

Today, standards are pushing for the deprecation of all versions of SSL and TLS that are not TLS versions 1.2 and TLS 1.3. Yet, due to legacy clients and servers, many libraries and applications continue to support older versions of the protocol (up to SSL version 3 sometimes!). This is not straightforward and, because of the number of vulnerabilities you need to defend against, many hard-to-implement mitigations must be maintained.

> **WARNING** Using TLS 1.3 (and TLS 1.2) is considered secure and best practice. Using any lower version means that you will need to consult experts and will have to figure out how to avoid known vulnerabilities.

By default, browsers still connect to web servers using HTTP, and websites still have to manually ask a CA to obtain a certificate. This means that with the current protocols, the web will never be fully encrypted, although some estimates show global web traffic to be 90% encrypted as of 2019.

The fact that, by default, your browser always uses an insecure connection is also an issue. Web servers nowadays usually redirect users accessing their pages using HTTP toward HTTPS. Web servers can also (and often do) tell browsers to use HTTPS for subsequent connections. This is done via an HTTPS response header called *HTTP Strict Transport Security* (HSTS). Yet, the first connection to a website is still unprotected (unless the user thinks about typing `https` in the address bar) and can be intercepted to remove the redirection to HTTPS.

In addition, other web protocols like *NTP* (to get the current time) and *DNS* (to obtain the IP behind a domain name) are currently largely unencrypted and vulnerable to MITM attacks. While there are research efforts to improve the status quo, these are attack vectors that one needs to be aware of.

There's another threat to TLS users—misbehaving CAs. What if, today, a CA decides to sign a certificate for your domain and a public key that it controls? If it can obtain a MITM position, it could start impersonating your website to your users. The obvious solution, if you control the client-side of the connection, is to either not use the web PKI (and rely on your own PKI) or to *pin* a specific certificate or public key.

Certificate or public key pinning are techniques where a server's certificate (usually rather a hash of it), or the public key, is directly hardcoded in the client code. If the server does not present the expected certificate, or the certificate does not contain the expected long-term public key, the client aborts the connection during the authentication phase of the handshake. This practice is often used in mobile applications, as they know exactly what the server's public key or certificate should look like (unlike browsers that have to connect to an infinite number of servers). Hardcoding certificates and public keys is not always possible, though, and two other mechanisms co-exist to deal with bad certificates:

- *Certificate revocation*—As the name indicates, this allows a CA to revoke a certificate and warn browsers about it.
- *Certificate monitoring*—This is a relatively new system that forces CAs to publicly log every certificate signed.

The story of certificate revocation has historically been bumpy. The first solution proposed was *Certificate Revocation Lists* (CRLs), which allowed CAs to maintain a list of revoked certificates, those that were no longer considered valid. The problem with CRLs is that they can grow quite large and one needs to constantly check them.

CRLs were deprecated in favor of *Online Certificate Status Protocol* (OCSP), which are simple web interfaces that you can query to see if a certificate is revoked or not. OCSP has its own share of problems: it requires CAs to have a highly available service that can answer to OCSP requests, it leaks web traffic information to the CAs, and browsers often decide to ignore OCSP requests that time out (to not disrupt the user's experience). The current solution is to augment OCSP with *OCSP stapling*: the website is in charge of querying the CA for a signed status of its certificate and attaches (staples) the response to its certificate during the TLS handshake. I review the three solutions in figure 9.9.

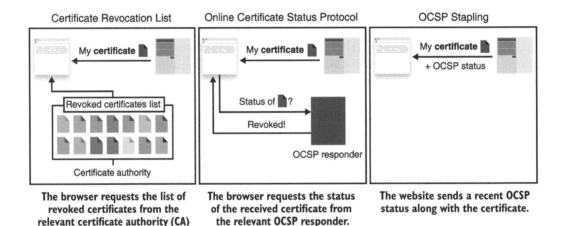

The browser requests the list of revoked certificates from the relevant certificate authority (CA) and checks if it contains the received certificate.

The browser requests the status of the received certificate from the relevant OCSP responder.

The website sends a recent OCSP status along with the certificate.

Figure 9.9   Certificate revocation on the web has had three popular solutions: Certificate Revocation Lists (CRLs), Online Certificate Status Protocol (OCSP), and OCSP stapling.

Certificate revocation might not seem to be a prime feature to support (especially for smaller systems compared to the World Wide Web) until a certificate gets compromised. Like a car seatbelt, certificate revocation is a security feature that is useless most of the time but can be a lifesaver in rare cases. This is what we in security call "defense in depth."

NOTE   For the web, certificate revocation has largely proven to be a good decision. In 2014, the Heartbleed bug turned out to be one of the most devastating bugs in the history of SSL and TLS. The most widely used SSL/TLS implementation (OpenSSL) was found to have a *buffer overread* bug (reading past the limit of an array), allowing anyone to send a specially crafted message to any OpenSSL server and receive a dump of its memory, often revealing its long-term private keys.

Yet, if a CA truly misbehaves, it can decide not to revoke malicious certificates or not to report them. The problem is that we are blindly trusting a non-negligible number of actors (the CAs) to do the right thing. To solve this issue at scale, *Certificate Transparency* was proposed in 2012 by Google. The idea behind a Certificate Transparency is to force CAs to add each certificate issued to a giant log of certificates for everyone to see. To do this, browsers like Chrome now reject certificates if they do not include proofs of inclusion in a public log. This transparency allows you to check if a certificate was wrongly issued for a domain you own (there should be no other certificates other than the ones you requested in the past).

Note that a Certificate Transparency relies on people monitoring logs for their own domain to catch bad certificates *after the fact*. CAs also have to react fast and revoke mis-issued certificates once detected. In extreme cases, browsers sometimes remove misbehaving CAs from their trust stores. Certificate Transparency is, thus, not as powerful as certificate or public key pinning, which mitigates CA misbehaviors.

9.4   *Other secure transport protocols*

You've now learned about TLS, which is the most popular protocol to encrypt communications. You're not done yet, though. TLS is not the only one in the secure transport protocol class. Many other protocols exist, and you might most likely be using them already. Yet, most of them are TLS-like protocols, customized to support a specific use case. This is the case, for example, with the following:

- *Secure Shell (SSH)*—The most widely used protocol and application to securely connect to a remote terminal on a different machine.
- *Wi-Fi Protected Access (WPA)*—The most popular protocol to connect devices to private network access points or to the internet.
- *IPSec*—One of the most popular virtual network protocols (VPNs) used to connect different private networks together. It is mostly used by companies to link different office networks. As its name indicates, it acts at the IP layer and is often found in routers, firewalls, and other network appliances. Another popular VPN is OpenVPN, which makes direct use of TLS.

All of these protocols typically reimplement the handshake/post-handshake paradigm and sprinkle some of their own flavors on it. Re-inventing the wheel is not without issues, as for example, several of the Wi-Fi protocols have been broken. To finish this chapter, I want to introduce you to the *Noise protocol framework*. Noise is a much more modern alternative to TLS.

9.5   *The Noise protocol framework:*
A modern alternative to TLS

TLS is now quite mature and considered a solid solution in most cases, due to the attention it gets. Yet, TLS adds a lot of overhead to applications that make use of it, due to historical reasons, backward compatibility constraints, and overall complexity.

Indeed, in many scenarios where you are in control of all the endpoints, you might not need all of the features that TLS has to offer. The next best solution is called the *Noise protocol framework.*

The Noise protocol framework removes the run-time complexity of TLS by avoiding all negotiation in the handshake. A client and a server running Noise follow a linear protocol that does not branch. Contrast this to TLS, which can take many different paths, depending on the information contained in the different handshake messages. What Noise does is that it pushes all the complexity to the design phase.

Developers who want to use the Noise protocol framework must decide what ad hoc instantiation of the framework they want their application to use. (This is why it is called a protocol *framework* and not a protocol.) As such, they must first decide what cryptographic algorithms will be used, what side of the connection is authenticated, if any pre-shared key is used, and so on. After that, the protocol is implemented and turns into a rigid series of messages, which can be a problem if one needs to update the protocol later while maintaining backward compatibility with devices that cannot be updated.

9.5.1   *The many handshakes of Noise*

The Noise protocol framework offers different *handshake patterns* that you can choose from. Handshake patterns typically come with a name that indicates what is going on. For example, the *IK* handshake pattern indicates that the client's public key is sent as part of the handshake (the first *I* stands for *immediate*), and that the server's public key is known to the client in advance (the *K* stands for *known*). Once a handshake pattern is chosen, applications making use of it will never attempt to perform any of the other possible handshake patterns. As opposed to TLS, this makes Noise a simple and linear protocol in practice.

In the rest of this section, I will use a handshake pattern called *NN* to explain how Noise works. It is simple enough for to explain, but insecure because of the two *N*'s indicating that no authentication takes place on both sides. In Noise's lingo, the pattern is written like this:

```
NN:
  -> e
  <- e, ee
```

Each line represents a message pattern, and the arrow indicates the direction of the message. Each message pattern is a succession of tokens (here, there are only two: e and ee) that dictates what both sides of the connection need to do:

- -> e—Means that the client must generate an ephemeral key pair and send the public key to the server. The server interprets this message differently: it must receive an ephemeral public key and store it.
- <- e, ee—Means that the server must generate an ephemeral key pair and send the public key to the client, then it must do a Diffie-Hellman (DH) key exchange

with the client's ephemeral (the first e) and its own ephemeral (the second e). On the other hand, the client must receive an ephemeral public key from the server, and use it to do a DH key exchange as well.

> **NOTE** Noise uses a combination of defined tokens in order to specify different types of handshakes. For example, the s token means a *static key* (another word for *long-term key*) as opposed to an ephemeral key, and the token es means that both participants must perform a DH key exchange using the client's ephemeral key and the server's static key.

There's more to it: at the end of each message pattern (-> e and <- e, ee), the sender also gets to transmit a payload. If a DH key exchange has happened previously, which is not the case in the first message pattern, -> e, the payload is encrypted and authenticated. At the end of the handshake both participants derive a set of symmetric keys and start encrypting communications similarly to TLS.

9.5.2 A handshake with Noise

One particularity of Noise is that it continuously authenticates its handshake transcript. To achieve this, both sides maintain two variables: a hash (h) and a chaining key (ck). Each handshake message sent or received is hashed with the previous h value. I illustrate this in figure 9.10.

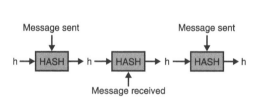

Figure 9.10 In the Noise protocol framework, each side of the connection keeps track of a digest h of all messages that have been sent and received during the handshake. When a message is sent and encrypted with an authenticated encryption with associated data (AEAD) algorithm, the current h value is used as associated data in order to authenticate the handshake up to this point.

At the end of each message pattern, a (potentially empty) payload is encrypted with an authenticated encryption with associated data (AEAD) algorithm (covered in chapter 4). When this happens, the h value is authenticated by the associated data field of the AEAD. This allows Noise to continuously verify that both sides of the connection are seeing the exact same series of messages and in the same order.

In addition, every time a DH key exchange happens (several can happen during a handshake), its output is fed along with the previous chaining key (ck) to HKDF, which derives a new chaining key and a new set of symmetric keys to use for authenticating and encrypting subsequent messages. I illustrate this in figure 9.11.

This makes Noise a simple protocol at run time; there is no branching and both sides of the connection simply do what they need to do. Libraries implementing Noise are also extremely simple and end up being a few hundred lines compared to hundreds of thousands of lines for TLS libraries. While Noise is more complex to use and

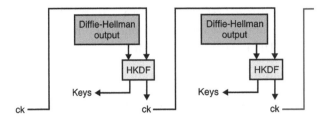

Figure 9.11   In the Noise protocol framework, each side of the connection keeps track of a *chaining key*, `ck`. This value is used to derive a new chaining key and new encryption keys to be used in the protocol every time a DH key exchange is performed.

will require developers who understand how Noise works to integrate it into an application, it is a strong alternative to TLS.

Summary

- Transport Layer Security (TLS) is a secure transport protocol to encrypt communications between machines. It was previously called Secure Sockets Layer (SSL) and is sometimes still referred to as SSL.
- TLS works on top of TCP and is used daily to protect connections between browsers, web servers, mobile applications, and so on.
- To protect sessions on top of User Datagram Protocol (UDP), TLS has a variant called Datagram Transport Layer Security (DTLS) that works with UDP.
- TLS and most other transport security protocols have a handshake phase (in which the secure negotiation is created) and a post-handshake phase (in which communications are encrypted using keys derived from the first phase).
- To avoid delegating too much trust to the web public key infrastructure, applications making use of TLS can use certificate and public key pinning to only allow secure communications with specific certificates or public keys.
- As a defense-in-depth measure, systems can implement certificate revocation (to remove compromised certificates) and monitoring (to detect compromised certificates or CAs).
- In order to avoid TLS complexity and size and whether you control both sides of the connection, you can use the Noise protocol framework.
- To use Noise, one must decide what variant of a handshake they want to use when designing the protocol. Due to this, it is much simpler and secure than TLS, but less flexible.

End-to-end encryption

Chapter 9 explained transport security via protocols like TLS and Noise. At the same time, I spent quite some time explaining where trust is rooted on the web: hundreds of certificate authorities (CAs) trusted by your browser and operating system. While not perfect, this system has worked so far for the web, which is a complex network of participants who know nothing of each other.

This problem of finding ways to trust others (and their public keys) and making it scale is at the center of real-world cryptography. A famous cryptographer was once heard saying, "Symmetric crypto is solved," to describe a field of research that had overstayed its welcome. And, for the most part, the statement was true. We seldom have issues encrypting communications, and we have strong confidence in the current encryption algorithms we use. When it comes to encryption, most engineering challenges are not about the algorithms themselves anymore, but about who Alice and Bob are and how to prove it.

Cryptography does not provide one solution to trust but many different ones that are more or less practical, depending on the context. In this chapter, I will survey some of the different techniques that people and applications use to create trust between users.

10.1 Why end-to-end encryption?

This chapter starts with a "why" instead of a "what." This is because end-to-end encryption is a concept more than a cryptographic protocol; it's a concept of securing communications between two (or more) participants across an adversarial path. I started this book with a simple example: Queen Alice wanted to send a message to Lord Bob without anyone in the middle being able to see it. Nowadays, many applications like email and messaging exist to connect users, and most of them seldom encrypt messages from soup to nuts.

You might ask, isn't TLS enough? In theory, it could be. You learned in chapter 9 that TLS is used in many places to secure communications. But end-to-end encryption is a concept that involves actual human beings. In contrast, TLS is most often used by systems that are "men-in-the-middle" by design (see figure 10.1). In these systems, TLS is only used to protect the communications between a central server and its users, allowing the server to see everything. Effectively, these MITM servers sit in between users, are necessary for the application to function, and are *trusted third parties* of the protocol. That is to say, we have to trust these parts of the system in order for the protocol to be considered secure (spoiler alert: that's not a great protocol).

In practice, much worse topologies exist. Communications between a user and a server can go through many network hops, and some of these hops might be machines

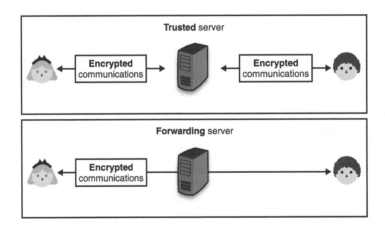

Figure 10.1   In most systems, a central server (top diagram) relays messages between users. A secure connection is usually established between a user and the central server, which can thus see all user messages. A protocol providing end-to-end encryption (bottom diagram) encrypts communications from one user up to its intended recipient, preventing any server in the middle from observing messages in cleartext.

that look at the traffic (often referred to as *middleboxes*). Even if traffic is encrypted, some middleboxes are set up to end the TLS connection (we say that they *terminate TLS*) and either forward the traffic in clear from that point on or start another TLS connection with the next hop. TLS termination is sometimes done for "good" reasons: to better filter traffic, balance connections geographically or within a data center, and so on. This adds to the attack surface as traffic is now visible in the clear in more places. Sometimes, TLS termination is done for "bad" reasons: to intercept, record, and spy on traffic.

In 2015, Lenovo was caught selling laptops with pre-installed custom CAs (covered in chapter 9) and software. The software was MITM'ing HTTPS connections using Lenovo's CAs and injecting ads into web pages. More concerning, large countries like China and Russia have been caught redirecting traffic on the internet, making it pass through their networks in order to intercept and observe connections. In 2013, Edward Snowden leaked a massive number of documents from NSA showing the abuses of many governments (not just the US) in spying on people's communications by intercepting the internet cables that link the world together.

Owning and seeing user data is also a liability for companies. As I've mentioned many times in this book, breaches and hacks happen way too often and can be devastating for the credibility of a company. From a legal standpoint, laws like the General Data Protection Regulation (GDPR) can end up costing organizations a lot of money. Government requests like the infamous National Security Letters (NSLs) that sometimes prevent companies and people involved from even mentioning that they have received the letters (so-called gag orders) can be seen as additional cost and stress to an organization, too, unless you have nothing much to share.

Bottom line, if you're using a popular online application, chances are that one or more governments already have access or have the ability to gain access to everything you wrote or uploaded there. Depending on an application's *threat model* (what the application wants to protect against) or the threat model of an application's most vulnerable users, end-to-end encryption plays a major role in ensuring confidentiality and privacy of end users.

This chapter covers different techniques and protocols that have been created in order to create trust between people. In particular, you will learn about how email encryption works today and how secure messaging is changing the landscape of end-to-end encrypted communications.

10.2   *A root of trust nowhere to be found*

One of the simplest scenarios for end-to-end encryption is the following: Alice wants to send an encrypted file to Bob over the internet. With all the cryptographic algorithms you learned about in the first chapters of this book, you can probably think of a way to do this. For example

1   Bob sends his public key to Alice.
2   Alice encrypts the file with Bob's public key and sends it to Bob.

Perhaps Alice and Bob can meet in real life or use another secure channel they already share to exchange the public key in the first message. If this is possible, we say that they have an *out-of-band* way of creating trust. This is not always the case, though. You can imagine me including my own public key in this book and asking you to use it to send me an encrypted message at some email address. Who says my copyeditor did not replace the public key with hers?

Same for Alice: how does she figure out if the public key she received truly is Bob's public key? It's possible that someone in the middle could have tampered with the first message. As you will see in this chapter, cryptography has no real answer to this issue of trust. Instead, it provides different solutions to help in different scenarios. The reason why there is no true solution is that we are trying to bridge reality (real human beings) with a theoretical cryptographic protocol.

> *This whole business of protecting public keys from tampering is the single most difficult problem in practical public key applications. It is the 'Achilles' heel' of public key cryptography, and a lot of software complexity is tied up in solving this one problem.*
>
> —Zimmermann et al. ("PGP User's Guide Volume I: Essential Topics," 1992)

Going back to our simple setup where Alice wants to send a file to Bob, and assuming that their untrusted connection is all they have, they have somewhat of an impossible trust issue at hand. Alice has no good way of knowing for sure what truly is Bob's public key. It's a chicken-and-egg type of scenario. Yet, let me point out that if no malicious *active* MITM attacker replaces Bob's public key in the first message, then the protocol is safe. Even if the messages are being passively recorded, it is too late for an attacker to come after the fact to decrypt the second message.

Of course, relying on the fact that your chances of being actively MITM'd are *not too high* is not the best way to undertake cryptography. We, unfortunately, often do not have a way to avoid this. For example, Google Chrome ships with a set of certificate authorities (CAs) that it chooses to trust, but how did you obtain Chrome in the first place? Perhaps you used the default browser of your operating system, which relies on its own set of CAs. But where did that come from? From the laptop you bought. But where did this laptop come from? As you can quickly see, it's "turtles all the way down." At some point, you will have to trust that something was done right.

A threat model typically chooses to stop addressing issues after a specific turtle and considers that any turtle further down is out-of-scope. This is why the rest of the chapter will assume that you have a secure way to obtain some *root of trust*. All systems based on cryptography work by relying on a root of trust, something that a protocol can build security on top of. A root of trust can be a secret or a public value that we start the protocol with or an out-of-band channel that we can use to obtain them.

10.3 The failure of encrypted email

Email was created as (and is still today) an *unencrypted* protocol. We can only blame a time where security was second thought. Email encryption started to become more than just an idea after the release of a tool called *Pretty Good Privacy* (PGP) in 1991. At the time, the creator of PGP, Phil Zimmermann, decided to release PGP in reaction to a bill that almost became law earlier in the same year. The bill would have allowed the US government to obtain all voice and text communications from any electronic communication company and manufacturer. In his 1994 essay "Why Do You Need PGP?", Philip Zimmermann ends with "PGP empowers people to take their privacy into their own hands. There's a growing social need for it. That's why I wrote it."

The protocol was finally standardized in RFC 2440 as *OpenPGP* in 1998 and caught traction with the release of the open source implementation, *GNU Privacy Guard* (GPG), around the same time. Today, GPG is still the main implementation, and people interchangeably use the terms GPG and PGP to pretty much mean the same thing.

10.3.1 PGP or GPG? And how does it work?

PGP, or OpenPGP, works by simply making use of hybrid encryption (covered in chapter 6). The details are in RFC 4880, the last version of OpenPGP, and can be simplified to the following steps:

1. The sender creates an email. At this point the email's content is compressed before it is encrypted.
2. The OpenPGP implementation generates a random symmetric key and symmetrically encrypts the email using the symmetric key.
3. The symmetric key is asymmetrically encrypted to each recipient's public key (using the techniques you learned in chapter 6).
4. All of the intended recipients' encrypted versions of the symmetric key are concatenated with the encrypted message. The email body is replaced with this blob of data and sent to all recipients.
5. To decrypt an email, a recipient uses their private key to decrypt the symmetric key, then decrypts the content of the email using the decrypted symmetric key.

Note that OpenPGP also defines how an email can be signed in order to authenticate the sender. To do this, the plaintext email's body is hashed and then signed using the sender's private key. The signature is then added to the message before being encrypted in step 2. Finally, so that the recipient can figure out what public key to use to verify the signature, the sender's public key is sent along the encrypted email in step 4. I illustrate the PGP flow in figure 10.2.

> **Exercise**
>
> Do you know why the email's content is compressed before it is encrypted and not after?

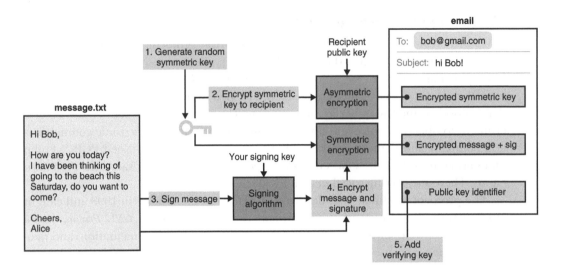

Figure 10.2   PGP's goal is to encrypt and sign messages. When integrated with email clients it does not care about hiding the subject or other metadata.

There's nothing inherently wrong with this design at first sight. It seems to prevent MITM attackers from seeing your email's content, although the subject and other email headers are not encrypted.

> **NOTE**   It is important to note that cryptography cannot always hide all metadata. In privacy-conscious applications, metadata is a big problem and can, in the worst cases, de-anonymize you! For example, in end-to-end encrypted protocols, you might not be able to decrypt messages between users, but you can probably tell what their IP addresses are, what the length of the messages they send and receive is, who they commonly talk to (their social graphs), and so on. A lot of engineering is put into hiding this type of metadata.

Yet, in the details, PGP is actually quite bad. The OpenPGP standard and its main implementation, GPG, make use of old algorithms, and backward compatibility prevents them from improving the situation. The most critical issue is that encryption is not authenticated, which means that anyone intercepting an email that hasn't been signed might be able to tamper with the encrypted content to some degree, depending on the exact encryption algorithm used. For this reason alone, I would not recommend anyone to use PGP today.

A surprising flaw of PGP comes from the fact that the signing and encryption operations are composed without care. In 2001, Don Davis pointed out that because of this naive composition of cryptographic algorithms, one can re-encrypt a signed email they received and send that to another recipient. This effectively allows Bob to send you the email Alice sent him as if you were the intended recipient!

If you're wondering, signing the ciphertext instead of the plaintext is still flawed as one could then simply remove the signature that comes with the ciphertext and add their own signature instead. In effect, Bob could pretend that he sent you an email that was actually coming from Alice. I recapitulate these two signing issues in figure 10.3.

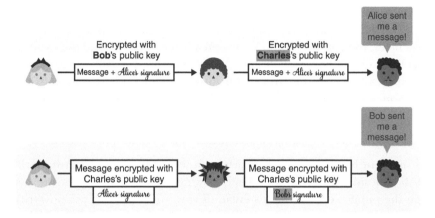

Figure 10.3 In the top diagram, Alice encrypts a message and signature over the message with Bob's public key. Bob can re-encrypt this message to Charles, who might believe that it was intended for him to begin with. This is the PGP flow. In the bottom diagram, this time Alice encrypts a message to Charles. She also signs the encrypted message instead of the plaintext content. Bob, who intercepts the encrypted message, can replace the signature with his own, fooling Charles into thinking that he wrote the content of the message.

Exercise
Can you think of an unambiguous way of signing a message?

The icing on the cake is that the algorithm does not provide *forward secrecy* by default. As a reminder, without forward secrecy, a compromise of your private key implies that all previous emails sent to you encrypted under that key can now be decrypted. You can still force forward secrecy by changing your PGP key, but this process is not straightforward (you can, for example, sign your new key with your older key) and most users just don't bother. To recap, remember that

- PGP uses old cryptographic algorithms.
- PGP does not have authenticated encryption and is, thus, not secure if used without signatures.
- Due to bad design, receiving a signed message doesn't necessarily mean we were the intended recipient.
- There is no forward secrecy by default.

10.3.2 Scaling trust between users with the web of trust

So why am I really talking about PGP here? Well, there is something interesting about PGP that I haven't talked about yet: how do you obtain and how can you trust other people's public keys? The answer is that in PGP, you build trust yourself!

OK, what does that mean? Imagine that you install GPG and decide that you want to encrypt some messages to your friends. To start, you must first find a secure way to obtain your friends' PGP public keys. Meeting them in real life is one sure way to do this. You meet, you copy their public keys on a piece of paper, and then you type those keys back into your laptop at home. Now, you can send your friends signed and encrypted messages with OpenPGP. But this is tedious. Do you have to do this for every person you want to email? Of course not. Let's take the following scenario:

- You have obtained Bob's public key in real life and, thus, you trust it.
- You do not have Mark's public key, but Bob does and he trusts it.

Take a moment here to think about what you could be doing to trust Mark's public key. Bob can simply sign Mark's key, showing you that he trusts the association between the public key and Mark's email. If you trust Bob, you can now trust Mark's public key and add it to your repertoire. This is the main idea behind PGP's concept of *decentralized* trust. It is called the *web of trust* (WOT) as figure 10.4 illustrates.

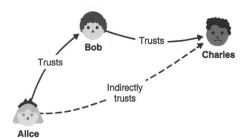

Figure 10.4   The web of trust (WOT) is the concept that users can transitively trust other users by relying on signatures. In this figure, we can see that Alice trusts Bob who trusts Charles. Alice can use Bob's signature over Charles's identity and public key to trust Charles as well.

You will sometimes see "key parties" at conferences, where people meet in real life and sign their respective public keys. But most of that is role-playing, and, in practice, few people rely on the WOT to enlarge their PGP circle.

10.3.3 Key discovery is a real issue

PGP did try another way to solve the issue of discovering public keys—*key registries*. The concept is pretty simple: publish your PGP public key and associated signatures from others that attest to your identity on some public list so that people can find it. In practice, this doesn't work as anyone can publish a key and associated signature purportedly matching your email. In fact, some attackers intentionally spoofed keys on key servers, although possibly more to cause havoc than to spy on emails. In some settings, we can relax our threat model and allow for a trusted authority to attest to identities and public keys. Think of a company managing their employees' emails, for example.

In 1995, the RSA company proposed *Secure/Multipurpose Internet Mail Extensions* (S/MIME) as an extension to the MIME format (which itself is an extension to the email standard) and as an alternative to PGP. S/MIME, standardized in RFC 5751, took an interesting departure from the WOT by using a public key infrastructure to build trust. That is pretty much the only conceptual difference that S/MIME has with PGP. As companies have processes in place to onboard and offboard employees, it makes sense for them to start using protocols like S/MIME in order to bootstrap trust in their internal email ecosystem.

It is important to note that both PGP and S/MIME are generally used over the *Simple Mail Transfer Protocol* (SMTP), which is the protocol used today for sending and receiving emails. PGP and S/MIME were also invented later, and for this reason, their integration with SMTP and email clients is far from perfect. For example, only the body of an email is encrypted not the subject or any of the other email headers. S/MIME, like PGP, is also quite an old protocol that uses outdated cryptography and practices. Like PGP, it does not offer authenticated encryption.

Recent research (Efail: "Breaking S/MIME and OpenPGP Email Encryption using Exfiltration Channels") on the integration of both protocols in email clients showed that most of them were vulnerable to *exfiltration attacks*, where an attacker who observes encrypted emails can retrieve the content by sending tampered versions to the recipients.

In the end, these shortcomings might not even matter, as most emails being sent and received in the world move along the global network unencrypted. PGP has proven to be quite difficult to use for nontechnical, as well as advanced, users who are required to understand the many subtleties and flows of PGP in order to encrypt their emails. For example, it's not uncommon to see users responding to an encrypted email without using encryption, quoting the whole thread in cleartext. On top of that, the poor (or nonexistent) support for PGP by popular email clients hasn't helped.

> *In the 1990s, I was excited about the future, and I dreamed of a world where everyone would install GPG. Now I'm still excited about the future, but I dream of a world where I can uninstall it.*
>
> —Moxie Marlinspike ("GPG and Me," 2015)

For these reasons, PGP has slowly been losing support (for example, Golang removed support for PGP from its standard library in 2019), while more and more real-world cryptography applications are aiming at replacing PGP and solving its usability problems. Today, it is hard to argue that email encryption will ever have the same level of success and adoption that, for example, HTTPS has.

> *If messages can be sent in plaintext, they will be sent in plaintext. Email is end-to-end unencrypted by default. The foundations of electronic mail are plaintext. All mainstream email software expects plaintext. In meaningful ways, the Internet email system is simply designed not to be encrypted.*
>
> —Thomas Ptacek ("Stop Using Encrypted Email," 2020)

10.3.4 *If not PGP, then what?*

I spent several pages talking about how a simple design like PGP can fail in a lot of different and surprising ways in practice. Yes, I would recommend against using PGP. While email encryption is still an unsolved problem, alternatives are being developed to replace different PGP use cases.

saltpack is a similar protocol and message format to PGP. It attempts to fix some of the PGP flaws I've talked about. In 2021, saltpack's main implementations are keybase (https://keybase.io) and keys.pub (https://keys.pub). Figure 10.5 illustrates the keys.pub tool.

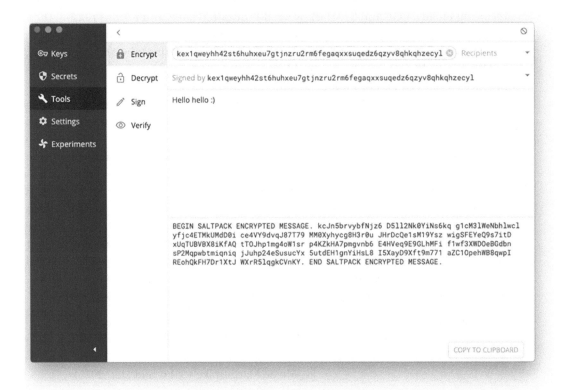

Figure 10.5   keys.pub is a native desktop application that implements the saltpack protocol. You can use it to import other people's public keys and to encrypt and sign messages to them.

These implementations have all moved away from WOT and allow users to broadcast their public keys on different social networks in order to instill their identity into their public keys (as figure 10.6 illustrates). PGP could obviously not have anticipated this key discovery mechanism as it predates the boom of social networks.

On the other hand, most secure communication nowadays is far from a one-time message, and the use of these tools is less and less relevant. In the next section, I talk

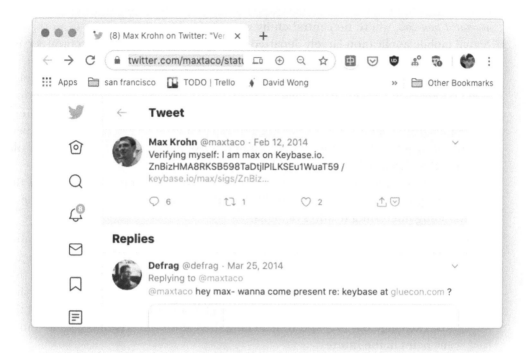

Figure 10.6   A keybase user broadcasting their public key on the Twitter social network. This allows other users to obtain additional proof that his identity is linked to a specific public key.

about *secure messaging*, one of the fields that aims to replace the communication aspect of PGP.

10.4   Secure messaging: A modern look at end-to-end encryption with Signal

In 2004, *Off-The-Record* (OTR) was introduced in a white paper titled "Off-the-Record Communication, or, Why Not To Use PGP." Unlike PGP or S/MIME, OTR is not used to encrypt emails but, instead, chat messages; specifically, it extends a chat protocol called the *Extensible Messaging and Presence Protocol* (XMPP).

One of the distinctive features of OTR was *deniability*—a claim that recipients of your messages and passive observers cannot use messages you sent them in a court of justice. Because messages you send are authenticated and encrypted symmetrically with a key your recipient shares with you, they could have easily forged these messages themselves. By contrast, with PGP, messages are signed and are, thus, the inverse of deniable—messages are *non-repudiable*. To my knowledge, none of these properties have actually been tested in court.

In 2010, the Signal mobile phone application (then called TextSecure) was released, making use of a newly created protocol called the *Signal protocol*. At the time, most secure communication protocols like PGP, S/MIME, and OTR were based on *federated protocols*, where no central entity was required for the network to work. The Signal mobile application largely departed from tradition by running a central service and offering a single official Signal client application.

While Signal prevents interoperability with other servers, the Signal protocol is open standard and has been adopted by many other messaging applications including Google Allo (now defunct), WhatsApp, Facebook Messenger, Skype, and many others. The Signal protocol is truly a success story, transparently being used by billions of people including journalists, targets of government surveillance, and even my 92-year-old grandmother (I swear I did not make her install it).

It is interesting to look at how Signal works because it attempts to fix many of the flaws that I previously mentioned with PGP. In this section, I will go over each one of the following interesting features of Signal:

- How can we do better than the WOT? Is there a way to upgrade the existing social graphs with end-to-end encryption? Signal's answer is to use a *trust on first use* (TOFU) approach. TOFU allows users to blindly trust other users the first time they communicate, relying on this first, insecure exchange to establish a long-lasting secure communication channel. Users are then free to check if the first exchange was MITM'd by matching their session secret out of band and at any point in the future.

- How can we upgrade PGP to obtain forward secrecy every time we start a conversation with someone? The first part of the Signal protocol is like most secure transport protocols: it's a key exchange, but a particular one called *Extended Triple Diffie-Hellman* (X3DH). More on that later.

- How can we upgrade PGP to obtain forward secrecy for every single message? This is important because conversations between users can span years, and a compromise at some point in time should not reveal years of communication. Signal addresses this with something called a *symmetric ratchet*.

- What if two users' session secrets are compromised at some point in time? Is that game over? Can we also recover from that? Signal introduces a new security property called *post-compromise security* (PCS) and addresses this with what is called a *Diffie-Hellman* (DH) *ratchet*.

Let's get started! First, we'll see how Signal's flavor of TOFU works.

10.4.1 More user-friendly than the WOT: Trust but verify

One of email encryption's biggest failures was its reliance on PGP and the WOT model to transform social graphs into *secure* social graphs. PGP's original design intended for people to meet in person to perform a *key-signing ceremony* (also called a *key-signing party*) to confirm one another's keys, but this was cumbersome and inconvenient in many and various ways. It is really rare today to see people signing each other's PGP keys.

The way most people use applications like PGP, OTR, Signal, and so on, is to blindly trust a key the first time they see it and to reject any future changes (as figure 10.7 illustrates). This way, only the first connection can be attacked (and this only by an active MITM attacker).

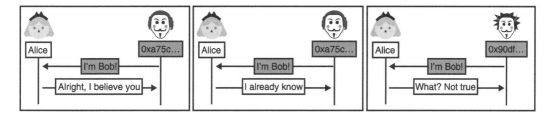

Figure 10.7   Trust on first use (TOFU) allows Alice to trust her first connection but not subsequent connections if they don't exhibit the same public key. TOFU is an easy mechanism to build trust when the chances that the first connection is actively MITM'd are low. The association between a public key and the identity (here Bob) can also be verified after the fact in a different channel.

While TOFU is not the best security model, it is often the best we have and has proven extremely useful. The Secure Shell (SSH) protocol, for example, is often used by trusting the server's public key during the initial connection (see figure 10.8) and by rejecting any future change.

Figure 10.8   SSH clients use trust on first use. The first time you connect to an SSH server (the left picture), you have the option to blindly trust the association between the SSH server and the public key displayed. If the public key of the SSH server later changes (right picture), your SSH client prevents you from connecting to it.

While TOFU systems trust the first key they see, they still allow the user to later verify that the key is, indeed, the right one and to catch any impersonation attempts. In real-world applications, users typically compare *fingerprints*, which are most often hexadecimal representations of public keys or hashes of public keys. This verification is, of course, done out of band. (If the SSH connection is compromised, then the verification is compromised as well.)

NOTE Of course, if users do not verify fingerprints, then they can be MITM'd without knowing it. But that is the kind of tradeoff that real-world applications have to deal with when bringing end-to-end encryption at scale. Indeed, the failure of the WOT shows that security-focused applications must keep usability in mind to get widely adopted.

In the Signal mobile application, a fingerprint between Alice and Bob is computed by:

1 Hashing Alice's identity key prefixed by her username (a phone number in Signal) and interpreting a truncation of that digest as a series of numbers
2 Doing the same for Bob
3 Displaying the concatenation of the two series of numbers to the user

Applications like Signal make use of *QR codes* to let users verify fingerprints more easily as these codes can be lengthy. Figure 10.9 illustrates this use case.

Figure 10.9 With Signal, you can verify the authenticity and confidentiality of the connection you have with a friend by using a different channel (just like in real life) to make sure the two fingerprints (Signal calls them *safety numbers*) of you and your friend match. This can be done more easily via the use of a QR code, which encodes this information in a scannable format. Signal also hashes the session secret instead of the two users' public keys, allowing them to verify one large string instead of two.

Next, let's see how the Signal protocol works under the hood—specifically, how Signal manages to be forward secure.

10.4.2 X3DH: the Signal protocol's handshake

Most secure messaging apps before Signal were *synchronous*. This meant that, for example, Alice wasn't able to start (or continue) an end-to-end encrypted conversation with Bob if Bob was not online. The Signal protocol, on the other hand, is *asynchronous* (like email), meaning that Alice can start (and continue) a conversation with people that are offline.

Remember that *forward secrecy* (covered in chapter 9) means that a compromise of keys does not compromise previous sessions and that forward secrecy usually means that the key exchanges are interactive because both sides have to generate ephemeral Diffie-Hellman (DH) key pairs. In this section, you will see how Signal uses *non-interactive* key exchanges (key exchanges where one side is potentially offline) that are still forward secure. OK, let's get going.

To start a conversation with Bob, Alice initiates a key exchange with him. Signal's key exchange, X3DH, combines three (or more) DH key exchanges into one. But before you learn how that works, you need to understand the three different types of DH keys that Signal uses:

- *Identity keys*—These are the long-term keys that represent the users. You can imagine that if Signal only used identity keys, then the scheme would be fairly similar to PGP, and there would be no forward secrecy.
- *One-time prekeys*—In order to add forward secrecy to the key exchange, even when the recipient of a new conversation is not online, Signal has users upload multiple *single-use* public keys. They are simply ephemeral keys that are uploaded in advance and are deleted after being used.
- *Signed prekeys*—We could stop here, but there's one edge case missing. Because the one-time prekeys that a user uploads can, at some point, be depleted, users also have to upload a *medium-term* public key that they sign: a signed prekey. This way, if no more one-time prekeys are available on the server under your username, someone can still use your signed prekey to add forward secrecy up to the last time you changed your signed prekey. This also means that you have to periodically rotate your signed prekey (for example, every week).

This is enough to preview what the flow of a conversation creation in Signal looks like. Figure 10.10 presents an overview.

Let's go over each of these steps in more depth. First, a user registers by sending the following:

- One identity key
- One signed prekey and its signature
- A defined number of one-time prekeys

Bob registers.

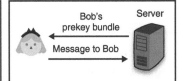

**Alice starts a
conversation with Bob.**

Bob connects to the server.

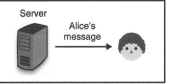

Bob publishes a long-term
identity key, a signed prekey,
and several one-time prekeys.

Alice requests a prekey bundle
for Bob. It is used to create a
message that the server can store.

Bob receives Alice's message.
He can decrypt it using Alice's
long-term public key and
Bob's private keys.

Figure 10.10   Signal's flow starts with a user registering with a number of public keys. If Alice wants to talk to Bob, she first retrieves Bob's public keys (called a *prekey bundle*), then she performs an X3DH key exchange with these keys and creates an initial message using the output of the key exchange. After receipt of the message, Bob can perform the same on his side to initialize and continue the conversation.

At this point, it is the responsibility of the user to periodically rotate the signed prekey and upload new one-time prekeys. I recap this flow in figure 10.11.

> **NOTE**   Signal makes use of the identity key to perform signatures over signed prekeys and key exchanges during the X3DH key exchange. While I've warned against using the same key for different purposes, Signal has deliberately analyzed that, in their case, there should be no issue. This does not mean that this would work in *your* case and with *your* key exchange algorithm. I would advise against using a key for different purposes in general.

After the step introduced in figure 10.11, Alice (going back to our example) would then start a conversation with Bob by retrieving:

- Bob's identity key.
- Bob's current signed prekey and its associated signature.
- If there are still some, one of Bob's one-time prekeys (the server then deletes the one-time prekey sent to Alice).

Alice can verify that the signature over the signed prekey is correct. She then performs the X3DH handshake with:

- All of the public keys from Bob
- An ephemeral key pair that she generates for the occasion in order to add forward secrecy
- Her own identity key

The output of X3DH is then used in a post-X3DH protocol, which is used to encrypt her messages to Bob (more on that in the next section). X3DH is composed of three

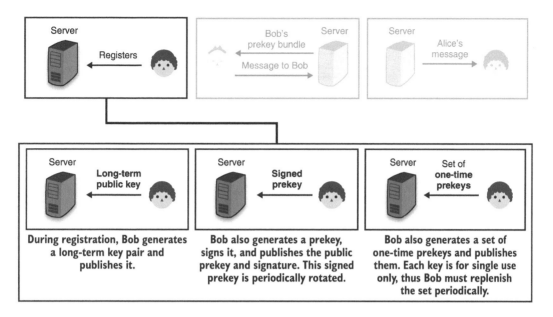

Figure 10.11 Building on figure 10.10, the first step is for a user to register by generating a number of DH key pairs and sending the public parts to a central server.

(optionally, four) DH key exchanges, grouped into one. The DH key exchanges are between:

1. The identity key of Alice and the signed prekey of Bob
2. The ephemeral key of Alice and the identity key of Bob
3. The ephemeral key of Alice and the signed prekey of Bob
4. If Bob still has a one-time prekey available, his one-time prekey and the ephemeral key of Alice

The output of X3DH is the concatenation of all of these DH key exchanges, passed to a key derivation function (KDF), which we covered in chapter 8. Different key exchanges provide different properties. The first and second ones are here for mutual authentication, while the last two are here for forward secrecy. All of this is analyzed in more depth in the X3DH specification (https://signal.org/docs/specifications/x3dh/), which I encourage you to read if you want to know more as it is well written. Figure 10.12 recaps this flow.

Alice now can send Bob her identity public key, the ephemeral public key she generated to start the conversation, and other relevant information (like which of Bob's one-time prekeys she used). Bob receives the message and can perform the exact same X3DH key exchange with the public keys contained in it. (For this reason, I skip illustrating the last step of this flow.) If Alice used one of Bob's one-time prekeys, Bob gets rid of it. What happens after X3DH is done? Let's look at that next.

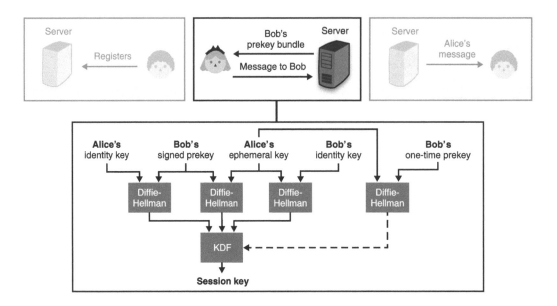

Figure 10.12   Building on figure 10.10, to send a message to Bob, Alice fetches a prekey bundle containing Bob's long-term key, Bob's signed prekey, and optionally, one of Bob's one-time prekeys. After performing different key exchanges with the different keys, all outputs are concatenated and passed into a KDF to produce an output used in a subsequent post-X3DH protocol to encrypt messages to Bob.

10.4.3 *Double Ratchet: Signal's post-handshake protocol*

The post-X3DH phase lives as long as the two users do not delete their conversations or lose any of their keys. For this reason, and because Signal was designed with SMS conversations in mind, where the time between two messages might be counted in months, Signal introduces *forward secrecy* at the message level. In this section, you will learn how this post-handshake protocol (called the *Double Ratchet*) works.

But first, imagine a simple post-X3DH protocol. Alice and Bob could have taken the output of X3DH as a session key and use it to encrypt messages between them as figure 10.13 illustrates.

Figure 10.13   Naively, a post-X3DH protocol could simply use the output of X3DH as a session key to encrypt messages between Alice and Bob.

We usually want to separate the keys used for different purposes though. What we can do is to use the output of X3DH as a *seed* (or *root key*, according to the Double Ratchet specification) to a KDF in order to derive two other keys. Alice can use one key to encrypt messages to Bob, and Bob can use the other key to encrypt messages to Alice. I illustrate this in figure 10.14.

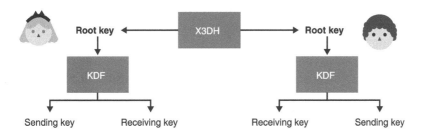

Figure 10.14 Building on figure 10.13, a better post-X3DH protocol would make use of a KDF with the output of the key exchanges to differentiate keys used to encrypt Bob's and Alice's messages. Here Alice's sending key is the same as Bob's receiving key, and Bob's sending key is the same as Alice's receiving key.

This approach could be enough, but Signal notes that texting sessions can last for years. This is unlike the TLS sessions of chapter 9 that are usually expected to be short-lived. Because of this, if at any point in time the session key is stolen, all previously recorded messages can be decrypted!

To fix this, Signal introduced what is called a *symmetric ratchet* (as figure 10.15 illustrates). The *sending key* is now renamed a *sending chain key* and is not used directly to

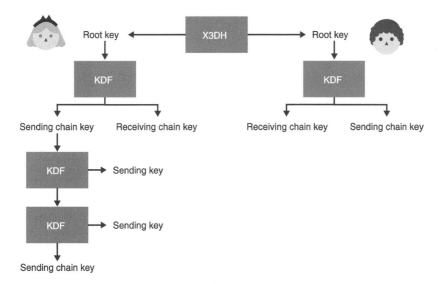

Figure 10.15 Building on figure 10.14, forward secrecy can be introduced in the post-X3DH protocol by *ratcheting* (passing into a KDF) a chain key every time one needs to send a message, and ratcheting another chain key every time one receives a message. Thus, the compromise of a sending or receiving chain key does not allow an attacker to recover previous ones.

encrypt messages. When sending a message, Alice continuously passes that sending chain key into a one-way function that produces the next sending chain key as well as the actual sending keys to encrypt her messages. Bob, on the other hand, will have to do the same but with the receiving chain key. Thus, by compromising one sending key or sending chain key, an attacker cannot recover previous keys. (And the same is true when receiving messages.)

Good. We now have forward secrecy baked into our protocol and at the message level. Every message sent and received protects all previously sent and received messages. Note that this is somewhat debatable as an attacker who compromises a key probably does this by compromising a user's phone, which will likely contain all previous messages in cleartext next to the key. Nevertheless, if both users in a conversation decide to delete previous messages (for example, by using Signal's "disappearing messages" feature), the forward secrecy property is achieved.

The Signal protocol has one last interesting thing I want to talk about: PCS (*post-compromise security*, also called *backward secrecy* as you learned in chapter 8). PCS is the idea that if your keys get compromised at some point, you can still manage to recover as the protocol will heal itself. Of course, if the attacker still has access to your device after a compromise, then this is for nothing.

PCS can work only by reintroducing new entropy that a nonpersistent compromise wouldn't have access to. The new entropy has to be the same for both peers. Signal's way of finding such entropy is by doing an ephemeral key exchange. To do this, the Signal protocol continuously performs key exchanges in what is called a *DH ratchet*. Every message sent by the protocol comes with the current ratchet public key as figure 10.16 illustrates.

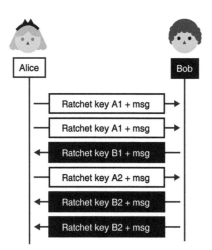

Figure 10.16   The Diffie-Hellman (DH) ratchet works by advertising a ratchet public key in every message sent. This ratchet public key can be the same as the previous one, or it can advertise a new ratchet public key if a participant decides to refresh theirs.

When Bob notices a new ratchet key from Alice, he must perform a new DH key exchange with Alice's new ratchet key and Bob's own ratchet key. The output can then be used with the symmetric ratchet to decrypt the messages received. I illustrate this in figure 10.17.

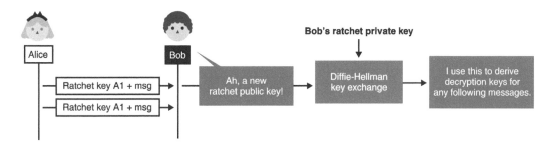

Figure 10.17   When receiving a new ratchet public key from Alice, Bob must do a key exchange with it and his own ratchet key to derive decryption keys. This is done with the symmetric ratchet. Alice's messages can then be decrypted.

Another thing that Bob must do when receiving a new ratchet key is to generate a new random ratchet key for himself. With his new ratchet key, he can perform another key exchange with Alice's new ratchet key, which he then uses to encrypt messages to her. This should look like figure 10.18.

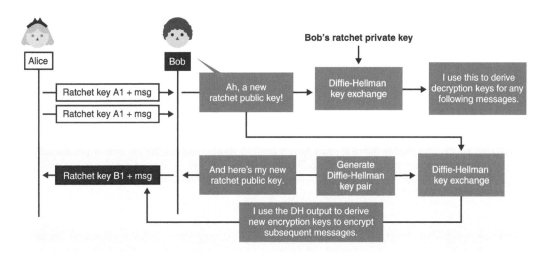

Figure 10.18   Building on figure 10.17, after receiving a new ratchet key Bob must also generate a new ratchet key for himself. This new ratchet key is used to derive encryption keys and is advertised to Alice in his next series of messages (up until he receives a new ratchet key from Alice).

This back and forth of key exchanges is mentioned as a "ping-pong" in the Double Ratchet specification:

This results in a "ping-pong" behavior as the parties take turns replacing ratchet key pairs. An eavesdropper who briefly compromises one of the parties might learn the value of a current ratchet private key, but that private key will eventually be replaced with an uncompromised one. At that point, the Diffie-Hellman calculation between ratchet key pairs will define a DH output unknown to the attacker.

—The Double Ratchet Algorithm

Finally, the combination of the DH ratchet and the symmetric ratchet is called the *Double Ratchet*. It's a bit dense to visualize as one diagram, but figure 10.19 attempts to do so.

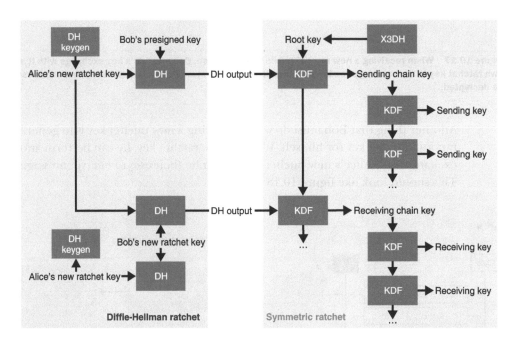

Figure 10.19   The Double Ratchet (from Alice's point of view) combines the DH ratchet (on the left) with the symmetric ratchet (on the right). This provides PCS as well as forward secrecy to the post-X3DH protocol. In the first message, Alice does not yet know Bob's ratchet key so she uses his presigned key instead.

I know this last diagram is quite dense, so I encourage you to take a look at Signal's specifications, which are published on https://signal.org/docs. They provide another well-written explanation of the protocol.

10.5 *The state of end-to-end encryption*

Today, most secure communications between users happen through secure messaging applications instead of encrypted emails. The Signal protocol has been the clear winner in its category, being adopted by many proprietary applications and also by open source and federated protocols like XMPP (via the OMEMO extension) and Matrix (a modern alternative to IRC). On the other hand, PGP and S/MIME are being dropped as published attacks have led to a loss of trust.

What if you want to write your own end-to-end encrypted messaging app? Unfortunately, a lot of what's being used in this field is ad hoc, and you would have to fill in many of the details yourself in order to obtain a full-featured and secure system. Signal has open sourced a lot of its code, but it lacks documentation and can be hard to use correctly. On the other hand, you might have better luck using a decentralized open source solution like Matrix, which might prove easier to integrate with. This is what the French government has done.

Before we close this chapter, there are also a number of open questions and active research problems that I want to talk about. For example

- Group messaging
- Support for multiple devices
- Better security assurances than TOFU

Let's start with the first item: *group messaging*. At this point, while implemented in different ways by different applications, group messaging is still being actively researched. For example, the Signal application has clients make sense of group chats. Servers only see pairs of users talking—never less, never more. This means that clients have to encrypt a group chat message to all of the group chat participants and send them individually. This is called *client-side fanout* and does not scale super well. It is also not too hard for the server to figure out what are the group members when it sees Alice, for example, sending several messages of the same length to Bob and Charles (figure 10.20).

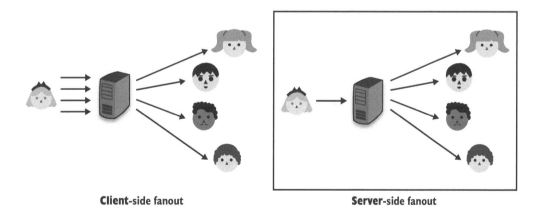

Client-side fanout   **Server**-side fanout

Figure 10.20   There are two ways to approach end-to-end encryption for group chats. A client-side fanout approach means that the client has to individually message each recipient using their already existing encrypted channel. This is a good approach to hide group membership from the server. A server-side fanout approach lets the server forward a message to each group chat participant. This is a good approach to reduce the number of messages sent from the client's perspective.

WhatsApp, on the other hand, uses a variant of the Signal protocol where the server is aware of group chat membership. This change allows a participant to send a single encrypted message to the server that, in turn, will have the responsibility to forward it to the group members. This is called *server-side fanout*.

Another problem of group chat is *scaling* to groups of a large memberset. For this, many players in the industry have recently gathered around a *Messaging Layer Security* (MLS) standard to tackle secure group messaging at scale. But there seems to be a lot of work to be done, and one can wonder, is there really any confidentiality in a group chat with more than a hundred participants?

> **NOTE**   This is still an area of active research, and different approaches come with different tradeoffs in security and usability. For example, in 2021, no group chat protocol seems to provide *transcript consistency*, a cryptographic property that ensures that all participants of a group chat see the same messages in the same order.

Support for multiple devices is either not a thing or implemented in various ways, most often by pretending that your different devices are different participants of a group chat. The TOFU model can make handling multiple devices quite complicated because having different identity keys per device can become a real key management problem. Imagine having to verify fingerprints for each of your devices and each of your friends' devices. Matrix, for example, has a user sign their own devices. Other users then can trust all your devices as one entity by verifying their associated signatures.

Finally, I mentioned that the TOFU model is also not the greatest as it is based on trusting a public key the first time we see it, and most users do not verify later that the fingerprints match. Can something be done about this? What if the server decides to impersonate Bob to Alice only? This is a problem that *Key Transparency* is trying to tackle. Key Transparency is a protocol proposed by Google, which is similar to the Certificate Transparency protocol that I talked about in chapter 9. There is also some research making use of the blockchain technology that I'll talk about in chapter 12 on cryptocurrencies.

Summary

- End-to-end encryption is about securing communications among real human beings. A protocol implementing end-to-end encryption is more resilient to vulnerabilities that can happen in servers sitting in between users and can greatly simplify legal requirements for companies.
- End-to-end encryption systems need a way to bootstrap trust between users. This trust can come from a public key that we already know or an out-of-band channel that we trust.
- PGP and S/MIME are the main protocols that are used to encrypt emails today, yet none of them are considered safe to use as they make use of old cryptographic

algorithms and practices. They also have poor integration with email clients that have been shown to be vulnerable to different attacks in practice.

- – PGP uses a web of trust (WOT) model, where users sign each other public keys in order to allow others to trust them.
- – S/MIME uses a public key infrastructure to build trust between participants. It is most commonly used in companies and universities.
- An alternative to PGP is saltpack, which fixes a number of issues while relying on social networks to discover other people's public keys.
- Emails will always have issues with encryption as the protocol was built without encryption in mind. On the other hand, modern messaging protocols and applications are considered better alternatives to encrypted emails as they are built with end-to-end encryption in mind.
  - – The Signal protocol is used by most messaging applications to secure end-to-end communications between users. Signal messenger, WhatsApp, Facebook Messenger, and Skype all advertise their use of the Signal protocol to secure messages.
  - – Other protocols, like Matrix, attempt to standardize federated protocols for end-to-end encrypted messaging. Federated protocols are open protocols that anyone can interoperate with (as opposed to centralized protocols that are limited to a single application).

User authentication

This chapter covers

- The difference between authenticating people and data
- User authentication to authenticate users based on passwords or keys
- User-aided authentication to secure connections between a user's devices

In the introduction of this book, I boiled cryptography down to two concepts: confidentiality and authentication. In real-world applications, confidentiality is (usually) the least of your problems; authentication is where most of the complexity arises. I know I've already talked a lot about authentication throughout this book, but it can be a confusing concept as it is used with different meanings in cryptography. For this reason, this chapter starts with an introduction of what authentication really is about. As usual with cryptography, no protocol is a panacea, and the rest of the chapter will teach you a large number of authentication protocols that are used in real-world applications.

11.1 A recap of authentication

By now, you have heard of authentication many times, so let's recap. You learned about

- Authentication in cryptographic primitives like message authentication codes (covered in chapter 3) and authenticated encryption (covered in chapter 4)
- Authentication in cryptographic protocols like TLS (covered in chapter 9) and Signal (covered in chapter 10), where one or more participants of a protocol can be authenticated

In the first case, authentication refers to the *authenticity* (or *integrity*) of messages. In the latter case, authentication refers to *proving who you are to someone else*. These are different concepts covered by the same word, which can be quite confusing! But both usages are correct as the Oxford English Dictionary (http://www.oed.com/) points out:

> *Authentication. The process or action of proving or showing something to be true, genuine, or valid.*

For this reason, you should think of authentication as a term used in cryptography to convey two different concepts depending on the context:

- *Message/payload authentication*—You're proving that a message is genuine and hasn't been modified since its creation. (For example, are these messages authenticated or can someone tamper with them?)
- *Origin/entity/identity authentication*—You're proving that an entity really is who they say they are. (For example, am I actually communicating with google.com?)

Bottom line: authentication is about proving that something is what it is supposed to be, and that something can be a person, a message, or something else. In this chapter, I will use the term *authentication* only to refer to identifying people or machines. In other words, *identity* authentication. By the way, you already saw a lot about this type of authentication:

- In chapter 9, on secure transport, you learned that machines can authenticate other machines at scale by using public key infrastructures (PKIs).
- In chapter 10, on end-to-end encryption, you learned about ways humans can authenticate one another at scale by using *trust on first use* (TOFU) (and verifying later) or by using the web of trust (WOT) techniques.

In this chapter, you will learn the following two other cases not previously mentioned. (I recap these in figure 11.1.)

- *User authentication*, or how machines authenticate humans—beep boop
- *User-aided authentication*, or how humans can help machines authenticate one another

Another aspect of identity authentication is the identity part. Indeed, how do we define someone like Alice in a cryptographic protocol? How can a machine authenticate you and me? There is, unfortunately (or fortunately), an inherent gap between flesh

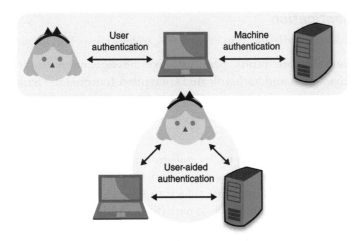

Figure 11.1   In this book, I talk about origin authentication in three types of scenarios. User authentication happens when a device authenticates a human being. Machine authentication happens when a machine authenticates another machine. User-aided authentication happens when a human is involved in a machine authenticating another machine.

and bits. To bridge reality and the digital world, we always assume that Alice is the only one who knows some secret data, and to prove her identity, she has to demonstrate knowledge of that secret data. For example, she could be sending her password or she could be signing a random challenge using the private key associated with her public key.

Alright, that's enough intro. If this section didn't make too much sense, the multitude of examples that are to follow will. Let's now first have a look at the many ways machines have found to authenticate us humans!

11.2   *User authentication, or the quest to get rid of passwords*

The first part of this chapter is about how machines authenticate humans or, in other words, *user authentication*. There are many ways to do this, and no solution is a panacea. But in most user authentication scenarios, we assume that

- The server is already authenticated.
- The user shares a secure connection with it.

For example, you can imagine that the server is authenticated to the user via the web public key infrastructure (PKI) and that the connection is secured via TLS (both covered in chapter 9). In a sense, most of this section is about upgrading a one-way authenticated connection to a mutually-authenticated connection as figure 11.2 illustrates.

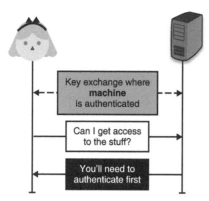

Figure 11.2 User authentication typically happens over a channel that is already secured but where only the server is authenticated. A typical example is when you browse the web using HTTPS and log into a web page using your credentials.

I have to warn you: user authentication is a vast land of broken promises. You must have used passwords many times to authenticate to different web pages, and your own experience probably resembles something like this:

1 You register with a username and password on a website.
2 You log into the website using your new credentials.
3 You change your password after recovering your account or because the website forces you to.
4 If you're out of luck, your password (or a hash of it) is leaked in a series of database breaches.

Sound familiar?

> **NOTE** I will ignore *password/account recovery* in this chapter, as they have little to do with cryptography. Just know that they are often tied to the way you first registered. For example, if you registered with the IT department at your workplace, then you'll probably have to go see them if you lose your password, and they can be the weakest link in your system if you are not careful. Indeed, if I can recover your account by calling a number and giving someone your birth date, then no amount of cool cryptography at login time will help.

A naive way to implement the previous user authentication flow is to store the user password at registration and then ask the user for it at login time. As mentioned in chapter 3, once successfully authenticated, a user is typically given a cookie that can be sent in every subsequent request instead of a username and password. But wait; if the server stores your password in cleartext, then any breach of its databases reveals your password to the attackers. These attackers will then be able to use it to log into any websites where you use the same password to register.

A better way to store passwords would be to use a *password hashing* algorithm like the standardized Argon2 you've learned about in chapter 2. This would effectively prevent a smash-and-grab type of attack on the database to leak your password, although an intruder that overextends their welcome would still be able to see your password every time you log in. Yet, a lot of websites and companies still store passwords in cleartext.

> **Exercise**
>
> Sometimes applications attempt to fix the issue of the server learning about the user passwords at registration by having the client hash (perhaps with a password hash) the password before sending it to the server. Can you determine if this really works?

Moreover, humans are naturally bad at passwords. We are usually most comfortable with small and easy-to-remember passwords. And, if possible, we would want to just reuse the same password everywhere.

81% of all hacking-related breaches leverage stolen or weak passwords.

—Verizon Data Breach Report (2017)

The problem of weak passwords and password reuse has led to many silly and annoying design patterns that attempt to force users to take passwords more seriously. For example, some websites require you to use special characters in your passwords or force you to change your password every 6 months, and so on. Furthermore, many protocols attempt to "fix" passwords or to get rid of them altogether. Every year, new security experts seem to think that the concept of "password" is dead. Yet, it is still the most widely used user authentication mechanism.

So here you have it, passwords are probably here to stay. Yet, there exist many protocols that improve or replace passwords. Let's take a look at those.

11.2.1 One password to rule them all: Single sign-on (SSO) and password managers

OK, password reuse is bad, so what can we do about it? Naively, users could use different passwords for different websites, but there are two problems with this approach:

- Users are bad at creating many different passwords.
- The mental load required to remember multiple passwords is impractical.

To alleviate these concerns, two solutions have been widely adopted:

- *Single sign-on* (SSO)—The idea of SSO is to allow users to connect to many different services by proving that they own the account of a single service. This way, the user only has to remember the password associated with that one service in order to be able to connect to many services. Think "connect with Facebook" type of buttons as figure 11.3 illustrates.
- *Password managers*—The previous SSO approach is convenient if the different services you use all support it, but this is obviously not scalable for scenarios like the web. A better approach in these extreme cases is to improve the clients as opposed to attempting to fix the issue on the server side. Nowadays, modern browsers have built-in password managers that can suggest complex passwords when you register on new websites, and they can remember all of your passwords as long as you remember one master password.

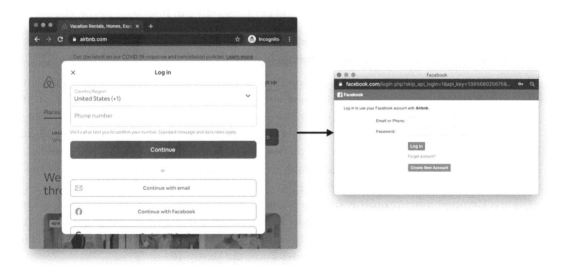

Figure 11.3 An example of single sign-on (SSO) on the web. By having an account on Facebook or Google, a user can connect to new services (in this example, Airbnb) without having to think about a new password.

The concept of SSO is not new in the enterprise world, but its success with normal end-users is relatively recent. Today, two protocols are the main competitors when it comes to setting up SSO:

- *Security Assertion Markup Language 2.0* (SAML)—A protocol using the Extensible Markup Language (XML) encoding.
- *OpenID Connect* (OIDC)—An extension to the OAuth 2.0 (RFC 6749) authorization protocol using the JavaScript Object Notation (JSON) encoding.

SAML is still widely used, mostly in an enterprise setting, but it is (at this point) a legacy protocol. OIDC, on the other hand, can be seen everywhere on web and mobile applications. You most likely already used it!

Authentication protocols are often considered hard to get right. OAuth2, the protocol OIDC relies on, is notorious for being easy to misuse. On the other hand, OIDC is well specified (see https://openid.net). Make sure that you follow the standards and that you look at best practices, as this can save you from a lot of trouble.

> **NOTE**   Here's another example of a pretty large company deciding *not* to follow this advice. In May 2020, the Sign-in with Apple SSO flow that took a departure from OIDC was found to be vulnerable. Anyone could have obtained a valid ID token for any Apple account just by querying Apple's servers.

SSO is great for users as it reduces the number of passwords they have to manage, but it does not remove passwords altogether. The user still has to use passwords to connect to OIDC providers. So next, let's see how cryptography can help hide passwords.

11.2.2 Don't want to see their passwords? Use an asymmetric password-authenticated key exchange

The previous section surveyed solutions that attempt to simplify identity management for users, allowing them to authenticate to multiple services using only one account linked to a single service. While protocols like OIDC are great, as they effectively decrease the number of passwords users have to manage, they don't change the fact that some service still needs to see the user's password in cleartext. Even if the password is stored after password hashing it, it is still sent in clear every time the user registers, changes their password, or logs in.

Cryptographic protocols called *asymmetric (or augmented) password-authenticated key exchanges* (PAKEs) attempt to provide user authentication without having users ever communicate their passwords directly to the server. This contrasts with *symmetric or balanced PAKEs* protocols, where both sides know the password.

The most popular asymmetric PAKE at the moment is the *Secure Remote Password* (SRP) protocol, which was standardized for the first time in 2000 in RFC 2944 ("Telnet Authentication: SRP") and later integrated into TLS via RFC 5054 ("Using the Secure Remote Password (SRP) Protocol for TLS Authentication"). It is quite an old protocol and has a number of flaws. For example, if the registration flow is intercepted by a MITM attacker, the attacker would then be able to impersonate and log in as the victim. It also does not play well with modern protocols as it cannot be instantiated on elliptic curves, and worse, it is incompatible with TLS 1.3.

Since the invention of SRP, many asymmetric PAKEs have been proposed and standardized. In the summer of 2019, the Crypto Forum Research Group (CFRG) of the IETF started a PAKE selection process with the goal to pick one algorithm to standardize for each category of PAKEs: symmetric/balanced and asymmetric/augmented. In March 2020, the CFRG announced the end of the PAKE selection process, selecting

- *CPace*—The recommended symmetric/balanced PAKE, invented by Haase and Benoît Labrique
- *OPAQUE*—The recommended asymmetric/augmented PAKE, invented by Stanislaw Jarecki, Hugo Krawczyk, and Jiayu Xu

In this section, I talk about OPAQUE, which (in early 2021) is still in the process of being standardized. In the second section of this chapter, you will learn more about symmetric PAKEs and CPace.

OPAQUE takes its name from the homonym *O-PAKE*, where *O* refers to the term *oblivious*. This is because OPAQUE relies on a cryptographic primitive that I have not yet mentioned in this book: an *oblivious pseudorandom function* (OPRF).

OBLIVIOUS PSEUDORANDOM FUNCTIONS (OPRFs)

OPRFs are a two-participant protocol that mimics the PRFs that you learned about in chapter 3. As a reminder, a PRF is somewhat equivalent to what one would expect of a MAC: it takes a key and an input and gives you a totally random output of a fixed length.

> **NOTE** The term *oblivious* in cryptography generally refers to protocols where one party computes a cryptographic operation without knowing the input provided by another party.

Here is how an OPRF works at a high level:

1. Alice wants to compute a PRF over an input but wants the input to remain secret. She "blinds" her input with a random value (called a *blinding factor*) and sends this to Bob.
2. Bob runs the OPRFs on this blinded value with his secret key, but the output is still blinded so it's useless for Bob. Bob then sends this back to Alice.
3. Alice finally "unblinds" the result using the same blinding factor she previously used to obtain the real output.

It is important to note that every time Alice wants to go over this protocol, she has to create a different blinding factor. But no matter what blinding factor she uses, as long as she uses the same input, she will always obtain the same result. I illustrate this in figure 11.4.

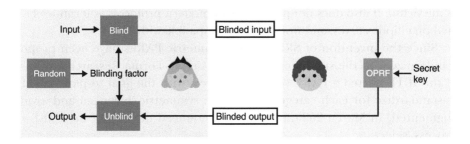

Figure 11.4   An oblivious PRF (OPRF) is a construction that allows one party to compute a PRF over the input of another party without learning that input. To do this, Alice first generates a random blinding factor, then blinds her input with that before sending it to Bob. Bob uses his secret key to compute the PRF over the blinded value, then sends the blinded output to Alice who can unblind it. The result does not depend on the value of the blinding factor.

Here's an example of an OPRF protocol implemented in a group where the discrete logarithm problem is hard:

1 Alice converts her input to a group element x.
2 Alice generates a random blinding factor r.
3 Alice blinds her input by computing $blinded\_input = x^r$.
4 Alice sends the $blinded\_input$ to Bob.
5 Bob computes $blinded\_output = blinded\_input^k$, where k is the secret key.
6 Bob sends the result back to Alice.
7 Alice can then unblind the produced result by computing $output = blinded\_output^{1/r} = x^k$, where $1/r$ is the inverse of r.

How OPAQUE uses this interesting construction is the whole trick behind the asymmetric PAKE.

THE OPAQUE ASYMMETRIC PAKE, HOW DOES IT WORK?

The idea is that we want a client, let's say Alice, to be able to do an authenticated key exchange with some server. We also assume that Alice already knows the server's public key or already has a way to authenticate it (the server could be an HTTPS website and, thus, Alice can use the web PKI). Let's see how we could build this to progressively understand how OPAQUE works.

First idea: use public key cryptography to authenticate Alice's side of the connection. If Alice owns a long-term key pair and the server knows the public key, she can simply use her private key to perform a mutually authenticated key exchange with the server, or she can sign a challenge given by the server. Unfortunately, an asymmetric private key is too long, and Alice can only remember her password. She could store a key pair on her current device, but she also wants to be able to log in from another device later.

Second idea: Alice can derive the asymmetric private key from her password, using a password-based key derivation function (KDF) like Argon2, which you learned about in chapter 2 and chapter 8. Alice's public key could then be stored on the server. If we want to avoid someone testing a password against the whole database in case of a database breach, we can have the server supply each user with a different salt that they have to use with the password-based KDF.

This is pretty good already, but there's one attack that OPAQUE wants to discard: a *precomputation attack*. I can try to log in as you, receive your salt, and then precompute a huge number of asymmetric private keys and their associated public keys *offline*. The day the database is compromised, I can quickly see if I can find your public key and the associated password in my huge list of precomputed asymmetric public keys.

Third idea: This is where the main trick of OPAQUE comes in! We can use the OPRF protocol with Alice's password in order to derive the asymmetric private key. If the server uses a different key per user, that's as good as having salts (attacks can only target one user at a time). This way, an attacker that wants to precompute asymmetric private keys based on guesses of our password has to perform *online* queries (preventing offline brute force attacks). Online queries are good because they can be rate-limited (preventing more than 10 sign-in attempts per hour, for example) in order to prevent these kinds of online brute force attacks.

Note that this is actually not how OPAQUE works: instead of having the user derive an asymmetric private key, OPAQUE has the user derive a symmetric key. The symmetric key is then used to encrypt a backup of your asymmetric key pair and some additional data (which can include the server's public key, for example). I illustrate the algorithm in figure 11.5.

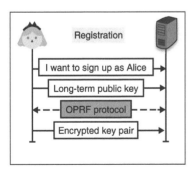 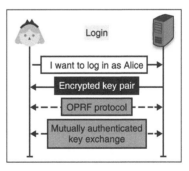

Figure 11.5 **To register to a server using OPAQUE, Alice generates a long-term key pair and sends her public key to the server, which stores it and associates it with Alice's identity. She then uses the OPRF protocol to obtain a strong symmetric key from her password and sends an encrypted backup of her key pair to the server. To log in, she obtains her encrypted key pair from the server, then performs the OPRF protocol with her password to obtain a symmetric key capable of decrypting her key pair. All that's left is to perform a mutually authenticated key exchange (or possibly sign a challenge) with this key.**

Before going to the next section, let's review what you've learned here. Figure 11.6 illustrates this.

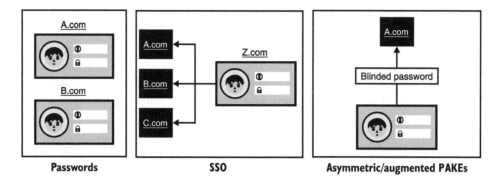

Passwords   **SSO**   **Asymmetric/augmented PAKEs**

Figure 11.6 Passwords are a handy way to authenticate users as they live in someone's head and can be used on any device. On the other hand, users have trouble creating strong passwords, and because users tend to reuse passwords across websites, password breaches can be damaging. SSO allows you to connect to many services using one (or a few) service(s), while asymmetric (or augmented) password-authenticated key exchanges allow you to authenticate without the server ever learning your real password.

11.2.3 One-time passwords aren't really passwords: Going passwordless with symmetric keys

Alright, so far so good. You've learned about different protocols that applications can leverage to authenticate users with passwords. But, as you've heard, passwords are also not that great. They are vulnerable to brute force attacks, tend to be reused, stolen, and so on. What is available to us if we can afford to avoid using passwords?

And the answer is—keys! And, as you know, there are two types of keys in cryptography and both types can be useful:

- Symmetric keys
- Asymmetric keys

This section goes over solutions that are based on symmetric keys, while the next section goes over solutions based on asymmetric keys. Let's imagine that Alice registers with a service using a symmetric key (often generated by the server and communicated to you via a QR code). A naive way to authenticate Alice later would be to simply ask her to send the symmetric key. This is, of course, not great, as a compromise of her secret would give an attacker unlimited access to her account. Instead, Alice can derive what are called *one-time passwords* (OTPs) from the symmetric key and send those in place of the longer-term symmetric key. Even though an OTP is not a password, the name indicates that an OTP can be used in place of a password and warns that it should never be reused.

The idea behind OTP-based user authentication is straightforward: your security comes from the knowledge of a (usually) 16- to 32-byte uniformly random symmetric key instead of a low-entropy password. This symmetric key allows you to generate OTPs on demand as figure 11.7 illustrates.

Figure 11.7   A one-time password (OTP) algorithm allows you to create as many one-time passwords as you want from a symmetric key and some additional data. The additional data is different, depending on the OTP algorithm.

OTP-based authentication is most often implemented in mobile applications (see figure 11.8 for a popular example) or in security keys (a small device that you can plug in the USB port of your computer). There are two main schemes that one can use to produce OTPs:

- The HMAC-based one-time password (HOTP) algorithm, standardized in RFC 4226, which is an OTP algorithm where the additional data is a counter.
- The time-based one-time password (TOTP) algorithm, standardized in RFC 6238, which is an OTP algorithm where the additional data is the time.

Most applications nowadays use TOTP because HOTP requires both the client and the server to store a state (a counter). Storing a state can lead to issues if one side falls out of synchrony and cannot produce (or validate) legitimate OTPs anymore.

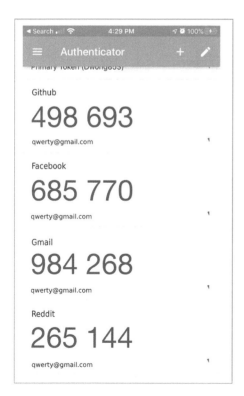

Figure 11.8   A screenshot of the Google Authenticator mobile app. The application allows you to store unique per-application symmetric keys that can then be used with the TOTP scheme to generate 6-digit, one-time passwords (OTPs), valid only for 30 seconds.

In most cases, this is how TOTP works:

- *When registering, the service communicates a symmetric key to the user (perhaps using a QR code).* The user then adds this key to a TOTP application.

- *When logging in, the user can use the TOTP application to compute a one-time password.* This is done by computing *HMAC(symmetric_key, time)*, where *time* represents the current time (rounded to the minute in order to make a one-time password valid for 60 seconds). Then

  a The TOTP application displays to the user the derived one-time password, truncated and in a human-readable base (for example, reduced to 6 characters in base 10 to make it all digits).

  b The user either copies or types the one-time password into the relevant application.

  c The application retrieves the user's associated symmetric key and computes the one-time password in the same way as the user did. If the result matches the received one-time password, the user is successfully authenticated.

Of course, the comparison between the user's OTP and the one computed on the server must be done in constant time. This is similar to MAC authentication tag checks. I demonstrate this flow in figure 11.9.

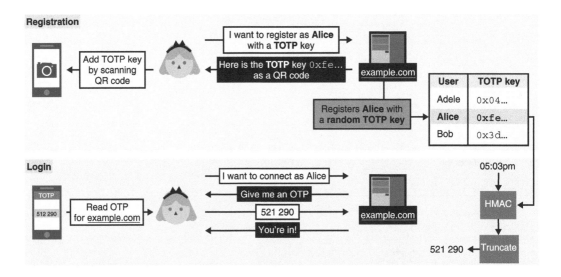

Figure 11.9   Alice registers with example.com using TOTP as authentication. She imports a symmetric key from the website into her TOTP application. Later, she can ask the application to compute a one-time password for example.com and use it to authenticate with the website. The website, example.com, fetches the symmetric key associated with Alice and computes the one-time password using HMAC and the current time. The website next compares the one-time password in constant time with what Alice sends.

This TOTP-based authentication flow is not ideal, though. There are a number of things that could be improved, for example:

- The authentication can be faked by the server as it also owns the symmetric key.
- You can be social-engineered out of your one-time password.

For this reason, symmetric keys are yet another *not-perfect replacement* for passwords. Next, let's see how using asymmetric keys can address these downsides.

Phishing

Phishing (or *social engineering*) is an attack that does not target vulnerabilities in the software but rather vulnerabilities in human beings. Imagine that an application requires you to enter a one-time password to authenticate. What an attacker could do in this case is to attempt to log in the application as you, and when prompted with a one-time password request, give you a call to ask you for a valid one (pretending that they work for the application).

You're telling me you wouldn't fall for it! Good social engineers are superior at spinning believable stories and fabricating a sense of urgency that would make the best of us spill the beans. If you think about it, all the protocols that we've talked about previously are vulnerable to these types of attacks.

11.2.4 Replacing passwords with asymmetric keys

Now that we're dealing with public key cryptography, there's more than one way we can use asymmetric keys to authenticate to a server. We can

- Use our asymmetric key inside a key exchange to authenticate our side of the connection
- Use our asymmetric key in an already secured connection with an authenticated server

Let's take a look at each method.

MUTUAL AUTHENTICATION IN KEY EXCHANGES

You've already heard about the first method: using the asymmetric key inside a key exchange. In chapter 9, I mentioned that a TLS server can request the client to use a *certificate* as part of the handshake. Often, companies will provision their employees' devices with a unique per-employee certificate that allows them to authenticate to internal services. Figure 11.10 provides an idea of what it looks like from a user's perspective.

Client-side certificates are pretty straightforward. For example, in TLS 1.3, a server can request the client to authenticate during the handshake by sending a `Certificate-Request` message. The client then responds by sending its certificate in a `Certificate` message, followed by a signature of all messages sent and received in a `Certificate-Verify` message (which includes the ephemeral public key used in the key exchange).

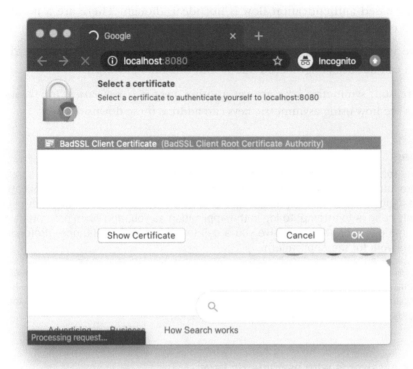

Figure 11.10 A page prompting the user's browser for a client certificate. The user can then select which certificate to use from a list of locally installed certificates. In the TLS handshake, the client certificate's key is then used to sign the handshake transcript, including the client's ephemeral public key, which is used as part of the handshake.

The client is authenticated if the server can recognize the certificate and successfully verify the client's signature. Another example is the Secure Shell (SSH) protocol, which also has the client sign parts of the handshake with a public key known to the server.

Note that signing is not the only way to authenticate with public key cryptography during the handshake phase. The Noise protocol framework (covered in chapter 9 as well) has several handshake patterns that enable client-side authentication using just DH key exchanges.

POST-HANDSHAKE USER AUTHENTICATION WITH FIDO2

The second type of authentication with asymmetric keys uses an already *secure* connection where only the server is authenticated. To do this, a server can simply ask the client to sign a *random* challenge. This way, replay attacks are prevented.

One interesting standard in this space is the *Fast IDentity Online 2* (FIDO2). FIDO2 is an open standard that defines how to use asymmetric keys to authenticate users. The standard specifically targets phishing attacks, and for this reason, FIDO2 is made to work only with *hardware authenticators.* Hardware authenticators are simply physical

Roaming authenticator   **Built-in** authenticator

Figure 11.11 Two types of hardware authenticators that can be used with FIDO2: (on the left) a Yubikey, a roaming authenticator, and (on the right) TouchID, a built-in authenticator.

components that can generate and store signing keys and can sign arbitrary challenges. FIDO2 is split into two specifications (figure 11.11):

- *Client to Authenticator Protocol* (CTAP)—CTAP specifies a protocol that *roaming authenticators* and *clients* can use to communicate with one another. Roaming authenticators are hardware authenticators that are external to your main device. A client in the CTAP specification is defined as the software that wants to query these authenticators as part of an authentication protocol. Thus, a client can be an operating system, a native application like a browser, and so on.
- *Web Authentication* (WebAuthn)—WebAuthn is the protocol that web browsers and web applications can use to authenticate users with hardware authenticators. It, thus, must be implemented by browsers to support authenticators. If you are building a web application and want to support user authentication via hardware authenticators, WebAuthn is what you need to use.

WebAuthn allows websites to use not only roaming authenticators but also *platform* authenticators. Platform authenticators are built-in authenticators provided by a device. They are implemented differently by various platforms and are often protected by biometrics (for example, a fingerprint reader, facial recognition, and so on).

We are now ending the first part of this chapter. But before I do this, figure 11.12 recaps the nonpassword-based authentication protocols I've talked about.

Now that you have learned about many different techniques and protocols that exist to either improve passwords or replace them with stronger cryptographic solutions, you might be wondering, which one you should use? Each of these solutions have their own caveats, and no single solution might do it. If not, combine multiple ones! This idea is called *multi-factor authentication* (MFA). Actually, chances are that you might have already used OTPs or FIDO2 as a second authentication factor in addition to (and not in place of) passwords.

This concludes the first half of this chapter on authenticating users. Next, let's take a look at how humans can help devices to authenticate each other.

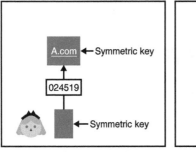 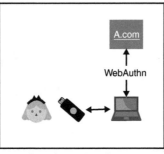 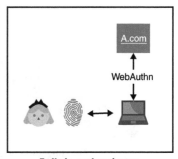

Figure 11.12 To authenticate without using a password, applications can allow users to either use symmetric keys via OTP-based protocols or use asymmetric keys via the FIDO2 standard. FIDO2 supports different types of authenticators, roaming authenticators (via the CTAP standard) or built-in authenticators.

11.3 User-aided authentication: Pairing devices using some human help

Humans help machines to authenticate one another every day—EVERY DAY! You've done it by pairing your wireless headphones with your phone, or by pairing your phone with your car, or by connecting some device to your home WiFi, and so on. And as with any pairing, what's underneath is most probably a key exchange.

The authentication protocols in the last section took place in already secured channels (perhaps with TLS), where the server was authenticated. Most of this section, in contrast, attempts to provide a secure channel to two devices that do not know how to authenticate each other. In that sense, what you'll learn in this section is how humans can help to *upgrade* an insecure connection into a *mutually authenticated connection.* For this reason, the techniques you will learn about next should be reminiscent of some of the trust establishment techniques in the end-to-end protocols of chapter 10, except that there, two humans were trying to authenticate themselves to each other.

Nowadays, the most common insecure connections that you will run into, those that do not go through the internet, are protocols based on short-range radio frequencies like Bluetooth, WiFi, and Near Field Communication (NFC). NFC is what you use to pay with your phone or with your bank card's "contactless" payment. Devices that use these communication protocols tend to range from low-power electronics to full-featured computers. This already sets some constraints for us:

- *The device you are trying to connect to might not offer a screen to display a key or a way to manually enter a key.* We call this *provisioning* the device. For example, most wireless audio headsets today only have a few buttons and that's it.
- *As a human is part of the validation process, having to type or compare long strings is often deemed impractical and not user-friendly.* For this reason, many protocols attempt to shorten security-related strings to 4- or 6-digit PINs.

> **Exercise**
> Imagine a protocol where you have to enter the correct 4-digit PIN to securely connect to a device. What are the chances to pick a correct PIN by just guessing?

You're probably thinking back at some of your device-pairing experiences and realizing now that a lot of them *just worked*. For example

1. You pushed a button on a device.
2. The device entered pairing mode.
3. You then tried to find the device in the Bluetooth list on your phone.
4. After clicking the device icon, it successfully paired the device with your phone.

If you read chapter 10, this should remind you of *trust on first use* (TOFU). Except, this time we also have a few more cards in our hand:

- *Proximity*—Both devices have to be close to each other, especially if using the NFC protocol.
- *Time*—Device pairing is often time-constrained. It is common that if, for example, in a 30-second window, the pairing is not successful, the process must be manually restarted.

Unlike TOFU though, these real-life scenarios usually do not allow you to validate after the fact that you've connected to the right device. This is not ideal, and one should strive for better security if possible.

> **NOTE** By the way, this is what the Bluetooth core specification actually calls the TOFU-like protocol: "Just Works." I should mention that all built-in Bluetooth security protocols are currently broken due to many attacks, including the latest KNOB attack released in 2019 (https://knobattack.com). The techniques surveyed in this chapter are nonetheless secure—if designed and implemented correctly.

What's next in our toolkit? This is what we will see in this section: ways for a human to help devices to authenticate themselves. Spoiler alert:

- You'll see that cryptographic keys are always the most secure approach but not necessarily the most user-friendly.
- You'll learn about symmetric PAKEs and how you can input the same password on two devices to connect them securely.
- You'll learn about protocols based on short authenticated strings (SAS), which authenticate a key exchange after the fact by having you compare and match two short strings displayed by the two devices.

Let's get started!

11.3.1 *Pre-shared keys*

Naively, the first approach to connect a user to a device would be to reuse protocols that you learned about in chapter 9 or chapter 10 (for example, TLS or Noise) and to provision both devices with a symmetric shared secret or, better, with long-term public keys in order to provide forward secrecy to future sessions. This means that you need two things for each device to learn the other device's public key:

- You need a way to *export* a public key from its device.
- You need a way for a device to *import* public keys.

As we will see, this is not always straightforward or user-friendly. But remember, we have a human in the mix who can observe and (maybe) play with the two devices. This is unlike other scenarios that we've seen before, and we can use this to our advantage!

> *The Authentication Problem - One of the main issues in cryptography is the establishment of a secure peer-to-peer (or group) communication over an insecure channel. With no assumption, such as availability of an extra secure channel, this task is impossible. However, given some assumption(s), there exists many ways to set up a secure communication.*
>
> —Sylvain Pasini ("Secure Communication Using Authenticated Channels," 2009)

All the protocols that follow are based on the fact that you (the human in charge) have an additional *out-of-band* channel. This allows you to securely communicate some information. The addition of this out-of-band channel can be modeled as the two devices having access to two types of channels (illustrated in figure 11.13):

- *An insecure channel*—Think about a Bluetooth or a WiFi connection with a device. By default, the user has no way of authenticating the device and can, thus, be MITM'd.
- *An authenticated channel*—Think about a screen on a device. The channel provides integrity/authenticity of the information communicated but poor confidentiality (someone could be looking over your shoulder).

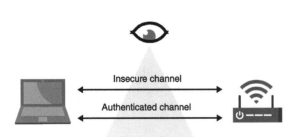

Figure 11.13   User-aided authentication protocols that allow a human to pair two devices are modeled with two types of channels between the devices: an insecure channel (for example, NFC, Bluetooth, WiFi, and so on), which we assume is adversary-controlled, and an authenticated channel (for example, real life), which does not provide confidentiality but can be used to exchange relatively small amounts of information.

Insecure channel

Authenticated channel

As this out-of-band channel provides poor confidentiality, we usually do not want to use it to export secrets but rather public data. For example, a public key or some digest can be displayed by the device's screen. But once you have exported a public key, you still need the other device to import it. For example, if the key is a QR code, then the other device might be able to scan it, or if the key is encoded in a human-readable format, then the user could manually type it in the other device using a keyboard. Once both devices are provisioned with each other's public keys, you can use any protocols I've mentioned in chapter 9 to perform a mutually authenticated key exchange with the two devices.

What I want you to get from this section is that using cryptographic keys in your protocol is always the most secure way to achieve something, but it is not always the most user-friendly way. Yet, real-world cryptography is full of compromise and trade-offs, and this is why the next two schemes not only exist, but are the most popular ways to authenticate devices.

Let's see how we can use *passwords* to bootstrap a mutually authenticated key exchange in cases where you cannot export and import long public keys. Then we'll look at how short *authenticated strings* can help in situations where importing data into one or both of the devices is just not possible.

11.3.2 *Symmetric password-authenticated key exchanges with CPace*

The previous solution is what you should be doing, if possible, as it relies on strong asymmetric keys as a root of trust. Yet, it turns out that, in practice, typing a long string representing a key with some cumbersome keypad manually is tedious. What about these dear passwords? They are so much shorter and, thus, easier to deal with. We love passwords right? Perhaps we don't, but users do, and real-world cryptography is full of compromises. So be it.

In the section on asymmetric password-authenticated key exchanges, I mentioned that a symmetric (or balanced) version exists where two peers who know a common password can perform a mutually authenticated key exchange. This is exactly what we need.

Composable Password Authenticated Connection Establishment (CPace) was proposed in 2008 by Björn Haase and Benoît Labrique and was chosen in early 2020 as the official recommendation of the CFRG (the Crypto Forum Research Group). The algorithm is currently being standardized as an RFC. The protocol, simplified, looks something like the following (figure 11.14 illustrates the algorithm):

- Two devices derive a generator (for some predetermined cyclic group) based on a common password.
- Then the two devices use this generator to perform an ephemeral DH key exchange on top of it.

The devil is in the details, of course, and as a modern specification, CPace targets elliptic curve "gotchas" and defines when one must verify that a received point is in

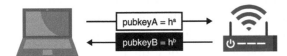

h = derive_group_element(**password**, metadata)

pubkeyA = hᵃ
pubkeyB = hᵇ

Figure 11.14 **The CPace PAKE works by having the two devices create a generator based on a password and then use it to perform as a base for the usual ephemeral DH key exchange.**

the right group (due to the trendy Curve25519 that, unfortunately, does not span a prime group). It also specifies how one derives a generator based on a password when in an elliptic curve group (using so-called hash-to-curve algorithms) and how to do this (using not only a common password but also an unique session ID and some additional contextual metadata like peer IP addresses and so on).

These steps are important as both peers must derive a generator h in a way that prevents them from knowing its discrete logarithm x such that $g^x = h$. Finally, the session key is derived from the DH key exchange output, the transcript (the ephemeral public keys), and the unique session ID.

Intuitively, you can see that impersonating one of the peers and sending a group element as part of the handshake means that you're sending a public key, which is associated with a private key you cannot know. This means that you can never perform a DH key exchange if you don't know the password. The transcript just looks like a normal DH key exchange, and so, no luck there (as long as DH is secure).

11.3.3 *Was my key exchange MITM'd? Just check a short authenticated string (SAS)*

In the second part of this chapter, you saw different protocols that allow two devices to be paired with the help of a human. Yet, I mentioned that some devices are so constrained that they cannot make use of those protocols. Let's take a look at a scheme that is used when the two devices cannot import keys but can display some limited amount of data to the user (perhaps via a screen, or by turning on some LEDs, or by emitting some sounds, and so on).

First, remember that in chapter 10, you learned about authenticating a session *post-handshake* (after the key exchange) using *fingerprints* (hashes of the transcript). We could use something like this as we have our out-of-band channel to communicate these fingerprints. If the user can successfully compare and match the fingerprints obtained from both devices, then the user knows that the key exchange was not MITM'd.

The problem with fingerprints is that they are long byte strings (typically, 32 bytes long), which might be hard to display to the user. They are also cumbersome to compare. But for device pairing, we can use much shorter byte strings because we are doing the comparison in real time! We call these *short authenticated strings* (SAS). SAS are used a lot, notably by Bluetooth, due to them being quite user-friendly (see figure 11.15 for an example).

There aren't any standards for SAS-based schemes, but most protocols (including Bluetooth's numeric comparison) implement a variant of the *Manually Authenticated*

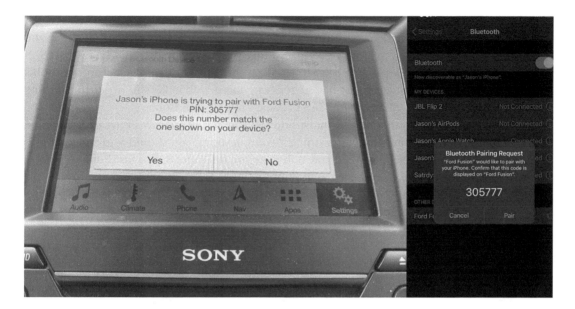

Figure 11.15 To pair a phone with a car via Bluetooth, the Numeric Comparison mode can be used to generate a short authenticated string (SAS) of the secure connection negotiated between the two devices. Unfortunately, as I stated earlier in this chapter, due to the KNOB attack, Bluetooth's security protocols are currently broken (as of 2021). If you control both devices, you need to implement your own SAS protocol.

Diffie-Hellman (MA-DH). MA-DH is a simple key exchange with an additional trick that makes it hard for an attacker to actively man-in-the-middle the protocol. You might ask, why not just create SAS from truncating a fingerprint? Why the need for a trick?

An SAS is typically a 6-digit number, which can be obtained by truncating a hash of the transcript to less than 20 bits and converting that to numbers in base 10. SAS is, thus, dangerously small, which makes it much easier for an attacker to obtain a *second pre-image* on the truncated hash. In figure 11.16, we take the example of two devices

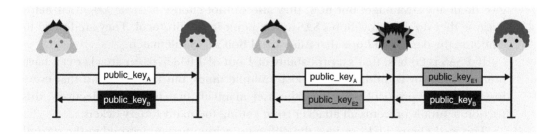

Figure 11.16 A typical unauthenticated key exchange (on the left) can be intercepted by an active MITM attacker (on the right), who can then substitute the public keys of both Alice and Bob. A MITM attack is successful if both Alice and Bob generate the same short authenticated string. That is, if *hash*(*public_key*$_A$ || *public_key*$_{E2}$) and *hash*(*public_key*$_{E1}$ || *public_key*$_B$) match.

(although we use Alice and Bob) performing an unauthenticated key exchange. An active MITM attacker can substitute Alice's public key with their own public key in the first message. Once the attacker receives Bob's public key, they would know what SAS Bob will compute (a truncated hash based on the attacker's public key and on Bob's public key). The attacker just has to generate many public keys in order to find one ($public\_key_{E2}$) that will make the SAS of Alice's match with Bob's.

Generating a public key to make both SAS match is actually pretty easy. Imagine that the SAS is 20 bits, then after only 2^{20} computations, you should find a second preimage that will have both Alice and Bob generate the same SAS. This should be pretty instant to compute, even on a cheap phone.

The trick behind SAS-based key exchanges is to prevent the attacker from being able to choose their second public key, forcing the two SAS to match. To do this, Alice simply sends a *commitment* of her public key before seeing Bob's public key (as in figure 11.17).

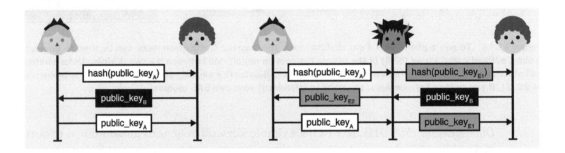

Figure 11.17   The diagram on the left pictures a secure SAS-based protocol in which Alice first sends a commitment of her public key. She then only reveals her public key after receiving Bob's public key. As she committed to it, she cannot freely choose her key pair based on Bob's key. If the exchange is actively MITM'd (diagram on the right), the attacker cannot choose either key pairs to force Alice's and Bob's SAS to match.

As with the previous insecure scheme, the attacker's choice of $public\_key_{E1}$ does not give them any advantage. But now, they also cannot choose a $public\_key_{E2}$ that helps because they do not know Bob's SAS at this point in the protocol. They are forced to "shoot in the dark" and hope that Alice's and Bob's SAS will match.

If a SAS is 20 bits, that's a probability of 1 out of 1,048,576. An attacker can have more chances by running the protocol multiple times, but keep in mind that every instance of the protocol must have the user manually match a SAS. Effectively, this friction naturally prevents an attacker from getting too many lottery tickets.

This is it! Figure 11.18 reviews the different techniques you learned in the second part of this chapter. I'll see you in chapter 12.

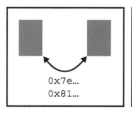 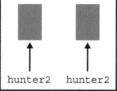 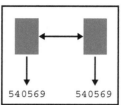

Exchange public keys out-of-band, then perform key exchange

Enter the same password on both devices

Verify the session key out-of-band

Figure 11.18 You've learned about three techniques to pair two devices: (1) a user can either help the devices obtain each other's public keys so that they can perform a key exchange; (2) a user can enter the same password on two devices so that they can perform a symmetric password-authenticated key exchange; or (3) a user can verify a fingerprint of the key exchange after the fact to confirm that no MITM attacker intercepted the pairing.

Story time

Interestingly, as I was writing chapter 10 on end-to-end encryption, I started looking into how users of the Matrix end-to-end encrypted chat protocol authenticated their communications. In order to make the verification more user-friendly, Matrix created their own variant of a SAS-based protocol. Unfortunately, it hashed the shared secret of an X25519 key exchange and did not include the public keys being exchanged in the hash.

In chapter 5, I mentioned that it is important to validate X25519 public keys. Matrix did not, and this allowed a MITM attacker to send incorrect public keys to users, forcing them to end up with the same predictable shared secret and, in turn, the same SAS. This completely broke the end-to-end encryption claim of the protocol and ended up being quickly fixed by Matrix.

Summary

- User authentication protocols (protocols for machines to authenticate humans) often take place over secure connections, where only the machine (server) has been authenticated. In this sense, it upgrades a one-way authenticated connection to a mutually authenticated connection.
- User authentication protocols make heavy use of passwords. Passwords have proven to be a somewhat practical solution and one that is widely accepted by users. But they have also led to many issues due to poor password hygiene, low entropy, and password database breaches.
- There are two ways to avoid having users carry multiple passwords (and possibly reuse passwords):
  - *Password managers*—Tools that users can use to generate and manage strong passwords for every application they use.

- *Single sign-on* (SSO)—A federated protocol that allows a user to use one account to register and log into other services.

- A solution for servers to avoid learning about and storing their users' passwords is to use an asymmetric password-authenticated key exchange (asymmetric PAKE). An asymmetric PAKE (like OPAQUE) allows users to authenticate to a known server using passwords but without having to actually reveal their passwords to the server.

- Solutions to avoid passwords altogether are for users to use symmetric keys via one-time passwords (OTP) algorithms or to use asymmetric keys via standards like FIDO2.

- User-aided authentication protocols often take place over insecure connections (WiFi, Bluetooth, NFC) and help two devices to authenticate each other. To secure connections in these scenarios, user-aided protocols assume that the two participants possess an additional authenticated (but not confidential) channel that they can use (for example, a screen on the device).

- Exporting a device's public key to another device could allow strongly mutually authenticated key exchanges to happen. These flows are, unfortunately, not user-friendly and sometimes not possible due to device constraints (no way to export or import keys, for example).

- Symmetric password-authenticated key exchanges (symmetric PAKEs) like CPace can decrease the burden for the user to import a long public key by only having to manually input a password in a device. Symmetric PAKEs are already used by most people to connect to their home WiFi, for example.

- Protocols based on short authenticated strings (SAS) can provide security for devices that cannot import keys or passwords but are able to display a short string after a key exchange takes place. This short string must be the same on both devices in order to ensure that the unauthenticated key exchange was not actively MITM'd.

Crypto as
in cryptocurrency?

This chapter covers

- Consensus protocols and how they make cryptocurrencies possible
- The different types of cryptocurrencies
- How the Bitcoin and Diem cryptocurrencies work in practice

Can cryptography be the basis for a new financial system? This is what cryptocurrencies have been trying to answer since at least 2008, when Bitcoin was proposed by Satoshi Nakamoto (who to this day has yet to reveal his or their identity). Before that, the term *crypto* was always used in reference to the field of cryptography. But since the creation of Bitcoin, I have seen its meaning quickly change, now being used to refer to cryptocurrencies as well. Cryptocurrency enthusiasts, in turn, have become more and more interested in learning about cryptography. This makes sense as cryptography is at the core of cryptocurrencies.

What's a *cryptocurrency*? It is two things:

- *It's a digital currency.* Simply put, it allows people to transact currency electronically. Sometimes a currency backed by a government is used (like the US dollar), and sometimes a made-up currency is used (like the bitcoin). You likely already use digital currencies—whenever you send money to someone on the internet or use a checking account, you are using a digital currency! Indeed, you don't need to send cash by mail anymore, and most money transactions today are just updates of rows in databases.

- *It's a currency that relies heavily on cryptography to avoid using a trusted third party and to provide transparency.* In a cryptocurrency, there is no central authority that one has to blindly trust, like a government or a bank. We often talk about this property as *decentralization* (as in "we are decentralizing trust"). Thus, as you will see in this chapter, cryptocurrencies are designed to tolerate a certain number of malicious actors, and to allow people to verify that they function properly.

Cryptocurrencies are relatively new as the first experiment to be successful was Bitcoin, proposed in 2008 in the middle of a global financial crisis. While the crisis started in the US, it quickly spread to the rest of the world, eroding the trust people had in financial systems and providing a platform for more transparent initiatives like Bitcoin. At that time, many people started to realize that the status quo for financial transactions was inefficient, expensive to maintain, and opaque to most people. The rest is history, and I believe this book is the first book on cryptography to include a chapter on cryptocurrencies.

12.1 A gentle introduction to Byzantine fault-tolerant (BFT) consensus algorithms

Imagine that you want to create a new digital currency. It's actually not too involved to build something that works. You could set up a database on a dedicated server, which would be used to track users and their balances. With this, you provide an interface for people to query their balance or let them send payments, which would reduce their balance in the database and increase the balance in another row. Initially, you could also randomly attribute some of your made-up currency to your friends so that they can start transferring money to your system. But such a simple system has a number of flaws.

12.1.1 A problem of resilience: Distributed protocols to the rescue

The system we just saw is a *single point of failure*. If you lose electricity, your users won't be able to use the system. Worse, if some natural disaster unexpectedly destroys your server, everybody might permanently lose their balance. To tackle this issue, there exist well-known techniques that you can use to provide more resilience to your system. The field of *distributed systems* studies such techniques.

In this case, the usual solution used by most large applications is to replicate the content of your database in (somewhat) real time to other backup servers. These servers can then be distributed across various geographical locations, ready to be used as backup or even to take over if your main server goes down. This is called *high availability*. You now have a *distributed database*.

For large systems that serve lots of queries, it is often the case that these backup databases are not just sitting on the sideline waiting to be useful, but instead, they are used to provide reads to the state. It is difficult to have more than one database accept writes and updates because then you could have conflicts (the same way two people editing the same document can be dangerous). Thus, you often want a single database to act as *leader* and order all writes and updates to the database, while others can be used to read the state.

Replication of database content can be slow, and it is expected that some of your databases will lag behind the leader until they catch up. This is especially true if they are situated further away in the world or are experiencing network delays due to some reason. This lag becomes a problem when the replicated databases are used to read the state. (Imagine that you see a different account balance than your friend because you are both querying different servers.)

In these cases, applications are often written in order to tolerate this lag. This is referred to as *eventual consistency* because eventually the states of the databases become consistent. (Stronger consistency models exist, but they are usually slow and impractical.) Such systems also have other problems: if the main database crashes, which one gets to become the main database? Another problem is if the backup databases were lagging behind when the main database crashed, will we lose some of the latest changes?

This is where stronger algorithms—*consensus algorithms* (also referred to as *log replication, state machine replication,* or *atomic broadcasts*)—come into play when you need the whole system to agree (or come to a consensus) on some decision. Imagine that a consensus algorithm solves the solution of a group of people trying to agree on what pizza to order. It's easy to see what the majority wants if everyone is in the same room. But if everyone is communicating through the network where messages can be delayed, dropped, intercepted, and modified, then a more complicated protocol is required.

Let's see how consensus can be used to answer the previous two questions. The first question of which database gets to take over in the case of a crash is called *leader election,*

and a consensus algorithm is often used to determine which will become the next leader. The second question is often solved by viewing database changes in two different steps: *pending* and *committed*. Changes to the database state are always pending at first and can only be set as committed if enough of the databases agree to commit it (this is where a consensus protocol can be used as well). Once committed, the update to the state cannot be lost easily as most of the database participanting have committed the change.

Some well-known consensus algorithms include Paxos (published by Lamport in 1989) and its subsequent simplification, Raft, (published by Ongaro and Ousterhout in 2013). You can use these algorithms in most distributed database systems to solve different problems. (For a great interactive explanation on Raft, check out https://thesecretlivesofdata.com/raft.)

12.1.2 *A problem of trust? Decentralization helps*

Distributed systems (from an operational perspective) provide a resilient alternative to systems that act as a single point of failure. The consensus algorithms used by most distributed database systems do not tolerate faults well. As soon as machines start crashing, or start misbehaving due to hardware faults, or start getting disconnected from some of the other machines like network partitions, problems arise. Moreover, there's no way to detect this from a user perspective, which is even more of an issue if servers become compromised.

If I query a server and it tells me that Alice has 5 billion dollars in her account, I just have to trust it. If the server includes in its response all the money transfers that she has received and sent since the beginning of time and sums it all up, I could verify that indeed it results with the 5 billion dollars she has in her account is correct. But what tells me the server didn't lie to me? Perhaps when Bob asks a different server, it returns a completely different balance and/or history for Alice's account. We call this a *fork* (two contradicting states presented as valid), a branch in history that should never have happened. And, thus, you can imagine that the compromise of one of the replicated databases can lead to pretty devastating consequences.

In chapter 9, I mentioned *certificate transparency*, a gossip protocol that aims at detecting such forks in the web public key infrastructure (PKI). The problem with money is that detection alone is not enough. You want to prevent forks from happening in the first place! In 1982, Lamport, the author of the Paxos consensus algorithm, introduced the idea of *Byzantine fault-tolerant* (BFT) *consensus algorithms*.

> *We imagine that several divisions of the Byzantine army are camped outside an enemy city, each division commanded by its own general. The generals can communicate with one another only by messenger. After observing the enemy, they must decide upon a common plan of action. However, some of the generals may be traitors, trying to prevent the loyal generals from reaching agreement.*
>
> —Lamport et al. ("The Byzantine Generals Problem," 1982)

With his Byzantine analogy, Lamport started the field of BFT consensus algorithms, aiming at preventing bad consensus participants from creating different conflicting views of a system when agreeing on a decision. These BFT consensus algorithms highly resemble previous consensus algorithms like Paxos and Raft, except that the replicated databases (the participants of the protocol) do not blindly trust one another anymore. BFT protocols usually make heavy use of cryptography to authenticate messages and decisions, which in turn, can be used by others to cryptographically validate the decisions output by the consensus protocol.

These BFT consensus protocols are, thus, solutions to both our resilience and trust issues. The different replicated databases can run these BFT algorithms to agree on new system states (for example, user balances), while policing each other by verifying that the state transitions (transactions between users) are valid and have been agreed on by most of the participants. We say that the trust is now *decentralized.*

The first real-world BFT consensus algorithm invented was *Practical BFT* (PBFT), published in 1999. PBFT is a leader-based algorithm similar to Paxos and Raft, where one leader is in charge of making proposals while the rest attempt to agree on the proposals. Unfortunately, PBFT is quite complex, slow, and doesn't scale well past a dozen participants. Today, most modern cryptocurrencies use more efficient variants of PBFT. For example, Diem, the cryptocurrency introduced by Facebook in 2019, is based on HotStuff, a PBFT-inspired protocol.

12.1.3 A problem of scale: Permissionless and censorship-resistant networks

One limitation of these PBFT-based consensus algorithms is that they all require a known and fixed set of participants. More problematic, past a certain number of participants, they start breaking apart: communication complexity increases drastically, they become extremely slow, electing a leader becomes complicated, etc.

How does a cryptocurrency decide who the consensus participants are? There are several ways, but the two most common ways are

- *Proof of authority* (PoA)—The consensus participants are decided in advance.
- *Proof of stake* (PoS)—The consensus participants are picked dynamically, based on which has the most at stake (and, thus, is less incentivized to attack the protocol). In general, cryptocurrencies based on PoS elect participants based on the amount of digital currency they hold.

Having said that, not all consensus protocols are classical BFT consensus protocols. Bitcoin, for example, took a different approach when it proposed a consensus mechanism that had no known list of participants. This was quite a novel idea at the time, and Bitcoin achieved this by relaxing the constraints of classical BFT consensus protocols. As you will see later in this chapter, because of this approach, Bitcoin can fork, and this introduces its own sets of challenges.

Without participants, how do you even pick a leader? You could use a PoS system (for example, the Ouroboros consensus protocol does this). Instead, Bitcoin's consensus relied on a probabilistic mechanism called *proof of work* (PoW). In Bitcoin, this translates to people attempting to find solutions to puzzles in order to become a participant and a leader. The puzzle is a cryptographic one as you will see later in this chapter.

Due to a lack of known participants, Bitcoin is called a *permissionless* network. In a permissionless network, you do not need extra permissions to participate in consensus; anyone can participate. This is in contrast to *permissioned* networks that have a fixed set of participants. I summarize some of these new concepts in figure 12.1.

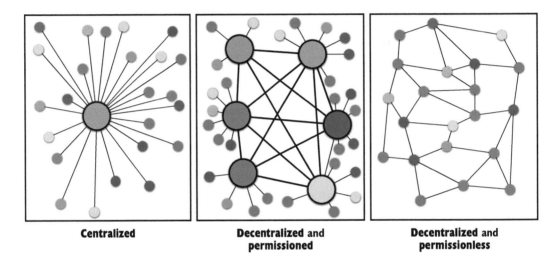

Centralized   **Decentralized and permissioned**   **Decentralized and permissionless**

Figure 12.1   A centralized network can be seen as a single point of failure, whereas a distributed and decentralized network are resilient to a number of servers shutting down or acting maliciously. A permissioned network has a known and fixed set of main actors, while in a permissionless network, anyone can participate.

Until recently, it was not known how to use classical BFT consensus protocols with a permissionless network, where anyone is allowed to join. Today, there exist many approaches using PoS to dynamically pick a smaller subset of the participants as consensus participants. One of the most notable ones is Algorand, published in 2017, which dynamically picks participants and leaders based on how much currency they hold.

Bitcoin also claims to be resistant to censorship because you cannot know in advance who will become the next leader and, therefore, cannot prevent the system from electing a new leader. It is less clear if this is possible in PoS systems where it might be easier to figure out the identities behind large sums of currency.

I should mention that not all BFT consensus protocols are leader-based. Some are *leaderless*, they do not work by having elected leaders decide on the next state transitions.

Instead, everyone can propose changes, and the consensus protocol helps everyone agree on the next state. In 2019, Avalanche launched such a cryptocurrency that allowed anyone to propose changes and participate in consensus.

Finally, if you thought that consensus was necessary at all for a decentralized payment system, it's not exactly right as well. Consensus-less protocols were proposed in 2018 in "AT2: Asynchronous Trustworthy Transfers" by Guerraoui, Kuznetsov, Monti, Pavlovic, and Seredinschi. With that in mind, I will not talk about consensus-less protocols in this chapter as they are a relatively new and haven't been battle-tested yet. In the rest of this chapter, I will go over two different cryptocurrencies in order to demonstrate different aspects of the field:

- *Bitcoin*—The most popular cryptocurrency based on PoW, introduced in 2008.
- *Diem*—A cryptocurrency based on the BFT consensus protocol, announced by Facebook and a group of other companies in 2019.

12.2 How does Bitcoin work?

On October 31, 2008, an anonymous researcher(s) published "Bitcoin: A Peer-to-Peer Electronic Cash System" under the pseudonym Satoshi Nakamoto. To this day, it remains unknown who Satoshi Nakamoto is. Not long after, "they" released the Bitcoin core client, a software that anyone can run in order to join and participate in the Bitcoin network. That was the only thing that Bitcoin needed: enough users to run the same software or at least the same algorithm. The first ever cryptocurrency was born— the bitcoin (or BTC).

Bitcoin is a true success story. The cryptocurrency has been running for more than a decade (at the time of this writing) and has allowed users from all around the world to undertake transactions using the digital currency. In 2010, Laszlo Hanyecz, a developer, bought two pizzas for 10,000 BTCs. As I am writing these lines (February 2021), a BTC is worth almost $57,000. Thus, one can already take away that cryptocurrencies can sometimes be extremely volatile.

12.2.1 How Bitcoin handles user balances and transactions

Let's dive deeper into the internals of Bitcoin, first looking at how Bitcoin handles user balances and transactions. As a user of Bitcoin, you directly deal with cryptography. You do not have a username and password to log into a website as with any bank; instead, you have an ECDSA (Elliptic Curve Digital Signature Algorithm) key pair that you generate yourself. A user's balance is simply an amount of BTC associated with a public key, and as such, to receive BTCs, you simply share your public key with others.

To use your BTCs, you sign a transaction with your private key. A transaction pretty much says what you think it says, "I send X BTC to public key Y," overlooking some details that I'll explain later.

NOTE In chapter 7, I mentioned that Bitcoin uses the secp256k1 curve with ECDSA. The curve is not to be confused with NIST's P-256 curve, which is known as secp256r1.

The safety of your funds is directly linked to the security your private key. And, as you know, key management is hard. In the past decade, key management issues in cryptocurrencies have led to the accidental loss (or theft) of keys worth millions of dollars. Be careful!

There exist different types of transactions in Bitcoin, and most of the transactions seen on the network actually hide the recipient's public key by hashing it. In these cases, the hash of a public key is referred to as the *address* of an account. (For example, this is my Bitcoin address: bc1q8y6p4x3rp32dz80etpyffh6764ray9842egchy.) An address effectively hides the actual public key of the account until the account owner decides to spend the BTCs (in which case, the pre-image of the address needs to be revealed so that others can verify the signature). This makes addresses shorter in size and prevents someone from retrieving your private key in case ECDSA one day breaks.

The fact that different types of transactions exist is an interesting detail of Bitcoin. Transactions are not just payloads containing some information; they are actually short scripts written in a made-up and quite limited instruction set. When a transaction is processed, the script needs to be executed before the produced output can determine if the transaction is valid, and if it is, what steps need to be taken to modify the state of all the accounts.

Cryptocurrencies like Ethereum have pushed this scripting idea to the limit by allowing much more complex programs (so-called *smart contracts*) to run when a transaction is executed. There are a few things here that I didn't touch on:

- What's in a transaction?
- What does it mean for a transaction to be executed? And who executes it?

I will explain the second item in the next section. For now, let's look at what is in a transaction.

A particularity of Bitcoin is that there is no real database of account balances. Instead, a user has pockets of BTCs that are available for them to spend and which are called *Unspent Transaction Outputs* (UTXOs). You can think of the concept of UTXOs as a large bowl, visible to everyone, and filled with coins that only their owners can spend. When a transaction spends some of the coins, the coins disappear from the bowl, and new ones appear for the payees of the same transaction. These new coins are just the outputs listed in the transaction.

To know how many BTCs you have in your account, you'd have to count all of the UTXOs that are assigned to your address. In other words, you'd have to count all of the money that was sent to you and that you haven't spent yet. Figure 12.2 gives an example that illustrates how UTXOs are used in transactions.

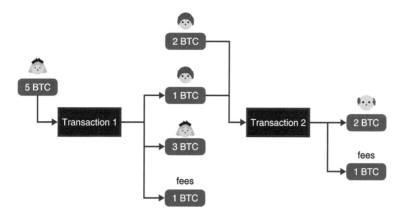

Figure 12.2   Transaction 1 is signed by Alice and transfers 1 BTC to Bob. Because it uses a UTXO of 5 BTCs, the transaction needs to also send back the change to Alice as well as reserve some of that change as fees. Transaction 2 is signed by Bob and combines two UTXOs to transfer 2 BTCs to Felix. (Note that in reality, fees are much lower.)

There's now a chicken-and-egg question: where did the first UTXOs come from? That, I will answer in the next section.

12.2.2 *Mining BTCs in the digital age of gold*

You now understand what's in a Bitcoin transaction and how you can manage your account or figure out someone's balance. But who actually keeps track of all these transactions? The answer is everyone!

Indeed, using Bitcoin means that every transaction must be publicly shared and recorded in history. Bitcoin is an *append-only ledger*—a book of transactions where each page is connected to the previous one. I want to emphasize here that append-only means that you can't go back and alter a page in the book. Note also that because every transaction is public, the only semblance of anonymity you get is that it might be hard to figure out who's who (in other words, what public key is linked to what person in real life).

One can easily inspect any transaction that has happened since the inception of Bitcoin by downloading a Bitcoin client and using it to download the whole history. By doing this, you become part of the network and must re-execute every transaction according to the rules encoded in the Bitcoin client. Of course, Bitcoin's history is pretty massive: at the time of this writing, it is around 300 GB, and it can take days, depending on your connection, to download the entire Bitcoin ledger. You can more easily inspect transactions by using an online service that does the heavy lifting for you (as long as you trust an online service). I give an example of these so-called *blockchain explorers* in figure 12.3.

Figure 12.3   A random transaction I chose to analyze on https://blockchain.com (http://mng.bz/n295). The transaction uses one input (of around 1.976 BTCs) and splits it in two outputs (of around 0.009 BTC and 1.967 BTCs). The difference between the total input amount and the total output amount is the transaction fee (not represented as an output). The other fields are the scripts written using Bitcoin's scripting language in order to either spend the UTXOs in the inputs or to make the UTXOs in the outputs spendable.

Bitcoin is really just a list of all the transactions that have been processed since its inception (we call that the *genesis*) up until now. This should make you wonder: who is in charge of choosing and ordering transactions in this ledger?

In order to agree on an ordering of transactions, Bitcoin allows anyone (even you) to propose a list of transactions to be included in the next page of the ledger. This proposal containing a list of transactions is called a *block* in Bitcoin's terms. But letting anyone propose a block is a recipe for disaster as there are a lot of participants in Bitcoin. Instead, we want just one person to make a proposal for the next block of transactions. To do this, Bitcoin makes everybody work on some probabilistic puzzle, and only allows the one who solves the puzzle first to propose their block. This is the proof of work (PoW) mechanism I talked about previously. Bitcoin's PoW is based on finding a block that hashes to a digest smaller than some value. In other words, the block's digest must have a binary representation starting with some given numbers of zeros.

In addition to the transactions you want to include, the block must contain the hash of the previous block. Hence the Bitcoin ledger is really a succession of blocks, where each block refers to the previous one, down to the very first block, the genesis block. This is what Bitcoin calls a *blockchain*. The beauty of the blockchain is that the slightest modification to a block would render the chain invalid as the block's digest would also change and consequently break the reference the next block had to it.

Note that as a participant who is looking to propose the next block, you don't have to change much in your block to derive a new hash from it. You can fix most of its content first (the transactions it includes, the hash of the block it extends, etc.) and then only modify a field (called the block's nonce) to impact the block's hash. You can treat this field as a counter, incrementing the value until you find a digest that fits the rules of the game, or you can generate a random value. I illustrate this idea of a blockchain in figure 12.4.

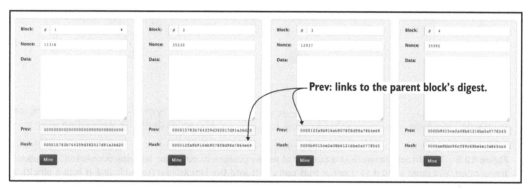

Valid blockchain

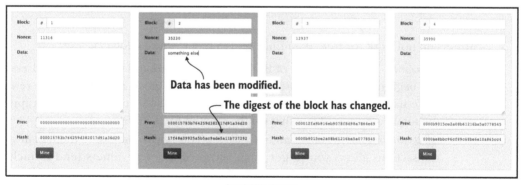

Invalid blockchain

Figure 12.4   On https://andersbrownworth.com/blockchain/blockchain, one can interactively play with a toy blockchain. Each block includes its parent's digest, and each block contains a random nonce that allows its digest to start with four 0s. Notice that this is true for the top blockchain, but the bottom one contains a block (number 2) that has been modified (its data was initially empty). As the modification changed the block's digest, it is no longer authenticated by subsequent blocks.

All of this works because everyone is running the same protocol using the same rules. When you synchronize with the blockchain, you download every block from other peers and verify that:

- Hashing each block indeed gives a digest that is smaller than some expected value.
- Each block refers back to the previous block in the history.

Not everyone has to propose blocks, but you can if you want. If you do so, you are called a *miner*. This means that in order to get your transactions in the blockchain, you need the miners' help (as figure 12.5 illustrates).

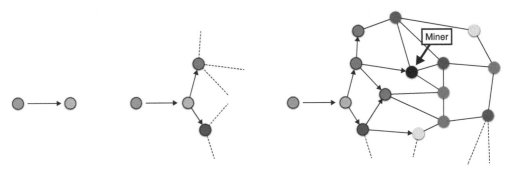

A client **submits** a transaction to a **node**.

The node **forwards** the transaction to other nodes.

Eventually the transaction reaches **miners** who will **include the transaction** when mining.

Figure 12.5   The Bitcoin network is a number of nodes (miners or not) that are interconnected. To submit a transaction, you must send it to a miner that can get it into the blockchain (by including it into a block). As you do not know which miner will be successful at mining a block, you must propagate your transaction through the network to reach as many miners as possible.

Miners do not work for free. If a miner finds a block, they collect:

- *A reward*—A fixed number of BTCs will get created and sent to your address. In the beginning, miners would get 50 BTCs per block mined. But the reward value halves every 210,000 blocks and will eventually be reduced to 0, capping the total amount of BTCs that can be created to 21 million.
- *All the transaction fees contained in the block*—This is why increasing the fees in your transactions allows you to get them accepted faster as miners tend to include transactions with higher fees in the blocks they mine.

This is how users of Bitcoin are incentivized in making the protocol move forward. A block always contains what is called a *coinbase*, which is the address that collects the reward and the fees. The miner usually sets the coinbase to their own address.

We can now answer the question we had at the beginning of the section: where did the first UTXOs come from? The answer is that all BTCs in history were, at some point or another, created as part of the block reward for miners.

12.2.3 *Forking hell! Solving conflicts in mining*

Bitcoin distributes the task of choosing the next set of transactions to be processed via a PoW-based system. Your chance to mine a block is directly correlated to the amount of hashes you can compute, and thus, the amount of computation you can put produce. A lot of computation power nowadays is directed at mining blocks in Bitcoin or other PoW-based cryptocurrencies.

> **NOTE** PoW can be seen as Bitcoin's way of addressing *sybil attacks*, which are attacks that take advantage of the fact that you can create as many accounts as you want in a protocol, giving you an asymmetric edge to dishonest participants. In Bitcoin, the only way to obtain more power is really to buy more hardware to compute hashes, not to create more addresses in the network.

There is still one problem though: the difficulty of finding a hash that is lower than some value can't be too easy. If it is, then the network will have too many participants mining a valid block at the same time. And, if this happens, which mined block is the legitimate next block in the chain? This is essentially what we call a *fork*.

To solve forks, Bitcoin has two mechanisms. The first is to *maintain the hardness of PoW*. If blocks get mined too quickly or too slowly, the Bitcoin algorithm that everyone is running dynamically adapts to the network conditions and increases or decreases the *difficulty* of the PoW. Simplified, miners have to find a block digest that has more or less zeros.

> **NOTE** If the difficulty dictates that a block digest needs to start with a 0 byte, you are expected to try 2^8 different blocks (more specifically different nonces as explained previously) until you can find a valid digest. Raise this to 2 bytes, and you are now expected to try 2^{16} different blocks. The time it takes for you to get there depends on the amount of power you have and whether you have specialized hardware to compute these hashes more rapidly. Currently, Bitcoin's algorithm dynamically changes the difficulty so that a block is mined every 10 minutes.

Our second mechanism is to make sure everyone has the same way of going forward if a fork does happen. To do this, the rule is to *follow the chain with the most amount of work*. The 2008 Bitcoin paper stated, "the longest chain not only serves as proof of the sequence of events witnessed, but proof that it came from the largest pool of CPU power," dictating that participants should honor what they see as the longest chain. The protocol was later updated to follow the chain with the highest cumulative amount of work, but this distinction does not matter too much here. I illustrate this in figure 12.6.

I said previously that the consensus algorithm of Bitcoin is not a BFT protocol. This is because the consensus algorithm allows such forks. Thus, if you are waiting for your transaction to be processed, you should absolutely *not* rely on simply observing your transaction being included in a block! The observed block could actually be a fork, and a losing one (to a longer fork) at that.

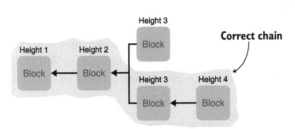

Figure 12.6   A fork in the blockchain: two miners publish a valid block at height 3 (meaning 3 blocks after genesis). Later, another miner mines a block at height 4 that points to the second block at height 3. As the second fork is now longer, it is the valid fork that miners should continue to extend. Note that arrows coming out of a block point to the parent block (the block they extend).

You need more assurance to decide when your transaction has been processed for real. Most wallets and exchange platforms wait for a number of *confirmation blocks* to be mined on top of your block. The more blocks on top of the one that includes your transaction, the less chance that chain will be reorganized into another, due to a longer existing fork.

The number of confirmation is typically set to 6 blocks, which makes the confirmation time for your transaction around an hour. That being said, Bitcoin still does not provide 100% assurance that a fork past 6 blocks would never happen. If the mining difficulty is well adjusted, then it should be fine, and we have reason to believe that this is true for Bitcoin.

Bitcoin's PoW difficulty has increased gradually over time as cryptocurrency becomes more popular. The difficulty is now so high that most people cannot afford the hardware required to have a chance at mining a block. Today, most miners get together in what are called *mining pools* to distribute the work needed to mine a block. They then share the reward.

> *With block 632874 [. . .] the expected cumulative work in the Bitcoin blockchain surpassed 2^{92} double-SHA256 hashes.*
>
> —Pieter Wuille (2020, http://mng.bz/aZNJ)

To understand why forks are disruptive, let's imagine the following scenario. Alice buys a bottle of wine from you, and you've been waiting for her to send you the 5 BTCs she has in her account. Finally, you observe a new block at height 10 (meaning 10 blocks after genesis) that includes her transaction. Being cautious, you decide to wait for 6 more blocks to be added on top of that. After waiting for a while, you finally see a block at height 16 that extends the chain containing your block at height 10. You send the bottle of wine to Alice and call it a day. But this is not the end of the story.

Later, a block at height 30 appears out of nowhere, extending a different blockchain that branched out just a block before yours (at height 9). Because the new chain is longer, it ends up being accepted by everyone as the legitimate chain. The previous chain you were on (starting from your block at height 10) gets discarded, and participants in the network simply reorganize their chain to now point to the new longest one. And as you can guess, this new chain doesn't has any block that includes Alice's transaction. Instead, it includes a transaction moving all of her funds to another address, preventing you from republishing the original transaction that moved her funds to your address. Alice effectively *double spent* her money.

This is a *51% attack*. The name comes from the amount of computation power Alice needed to perform the attack; she needed just a bit more than everyone else. (https://crypto51.app has an interesting table that lists the cost of performing a 51% attack on different cryptocurrencies based on PoW.) This is not just a theoretical attack! 51% attacks happen in the real world. For example, in 2018, an attacker managed to double-spend a number of funds in a 51% attack on the Vertcoin currency.

> The attacker essentially rewrote part of the ledger's history and then, using their dominant hashing power to produce the longest chain, convinced the rest of the miners to validate this new version of the blockchain. With that, he or she could commit the ultimate crypto crime: a double-spend of prior transactions, leaving earlier payees holding invalidated coins.
>
> —Michael J. Casey ("Vertcoin's Struggle Is Real:
> Why the Latest Crypto 51% Attack Matters," 2018)

In 2019, the same thing happened to Ethereum Classic (a variant of Ethereum), causing losses of more than $1 million at the time with several reorganizations of more than 100 blocks of depth. In 2020, Bitcoin Gold (a variant of Bitcoin) also suffered from a 51% attack, removing 29 blocks from the cryptocurrency's history and double-spending more than $70,000 in less than two days.

12.2.4 Reducing a block's size by using Merkle trees

One last interesting aspect of Bitcoin that I want to talk about is how it compresses some of the information available. A block in Bitcoin actually does not contain any transactions! Transactions are shared separately, and instead, a block contains a single digest that authenticates a list of transactions. That digest could simply be the hash of all the transactions contained in the block, but it's a bit more clever than that. Instead, the digest is the root of a *Merkle tree*.

What's a Merkle tree? Simply put, it's a tree (data structure) where internal nodes are hashes of their children. This might be a tad confusing, and a picture is worth a thousand words, so check out figure 12.7.

Merkle trees are useful structures, and you will find them in all types of real world protocols. They can compress a large amount of data into a small, fixed-size value—the root of the tree. Not only that, you do not necessarily need all the leaves to reconstruct the root.

For example, imagine that you know the root of the Merkle tree due to its inclusion in a Bitcoin block, and you want to know if a transaction (a leaf in the tree) is included in the block. If it is in the tree, what I can do is to share with you the neighbor

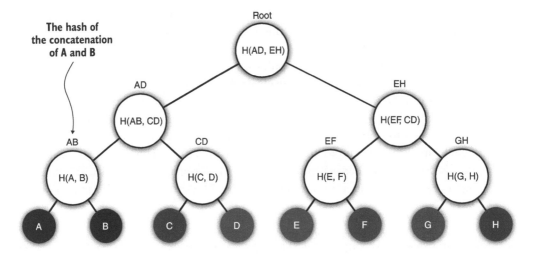

Figure 12.7   A Merkle tree, a data structure that authenticates the elements in its leaves. In the tree, an internal node is the hash of its children. The root hash can be used to authenticate the whole structure. In the diagram, H() represents a hash function, and the comma-separated inputs can be implemented as a concatenation (as long as there is no ambiguity).

nodes in the path up to the root as a *membership proof.* (A proof that is logarithmic in the depth of the tree in size.) What's left for you is to compute the internal nodes up to the root of the tree by hashing each pair in the path. It's a bit complicated to explain this in writing, so I illustrate the proof in figure 12.8.

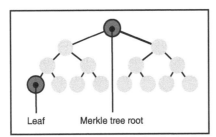

1. Proof of membership for the leaf with knowledge of the root

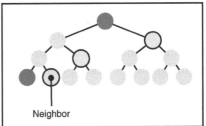

2. Using the neighbor nodes verifies if it leads to the root.

Figure 12.8   Knowing the root of a Merkle tree, one can verify that a leaf belongs to the tree by reconstructing the root hash from all the leaves. To do this, you would need all the leaves in the first place, which in our diagram is 8 digests (assuming leaves are the hashes of some object). There's a more efficient way to construct a proof of membership if you don't need all the other leaves: you only need the neighbor nodes in the path from the leaf to the root, which is 4 digests including your leaf. A verifier can then use these neighbor nodes to compute the hash of all the missing nodes in the path to the root until they reconstruct the root hash and see if it matches what they were expecting.

The reason for using Merkle trees in a block instead of listing all transactions directly is to lighten the information that needs to be downloaded in order to perform simple queries on the blockchain. For example, imagine that you want to check that your recent transaction is included in a block without having to download the whole history of the Bitcoin blockchain. What you can do is to only download the block headers, which are lighter as they do not contain the transactions, and once you have that, ask a peer to tell you which block included your transaction. If there is such a block, they should be able to provide you with a proof that your transaction is in the tree authenticated by the digest you have in the block header.

There's a lot more to be said about Bitcoin, but there's only so many pages left in this book. Instead, I will use the remaining space in this chapter to give you a tour of the field and to explain how the classical BFT consensus protocols work.

12.3 A tour of cryptocurrencies

Bitcoin is the first successful cryptocurrency and has remained the cryptocurrency with the largest market share and value in spite of hundreds of other cryptocurrencies being created. What's interesting is that Bitcoin had, and still has, many issues that other cryptocurrencies have attempted to tackle (and some with success). Even more interesting, the cryptocurrency field has made use of many cryptographic primitives that until now did not have many practical applications or did not even exist! So without further ado, the following sections list the issues that have been researched since the advent of Bitcoin.

12.3.1 Volatility

Most people currently use cryptocurrencies as speculation vehicles. The price of Bitcoin obviously helps that story as it has shown that it can easily move thousands of dollars up or down in a single day. Some people claim that the stability will come over time, but the fact remains that Bitcoin is not usable as a currency nowadays. Other cryptocurrencies have experimented with the concept of *stablecoin*, by tying the price of their token to an existing fiat currency (like the US dollar).

12.3.2 Latency

You can measure the efficiency of a cryptocurrency in many ways. The *throughput* of a cryptocurrency is the number of transactions per second that it can process. Bitcoin's throughput, for example, is quite low with only 7 transactions per second. On the other hand, *finality* is the time it takes for your transaction to be considered finalized once it is included in the blockchain. Due to forks, Bitcoin's finality is never completely achieved. It is considered that at least one hour after a transaction is included in a new block, the probability of the transaction getting reverted becomes acceptable. Both numbers greatly impact the *latency*, which is the amount of time it takes for a transaction to be finalized from the point of view of the user.

In Bitcoin, latency includes the creation of the transaction, the time it takes to propagate it through the network, the time it takes for it to get included in a block, and finally, the wait time for the block to be confirmed.

The solution to these speed issues can be solved by BFT protocols, which usually provide finality of mere seconds with an insurance that no forks are possible, as well as throughput in the order of thousands of transactions per second. Yet, this is sometimes still not enough, and different technologies are being explored. So-called *layer 2 protocols* attempt to provide additional solutions that can enact faster payments off-chain while saving progress periodically on the main blockchain (referred to as the layer 1 in comparison).

12.3.3   Blockchain size

Another common problem with Bitcoin and other cryptocurrencies is that the size of the blockchain can quickly grow to impractical sizes. This creates usability issues when users who want to use the cryptocurrency (for example, to query their account's balance) are expected to first download the entire chain in order to interact with the network. BFT-based cryptocurrencies that process a large number of transactions per second are expected to easily reach terabytes of data within months or even weeks. Several attempts exist for solving this.

One of the most interesting ones is Mina, which doesn't require you to download the whole history of the blockchain in order to get to the latest state. Instead, Mina uses zero-knowledge proofs (ZKPs), mentioned in chapter 7 and that I'll cover more in depth in chapter 15, to compress all the history into a fixed-size 11 KB proof. This is especially useful for lighter clients like mobile phones that usually have to trust third-party servers in order to query the blockchain.

12.3.4   Confidentiality

Bitcoin provides *pseudo-anonymity* in that accounts are only tied to public keys. As long as nobody can tie a public key to a person, the associated account remains anonymous. Remember that all the transactions from and to that account are publicly available, and social graphs can still be created in order to understand who tends to trade more often with whom, and who owns how much of the currency.

There are many cryptocurrencies that attempt to solve these issues using ZKPs or other techniques. *Zcash* is one of the most well-known confidential cryptocurrencies as its transactions can encrypt the sender address, receiver address, and the amount being transacted. All of that using ZKPs!

12.3.5   Energy efficiency

Bitcoin has been criticized heavily for being too consuming in terms of electricity. Indeed, the University of Cambridge recently evaluated that all of the energy spent mining BTCs brings Bitcoin to the top 30 energy users in the world (if seen as a country), consuming more energy in a year than a country like Argentina (February

2021; https://cbeci.org/). BFT protocols on the other hand do not rely on PoW and so avoid this heavy overhead. This is most certainly why any modern cryptocurrency seems to avoid a consensus based on PoW, and even important PoW-based cryptocurrencies like Ethereum have announced plans to move towards greener consensus protocols. Before going to the next chapter, let's take a look at these cryptocurrencies based on BFT consensus protocols.

12.4 DiemBFT: A Byzantine fault-tolerant (BFT) consensus protocol

Many modern cryptocurrencies have ditched the PoW aspect of Bitcoin for greener and more efficient consensus protocols. Most of these consensus protocols are based on classical BFT consensus protocols, which are mostly variants of the original PBFT protocol. In this last section, I will use Diem to illustrate such BFT protocols.

Diem (previously called Libra) is a digital currency initially announced by Facebook in 2019, and governed by the Diem Association, an organization of companies, universities, and nonprofits looking to push for an open and global payment network. One particularity of Diem is that it is backed by real money, using a reserve of fiat currencies. This allows the digital currency to be stable unlike its older cousin Bitcoin. To run the payment network in a secure and open manner, a BFT consensus protocol called *DiemBFT* is used, which is a variant of HotStuff. In this section, let's see how DiemBFT works.

12.4.1 Safety and liveness: The two properties of a BFT consensus protocol

A BFT consensus protocol is meant to achieve two properties, even in the presence of a tolerated percentage of malicious participants. These properties include

- *Safety*—No contradicting states can be agreed on, meaning that forks are not supposed to happen (or happen with a negligible probability).
- *Liveness*—When people submit transactions, the state will eventually end up processing them. In other words, nobody can stop the protocol from doing its thing.

Note that a participant is generally seen as malicious (also called *byzantine*) if they do not behave according to the protocol. This could mean that they're not doing anything, or that they're not following the steps of the protocol in the correct order, or that they're not respecting some mandatory rule meant to ensure that there is no fork, and so on.

It's usually quite straightforward for BFT consensus protocols to achieve safety, while liveness is known to be more difficult. Indeed, there's a well-known impossibility result from Fischer, Lync, and Paterson ("Impossibility of distributed consensus with one faulty process") dating from 1985 and linked to BFT protocols that states that no *deterministic* consensus protocol can tolerate failures in an *asynchronous* network (where messages can take as much time as they want to arrive). Most BFT protocols avoid this impossibility result by considering the network somewhat *synchronous* (and indeed, no protocol is useful if your network goes down for a long period of time) or by introducing randomness in the algorithm.

For this reason, DiemBFT never forks, even under extreme network conditions. In addition, it always makes progress even when there's network partitions where different parts of the network can't reach other parts of the network, as long as the network ends up healing and stabilizing for a long enough period.

12.4.2 A round in the DiemBFT protocol

Diem runs in a permissioned setting where participants (called *validators*) are known in advance. The protocol advances in strictly increasing rounds (round 1, 2, 3, etc.), during which validators take turns to propose blocks of transactions. In each round

1. The validator that is chosen to lead (deterministically) collects a number of transactions, groups them into a new block extending the blockchain, then signs the block and sends it to all other validators.
2. Upon receiving the proposed block, other validators can vote to certify it by signing it and sending the signature to the leader of the next round.
3. If the leader of the next round receives enough votes for that block, they can bundle all of them in what is called a *quorum certificate* (QC), which certifies the block, and use the QC to propose a new block (in the next round) extending the now certified block.

Another way to look at this is that whereas in Bitcoin a block only contains the hash of the block it extends, in DiemBFT, a block also contains a number of signatures over that hash. (The number of signatures is important, but more on that later.)

Note that if validators do not see a proposal during a round (because the leader is AFK, for example), they can timeout and warn other validators that nothing happened. In this case, the next round is triggered and the proposer can extend whatever is the highest certified block that they have seen. I recap this in figure 12.9.

12.4.3 How much dishonesty can the protocol tolerate?

Let's imagine that we want to be able to tolerate f malicious validators at most (even if they all collude), then DiemBFT says that there needs to be at least $3f + 1$ validators to participate in the protocol (in other words, for f malicious validators there needs to be at least $2f + 1$ honest validators). As long as this assumption is true, the protocol provides safety and liveness.

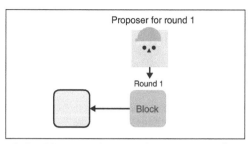

1. A validator who is elected for a round can **sign** and broadcast a **block of transactions**.

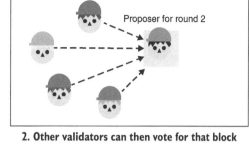

2. Other validators can then vote for that block by **signing** a message and sending it to the **next proposer**.

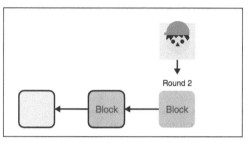

3. If **enough votes** are gathered the next proposer proposes a block carrying them, **certifying** the block voted on.

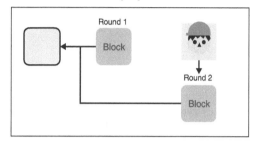

4. If the round times out and not enough votes are observed, the next proposer extends the **certified block** in the **highest round** they have seen.

Figure 12.9   Each round of DiemBFT starts with the designated leader proposing a block that extends the last one they've seen. Other validators can then vote on this block by sending their vote to the next round's leader. If the next round's leader gathers enough votes to form a quorum certificate (QC), they can propose a new block containing the QC, effectively extending the previously seen block.

With that in mind, QCs can only be formed with a majority of honest validators' votes, which is $2f + 1$ signatures if there are $3f + 1$ participants. These numbers can be a bit hard to visualize, so I show how they impact confidence in the votes we observe in figure 12.10.

12.4.4 The DiemBFT rules of voting

Validators must follow two voting rules at all times, without which, they are considered byzantine:

1   They can't vote in the past (for example, if you just finished voting in round 3, you can only vote in round 4 and above).

2   They can only vote for a block extending a block at their preferred round or higher.

What's a *preferred round*? By default, it is 0, but if you vote for a block that extends a block that extends a block (and by that I mean you voted for a block that has a

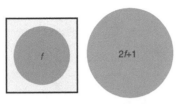

If *f* have voted for a block,
then they could be **all malicious votes**.

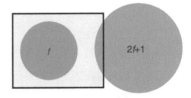

If *f* +1 have voted for a block,
then **at least one honest** node voted.

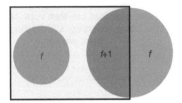

If **2*f* +1** (a **quorum**) have voted for a block,
then **at least *f* +1 honest** nodes voted.

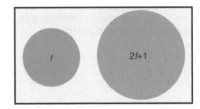

If **3*f* +1** have voted for a block,
then **everybody** has voted.

Figure 12.10 In the DiemBFT protocol, at least two thirds of the validators must be honest for the protocol to be safe (it won't fork) and live (it will make progress). In other words, the protocol can tolerate *f* dishonest validators if at least 2*f* + 1 validators are honest. A certified block has received at least 2*f* + 1 votes as it is the lowest number of votes that can represent a majority of honest validators.

grandparent block), then that grandparent block's round becomes your preferred round unless your previous preferred round was higher. Complicated? I know, that's why I made figure 12.11.

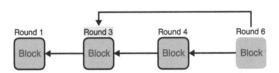

If I vote for the block at round 6, my **preferred round** becomes round 3.

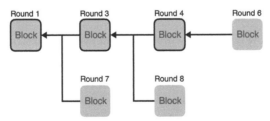

Then I **cannot vote** for the block at round 7, but I **can vote** for the block at round 8.

Figure 12.11 After voting for a block, a validator sets their preferred round to the round of the grandparent block if it is higher than their current preferred round. To vote on a block, its parent block must have a round greater or equal to the preferred round.

12.4.5 When are transactions considered finalized?

Note that blocks that are certified are not finalized yet, or as we also say, *committed*. Nobody should assume that the transactions contained in the pending blocks won't be reverted. Blocks and the transactions they contain can only be considered finalized once the *commit rule* is triggered. The commit rule (illustrated in figure 12.12) says that a block and all the pending blocks it extends become committed if:

- The block starts a chain of 3 blocks that are proposed in *contiguous rounds* (for example, in round 1, 2, and 3).
- The last block of the 3-block chain become certified.

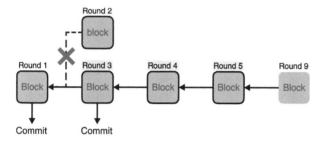

Figure 12.12   Three contiguous rounds (3, 4, 5) happen to have a chain of certified blocks. Any validator observing the certification of the last block in round 5 by the QC of round 9 can commit the first block of the chain at round 3, as well as all of its ancestors (here the block of round 1). Any contradicting branches (for example, the block of round 2) get dropped.

And this is all there is to the protocol at a high level. But, of course, once again, the devil is in the details.

12.4.6 The intuitions behind the safety of DiemBFT

While I encourage you to read the one-page safety proof on the DiemBFT paper, I want to use a couple pages here to give you an intuition on why it works. First, we notice that two different blocks cannot be certified during the same round. This is an important property, which I explain visually in figure 12.13.

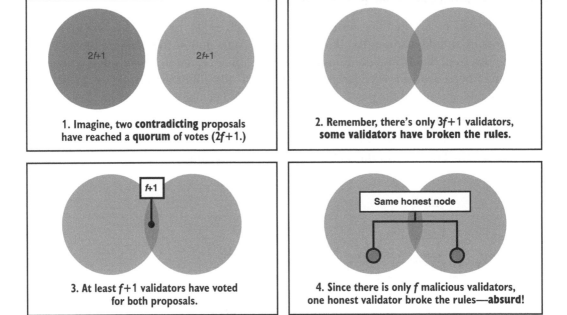

1. Imagine, two **contradicting** proposals have reached a **quorum** of votes (2f+1.)

2. Remember, there's only 3f+1 validators, **some validators have broken the rules.**

3. At least f+1 validators have voted for both proposals.

4. Since there is only f malicious validators, one honest validator broke the rules—**absurd!**

Figure 12.13   Assuming that there can only be up to f malicious validators in a protocol of 3f + 1 validators, and that a quorum certificate is created from 2f + 1 signed votes, then there can only be one certified block per round. The diagram shows a *proof by contradiction*, a proof that this cannot be because then it would contradict our initial assumptions.

Using the property that only one block can get certified at a given round, we can simplify how we talk about blocks: block 3 is at round 3, block 6 is at round 6, and so on. Now, take a look at figure 12.14 and take a moment to figure out why a certified block,

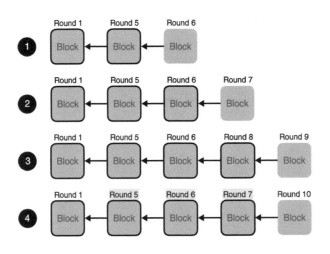

Figure 12.14   In all these scenarios, committing block 5 could lead to a fork. Only in scenario number 4 is committing block 5 safe. Can you tell why it is dangerous to commit block 5 in all scenarios but 4?

or two certified blocks, or three certified blocks at noncontiguous rounds cannot lead to a commit without risking a fork.

Did you manage to find out answers for all the scenarios? The short answer is that all scenarios, with the exception of the last one, leave room for a block to extend round 1. This late block effectively branches out and can be further extended according to the rules of the consensus protocol. If this happens, block 5 and other blocks extending it will get dropped as another earlier branch gets committed. For scenarios 1 and 2, this can be due to the proposer not seeing the previous blocks. In scenario 3, an earlier block could appear later than expected, perhaps due to network delays, or worse, due to a validator withholding it up to the right moment. I explain this further in figure 12.15.

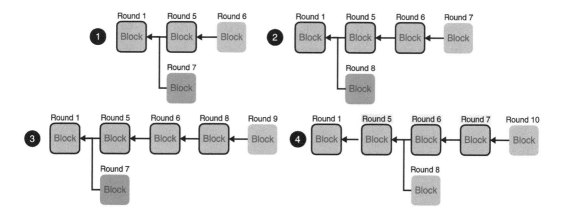

Figure 12.15 Building on figure 12.14, all scenarios except the last one allow for a parallel chain that can eventually win and discard the branch of block 5. The last scenario has a chain of three certified blocks in contiguous rounds. This means that block 7 has had a majority of honest voters, who, in turn, updated their preferred round to round 5. After that, no block can branch out before block 5 and obtain a QC at the same time. The worst that can happen is that a block extends block 5 or block 6, which will eventually lead to the same outcome—block 5 is committed.

Summary

- Cryptocurrencies are about decentralizing a payment network to avoid a single point of failure.
- To have everyone agree on the state of a cryptocurrency, we can use consensus algorithms.
- Byzantine fault-tolerant (BFT) consensus protocols were invented in 1982 and have evolved to become faster and simpler to understand.
- BFT consensus protocols need a known and fixed set of participants to work (permissioned network). Such protocols can decide who is part of this participant set (proof of authority or PoA) or dynamically elect the participant set based on the amount of currency they hold (proof of stake or PoS).

- Bitcoin's consensus algorithm (the Nakamoto consensus) uses proof of work (PoW) to validate the correct chain and to allow anyone to participate (permissionless network).

- Bitcoin's PoW has participants (called miners) compute a lot of hashes in order to find some with specific prefixes. Successfully finding a valid digest allows a miner to decide on the next block of transaction and collect a reward as well as transaction fees.

- Accounts in Bitcoin are simply ECDSA key pairs using the secp256k1 curve. A user knows how much BTCs their account holds by looking at all transaction outputs that have not yet been spent (UTXOs). A transaction is, thus, a signed message authorizing the movement of a number of older transaction outputs to new outputs, spendable to different public keys.

- Bitcoin uses Merkle trees to compress the size of a block and allow verification of transaction inclusion to be small in size.

- Stablecoins are cryptocurrencies that attempt to stabilize their values, most often by pegging their token to the value of a fiat currency like the US dollar.

- Cryptocurrencies use so-called layer 2 protocols in order to decrease their latency by processing transactions off-chain and saving progress on-chain periodically.

- Zero-knowledge proofs (ZKPs) are used in many different blockchain applications (for example, in Zcash to provide confidentiality and in Mina to compress the whole blockchain to a short proof of validity).

- Diem is a stablecoin that uses a BFT consensus protocol called DiemBFT. It remains both safe (no forks) and live (progress is always made) as long as no more than f malicious participants exist out of $3f + 1$ participants.

- DiemBFT works by having rounds in which a participant proposes a block of transactions extending a previous block. Other participants can then vote for the block, potentially creating a quorum certificate (QC) if enough votes are gathered ($2f + 1$).

- In DiemBFT, blocks and their transactions are finalized when the commit rule (a chain of 3 certified blocks at contiguous rounds) is triggered. When this happens, the first block of the chain and the blocks it extends are committed.

Hardware cryptography

13

This chapter covers

- Cryptography issues in highly adversarial environments
- Hardware solutions to increase the attacker's cost
- Side-channel attacks and software mitigations

Cryptographic primitives and protocols are often described as isolated building blocks as if they were running in a galaxy far, far away from any adversary. In practice, this is an unrealistic assumption that has often proven wrong. In the real world, cryptography runs in all kinds of environments and is subject to all sorts of threats. In this chapter, we'll look at the more extreme scenarios—*the highly adversarial environments*—and what you can do to protect your keys and your data in these situations. (Spoiler alert: it involves using specialized hardware.)

13.1   *Modern cryptography attacker model*

> *Present-day computer and network security starts with the assumption that there is a domain that we can trust. For example: if we encrypt data for transport over the Internet, we generally assume the computer that's doing the encrypting is not compromised and that there's some other "endpoint" at which it can be safely decrypted.*
>
> —Joanna Rutkowska ("Intel x86 considered harmful," 2015)

Cryptography used to be about "Alice wants to encrypt a message to Bob without Eve being able to intercept it." Today, a lot of it has moved to something more like "Alice wants to encrypt a message to Bob, but Alice has been compromised." It's a totally different attacker model, which is often not anticipated for in theoretical cryptography. What do I mean by this? Let me give you some examples:

- Using your credit card on an automated teller machine (ATM) that might be augmented with a *skimmer*, which is a device that a thief can place on top of the card reader in order to copy the content of your bank card (see figure 13.1)
- Downloading an application on your mobile phone that compromises the operating system (OS)
- Hosting a web server in a shared web-hosting service, where another malicious customer might be sharing the same machine as you
- Managing highly sensitive secrets in a data center that gets visited by spies from a different country

SKIMMER

Figure 13.1   **A skimmer, a malicious device that can be placed in front of ATM or payment terminal card readers in order to copy data contained in the card magnetic stripe. The magnetic stripe usually contains the account number, the expiration date, and other metadata that's used by you to pay online or in a number of payment terminals. Skimmers are sometimes accompanied with a hidden camera to obtain your PIN as well, potentially enabling the thief to use ATM withdrawals and payment terminals enforcing PIN entry.**

All of these examples are a modern use of cryptography in a threat model that many cryptographers ignore or are totally unaware of. Indeed, most of the cryptographic primitives that you read about in the literature will just assume that Alice, for example, has total control of her execution environment, and only when ciphertext (or a signature or a public key or . . .) leaves her computer to go over the network will man-in-the-middle (MITM) attackers be able to perform their tricks. But, in reality and in these modern times, we often use cryptography in much more adversarial models.

WARNING Security is, after all, a product of your assumptions and what you expect of a potential attacker. If your assumptions are wrong, you're in for a bad time.

How do real-world applications reconcile theoretical cryptography with these more powerful attackers? They make *compromises*. In other words, they try to make the attackers' lives more difficult. The security of such systems is often calculated in *cost* (how much does the attacker have to spend to break the system?) rather than computational complexity.

A lot of what you'll learn in this chapter will be *imperfect* cryptography, which in the real world, we call *defense in depth*. There's a lot to learn, and this chapter comes with lots of new acronyms and different solutions that different vendors and their marketing teams and sales people have come up with. So let's get started and learn about trusted systems in untrusted environments.

13.2 Untrusted environments: Hardware to the rescue

There are different ways to attack a system in practice. One way to categorize them is to think:

- *Software attacks*—Attacks that leverage code run on your device
- *Hardware attacks*—Attacks that require the adversary to be physically close to your device

While I already talked repeatedly about software attacks that target cryptography and how to mitigate them in previous chapters, there are some software attacks that are easier to defend if you leverage hardware solutions. For example, by generating and using cryptographic keys on a separate device connected to your computer, a virus hitting your computer wouldn't be able to extract the keys.

Hardware attacks, however, are more tricky because attackers who get access to a device can pretty much do anything they want: data on disk can be arbitrarily modified, lasers can be shot on targeted places to force a computation to produce an erroneous value (so-called *fault attacks*), chips can be opened to reveal their parts, focused ion beam (FIB) microscopes can be used to reverse-engineer components, and so on. The sky's the limit, and it is hard to protect against such motivated attackers. Typically, the different solutions available boil down to adding as many layers of defenses as you can in an attempt to make the attacker's life much more difficult. It is all about raising the costs!

Evil maid attacks

Not all hardware attackers are the same. For example, some attackers are able to spend some quality time with your devices, while others might have a limited amount of time. Imagine the following scenario: you leave your phone or laptop unattended in your hotel room, and a "malicious" maid comes in, opens the device, uses a low-budget, off-the-shelf tool to modify the system, and then leaves the device appearing

(continued)

untouched where it was found before you get back to your room. In the literature, this is known as an *evil maid attack* and can be generalized for many situations (for example, carrying devices in check-in luggages while flying, storing sensitive keys in an insecure data center, and so forth).

Of course, all systems don't necessarily need to defend against the most powerful hardware attacks, and not all applications deal with the same level of threat. Different hardware solutions exist for different contexts, so the rest of this section is about understanding the differences between "such and such."

13.2.1 White box cryptography, a bad idea

Before getting into hardware solutions for untrusted environments, why not use software solutions? Can cryptography provide primitives that do not leak their own keys?

White box cryptography is exactly this: a field of cryptography that attempts to scramble a cryptographic implementation with the key it uses. The goal is to prevent extraction of the key from observers. The attacker obtains the source code of some white box AES implementation with a fixed key, and it encrypts and decrypts just fine, but the key is mixed so well with the implementation that it is too hard for anyone to extract it from the algorithm. That's the theory at least. In practice, no published white box crypto algorithm has been found to be secure, and most commercial solutions are closed-source due to this fact.

> **NOTE** *Security through obscurity and obfuscation* (scrambling code to make it look unintelligible) are techniques that are generally frowned on as they haven't been proven to work effectively. That being said, in the real world, these techniques sometimes have their place and can be used to delay and frustrate adversaries.

All in all, white box cryptography is a big industry that sells dubious products to businesses in need of *digital rights management* (DRM) solutions (tools that control how much access a customer can get to a product they bought). For example, you can find these white-box solutions in the hardware that plays movies you bought in a store or in the software that plays movies you are watching on a streaming service. In reality, DRM does not strongly prevent these attacks; it just makes the life of their customers more difficult. On a more serious note, there is a branch of cryptography called *indistinguishability obfuscation* (iO) that attempts to do this cryptographically. iO is a theoretical, impractical, and so far, not-a-really-proven field of research. We'll see how that one goes, but I wouldn't hold my breath.

13.2.2 *They're in your wallet: Smart cards and secure elements*

White box cryptography is not great, but that's pretty much the best software solution for defending against powerful adversaries. So let's turn to the hardware side for solutions. (Spoiler alert: things are about to get much more complicated and confusing.) If you thought that real-world cryptography was messy and that there were too many standards or ways to do the same thing, wait until you read what's going on in the hardware world. Different terms have been made up and used in different ways, and standards have, unfortunately, proliferated as much as (if not more than) cryptography standards.

To understand what all of these hardware solutions are and how they differ from one another, let's start with some necessary history. *Smart cards* are small chips usually seen packaged inside plastic cards (like bank cards) and were invented in the early 1970s following advances in microelectronics. Smart cards started out as a practical way to get everyone a pocket computer! Indeed, a modern smart card embeds its own CPU, different types of programmable or non-programmable memory (ROM, RAM, and EEPROM), inputs and outputs, a hardware random number generator (also called TRNG as you learned in chapter 8), and so on.

They're "smart" in the sense that they can run programs, unlike the not-so-smart cards that could only store data via a magnetic stripe, which could be easily copied via the skimmers I talked about previously. Most smart cards allow developers to write small, contained applications that can run on the card. The most popular standard supported by smart cards is *JavaCard*, which allows developers to write Java-like applications.

To use a smart card, you first need to activate it by inserting it into a card reader. More recently, cards have been augmented with the Near Field Communication (NFC) protocol to achieve the same result via radio frequencies. This allows you to use the card by getting close to a card reader, as opposed to physically touching it.

Banks and legacy cryptography

By the way, banks make use of smart cards to store a unique per-card secret that's capable of saying, "I am indeed the card that you gave to this customer." Intuitively, you might think that this is implemented via public key cryptography, but the banking industry is still stuck in the past and uses symmetric cryptography (due to the vast amount of legacy software and hardware still in use)!

More specifically, most bank card stores a *triple-DES* (3DES) symmetric key, an old 64-bit block cipher that seeks to make the insecure Data Encryption Standard (DES) secure. The algorithm is used not to encrypt, but to produce a MAC (message authentication code) over some challenge. The bank who holds every customer's current 3DES symmetric key can verify the MAC. This is an excellent example of what real-world cryptography is often about: legacy algorithms used all over the place in a risky way. (And this is also why key rotation is such an important concept and why you have to change your bank cards periodically.)

Smart cards mix a number of physical and logical techniques to prevent observation, extraction, and modification of their execution environment and parts of their memory (where secrets are stored). There exist many attacks that attempt to break these cards and hardware devices in general. These attacks can be classified in three different categories:

- *Non-invasive attacks*—Attacks that do not affect the targeted device. For example, differential power analysis (DPA) attacks evaluate the power consumption of a smart card while it simultaneously performs cryptographic operations in order to extract its keys.
- *Semi-invasive attacks*—Attacks that use access to the chip's surface in a non-damaging way to mount exploits. For example, differential fault analysis (DFA) attacks make use of heat, lasers, and other techniques to modify the execution of a program running on the smart card in order to leak keys.
- *Invasive attacks*—Attacks that open the chip to probe or modify the circuitry in the silicon itself in order to alter the chip's function and reveal its secrets. These attacks are noticeable because they can damage devices and have a greater chance of rendering devices unusable.

The fact that hardware chips are extremely small and tightly packaged can make attacks difficult. But specialized hardware usually goes much further by using different layers of materials to prevent depackaging and physical observation and by using hardware techniques to increase the inaccuracy of known attacks.

Smart cards got really popular really fast, and it became obvious that having such a secure black box in other devices could be useful. The concept of a *secure element* was born: a tamper-resistant microcontroller that can be found in pluggable form (for example, the SIM card in your phone required to access your carrier's network) or directly bonded on chips and motherboards (for example, the embedded secure element attached to an iPhone's NFC chip for payments). A secure element is really just a small, separate piece of hardware meant to protect your secrets and their usage in cryptographic operations.

Secure elements are an important concept to protect cryptographic operations in the *Internet of Things* (IoT), a colloquial (and overloaded) term referring to devices that can communicate with other devices (think credit cards, phones, biometric passports, garage keys, smart home sensors, and so on). You can see all of the solutions that follow in this section as secure elements implemented in different form factors, using different techniques to achieve pretty much the same thing, but providing different levels of security and speed.

The main definitions and standards around secure elements have been produced by Global Platform, a nonprofit association created from the need of the different players in the industry to facilitate interoperability among different vendors and systems. There exist more standards and certifications that focus on the security claims of secure elements from standard bodies like Common Criteria (CC), NIST, or the EMV (for Europay, Mastercard, and Visa).

As secure elements are highly secretive recipes, integrating them in your product means that you will have to sign nondisclosure agreements and use closed-source hardware and firmware. For many projects, this is seen as a serious limitation in transparency, but can be understood, as part of the security in these chips come from the obscurity of their design.

13.2.3 Banks love them: Hardware security modules (HSMs)

If you understood what a secure element is, well a *hardware security module* (HSM) is basically a bigger and faster secure element, and like some secure elements, some HSMs can run arbitrary code as well. This is not always true, however. Some HSMs are small (like the YubiHSM, a tiny USB dongle that resembles a YubiKey), and the term *hardware security module* can be used to mean different things by different people.

Many would argue that all of the hardware solutions discussed so far are HSMs of different forms and that secure elements are just HSMs specified by GlobalPlatform, while TPMs (Trusted Platform Modules) are HSMs specified by the Trusted Computing Group. But most of the time, when people talk about HSMs, they mean the big stuff.

HSMs are often classified according to FIPS 140-2, "Security Requirements for Cryptographic Modules." The document is quite old, published in 2001, and naturally, does not take into account a number of attacks discovered after its publication. Fortunately, in 2019, it was superseded by the more modern version, FIPS 140-3. FIPS 140-3 now relies on two international standards:

- *ISO/IEC 19790:2012*—Defines four security levels for hardware security modules. Level 1 HSMs do not provide any protection against physical attacks (you can think of these as pure software implementations), while level 3 HSMs wipe their secrets if they detect any intrusion!
- *ISO 24759:2017*—Defines how HSMs must be tested in order to standardize certifications for HSM products.

Unfortunately, the two standards are not free. You'll have to pay if you want to read them.

The US, Canada, and some other countries mandate certain industries like banks to use devices that have been certified according to the FIPS 140 levels. Many companies worldwide follow these same recommendations as well.

> **NOTE** Wiping secrets is a practice called *zeroization*. Unlike level 3 HSMs, level 4 HSMs can overwrite secret data multiple times, even in cases of power outages, thanks to backup internal batteries.

Typically, you find an HSM as an external device with its own shelf on a rack (see figure 13.2) plugged to an enterprise server in a data center, as a PCIe card plugged into a server's motherboard, or even as small dongles that resemble hardware security

**Figure 13.2   An IBM 4767 HSM as a PCI card. Photo from Wikipedia
(http://mng.bz/XrAG).**

tokens. They can be plugged into your hardware via USB devices (if you don't mind the lower performance). To go full circle, some of these HSMs can be administered using smart cards to install applications, to back up secret keys, and so on.

Some industries highly utilize HSMs. For example, every time you enter your PIN in an ATM, the PIN ends up being verified by an HSM somewhere. Whenever you connect to a website via HTTPS, the root of trust comes from a certificate authority (CA) that stores its private key in an HSM, and the TLS connection is possibly terminated by an HSM. Do you have an Android or iPhone? Chances are that Google or Apple keep a backup of your phone safe with a fleet of HSMs. This last case is interesting because the threat model is reversed: the user does not trust the cloud with its data and, thus, the cloud service provider claims that its service can't see the user's encrypted backup nor can it access the keys used to encrypt it.

HSMs don't really have a standard interface, but most of them will, at least, implement *Public Key Cryptography Standard 11* (PKCS#11), one of the old standards that were started by the RSA company and that were progressively moved to the OASIS organization in 2012 to facilitate adoption of the standards. While the last version of PKCS#11 (v2.40) was released in 2015, it is merely an update of a standard that originally started in 1994. For this reason, it specifies a number of old cryptographic algorithms, or old ways of doing things, which can lead to vulnerabilities. Nevertheless, it is good enough for many uses and specifies an interface that allows different systems to easily interoperate with each other. The good news is that PKCS#11 v3.0 was released in 2020, including a lot of modern cryptographic algorithms like Curve25519, EdDSA, and SHAKE to name a few.

While the real goal for HSMs is to make sure nobody can extract key material from them, their security is not always shining. A lot about the security of these hardware solutions really relies on their high price, the hardware defense techniques not being disclosed, and the certifications (like FIPS and Common Criteria) that mostly focus on the hardware side of things. In practice, devastating software bugs were found, and it is not always straightforward if the HSM you use is at risk to any of these vulnerabilities. In 2018, Jean-Baptiste Bédrune and Gabriel Campana showed in their research ("Everybody be Cool, This is a Robbery") a software attack to extract keys out of popular HSMs.

> **NOTE** Not only is the price of one HSM high (it can easily be tens of thousands of dollars depending on the security level), but in addition to one HSM, you often have at least another HSM you use for testing and at least one more for backup (in case your first HSM dies with its keys in it). It can add up!

Furthermore, I still haven't touched on the "elephant in the room" with all of these solutions: while you might prevent most attackers from reaching your secret keys, you can't prevent attackers from compromising the system and making their own calls to the HSM (unless the HSM has logic that requires several signatures or the presence of a threshold of smart cards to operate). But, in most cases, the only service that an HSM provides is to prevent an attacker from stealthily stealing secrets and using those at some other time. When integrating hardware solutions like HSMs, it is good to first understand your threat model, the types of attacks you're looking to thwart, and if threshold schemes like the multi-signatures I mentioned in chapter 8 aren't a better solution.

13.2.4 *Trusted Platform Modules (TPMs): A useful standardization of secure elements*

While secure elements and HSMs prove to be useful, they are limited to specific use cases, and the process to write custom applications is known to be tedious. For this reason, the *Trusted Computing Group* (TCG) (another nonprofit organization formed by industry players) came up with a ready-to-use alternative that targets personal as well as enterprise computers. This is known as the *Trusted Platform Module* (TPM).

The TPM is not a chip but, instead, a standard (the TPM 2.0 standard); any vendor who so chooses can implement it. A TPM complying with the TPM 2.0 standard is a secure microcontroller that carries a hardware random number generator, secure memory for storing secrets, can perform cryptographic operations, and the whole thing is tamper-resistant. This description might sound familiar, and indeed, it is common to see TPMs implemented as a repackaging of secure elements. You usually find a TPM directly soldered or plugged into the motherboard of enterprise servers, laptops, and desktop computers (see figure 13.3).

Unlike smart cards and secure elements, a TPM does not run arbitrary code. Instead, it offers a well-defined interface that a greater system can take advantage of. TPMs are usually pretty cheap, and today many commodity laptops carry one.

Now the bad: the communication channel between a TPM and a processor is usually just a bus interface, which can easily be intercepted if you manage to steal or gain

Figure 13.3   A chip implementing the TPM 2.0 standard, plugged into a motherboard. This chip can be called by the system's motherboard components as well as user applications running on the computer's OS. Photo from Wikipedia (http://mng.bz/Q2je).

temporary physical access to the device. While many TPMs provide a high level of resistance against physical attacks, the fact that their communication channel is somewhat open does reduce their use cases to mostly defending against software attacks.

To solve these issues, there's been a move to TPM-like chips that are integrated directly into the main processor. For example, Apple has the Secure Enclave and Microsoft has Pluton. Unfortunately, none of these security processors seem to follow a standard, which means it could be difficult, perhaps impossible, for user applications to leverage their functionalities. Let's see some examples to get an idea of what hardware security chips like TPMs can do.

The simplest use case for TPMs is to protect data. To protect keys, it's easy: just generate them in the secure chip and disallow extraction. If you need the keys, ask the chip to perform the cryptographic operations. To protect data, encrypt it. That concept is called *file-based encryption* (FBE) if you're encrypting individual files and *full-disk encryption* (FDE) if it's the whole disk. FDE sounds much better as it's an all or nothing approach. That's what most laptops and desktops use. In practice, FDE is not that great though: it doesn't take into account how we, human beings, use our devices. We often leave our devices locked, as opposed to turned off, so that background functionalities can keep running. Computers deal with this by keeping the data-encryption key (DEK) around, even if your computer is locked. (Think about that the next time you go to the restroom at Starbucks, leaving your locked computer unattended.) Modern phones offer more security, encrypting different types of files depending on whether your phone is locked or turned off.

> **NOTE** In practice, both FDE and FBE have many implementation issues. In 2019, Meijer and Gastel (in "Self-encrypting deception: Weaknesses in the encryption of solid state drives (SSDs)") showed that several SSD vendors had completely insecure solutions. In 2021, Zinkus et al., (in "Data Security on Mobile Devices: Current State of the Art, Open Problems, and Proposed Solutions") found that phone disk encryption also had many issues.

Of course, the user should be authenticated before data can be decrypted. This is often done by asking the user for a PIN or password. A PIN or password is not enough though, as it would allow simple brute force attacks (especially on 4- or 6-digit PINs). In general, solutions try to tie the DEK to both a user credential and a symmetric key kept on the enclave.

But a chip manufacturer can't hardcode the same key in every device they produce; it leads to attacks like the DUHK attack (https://duhkattack.com), where thousands of devices were found hardcoding the same secret. This, in turn, means that the compromise of one device leads to the compromise of all the devices! The solution is a per-device key that is either fused into the chip at manufacturing time or created by the chip itself via hardware components called *physical unclonable functions*. For example, each Apple Secure Enclave has a UID, each TPM has a unique endorsement key and attestation key, etc. To prevent brute force attacks, Apple's Secure Enclave mixes both the UID key and the user PIN with a password-based key derivation function (we covered this in chapter 2) to derive the DEK. Except that I lied: to allow users to change their PIN quickly, the DEK is not derived directly, but instead encrypted by a key encryption key (KEK).

Another example is *secure boot*. When booting your computer, there are different stages that run until you finally get to the screen you want. One problem users face are viruses and malwares, and how if they infect the boot process, you then run on an evil OS.

To protect the integrity of boot, TPMs and integrated secure chips provide a root of trust, something that we trust 100% and that allows us to trust other stuff down the line. This root of trust is generally some read-only memory (ROM) that cannot be overwritten (also called *one-time programmable memory* as it's written during manufacturing and can't be changed). For example, when powering up a recent Apple device, the first code that gets executed is the boot ROM, located inside the Apple's Secure Enclave ROM. That boot ROM is tiny, so usually the only thing it does is:

1   Prepare some protected memory and load the next program to run there (usually some other boot loader)

2   Hash the program and verify its signature against the hardcoded public key in the ROM

3   Execute the program

The next boot loader does the same thing, and so on, until finally a boot loader starts the OS. This is, by the way, how OS updates that are not signed by Apple can't be installed on your phone.

TPMs and integrated TPM-like chips are an interesting development, and they greatly increased the security of our devices in recent years. As they become cheaper and a winning standard arises, more devices will be able to benefit from them.

13.2.5 *Confidential computing with a trusted execution environment (TEE)*

Smart cards, secure elements, HSMs, and TPMs are standalone chips or modules; they carry their own CPU, memory, TRNG, and so on, and other components can talk to them via some wires or radio frequency in NFC-enabled chips. TPM-like chips (Microsoft's Pluton and Apple's Secure Enclave) are standalone chips as well, although tightly coupled with the main processor inside of a system on chip (SoC). In this section, I will talk about the next logical step you can take in this taxonomy of security hardware, *integrated security*, hardware-enforced security within the main processor itself.

Processors that integrate security are said to create a *trusted execution environment* (TEE) for user code by extending the instruction set of a processor to allow for programs to run in a separate, secure environment. The separation between this secure environment and the ones we are used to dealing with already (often called a *rich execution environment*) is done via hardware. What ends up happening is that modern CPUs run both a normal OS as well as a secure OS simultaneously. Both have their own set of registers but share most of the rest of the CPU architecture. By using CPU-enforced logic, data from the secure world cannot be accessed from the normal world. For example, a CPU usually splits its memory, giving one part for the exclusive use of the TEE. Because a TEE is implemented directly on the main processor, not only does this mean a TEE is a faster and cheaper product than a TPM or secure element, it also comes for free in a lot of modern CPUs.

The TEE, like all other hardware solutions, is a concept developed independently by different vendors and a standard (by Global Platform) trying to play catch-up. The most known TEEs are Intel's Software Guard Extensions (SGX) and ARM's TrustZone.

What are TEEs good for? Let's look at an example. For the last few years, there's a new paradigm—the cloud—with big companies running servers to host your data. Amazon has AWS, Google has GCP, and Microsoft has Azure. Another way to put this is that people are moving from running things themselves to running things on someone else's computer. This creates some issues in some scenarios where privacy is important. To fix that, *confidential computing* attempts to offer solutions to run client code without being able to see it or modify its behavior. SGX's primary use case seems to be exactly that these days: clients running code that servers can't see or tamper with.

One interesting problem that arises is how can one trust that the response from a request came from SGX, for example, and not from some impersonator. This is what *attestation* tries to solve. There are two kinds of attestation:

- *Local attestation*—Two enclaves running on the same platform need to communicate and prove to each other that they are secure enclaves.
- *Remote attestation*—A client queries a remote enclave and needs to make sure that it is the legitimate enclave that produced the result from the request.

Each SGX chip is provided with unique key pairs (the *Root Sealing Keys*) at manufacturing time. The public key part is then signed by some Intel CA. The first assumption, if we ignore the assumption that the hardware is secure, is that Intel is correctly signing public keys for secure SGX chips only. With that in mind, you can now obtain a signed attestation from Intel's CA that you're talking to a real SGX enclave and that it is running some specific code.

TEE's goal is to first and foremost thwart *software attacks.* While the claimed software security seems to be attractive, it is, in practice, hard to segregate execution on the same chip due to the extreme complexity of modern CPUs and their dynamic states. This is attested to by the many software attacks against SGX and TrustZone (https://foreshadowattack.eu, https://mdsattacks.com, https://plundervolt.com, and https://sgaxe.com).

TEE as a concept provides some resistance against physical attacks because things at this microscopic level are way too tiny and tightly packaged together to analyze without expensive equipment. Against a motivated attacker, things might be different.

13.3 What solution is good for me?

You have learned about many hardware products in this chapter. As a recap, here's the list, which I illustrate in figure 13.4 as well:

- *Smart cards are microcomputers that need to be turned on by an external device like a payment terminal.* They can run small custom Java-like applications. Bank cards are an example of a widely used smart card.
- *Secure elements are a generalization of smart cards, which rely on a set of Global Platform standards.* SIM Cards are an example of secure elements.
- *HSMs (hardware security modules) can be seen as larger pluggable secure elements for enterprise servers.* They are faster and more flexible and are seen mostly in data centers to store secret keys, making attacks on keys more obvious.
- *TPMs (Trusted Platform Modules) are repackaged secure elements plugged into personal and enterprise computer motherboards.* They follow a standardized API by the Trusted

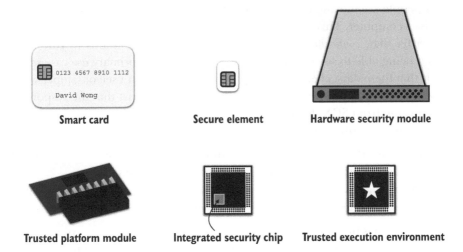

Figure 13.4   The different hardware solutions you learned in this chapter and an idea of what they look like.

Computing Group that can provide functionalities for operating systems and end users.

- *Security processors are TPM-like chips built extremely close to the main processor and are not programmable.* They follow no standards, and different players have come out with different technologies.
- *TEEs (trusted execution environments) like TrustZone and SGX can be thought of as programmable secure elements implemented within the CPU instruction set.* They are faster and cheaper, mostly providing resistance against software attacks. Most modern CPUs ship with TEEs and various levels of defense against hardware attacks.

What is the best solution for you? Try to narrow your choice by asking yourself some questions:

- *In what form factor?* For example, the need for a secure element in a small device dictates what solutions you won't be able to use.
- *How much speed do you need?* Applications that need to perform a high number of cryptographic operations per second will be highly constrained in the solutions they can use, probably limited to HSMs and TEEs.
- *How much security do you need?* Certifications and claims by vendors correspond to different levels of software or hardware security. The sky's the limit.

Keep in mind that no hardware solution is the panacea; you're only increasing the attack's cost. Against a sophisticated attacker all of this is pretty much useless. Design your system so that one compromised device doesn't imply that all devices are compromised.

13.4 Leakage-resilient cryptography or how to mitigate side-channel attacks in software

We saw how hardware attempts to prevent direct observation and extraction of secret keys, but there's only so much that hardware can do. At the end of the day, it is possible for the software to not care and give out the key despite all of this hardware hardening. The software can do so somewhat directly (like a backdoor) or it can do it indirectly by leaking enough information for someone to reconstruct the key. This latter option is called a *side channel*, and side-channel vulnerabilities are unintentional bugs most of the time (at least one would hope).

I mentioned timing attacks in chapter 3, where you learned that MAC authentication tags had to be compared in constant time; otherwise, attackers could infer the correct tag after sending you many incorrect ones and measuring how long they waited for you to respond. Timing attacks are usually taken seriously in all areas of real-world cryptography as they can potentially be remotely performed over the network, unlike physical side channels.

The most important and known side channel is *power consumption*, which I mentioned earlier in this chapter. This was discovered as an attack, called *differential power analysis* (DPA), by Kocher, Jaffe, and Jun in 1998, when they realized that they could hook an oscilloscope to a device and observe variance in the electricity consumed by the device over time while performing encryptions of known plaintexts. This variance clearly depends on the bits of the key used, and the fact that operations like XORing would consume more or less power, depending if the operand bits were set or not. This observation led to a *key-extraction attack* (so-called *total breaks*).

This concept can be illustrated with *simple power analysis* (SPA) attack. In ideal situations and when no hardware or software mitigations are implemented against power analysis attacks, it suffices to measure and analyze the power consumption of a single cryptographic operation involving a secret key. I illustrate this in figure 13.5.

Power is not the only physical side channel. Some attacks rely on electromagnetic radiations, vibrations, and even the sound emitted by the hardware. Let me still mention two other nonphysical side-channels. I know we are in a hardware-focused chapter, but these nonphysical side-channel attacks are important as they need to be mitigated in many real-world cryptographic applications.

First, returned errors can sometimes leak critical information. For example, in 2018, the ROBOT attack figured out a way to exploit the Bleichenbacher attack (mentioned in chapter 6) on a number of servers that implemented RSA PKCS#1 v1.5 decryption in the TLS protocol (covered in chapter 9). Bleichenbacher's attack only works if you can distinguish if an RSA ciphertext has a valid padding or not. To protect against that attack, safe implementations perform the padding validation in constant time and avoid returning early if they detects that the padding is invalid. For example, in an RSA key exchange in TLS, the server has to fake its response as if it completed a successful handshake if the padding of the RSA payload is incorrect. Yet, if at the end of the padding validation an implementation decides to return a

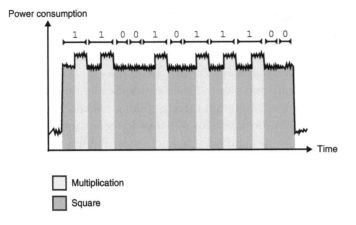

Figure 13.5 Some cryptographic algorithms leak so much information via their power consumption that a simple power analysis of a single power trace (a measure of the power consumed in time) can leak the private key of the algorithm. For example, this figure represents a trace of an RSA exponentiation (the message being exponentiated to the private exponent; see chapter 6). The RSA exponentiation is implemented with a square-and-multiply algorithm that iterates through the bits of the private exponent; for each bit it applies a square operation followed by a multiply operation only if the bit is set. In this example, multiplication is obviously consuming more power; hence, the clarity of the power trace.

different error to the client (based on the validity of the padding), then this was all for nothing.

Second, accessing memory can take more or less time, depending if the data was previously accessed or not. This is due to the numerous layers of caching that exist in a computer. For example if the CPU needs something, it first checks if it has been cached in its internal memory. If not, it then reaches into caches that are further and further away from it. The further away the cache, the more time it'll take. Not only that, but some caches are specific to a core (L1 cache, for example), while some caches are shared among cores in a multicore machine (L3 cache, RAM, disk).

Cache attacks exploit the fact that it is possible for a malicious program to run on the same machine, using the same cryptographic library as a sensitive cryptographic program. For example, many cloud services host different virtual servers on the same machine, and many servers use the OpenSSL library for cryptographic operations or for serving TLS pages. Malicious programs find ways to evict parts of the library that have been loaded in a cache shared with the victim's process and then periodically measure the time it takes to reread some parts of that library. If it takes a long time, then the victim did not execute this part of the program; if it doesn't take a long time, then the victim accessed this part of the program and repopulated the cache to avoid having to fetch again the program to a far away cache or worse from disk. What you obtain is a trace that resembles a power trace, and it is indeed exploitable in similar ways!

OK, that's enough for side-channel attacks. If you're interested in attacking cryptography via these side channels, there are better resources than this book. In this section, I want to only talk about software mitigations that cryptographic implementations can and should implement to protect against side-channel attacks in general. This whole field of study is called *leakage-resilient cryptography*, as the cryptographer's goal here is to not leak anything.

Defending against physical attackers is an endless battle, which explains why many of these mitigations are proprietary and akin to obfuscation. This section is obviously not exhaustive but should give you an idea of the type of things applied cryptographers are working on to address side-channel attacks.

13.4.1 *Constant-time programming*

The first line of defense for any cryptographic implementation is to implement its cryptographic sensitive parts (think any computation that involves a secret) in constant time. It is obvious that implementing something in constant time cancels timing attacks, but this also gets rid of many classes of attacks like cache attacks and simple power analysis attacks.

How do you implement something in constant time? Never *branch*. In other words, no matter what the input is, always do the same thing. For example, listing 13.1 shows how the Golang language implements a constant-time comparison of authentication tags for the HMAC algorithm. Intuitively, if two bytes are equal, then their XOR will be 0. If this property is verified for every pair of bytes we compare, then ORing them will also lead to a 0 value (and a nonzero value otherwise). Note that it can be quite disconcerting to read this code if this is the first time you're looking at constant-time tricks.

> **Listing 13.1   How Golang implements a constant-time comparison between two bytearrays**

```
func ConstantTimeCompare(x, y []byte) byte {
    if len(x) != len(y) {        There is no point comparing two strings in
        return 0                 constant time if they are of different lengths.
    }

    var v byte
    for i := 0; i < len(x); i++ {   Here is where the magic happens.
        v |= x[i] ^ y[i]            The loop OR accumulates the XOR
    }                               of every byte into a value v.

    return v        Returns 0 only if v is equal to 0 and
}                   returns a nonzero value otherwise
```

For a MAC authentication tag comparison, it is enough to stop here to check if the result is 0 or not by branching (using a conditional expression such as `if`). Another interesting example is *scalar multiplication* in elliptic curve cryptography, which, as you learned in chapter 5, consists of adding a point to itself x number of times, where x is what we call a scalar. This process can be somewhat slow, and thus clever algorithms exist to speed up this part. One of the popular ones is called Montgomery's ladder and is pretty much the equivalent to the RSA's square-and-multiply algorithm I mentioned earlier (but in a different group).

Montgomery ladder's algorithm alternates between the addition of two points and doubling of a point (adding the point to itself). Both the RSA's square-and-multiply and Montgomery ladder's algorithms have a simple way to mitigate timing attacks: they do not branch and always perform both operations. (And this is why the RSA exponentiation algorithm in constant time is usually referred to as *square and multiply always*.)

> **NOTE** In chapter 7, I mentioned that signature schemes can go wrong in multiple ways and that key recovery attacks exist against implementations that leak a few bytes of the nonces they use (in signature schemes like ECDSA). This is what happened in the Minerva and TPM-Fail attacks, which happened around the same time. Both attacks found that a number of devices were vulnerable due to the amount of timing variation the signing operation takes.

In practice, mitigating timing attacks is not always straightforward as it is not always clear if CPU instructions for multiplications or conditional moves are in constant time. Additionally, it is not always clear how the compiler will compile high-level code when used with different compilation flags. For this reason, a manual review of the assembly generated is sometimes performed in order to obtain more confidence in the constant-time code written. Different tools to analyze constant-time code exist (like ducdect, ct-verif, SideTrail, and so on), but they are rarely used in practice.

13.4.2 *Don't use the secret! Masking and blinding*

Another common way of thwarting or at least confusing attackers is to add layers of indirection to any operation involving secrets. One of these techniques is called *blinding*, which is often possible thanks to the arithmetic structure of public key cryptography algorithms. You saw blinding used in oblivious algorithms like password-authenticated key exchange algorithms in chapter 11, and we can use blinding in the same way where we want the oblivious party to be the attacker observing leaks from our computations. Let's talk about RSA as an example.

Remember, RSA decrypts by taking a ciphertext c and raising it to the private exponent d, where the private exponent d cancels the public exponent e, which was used to compute the ciphertext as $m^e \bmod N$. If you don't remember the details, make sure to consult chapter 6. One way to add indirection is to perform the decryption operation on a value that is not the ciphertext known to the attacker. This method is called *base blinding* and goes like this:

1 Generate a random blinding factor r
2 Compute *message* $= (ciphertext \times r^e)^d \bmod N$
3 Unblind the result by computing *real_message* $=$ *message* $\times r^{-1} \bmod N$, where r^{-1} is the inverse of r

This method blinds the value being used with the secret, but we can also blind the secret itself. For example, elliptic curve scalar multiplication is usually used with a secret scalar. But as computations take place in a cyclic group, adding a multiple of order to that secret does not change the computation result. This technique is called *scalar blinding* and goes like this:

1 Generate a random value k_1
2 Compute a scalar $k_2 = d + k_1 \times order$, where d is the original secret scalar and *order* is its order
3 To compute $Q = [d]\ P$, instead compute $Q = [k_2]\ P$, which results in the same point

All of these techniques have been proven to be more or less efficient and are often used in combinations with other software and hardware mitigations. In symmetric cryptography, another somewhat similar technique, called *masking*, is used.

The concept of masking is to transform the input (the plaintext or ciphertext in the case of a cipher) before passing it to the algorithm. For example, by XORing the input with a random value. The output is then unmasked in order to obtain the final correct output. As any intermediate state is thus masked, this provides the cryptographic computation some amount of decorrelation from the input data and makes side-channel attacks much more difficult. The algorithm must be aware of this masking to correctly perform internal operations while keeping the correct behavior of the original algorithm.

13.4.3 *What about fault attacks?*

I previously talked about *fault attacks*, a more intrusive type of side-channel attacks that modify the execution of the algorithm by inducing faults. Injecting faults can be done in many creative ways, physically, by increasing the heat of the system, for example, or even by shooting lasers at calculated points in the targeted chip.

Surprisingly, faults can also be induced via software. An example was found independently in the Plundervolt and V0LTpwn attacks, which managed to change the voltage of a CPU to introduce natural faults. This also happened in the infamous rowhammer attack, which discovered that repeatedly accessing memory of some DRAM devices could flip nearby bits. These types of attacks can be difficult to achieve but are extremely powerful. In cryptography, computing a bad result can sometimes leak the key. This is, for example, the case with RSA signatures that are implemented with some specific optimizations.

While it is impossible to fully mitigate these attacks, some techniques exist that can increase the complexity of a successful attack; for example, by computing the same operation several times and comparing the results to make sure they match before releasing it or by verifying the result before releasing it. For signatures, one can verify the signature via the public key before returning it.

Fault attacks can also have dramatic consequences against random number generators. One easy solution is to use algorithms that do not use new randomness every time they run. For example, in chapter 7, you learned about EdDSA, a signature algorithm that requires no new randomness to sign as opposed to the ECDSA signature algorithm.

All in all, none of these techniques are foolproof. Doing cryptography in highly adversarial environments is always about how much more cost you can afford to incur to the attackers.

Summary

- The threat today is not just an attacker intercepting messages over the wire, but an attacker stealing or tampering with the device that runs your cryptography. Devices in the so-called Internet of Things (IoT) often run into threats and are, by default, unprotected against sophisticated attackers. More recently, cloud services are also considered in the threat model of their users.

- Hardware can help protect cryptography applications and their secrets in a highly adversarial environment. One of the ideas is to provide a device with a tamper-resistant chip to store and perform crypto operations. That is, if the device falls in the hands of an attacker, extracting keys or modifying the behavior of the chip will be difficult.

- It is generally accepted that one has to combine different software and hardware techniques to harden cryptography in adversarial environments. But hardware-protected cryptography is not a panacea; it is merely defense in-depth, effectively slowing down and increasing the cost of an attack. Adversaries with unlimited time and money will always break your hardware.

- Decreasing the impact of an attack can also help deter attackers. This must be done by designing a system well (for example, by making sure that the compromise of one device does not imply a compromise of all devices).

- While there are many hardware solutions, the most popular ones are as follows:
  - Smart cards were one of the first such secure microcontrollers that could be used as a microcomputer to store secrets and perform cryptographic operations. They are supposed to use a number of techniques to discourage physical attackers. The concept of a smart card was generalized as a secure element, which is a term employed differently in different domains, but boils down to a smart card that can be used as a coprocessor in a greater system that already has a main processor.
  - Hardware security modules (HSMs) are often referred to as pluggable cards that act like secure elements. They do not follow any standard interface but usually implement the PKCS#11 standard for cryptographic operations. HSMs can be certified with different levels of security via some NIST standard (FIPS 140-3).
  - Trusted Platform Modules (TPMs) are similar to secure elements with a specified interface standardized as TPM 2.0. A TPM is usually seen plugged into a laptop or server motherboard.

- Trusted execution environment (TEE) is a way to segregate an execution environment between a secure one and a potentially insecure one. TEEs are usually implemented as an extension of a CPU's instruction set.

- Hardware is not enough to protect cryptographic operations in highly adversarial environments as software and hardware side-channel attacks can exploit leakage that occurs in different ways (timing, power consumption, electromagnetic radiations, and so on). In order to defend against side-channel attacks cryptographic algorithms implement software mitigations:

  - Serious cryptographic implementations are based on constant-time algorithms and avoid all branching as well as memory accesses that depend on secret data.

  - Mitigation techniques based on blinding and masking decorrelate sensitive operations from either the secret or the data known to be operated on.

  - Fault attacks are harder to protect against. Mitigations include computing an operation several times and comparing and verifying the result of an operation (for example, verifying a signature with the public key) before releasing the result.

- Hardening cryptography in adversarial settings is a never-ending battle. One should use a combination of software and hardware mitigations to increase the cost and the time for a successful attack up to a desired accepted risk. One should also decrease the impact of an attack by using unique keys per device and, potentially, unique keys per cryptographic operation.

14
Post-quantum cryptography

This chapter covers

- Quantum computers and their impact on cryptography
- Post-quantum cryptography to defend against quantum computers
- The post-quantum algorithms of today and tomorrow

"Quantum computers can break cryptography," implied Peter Shor, a professor of mathematics at MIT. It was 1994, and Shor had just come up with a new algorithm. His discovery unlocked efficient factoring of integers, destroying cryptographic algorithms like RSA if quantum computers ever were to become a reality. At the time, the quantum computer was just a theory, a concept of a new class of computer based on quantum physics. The idea remained to be proven. In mid-2015, the National Security Agency (NSA) took everybody by surprise after announcing their plans to transition to *quantum-resistant algorithms* (cryptographic algorithms not vulnerable to quantum computers).

> *For those partners and vendors that have not yet made the transition to Suite B elliptic curve algorithms, we recommend not making a significant expenditure to do so at this point but instead to prepare for the upcoming quantum resistant algorithm*

transition. [. . .] Unfortunately, the growth of elliptic curve use has bumped up against the fact of continued progress in the research on quantum computing, which has made it clear that elliptic curve cryptography is not the long term solution many once hoped it would be. Thus, we have been obligated to update our strategy.

—National Security Agency ("Cryptography Today," 2015)

While the idea of *quantum computing* (building a computer based on physical phenomena studied in the field of quantum mechanics) was not new, it had witnessed a huge boost in research grants as well as experimental breakthroughs in recent years. Still, no one was able to demonstrate a break of cryptography using a quantum computer. Did the NSA know something we didn't? Were quantum computers really going to break cryptography? And what is quantum-resistant cryptography? In this chapter, I will attempt to answer all your questions!

14.1 What are quantum computers and why are they scaring cryptographers?

Since NSA's announcement, quantum computers have repeatedly made the news as many large companies like IBM, Google, Alibaba, Microsoft, Intel, and so on have invested significant resources into researching them. But what are these quantum computers and why are they so scary? It all began with *quantum mechanics* (also called *quantum physics*), a field of physics that studies the behavior of small stuff (think atoms and smaller). As this is the basis of quantum computers, this is where our investigation starts.

There was a time when the newspapers said that only twelve men understood the theory of relativity. I do not believe there ever was such a time. There might have been a time when only one man did, because he was the only guy who caught on, before he wrote his paper. But after people read the paper, a lot of people understood the theory of relativity in some way or other, certainly more than twelve. On the other hand, I think I can safely say that nobody understands quantum mechanics.

—Richard Feynman (*The Character of Physical Law*, MIT Press, 1965)

14.1.1 Quantum mechanics, the study of the small

Physicists have long thought that the whole world is deterministic, like our cryptographic pseudorandom number generators: if you knew how the universe worked and if you had a computer large enough to compute the "universe function," all you would need is the *seed* (the information contained in the Big Bang) and you could predict everything from there. Yes *everything*, even the fact that merely 13.7 billion years after the start of the universe you were going to read this line. In such a world, there is no room for randomness. Every decision that you make is predetermined by past events, even by those that happened before you were born.

While this view of the world has bemused many philosophers—"Do we really have free will, then?" they asked—an interesting field of physics started growing in the 1990s, which has puzzled many scientists since then, We call this the field of *quantum physics* (also called *quantum mechanics*). It turns out that very small objects (think atoms and smaller) tend to behave quite differently from what we've observed and theorized so far using what we call classical physics. On this (sub)atomic scale, particles seem to behave like waves sometimes, in the sense that different waves can superpose to merge into a bigger wave or cancel each other for a brief moment.

One measurement we can perform on particles like electrons is their *spin*. For example, we can measure whether an electron is spinning up or down. So far, nothing too weird. What's weird is that quantum mechanics says that a particle can be in these two states *at the same time*, spinning up *and* down. We say that the particle is in *quantum superposition*.

This special state can be induced manually using different techniques depending on the type of particle. A particle can remain in a state of superposition until we measure it; in which case, the particle *collapses* into only one of these possible states (spinning up or down). This quantum superposition is what quantum computers end up using: instead of having a bit that can either be a 1 or a 0, a *quantum bit* or *qubit* can be both 0 and 1 at the same time.

Even weirder, quantum theory says that it is only when a measurement happens, and not before, that a particle in superposition decides at random which state it is going to take (each state having a 50% chance of being observed). If this seems weird, you are not alone. Many physicists could not conceive how this would work in the deterministic world they had painted. Einstein, convinced that something was wrong with this new theory, once said "God does not play dice." Yet cryptographers were interested, as this was a way to finally obtain *truly* random numbers! This is what *quantum random number generators* (QRNGs) do by continuously setting particles like photons in a superposed state and then measuring them.

Physicists have also theorized what quantum mechanics would look like with objects at our scale. This led to the famous experiment of *Schrödinger's cat*: a cat in a box is both dead and alive until an observer takes a look inside (which has led to many debates on what exactly constitutes an observer).

> *A cat is penned up in a steel chamber, along with the following device (which must be secured against direct interference by the cat): in a Geiger counter, there is a tiny bit of radioactive substance, so small, that perhaps in the course of the hour one of the atoms decays, but also, with equal probability, perhaps none; if it happens, the counter tube discharges and through a relay releases a hammer that shatters a small flask of hydrocyanic acid. If one has left this entire system to itself for an hour, one would say that the cat still lives if meanwhile no atom has decayed. The first atomic decay would have poisoned it. The psi-function of the entire system would express this by having in it the living and dead cat (pardon the expression) mixed or smeared out in equal parts.*

> —Erwin Schrödinger ("The Present Situation in
> Quantum Mechanics," 1935)

All of that is highly unintuitive to us because we've never encountered quantum behavior in our day-to-day lives. Now, let's add even more weirdness!

Sometimes particles interact with each other (for example, by colliding into one another) and end up in a state of strong *correlation*, where it is impossible to describe one particle without the others. This phenomenon is called *quantum entanglement*, and it is one of the secret sauces behind the performance boost of quantum computers. If, let's say, two particles are entangled, then when one of them is measured, both particles collapse and the state of one is known to be perfectly correlated to the state of the other. OK, that was confusing. Let's take an example: if two electrons are entangled and one of them is then measured and found to be spinning up, we know that the other one is then spinning down (but not before the first one is measured). Furthermore, any such experiment always turns out the same.

This is hard to believe, but even more mind-blowing, it was shown that entanglement works even across very long distances. Einstein, Podolsky, and Rosen famously argued that the description of quantum mechanics was incomplete, most probably missing *hidden variables*, which would explain entanglement (as in, once the particles are separated, they know exactly what their measurement will be).

Einstein, Podolsky, and Rosen also described a thought experiment (the *EPR paradox*, named after the first letters of their last names) in which two entangled particles are separated by a large distance (think light-years away) and then measured at approximately the same time. According to quantum mechanics, the measurement of one of the particles would instantly affect the other particle, which would be impossible as no information can travel faster than the speed of light, according to the theory of relativity (thus the paradox). This strange thought experiment is what Einstein famously called "spooky action at a distance."

John Bell later stated an inequality of probabilities known as *Bell's theorem*; the theorem, if shown to be true, would prove the existence of the hidden variables mentioned by the authors of the EPR paradox. The inequality was later violated experimentally (many, many times), enough to convince us that entanglement is real, discarding the presence of any hidden variables.

Today, we say that a measurement of entangled particles leads to the particles coordinating with each other, which bypasses the relativistic prediction that communication cannot go faster than the speed of light. Indeed, try to think of a way you could use entanglement to devise a communication channel, and you'll see that it is not possible. For cryptographers, though, the spooky action at a distance meant that we could develop novel ways to perform key exchanges; this idea is called *quantum key distribution* (QKD).

Imagine distributing two entangled particles to two peers: who would then measure their respective particles in order to start forming the same key (as measuring one particle would give you information about the measurement of the other)? QKD's concept is made even more sexy by the *no-cloning theorem*, which states that you can't passively observe such an exchange and create an exact copy of one of the particles being sent on that channel. Yet, these protocols are vulnerable to trivial man-in-the-middle (MITM) attacks and are sort of useless without already having a way to authenticate data. This flaw has led some cryptographers like Bruce Schneier to state that "QKD as a product has no future."

This is all I'll say about quantum physics as this is already too much for a book on cryptography. If you don't believe any of the bizarre things that you just read, you are not alone. In his book, *Quantum Mechanics for Engineers,* Leon van Dommelen writes "Physics ended up with quantum mechanics not because it seemed the most logical explanation, but because countless observations made it unavoidable."

14.1.2 *From the birth of quantum computers to quantum supremacy*

In 1980, the idea of *quantum computing* was born. It is Paul Benioff who is first to describe what a quantum computer could be: a computer built from the observations made in the last decades of quantum mechanics. Later that same year, Paul Benioff and Richard Feynman argue that this is the only way to simulate and analyze quantum systems, short of the limitations of classical computers.

It is only 18 years later when a quantum algorithm running on an actual quantum computer is demonstrated for the first time by IBM. Fast forward to 2011, D-Wave Systems, a quantum computer company, announces the first commercially available quantum computer, launching an entire industry forward in a quest to create the first scalable quantum computer.

There's still a long way to go, and a useful quantum computer is something that hasn't been achieved yet. The most recent notable result at the time of this writing (2021) is Google, claiming in 2019 to have reached *quantum supremacy* with a 53-qubit quantum computer. Quantum supremacy means that, for the first time ever, a quantum computer achieved something that a classical computer couldn't. In 3 minutes and 20 seconds, it performed some analysis that would have taken a classical computer around 10,000 years to finish. That is, before you get too excited, it outperformed a classical computer at a task that wasn't useful. Yet, it is an incredible milestone, and one can only wonder where this will all lead us.

A quantum computer pretty much uses the quantum physics phenomena (like superposition and entanglement) the same way classical computers use electricity to perform computations. Instead of bits, quantum computers use *quantum bits* or *qubits*, which can be transformed via *quantum gates* to set them to specific values or put them in a state of superposition and, even, entanglement. This is somewhat similar to how gates are used in circuits in classical computers. Once a computation is done, the qubits can be measured in order to be interpreted in a classical way—as 0s and 1s. At that point, one can interpret the result further with a classical computer in order to finish a useful computation.

In general, N entangled qubits contain information equivalent to 2^N classical bits. But measuring the qubits at the end of a computation only gives you N number of 0s or 1s. Thus, it is not always clear how a quantum computer can help, and quantum computers are only found to be useful for a limited number of applications. It is possible that they will appear more and more useful as people find clever ways to leverage their power.

Today, you can already use a quantum computer from the comfort of your home. Services like IBM Quantum (https://quantum-computing.ibm.com) allow you to build quantum circuits and execute those on real quantum computers hosted in the cloud. Of course, such services are quite limited at the moment (early 2021), with only a few qubits available. Still, it is quite a mind-blowing experience to create your own circuit and wait for it to run on a real quantum computer, and all of that for free.

14.1.3 *The impact of Grover and Shor's algorithms on cryptography*

Unfortunately, as I said earlier, quantum computers are not useful for every type of computation, and thus, are not a more powerful drop-in replacement for our classical computers. But then, what are they good for?

In 1994, at a time where the concept of a quantum computer was just a thought experiment, Peter Shor proposed a quantum algorithm to solve the discrete logarithm and the factorization problems. Shor had the insight that a quantum computer could be used to quickly compute solutions to problems that could be related to the hard problems seen in cryptography. It turns out that there exists an efficient quantum algorithm that helps in finding a *period* such that $f(x + period) = f(x)$ for any given x. For example, finding the value *period* such that $g^{x+period} = g^x \bmod N$. This, in turn, leads to algorithms that can efficiently solve the factorization and the discrete logarithm problems, effectively impacting algorithms like RSA (covered in chapter 6) and Diffie-Hellman (covered in chapter 5).

Shor's algorithm is devastating for *asymmetric cryptography*, as most of the asymmetric algorithms in use today rely on the discrete logarithm or the factorization problem—most of what you saw throughout this book actually. You could think that discrete logarithm and factorization are still hard mathematical problems and that we could (maybe) increase the size of our algorithms' parameters in order to upgrade their defense against quantum computers. Unfortunately, it was shown in 2017, by Bernstein and others, that while raising parameters works, it would be highly impractical. The research estimated that RSA could be made quantum resistant by increasing its parameters to 1 terabyte. Unrealistic, to say the least.

> *Shor's algorithm shatters the foundations for deployed public key cryptography: RSA and the discrete-logarithm problem in finite fields and elliptic curves. Long-term confidential documents such as patient health-care records and state secrets have to guarantee security for many years, but information encrypted today using RSA or elliptic curves and stored until quantum computers are available will then be as easy to decipher as Enigma-encrypted messages are today.*
>
> —PQCRYPTO: Initial recommendations of long-term
> secure post-quantum systems (2015)

For *symmetric cryptography*, things are much less worrisome. Grover's algorithm was proposed in 1996, by Lov Grover, as a way to optimize a search in an unordered list. A search in an unordered list of N items takes $N/2$ operations on average with a classical computer; it would take $\sqrt{N}$ operations with a quantum computer. Quite a speed-up!

Grover's algorithm is quite a versatile tool that can be applied in lots of ways in cryptography, for example, to extract a cipher's symmetric key or find a collision in a hash function. To search for a key of 128 bits, Grover's algorithm would run in 2^{64} operations on a quantum computer as opposed to 2^{127} on a classical computer. This is quite a scary statement for all of our symmetric cryptography algorithms, yet we can simply bump security parameters from 128 bits to 256 bits and it's enough to counter Grover's attack. Hence, if you want to protect your symmetric cryptography against quantum computers, you can simply use SHA-3-512 instead of SHA-3-256, AES-256-GCM instead of AES-128-GCM, and so on.

To summarize, symmetric cryptography is mostly fine, asymmetric cryptography is not. This is even worse than you might think at first sight: symmetric cryptography is often preceded by a key exchange, which is vulnerable to quantum computers. So is this the end of cryptography as we know it?

14.1.4 Post-quantum cryptography, the defense against quantum computers

Fortunately, this was not the end of the world for cryptography. The community quickly reacted to the quantum threat by organizing itself and by researching old and new algorithms that would *not* be vulnerable to Shor's and Grover's attacks. The field of *quantum-resistant cryptography*, also known as *post-quantum cryptography*, was born. Standardization efforts exist in different places on the internet, but the most well-regarded effort is from the NIST, which in 2016, started a post-quantum cryptography standardization process.

> *It appears that a transition to post-quantum cryptography will not be simple as there is unlikely to be a simple "drop-in" replacement for our current public key cryptographic algorithms. A significant effort will be required in order to develop, standardize, and deploy new post-quantum cryptosystems. In addition, this transition needs to take place well before any large-scale quantum computers are built, so that any information that is later compromised by quantum cryptanalysis is no longer sensitive when that compromise occurs. Therefore, it is desirable to plan for this transition early.*
>
> —Post-Quantum Cryptography page of the NIST
> standardization process (2016)

Since the NIST started this process, 82 candidates applied and 3 rounds have passed, narrowing down the list of candidates to 7 finalists and 8 alternate finalists (unlikely to be considered for standardization, but unique enough to be a good option if one of the paradigms used by the finalists end up being broken). The NIST standardization effort seeks to replace the most common type of asymmetric cryptography primitives, which include signature schemes and asymmetric encryption. The latter can also easily serve as a key exchange primitive, as you learned in chapter 6.

In the rest of this chapter, I will go over the different types of post-quantum cryptography algorithms that are being considered for standardization and point out which ones you can make use of today.

14.2 Hash-based signatures: Don't need anything but a hash function

While all practical signature schemes seem to use hash functions, ways exist to build signature schemes that make use of only hash functions, and nothing else. Even better, these schemes tend to rely only on the pre-image resistance of hash functions and not their collision resistance. This is quite an attractive proposition, as a huge part of applied cryptography is already based on solid and well-understood hash functions.

Modern hash functions are also resistant to quantum computers, which make these hash-based signature schemes naturally quantum-resistant. Let's take a look at what these hash-based signatures are and how they work.

14.2.1 One-time signatures (OTS) with Lamport signatures

On October 18, 1979, Leslie Lamport published his concept of *one-time signatures* (OTS): key pairs that you can only use to sign once. Most signature schemes rely (in part) on one-way functions (typically hash functions) for their security proofs. The beauty of Lamport's scheme is that his signature solely relies on the security of such one-way functions.

Imagine that you want to sign a single bit. First, you generate a key pair by

1. Generating two random numbers, x and y, which will be the private key
2. Hashing x and y to obtain two digests $h(x)$ and $h(y)$, which you can publish as the public key

To sign a bit set to 0, reveal the x part of your private key; to sign a bit set to 1, reveal the y part. To verify a signature, simply hash it to check that it matches the correct part of the public key. I illustrate this in figure 14.1.

Signing a bit is not that useful, you say. No problem; a Lamport signature works for larger inputs simply by creating more pairs of secrets, one per bit, to sign (see

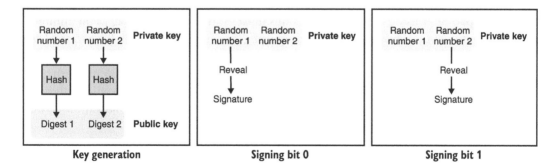

Figure 14.1 A Lamport signature is a one-time signature (OTS) based only on hash functions. To generate a key pair that can sign a bit, generate two random numbers, which will be your private key, and hash each of those individually to produce the two digests of your public key. To sign a bit set to 0, reveal the first random number; to sign a bit set to 1, reveal the second random number.

figure 14.2). Obviously, if your input is larger than 256 bits, you would first hash it and then sign it.

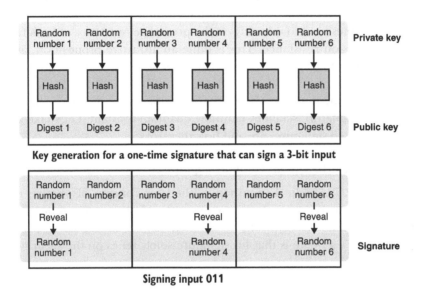

Key generation for a one-time signature that can sign a 3-bit input

Signing input 011

Figure 14.2 **To generate a Lamport signature key pair that can sign an *n*-bit message, generate 2*n* random numbers, which will be your private key, and hash each of those individually to produce the 2*n* digests of your public key. To sign, go through pairs of secrets and *n* bits, revealing the first element to sign a bit set to 0 or the second element to sign a bit set to 1.**

A major limitation of this scheme is that you can only use it to sign once; if you use it to sign twice, you end up authorizing someone else to mix the two signatures to forge other valid signatures. We can improve the situation naively by generating a large number of one-time key pairs instead of a single one, then making sure to discard a key pair after using it. Not only does this make your public key as big as the number of signatures you think you might end up using, but it also means you have to track what key pairs you've used (or better, get rid of the private keys you've used). For example, if you know you'll want to sign a maximum of 1,000 messages of 256 bits with a hash function with a 256-bit output size, your private key and public key would both have to be 1000 × (256 × 2 × 256) bits, which is around 16 megabytes. That's quite a lot for only 1,000 signatures.

Most of the hash-based signature schemes proposed today build on the foundations created by Lamport to allow for many more signatures (sometimes a practically unlimited amount of signatures), stateless private keys (although some proposed schemes are still stateful), and more practical parameter sizes.

14.2.2 Smaller keys with Winternitz one-time signatures (WOTS)

A few months after Lamport's publication, Robert Winternitz of the Stanford Mathematics Department proposed to publish hashes of hashes of a secret $h(h(...h(x))) = h^w(x)$ instead of publishing multiple digests of multiple secrets in order to optimize the size of a private key (see figure 14.3). This scheme is called *Winternitz one-time signature* (WOTS) after the author.

For example, choosing $w = 16$ allows you to sign 16 different values or, in other words, inputs of 4 bits. You start by generating a random value x that serves as your private key and hash that 16 times to obtain your public key, $h^{16}(x)$. Now imagine you want to sign the bits 1001 (9 in base 10); you publish the ninth iteration of the hash, $h^9(x)$. I illustrate this in figure 14.3.

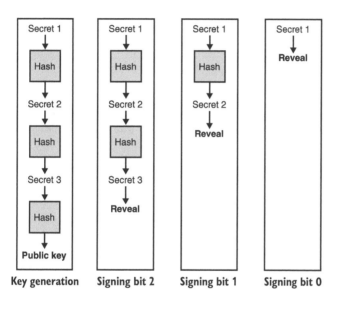

Figure 14.3   The Winternitz one-time signature (WOTS) scheme optimizes Lamport signatures by only using one secret that is hashed iteratively in order to obtain many other secrets and, finally, a public key. Revealing a different secret allows one to sign a different number.

Take a few minutes to understand how this scheme works. Do you see a problem with it? One major problem is that this scheme allows for *signature forgeries*. Imagine that you see someone else's signature for bit 1001, which would be $h^9(x)$ according to our previous example. You can simply hash it to retrieve any other iterations like $h^{10}(x)$ or $h^{11}(x)$, which would give you a valid signature for bits 1010 or 1011. This can be circumvented by adding a short authentication tag after the message, which you would have to sign as well. I illustrate this in figure 14.4. To convince yourself that this solves the forgery issue, try to forge a signature from another signature.

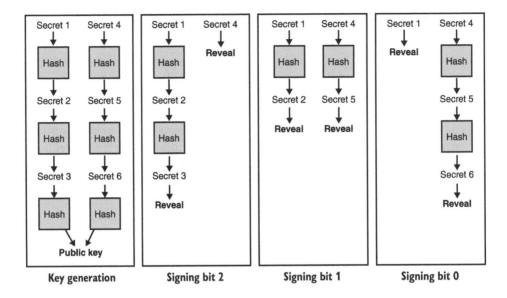

Figure 14.4 WOTS uses an additional signing key to authenticate a signature in order to prevent tampering. It works like this: when signing, the first private key is used to sign the message, and the second private key is used to sign the complement of the message. It should be clear that in any of the scenarios illustrated, tampering with a signature cannot lead to a new valid signature.

14.2.3 *Many-times signatures with XMSS and SPHINCS+*

So far, you've seen ways of signing things using only hash functions. While Lamport signatures work, they have large key sizes, so WOTS improved on those by reducing the key sizes. Yet, both these schemes still don't scale well as they are both one-time signatures (reuse a key pair and you break the scheme), and thus, their parameters linearly increase in size depending on the number of signatures you think you'll need.

Some schemes that tolerate reuse of a key pair for a few signatures (instead of a single one) do exist. These schemes are called *few-time signatures* (FTS) and will break, allowing signature forgeries if reused too many times. FTS rely on low probabilities of reusing the same combination of secrets from a pool of secrets. This is a small improvement on one-time signatures, allowing a decrease in the risk of key reuse. But we can do better.

What is one technique you learned about in this book that compresses many things into one thing? The answer is Merkle trees. As you may recall from chapter 12, a *Merkle tree* is a data structure that provides short proofs for questions like is my data in this set? In the 1990s, the same Merkle who proposed Merkle trees also invented a signature scheme based on hash functions that compresses a number of one-time signatures into a Merkle tree.

The idea is pretty straightforward: each leaf of your tree is the hash of a one-time signature, and the root hash can be used as a public key, reducing its size to the output size of your hash function. To sign, you pick a one-time signature that you haven't used previously and then apply it as explained in section 14.2.2. The signature is the one-time signature, along with the Merkle proof that it belongs in your Merkle tree (all the neighbors). This scheme is obviously stateful as one should be careful not to reuse one of the one-time signatures in the tree. I illustrate this in figure 14.5.

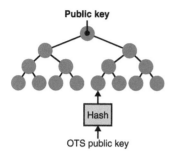

Figure 14.5 **The Merkle signature scheme is a stateful hash-based algorithm that makes use of a Merkle tree to compress many OTS public keys into a smaller public key (the root hash). The larger the tree, the more signatures it can produce. Note that signatures now have the overhead of a** *membership proof,* **which is a number of neighbor nodes that allow one to verify that a signature's associated OTS is part of the tree.**

The *extended Merkle signature scheme* (XMSS), standardized in RFC 8391, sought to productionize Merkle signatures by adding a number of optimizations to Merkle's scheme. For example, to produce a key pair capable of signing N messages, you must generate N OTS private keys. While the public key is now just a root hash, you still have to store N OTS private keys. XMSS reduces the size of the private key you hold by deterministically generating each OTS in the tree using a seed and the leaf position in the tree. This way, you only need to store the seed as a private key, instead of all the OTS private keys, and can quickly regenerate any OTS key pair from its position in the tree and the seed. To keep track of which leaf/OTS was used last, the private key also contains a counter that is incremented every time it is used to sign.

Having said that, there's only so much OTS you can hold in a Merkle tree. The larger the tree, the longer it'll take to regenerate the tree in order to sign messages (as you need to regenerate all the leaves to produce a Merkle proof). The smaller the tree, the fewer OTS private keys need to be regenerated when signing, but this obviously defeats the purpose: we are now back to having a limited amount of signatures. The solution is to use a smaller tree where the OTS in its leaves are not used to sign messages but, instead, used to sign the root hash of other Merkle trees of OTS. This transforms our initial tree into a *hypertree*—tree of trees—and is one of the variants of XMSS called XMSS^{MT}. With XMSS^{MT}, only the trees involved in the path of an OTS need to be regenerated, based on the same technique. I illustrate this in figure 14.6.

Note that the statefulness of XMSS and XMSS^{MT} might not be an issue in some situations, but it is not a desirable property, in general. Having to keep track of a counter is counterintuitive as it is not expected from users of mainstream signature schemes. This change of practice can lead to OTS reuse (and, thus, to signature forgery) in case of misuse. For example, rollbacks to a previous state of the filesystem or using the

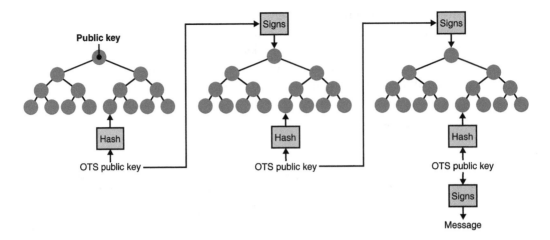

Figure 14.6   The XMSS^MT stateful hash-based signature scheme uses multiple trees to increase the amount of signatures supported by the scheme while reducing the work at key generation and signing time. Each tree is deterministically generated only when they are used in the path to the final leaf that contains the OTS used to sign a message.

same signing key on multiple servers might induce the same path in the hypertree being used twice to sign a message.

To fix one the biggest downsides of XMSS (its statefulness) and expose an interface similar to the signature schemes we're used to, the *SPHINCS+ signature scheme* was proposed as part of the NIST's post-quantum cryptography competition. The stateless signature scheme augments XMSS^MT with three major changes:

- *Signing the same message twice leads to the same signature.* In a similar fashion to EdDSA (covered in chapter 7), the path used in the hypertree is deterministically derived, based on the private key and the message. This ensures that signing the same message twice leads to the same OTS and, thus, the same signature; and because the private key is used, attackers are also unable to predict which path you'll take to sign their messages if you somehow sign other people's messages.

- *Using more trees.* XMSS^MT avoids reusing the same OTS twice by keeping track of which OTS was used last. As the whole point of SPHINCS+ is to avoid keeping track of a state, it needs to avoid collisions when it chooses a path pseudorandomly. To do this, SPHINCS+ simply uses a much larger amount of OTS, reducing the probability of reusing the same one twice. Because SPHINCS+ also uses a hypertree, this translates into more trees.

- *Using few-time signatures* (FTS). As the security of the scheme is based on the probability of reusing the same path twice, SPHINCS+ also replaces the final OTS used to sign messages with the FTS I mentioned earlier. This way, reusing the same path to sign two different messages still doesn't directly contribute to a break of the signature scheme.

While SPHINCS+ is being considered for standardization in the NIST post-quantum cryptography competition, it's not the main contender. SPHINCS+ is not only slow, its signatures are large compared to the proposed alternatives (like lattice-based ones, which you'll learn about later in this chapter). Stateful hash-based signature schemes like XMSS offer faster speed and better signature sizes (under 3 KB compared to the minimum of 8 KB for SPHINCS+). (In terms of public key sizes, both schemes provide sizes similar to pre-quantum signatures schemes like ECDSA and Ed25519.) Due to the more realistic parameter sizes and the well-understood security, XMSS is recommended as an early standard by the NIST in SP 800-208, "Recommendation for Stateful Hash-Based Signature Schemes."

Next, let's take a look at two other ways to build quantum-resistant cryptographic primitives. A gentle warning: they are much more math-heavy!

14.3 Shorter keys and signatures with lattice-based cryptography

A large number of post-quantum cryptography schemes are based on lattices, a mathematical structure that you'll learn about in this section. The NIST post-quantum cryptography competition itself has elected lattice-based schemes for half of its finalists. This makes lattice-based cryptography the most likely paradigm to win and obtain a standard from the NIST. In this section, I will tell you about two lattice-based algorithms: Dilithium, a signature scheme, and Kyber, a public key encryption primitive. But before that, though, let's see what lattices are.

14.3.1 What's a lattice?

First, lattice-based probably doesn't mean what you think it means. Take RSA (covered in chapter 6), which we say is based on the factorization problem. This does not mean that we use factorization in RSA, it instead means that factorization is how you attack RSA, and because factorization is hard, we say that RSA is secure. It's the same with lattice-based cryptosystems: *lattices* are structures that have hard problems, and these cryptosystems are safe as long as these problems remain hard.

With that being said, what is a lattice? Well, it's like a *vector space* but with integers. If you don't remember what a vector space is, it's the set of all vectors that can be created using:

- *A basis*—A set of vectors; for example, (0,1) and (1,0).
- *An operation between vectors*—The vectors can be added together; for example, (0,1) + (1,0) = (1,1).
- *A scalar operation*—A vector can be multiplied by what we call scalars; for example, $3 \times (1,2) = (3,6)$.

In our example, the vector space contains all the vectors that can be expressed as a linear combination of the basis, which translates to any vector that can be written as $a \times (0,1) + b \times (1,0)$ for any scalars a and b. For example, $0.5 \times (0,1) + 3.87 \times (1,0) = (3.87,0.5)$ is in our vector space, so is $99 \times (0,1) + 0 \times (1,0) = (0,99)$, and so on.

A lattice is a vector space where all of the numbers involved are integers. Yup, in cryptography, we like integers. I illustrate this in figure 14.7.

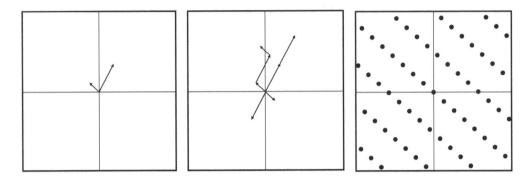

Figure 14.7   On the left, a basis of two vectors is drawn on a graph. A lattice can be formed by taking all of the possible integer linear combinations of these two vectors (middle figure). The resulting lattice can be interpreted as a pattern of points repeating forever in space (right figure).

There are several well-known hard problems in the lattice space, and for each of these problems, we have algorithms to solve them. These algorithms are often the best we could think of, but it doesn't necessarily mean that they are efficient or even practical. Thus, the problems are said to be hard at least until an more efficient solution is found. The two most well-known hard problems are as follows. (I illustrate both of these problems in figure 14.8.)

- *The shortest vector problem* (SVP)—Answers the question, what is the shortest non-zero vector in your lattice?
- *The closest vector problem* (CVP)—Given a coordinate that is not on the lattice, finds the closest point to that coordinate on the lattice.

Generally, we use algorithms like LLL (the Lenstra–Lenstra–Lovász algorithm) or BKZ (the Block-Korkine-Zolotarev algorithm) to solve both of these problems (CVP can be reduced to SVP). These are algorithms that reduce the basis of a lattice, meaning that they attempt to find a set of vectors that are shorter than the ones given and that managed to produce the exact same lattice.

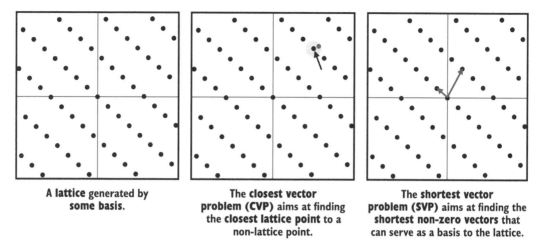

A lattice generated by some basis.

The **closest vector problem (CVP)** aims at finding the **closest lattice point** to a non-lattice point.

The **shortest vector problem (SVP)** aims at finding the **shortest non-zero vectors** that can serve as a basis to the lattice.

Figure 14.8 An illustration of the two major lattice problems used in cryptography: the shortest vector problem (SVP) and the closest vector problem (CVP)

14.3.2 Learning with errors (LWE), a basis for cryptography?

In 2005, Oded Regev introduced the *learning with errors* (LWE) problem, which became the basis for many cryptographic schemes including some of the algorithms in this chapter. Before going further, let's see what the LWE problem is about. Let's start with the following equations, which are linear combinations of the same integers s_0 and s_1:

- $5 \, s_0 + 2 \, s_1 = 27$
- $2 \, s_0 + 0 \, s_1 = 6$

We know that by using the *Gaussian elimination* algorithm, we can quickly and efficiently learn what s_0 and s_1 are, as long as we have enough of these equations. Now what's interesting is that if we add some noise to these equations, the problem becomes much harder:

- $5 \, s_0 + 2 \, s_1 = 28$
- $2 \, s_0 + 0 \, s_1 = 5$

While it probably isn't too hard to figure out the answer given more noisy equations, it becomes a hard problem once you increase the size of the numbers involved and the number of s_i.

This is essentially what the LWE problem is, albeit often stated with vectors instead. Imagine that you have a secret vector **s** with coordinates modulo some large number. Given an arbitrary number of random vectors a_i of the same size and the computations $a_i s + e_i$, where e_i is a random small error, can you find the value **s**?

NOTE For two vectors **v** and **w**, the product **vw** can be calculated using a *dot product*, which is the sum of the product of each pair of coordinates. Let's look at an example: if $v = (v_0, v_1)$ and $w = (w_0, w_1)$, then $vw = v_0 \times w_0 + v_1 \times w_1$.

For example, if I use the secret **s** = (3,6) and I give you the random vectors $\mathbf{a}_0$ = (5,2) and $\mathbf{a}_1$ = (2,0), I get back the equations I started the example with. As I said earlier, lattice-based schemes actually don't make any use of lattices; rather, they are proven secure if the SVP remains hard (for some definition of hard). The reduction can only be seen if we write the previous equations in a matrix form, as shown in figure 14.9.

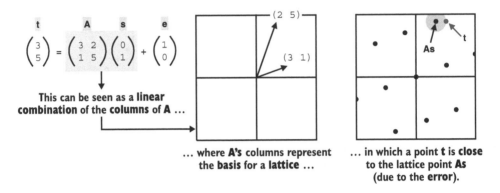

... where **A's** columns represent the **basis** for a **lattice** ...

... in which a point **t** is **close** to the lattice point **As** (due to the **error**).

Figure 14.9   **The learning with errors problem (LWE) is said to be a lattice-based construction due to the existence of a reduction to a lattice problem: the CVP. In other words, if we can find a solution to the CVP, then we can find a solution to the LWE problem.**

This matrix form is important as most LWE-based schemes are expressed and easier to explain in this form. Take a few minutes to brush up on matrix multiplication. Also, in case you haven't noticed, I used some common notational tricks that are quite helpful to read equations that involve matrices and vectors: both are written in bold, and matrices are always uppercase letters. For example, **A** is a matrix, **a** is a vector, and b is just a number.

> **NOTE**   There exist several variants of the LWE problem (for example, the ring-LWE or module-LWE problems), which are basically the same problem but with coordinates in different types of groups. These variants are often preferred due to the compactness and the optimizations they unlock. The difference between the variants of LWE does not affect the explanations that follow.

Now that you know what the LWE problem is, let's learn about some post-quantum cryptography based on it: the *Cryptographic Suite for Algebraic Lattices* (CRYSTALS). Conveniently, CRYSTALS encompasses two cryptographic primitives: a key exchange called *Kyber* and a signature scheme called *Dilithium*.

14.3.3   *Kyber, a lattice-based key exchange*

Two NIST finalist schemes are closely related: CRYSTALS-Kyber and CRYSTALS-Dilithium, which are candidates from the same team of researchers and are both based on the LWE problem. *Kyber* is a public key encryption primitive that can be used as a key exchange primitive, which I will explain in this section. *Dilithium* is a signature scheme, which I will explain in the next section. Also note that as these algorithms are still in flux, I will only write about the ideas and the intuitions behind both of the schemes.

First, let's assume that all operations happen in a group of integers modulo a large number q. Let's also say that errors and private keys are *sampled* (chosen uniformly at random) from a small range centered at 0 that we will call the *error range*. Specifically, the error range is the range $[-B, B]$ where B is much smaller than q. This is important as some terms need to be smaller than some value to be considered errors.

To generate the private key, simply generate a random vector $\mathbf{s}$, where every coefficient is in the error range. The first part of the public key is a list of random vectors $\mathbf{a}_i$ of the same size, and the second part is the associated list of noisy dot products $\mathbf{t}_i = \mathbf{a}_i s + \mathbf{e}_i \bmod q$. This is exactly the LWE problem we learned about previously. Importantly for the rest, we can rewrite this with matrices:

$$\mathbf{t} = \mathbf{As} + \mathbf{e}$$

where the matrix $\mathbf{A}$ contains the random vectors $\mathbf{a}_i$ as rows, and the error vector $\mathbf{e}$ contains the individual errors $\mathbf{e}_i$.

To perform a key exchange with Kyber, we encrypt a symmetric key of 1 bit (yes, a single bit!) with the scheme. This is akin to the RSA key encapsulation mechanism you saw in chapter 6. The following four steps shows how the encryption works:

1 Generate an ephemeral private key vector $\mathbf{r}$ (where coefficients are in the error range) and its associated ephemeral public key $\mathbf{rA} + \mathbf{e}_1$ with some random error vector $\mathbf{e}_1$, using the other peer's $\mathbf{A}$ matrix as a public parameter. Note that the matrix multiplication is done on the right, which involves multiplying the vector $\mathbf{r}$ with the columns of $\mathbf{A}$ instead of computing $\mathbf{Ar}$ (a multiplication of the vector $\mathbf{r}$ with the rows of $\mathbf{A}$). It is a detail, but it's necessary for the decryption step to work.

2 We shift our message to the left by multiplying it with $q/2$ in order to avoid small errors from impacting our message. Note that $q/2$ modulo q usually means q multiplied with the inverse of 2 modulo q, but here it simply means the closest integer to $q/2$.

3 Compute a shared secret with the dot product of our ephemeral private key and the public key of the peer.

4 Encrypt your (shifted) message by adding it to the shared secret as well as a random error $\mathbf{e}_2$. This produces a ciphertext.

After performing the steps, we can send both the ephemeral public key and the ciphertext to the other peer. After receiving both the ephemeral public key and the ciphertext, we can follow these steps to decrypt the message:

1 Obtain the shared secret by computing the dot product of your secret with the ephemeral public key received.

2 Subtract that shared secret from the ciphertext (the result contains the shifted message and some error).

3 Shift your message back to where it was originally by dividing it with $q/2$, effectively removing the error.

4 The message is 1 if it is closer to $q/2$ than 0, and it is 0 otherwise.

Of course, 1 bit is not enough, so current schemes employ different techniques to overcome this limitation. I recapitulate all three algorithms in figure 14.10.

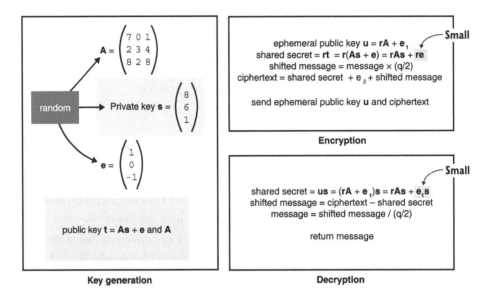

Figure 14.10   The Kyber public key encryption scheme. Note that the shared secret is approximately the same during encryption and decryption as re and e_1s are both small values because r, s, and the errors are much smaller than $q/2$). Thus, the last step of the decryption (dividing by $q/2$, which can be seen as a bitwise shift to the right) gets rid of any discrepancy between the two shared secrets. Note that all operations are done modulo q.

In practice, for a key exchange, the message you encrypt to your peer's public key is a random secret. The result is then derived deterministically from both the secret and the transcript of the key exchange, which includes the peer's public key, your ephemeral key, and the ciphertext.

The recommended parameters for Kyber leads to public keys and ciphertexts of around 1 kilobytes, which is much bigger than the pre-quantum schemes we use but still in the realm of the practical for most use cases. While time will tell if we can further reduce the communication overhead of these schemes, it seems like, so far, post-quantum rhymes with larger sizes.

14.3.4 *Dilithium, a lattice-based signature scheme*

The next scheme I'll explain, *Dilithium*, is also based on LWE and is the sister candidate of Kyber. As with other types of signatures we've seen (like Schnorr's signature in chapter 7), Dilithium is based on a zero-knowledge proof that is made non-interactive via the Fiat-Shamir trick.

For key generation, Dilithium is similar to the previous scheme, except that we keep the error as part of the private key. We first generate the two random vectors that serve as the private key, s_1 and s_2, then compute the public key as $t = As_1 + s_2$, where A is a matrix obtained in a similar manner as Kyber. The public key is t and A. Note that we consider the error s_2 as being part of the private key because we need to reuse it every time we sign a message (unlike in Kyber, where the error could be discarded after the key generation step).

To sign, we create a sigma protocol and then convert that to a non-interactive, zero-knowledge proof via the Fiat-Shamir transformation, which is similar to how the Schnorr identification protocol gets converted to a Schnorr signature in chapter 7. The interactive protocol looks like this:

1 The prover commits on two random vectors, y_1 and y_2, by sending $Ay_1 + y_2$.

2 Upon reception of this commit, the verifier responds with a random challenge c.

3 The prover then computes the two vectors $z_1 = cs_1 + y_1$ and $z_2 = cs_2 + y_2$ and sends them to the verifier only if they are small values.

4 The verifier checks if $Az_1 + z_2 - ct$ and $Ay_1 + y_2$ are the same values.

The Fiat-Shamir trick replaces the role of the verifier in step 2 by having the prover generate a challenge from a hash of the message to sign and the committed $Ay_1 + y_2$ value. I recap this transformation in figure 14.11, using a similar diagram from chapter 7.

Dilithium interactive zero-knowledge proof   Dilithium signature

Figure 14.11 A Dilithium signature is a proof of knowledge of a secret vector s made non-interactive via the Fiat-Shamir transformation. The diagram on the left shows the interactive proof protocol, while the diagram on the right shows a non-interactive version where the challenge is computed as a commitment of both y and the message to sign.

Again, this is a gross simplification of the signature scheme. Many more optimizations are used in practice to reduce the key and the signature sizes. Usually, these optimizations look at reducing any random data by deterministically generating it from a smaller random value and by reducing non-random data by compressing it via custom methods, not necessarily via known compression algorithms. There are also a number of additional optimizations that are possible due to the unique structure of LWE.

At the recommended security level, Dilithium offers signatures of around 3 KB and public keys of less than 2 KB. This is obviously much more than the 32-byte public keys and 64-byte signatures of pre-quantum schemes, but it is also much better than the stateless hash-based signatures. It is good to keep in mind that these schemes are still pretty new, and it is possible that better algorithms will be found to solve the LWE problem, potentially increasing the sizes of public keys and signatures. It is also possible that we will find better techniques to reduce the sizes of these parameters. In general, it's likely that quantum resistance will always come with a cost in size.

This is not all there is to post-quantum cryptography; the NIST post-quantum cryptography competition has a number of other constructions based on different paradigms. NIST has announced that an initial standard will be published in 2022, but I expect that the field will continue to move quickly, at least as long as post-quantum computers continue to be seen as a legitimate threat. While there's still a lot of unknowns, it also means that there's a lot of exciting room for research. If this is interesting to you, I recommend taking a look at the NIST reports (https://nist.gov/pqcrypto).

14.4   *Do I need to panic?*

To summarize, quantum computers are a huge deal for cryptography if they are realized. What's the take away here? Do you need to throw everything you're doing and transition to post-quantum algorithms? Well, it's not that simple.

Ask any expert and you'll receive different kinds of answers. For some, it's 5 to 50 years away; for others, it'll never happen. Michele Mosca, the director of the Institute for Quantum Computing, estimated "a 1/7 chance of breaking RSA-2048 by 2026 and a 1/2 chance by 2031," while Mikhail Dyakonov, a researcher at the CNRS in France, stated publicly "Could we ever learn to control the more than 10^{300} continuously variable parameters defining the quantum state of such a system? My answer is simple. No, never." While physicists, not cryptographers, know better, they can still be incentivized to hype their own research in order to get funding. As I am no physicist, I will simply say that we should remain skeptical of extraordinary claims, while preparing for the worst. The question is not "Will it work?"; rather, it's "Will it scale?"

There exist many challenges for scalable quantum computers (which can destroy cryptography) to become a reality; the biggest ones seem to be about the amount of noise and errors that is difficult to reduce or correct. Scott Aaronson, a computer scientist at the University of Texas, puts it as "You're trying to build a ship that remains the same ship, even as every plank in it rots and has to be replaced."

But what about what the NSA said? One needs to remember that the government's need for confidentiality most often exceeds the needs of individuals and private companies. It is not crazy to think that the government might want to keep some top secret data classified for more than 50 years. Nevertheless, this has puzzled many cryptographers (see, for example, "A Riddle Wrapped In An Enigma" by Neal Koblitz and

Alfred J. Menezes), who have been wondering why we would protect ourselves against something that doesn't exist yet or might never exist.

In any case, if you're really worried and the confidentiality of your assets needs to remain for long periods of time, it is not crazy and relatively easy to increase the parameters of every symmetric cryptographic algorithm you're using. That being said, if you're doing a key exchange in order to obtain an AES-256-GCM key, that asymmetric cryptography part is still vulnerable to quantum computers, and protecting the symmetric cryptography alone won't be enough.

For asymmetric cryptography, it is too early to really know what is safe to use. Best wait for the end of the NIST competition in order to obtain more cryptanalysis, and in turn, more confidence in these novel algorithms.

> *At present, there are several post-quantum cryptosystems that have been proposed, including lattice-based cryptosystems, code-based cryptosystems, multivariate cryptosystems, hash-based signatures, and others. However, for most of these proposals, further research is needed in order to gain more confidence in their security (particularly against adversaries with quantum computers) and to improve their performance.*
>
> —NIST Post-Quantum Cryptography Call for Proposals (2017)

If you're too impatient and can't wait for the result of the NIST competition, one thing you can do is to use both a current scheme *and* a post-quantum scheme in your protocol. For example, you could cross-sign messages using Ed25519 and Dilithium or, in other words, attach a message with two signatures from two different signature schemes. If it turns out that Dilithium is broken, an attacker would still have to break Ed25519, and if it turns out that quantum computers are real, then the attacker would still have the Dilithium signature that they can't forge.

NOTE This is what Google did in 2018, and then again in 2019, with Cloudflare, experimenting with a hybrid key exchange scheme in TLS connections between a small percentage of Google Chrome users and servers from both Google and Cloudflare. The hybrid scheme was a mix of X25519 and one post-quantum key exchange (New Hope in 2018, HRSS and SIKE in 2019), where both the output of the current key exchange and the post-quantum key exchange were mixed together into HKDF to produce a single shared secret.

Finally, I will re-emphasize that hash-based signatures are well studied and well understood. Even though they present some overhead, schemes like XMSS and SPHINCS+ can be used now, and XMSS has ready-to-use standards (RFC 8391 and NIST SP 800-208).

Summary

- Quantum computers are based on quantum physics and can provide a non-negligible speed up for specific computations.
- Not all algorithms can run on a quantum computer, and not all algorithms can compete with a classical computer. Two notable algorithms that worry cryptographers are

- Shor's algorithm, which can efficiently solve the discrete logarithm problem and the factorization problem. It breaks most of today's asymmetric cryptography.
- Grover's algorithm, which can efficiently search for a key or value in a space of 2^{128} values, impacts most symmetric algorithms with 128-bit security. Boosting a symmetric algorithm's parameters to provide 256-bit security is enough to thwart quantum attacks.

- The field of post-quantum cryptography aims at finding novel cryptographic algorithms to replace today's asymmetric cryptographic primitives (for example, asymmetric encryption, key exchanges, and digital signatures).

- NIST started a post-quantum cryptography standardization effort in 2016. There are currently seven finalists and the effort is now entering its final round of selection.

- Hash-based signatures are signature schemes that are only based on hash functions. The two main standards are XMSS (a stateful signature scheme) and SPHINCS+ (a stateless signature scheme).

- Lattice-based cryptography is promising as it provides shorter keys and signatures. Two of the most promising candidates are based on the LWE problem: Kyber is an asymmetric encryption and key exchange primitive, and Dilithium is a signature scheme.

- Other post-quantum schemes exist and are being proposed as part of the NIST post-quantum cryptography competition. These include schemes based on code theory, isogenies, symmetric-key cryptography, and multivariate polynomials. NIST's competition is scheduled to end in 2022, which still leaves a lot of room for new attacks or optimizations to be discovered.

- It is not clear when quantum computers will be efficient enough to destroy cryptography, or if it is possible for them to get there.

- If you have requirements to protect data for a long period of time, you should consider transitioning to post-quantum cryptography:
  - Upgrade all usage of symmetric cryptographic algorithms to use parameters that provide 256-bit security (for example, move from AES-128-GCM to AES-256-GCM, and from SHA-3-256 to SHA-3-512).
  - Use hybrid schemes that mix post-quantum algorithms with pre-quantum algorithms. For example, always sign messages with both Ed25519 and Dilithium, or always perform a key exchange with both X25519 and Kyber (deriving a shared secret from the two key exchange outputs obtained).
  - Use hash-based signatures like XMSS and SPHINCS+, which are well-studied and well-understood. XMSS has the advantage of having already been standardized and approved by the NIST.

Is this it?
Next-generation
cryptography

This chapter covers

- Getting rid of trusted third parties via secure multi-party computation (MPC)
- Allowing others to act on encrypted data via fully homomorphic encryption (FHE)
- Hiding parts of a program execution via zero-knowledge proofs (ZKPs)

I started this book with the idea that readers who would get through most of the chapters would also be interested in the future of real-world cryptography. While you're reading an applied and practical book with a focus on what is in use today, the field of cryptography is rapidly changing (as we saw in recent years with cryptocurrencies, for example).

As you're reading this book, a number of theoretical cryptographic primitives and protocols are making their ways into the applied cryptography world—maybe because these theoretical primitives are finally finding a use case or because they're finally becoming efficient enough to be used in real-world applications. Whatever the reason, the real world of cryptography is definitely growing and getting more exciting. In this chapter, I give you a taste of what the future of real-world cryptography might look like (perhaps in the next 10 to 20 years) by briefly introducing three primitives:

- *Secure multi-party computation* (MPC)—A subfield of cryptography that allows different participants to execute a program together without necessarily revealing their own input to the program.
- *Fully homomorphic encryption* (FHE)—The holy grail of cryptography, a primitive used to allow arbitrary computations on encrypted data.
- *General-purpose zero-knowledge proofs* (ZKPs)—The primitive you learned about in chapter 7 that allows you to prove that you know something without revealing that something, but this time, applied more generally to more complex programs.

This chapter contains the most advanced and complicated concepts in the book. For this reason, I recommend that you glance at it and then move on to chapter 16 to read the conclusion. When you are motivated to learn more about the inners of these more advanced concepts, come back to this chapter. Let's get started!

15.1   *The more the merrier: Secure multi-party computation (MPC)*

Secure multi-party computation (MPC) is a field of cryptography that came into existence in 1982 with the famous Millionaires' problem. In his 1982 paper "Protocols for Secure Computations," Andrew C. Yao wrote, "Two millionaires wish to know who is richer; however, they do not want to find out inadvertently any additional information about each other's wealth. How can they carry out such a conversation?" Simply put, MPC is a way for multiple participants to compute a program together. But before learning more about this new primitive, let's see why it's useful.

We know that with the help of a trusted third party, any distributed computation can easily be worked out. This trusted third party can perhaps maintain the privacy of each participant's input, as well as possibly restricting the amount of information revealed by the computation to specific participants. In the real world, though, we don't like trusted third parties too much; we know that they are pretty hard to come by, and they don't always respect their commitments.

MPC allows us to completely remove trusted third parties from a distributed computation and enables participants to compute the computation by themselves without revealing their respective inputs to one another. This is done through a cryptographic protocol. With that in mind, using MPC in a system is pretty much the equivalent to using a trusted third party (see figure 15.1).

Note that you already saw some MPC protocols. Threshold signatures and distributed key generations, covered in chapter 8, are examples of MPC. More specifically, these examples are part of a subfield of MPC called *threshold cryptography*, which has been receiving a lot of love in more recent years with, for example, NIST in mid-2019 kicking off a standardization process for threshold cryptography.

Figure 15.1 **A secure multi-party computation (MPC) protocol turns a distributed computation that can be calculated via a trusted third party (image on the left) into a computation that doesn't need the help of a trusted third party (image on the right).**

15.1.1 *Private set intersection (PSI)*

Another well-known subfield of MPC is the field of *private set intersection* (PSI), which poses the following problem: Alice and Bob have a list of words, and they want to know which words (or perhaps just how many) they have in common without revealing their respective list of words. One way to solve this problem is to use the oblivious pseudorandom function (OPFR) construction you learned about in chapter 11. (I illustrate this protocol in figure 15.2.) If you recall

1. Bob generates a key for the OPRF.
2. Alice obtains the random values, *PRF*(*key, word*), for every word in her list using the OPRF protocol (so she doesn't learn the PRF key and Bob doesn't learn the words).

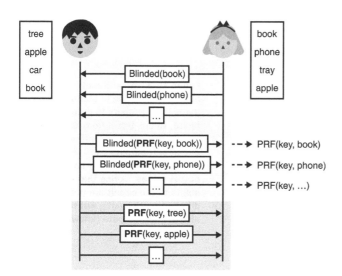

Figure 15.2 **Private set intersection (PSI) allows Alice to learn what words she has in common with Bob. First, she blinds every word she has in her list and uses the OPRF protocol with Bob to apply a PRF using Bob's key on each of her words. Finally, Bob sends her the PRF of his key with his words. Alice can then see if anything matches to learn what words they have in common.**

3 Bob then can compute the list of *PRF* (*key, word*) values for his own words and send it to Alice, who is then able to compare it with her own PRF outputs to see if any of Bob's PRF outputs matches.

PSI is a promising field that is starting to see more and more adoption in recent years, as it has shown to be much more practical than it used to be. For example, Google's Password Checkup feature integrated into the Chrome browser uses PSI to warn you when some of your passwords have been detected in password dumps following password breaches without actually seeing your passwords. Interestingly, Microsoft also does this for its Edge browser but uses fully homomorphic encryption (which I'll introduce in the next section) to perform the private set intersection. On the other hand, the developers of the Signal messaging application (discussed in chapter 10) decided that PSI was too slow to perform contact discovery in order to figure out who you can talk to based on your phone's contact list, and instead, used SGX (covered in chapter 13) as a trusted third party.

15.1.2 General-purpose MPC

More generally, MPC has many different solutions aiming at the computation of arbitrary programs. General-purpose MPC solutions all provide different levels of efficiency (from hours to milliseconds) and types of properties. For example, how many dishonest participants can the protocol tolerate? Are participants malicious or just honest but curious (also called *semi-honest,* a type of participant in MPC protocols that is willing to execute the protocol correctly but might attempt to learn the other participants' inputs)? Is it fair to all participants if some of them terminate the protocol early?

Before a program can be securely computed with MPC, it needs to be translated into an *arithmetic circuit.* Arithmetic circuits are successions of additions and multiplications, and because they are Turing complete, they can represent *any* program! For an illustration of an arithmetic circuit, see figure 15.3.

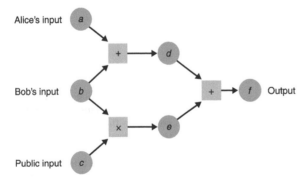

Figure 15.3   **An arithmetic circuit is a number of addition or multiplication gates linking inputs to outputs. In the figure, values travel from left to right. For example, *d = a + b*. Here, the circuit only outputs one value *f = a + b + bc*, but it can in theory have multiple output values. Notice that different inputs to the circuit are provided by different participants, but they could also be public inputs (known to everyone).**

Before taking a look at the next primitive, let me give you a simplified example of an (honest-majority) general-purpose MPC built via Shamir's secret sharing. Many more schemes exist, but this one is simple enough to fit here in a three-step explanation: share enough information on each input in the circuit, evaluate every gate in the circuit, and reconstruct the output. Let's look at each step in more detail.

The first step is for every participant to have enough information about each input of the circuit. Public inputs are shared publicly, while private inputs are shared via Shamir's secret sharing (covered in chapter 8). I illustrate this in figure 15.4.

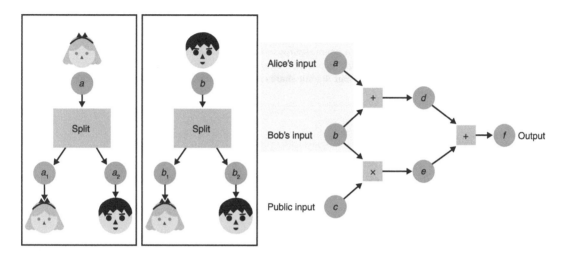

Figure 15.4 **The first step of a general-purpose MPC with secret sharing is to have participants split their respective secret inputs (using Shamir's secret sharing scheme) and distribute the parts to all participants. For example, here Alice splits her input *a* into a_1 and a_2. Because there are only two participants in this example, she gives the first share to herself and gives Bob the second one.**

The second step is to evaluate every gate of the circuit. For technical reasons I'll omit here, addition gates can be computed locally, while multiplication gates must be computed interactively (participants must exchange some messages). For an addition gate, simply add the input shares you have; for a multiplication gate, multiply the input shares. What you get is a share of the result as figure 15.5 illustrates. At this point, the shares can be exchanged (in order to reconstruct the output) or kept separate to continue the computation (if they represent an intermediate value).

The final step is to reconstruct the output. At this point, the participants should all own a share of the output, which they can use to reconstruct the final output using the final step of Shamir's secret sharing scheme.

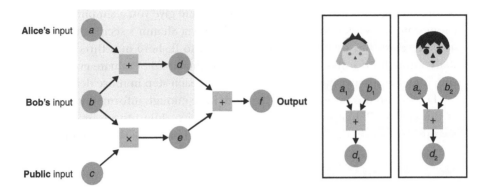

Figure 15.5   The second step of a general-purpose MPC with secret sharing is to have participants compute each gate in the circuit. For example, a participant can compute an addition gate by adding the two input Shamir shares that they have, which produces a Shamir share of the output.

15.1.3 *The state of MPC*

There's been huge progress in the last decade to make MPC practical. It is a field of many different use cases, and one should be on the lookout for the potential applications that can benefit from this newish primitive. Note that, unfortunately, no real standardization effort exists, and while several MPC implementations can be considered practical for many use cases today, they are not easy to use.

Incidentally, the general-purpose MPC construction I explained earlier in this section is based on secret sharing, but there are more ways to construct MPC protocols. A well-known alternative is called *garbled circuits*, which is a type of construction first proposed by Yao in his 1982 paper introducing MPC. Another alternative is based on fully homomorphic encryption, a primitive you'll learn about in the next section.

15.2 *Fully homomorphic encryption (FHE) and the promises of an encrypted cloud*

For a long time in cryptography, a question has troubled many cryptographers: is it possible to compute arbitrary programs on encrypted data? Imagine that you could encrypt the values a, b, and c separately, send the ciphertexts to a service, and ask that service to return the encryption of $a \times 3b + 2c + 3$, which you could then decrypt. The important idea here is that the service never learns about your values and always deals with ciphertexts. This calculation might not be too useful, but with additions and multiplications, one can compute actual programs on the encrypted data.

This interesting concept, originally proposed in 1978 by Rivest, Adleman, and Dertouzos, is what we call *fully homomorphic encryption* (FHE) (or as it used to be called, the *holy grail of cryptography*). I illustrate this cryptographic primitive in figure 15.6.

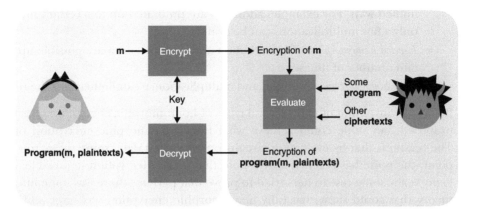

Figure 15.6 Fully homomorphic encryption (FHE) is an encryption scheme that allows for arbitrary computations over encrypted content. Only the owner of the key can decrypt the result of the computation.

15.2.1 An example of homomorphic encryption with RSA encryption

By the way, you already saw some cryptographic schemes that should make you feel like you know what I'm talking about. Think of RSA (covered in chapter 6): given a *ciphertext* = *message^e* mod *N*, someone can easily compute some restricted function of the ciphertext

$$n^e \times \textit{ciphertext} = (n \times \textit{message})^e \bmod N$$

for any number *n* they want (although it can't be too big). The result is a ciphertext that decrypts to

$$n \times \textit{message}$$

Of course, this is not a desired behavior for RSA, and it has led to some attacks (for example, Bleichenbacher's attack mentioned in chapter 6). In practice, RSA breaks the homomorphism property by using a padding scheme. Note that RSA is homomorphic only for the multiplication, which is not enough to compute arbitrary functions, as both multiplication and addition are needed for those. Due to this limitation, we say that RSA is *partially homomorphic*.

15.2.2 The different types of homomorphic encryption

Other types of homomorphic encryptions include

- *Somewhat homomorphic*—Which means partially homomorphic for one operation (addition or multiplication) and homomorphic for the other operation in limited ways. For example, additions are unlimited up to a certain number but only a few multiplications can be done.

- *Leveled homomorphic*—Both addition and multiplication are possible up to a certain number of times.
- *Fully homomorphic*—Addition and multiplication are unlimited (it's the real deal).

Before the invention of FHE, several types of homomorphic encryption schemes were proposed, but none could achieve what fully homomorphic encryption promised. The reason is that by evaluating circuits on encrypted data, some *noise* grows; after a point, the noise has reached a threshold that makes decryption impossible. And, for many years, some researchers tried to prove that perhaps there was some information theory that could show that fully homomorphic encryption was impossible; that is, until it was shown to be possible.

15.2.3 Bootstrapping, the key to fully homomorphic encryption

One night, Alice dreams of immense riches, caverns piled high with silver, gold and diamonds. Then, a giant dragon devours the riches and begins to eat its own tail! She awakes with a feeling of peace. As she tries to make sense of her dream, she realizes that she has the solution to her problem.

—Craig Gentry ("Computing Arbitrary Functions
of Encrypted Data," 2009)

In 2009, Craig Gentry, a PhD student of Dan Boneh, proposed the first-ever fully homomorphic encryption construction. Gentry's solution was called *bootstrapping*, which in effect was to evaluate a decryption circuit on the ciphertext every so often in order to reduce the noise to a manageable threshold. Interestingly, the decryption circuit itself does not reveal the private key and can be computed by the untrusted party. Bootstrapping allowed turning a leveled FHE scheme into an FHE scheme. Gentry's construction was slow and quite impractical, reporting about 30 minutes per basic bit operation, but as with any breakthrough, it only got better with time. It also showed that fully homomorphic encryption was possible.

How does bootstrapping work? Let's see if we can gain some insight. First, I need to mention that we'll need not a symmetric encryption system, but a public key encryption system, where a public key can be used to encrypt and a private key can be used to decrypt. Now, imagine that you execute a certain number of additions and multiplications on a ciphertext and reach some level of noise. The noise is low enough to still allow you to decrypt the ciphertext correctly, but too high that it won't let you perform more homomorphic operations without destroying the encrypted content. I illustrate this in figure 15.7.

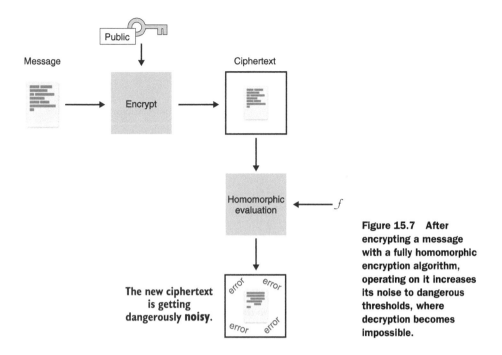

Figure 15.7   After encrypting a message with a fully homomorphic encryption algorithm, operating on it increases its noise to dangerous thresholds, where decryption becomes impossible.

You could think that you're stuck, but bootstrapping unsticks you by removing the noise out of that ciphertext. To do that, you re-encrypt the noisy ciphertext under another public key (usually called the *bootstrapping key*) to obtain an encryption of that noisy ciphertext. Notice that the new ciphertext has no noise. I illustrate this in figure 15.8.

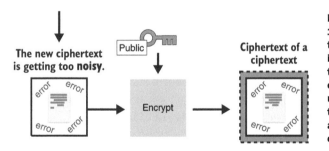

Figure 15.8   Building on figure 15.7, to eliminate the noise of the ciphertext, you can decrypt it. But because you don't have the secret key, instead you re-encrypt the noisy ciphertext under another public key (called the bootstrapping key) to obtain a new ciphertext of a noisy ciphertext without error.

Now comes the magic: you are provided with the initial private key, not in cleartext, but encrypted under that bootstrapping key. This means that you can use it with a decryption circuit to homomorphically decrypt the inner noisy ciphertext. If the decryption circuit produces an acceptable amount of noise, then it works, and you will end up with the result of the first homomorphic operation encrypted under the bootstrapping key. I illustrate this in figure 15.9.

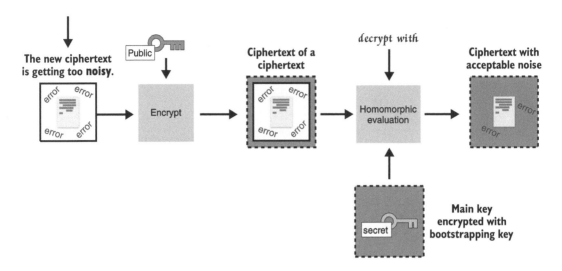

Figure 15.9   Building on figure 15.9, you use the initial secret key encrypted to the bootstrapping key to apply the decryption circuit to that new ciphertext. This effectively decrypts the noisy ciphertext in place, removing the errors. There will be some amount of errors due to the decryption circuit.

If the remaining amount of errors allows you to do at least one more homomorphic operation (+ or ×), then you are gold: you have a fully homomorphic encryption algorithm because you can always, in practice, run the bootstrapping after or before every operation. Note that you can set the bootstrapping key pair to be the same as the initial key pair. It's a bit weird as you get some circular security oddity, but it seems to work and no security issues are known.

15.2.4 *An FHE scheme based on the learning with errors problem*

Before moving on, let's see one example of an FHE scheme based on the learning with errors problem we saw in chapter 14. I'll explain a simplified version of the GSW scheme, named after the authors Craig Gentry, Amit Sahai, and Brent Waters. To keep things simple, I'll introduce a secret key version of the algorithm, but just keep in mind that it is relatively straightforward to transform such a scheme into a public key variant, which we need for bootstrapping. Take a look at the following equation where **C** is a square matrix, **s** is a vector, and *m* is a scalar (a number):

$$\mathbf{C}\mathbf{s} = m\mathbf{s}$$

In this equation, **s** is called an *eigenvector* and *m* is an *eigenvalue*. If these words are foreign to you, don't worry about it; they don't matter much here.

The first intuition in our FHE scheme is obtained by looking at the eigenvectors and eigenvalues. The observation is that if we set *m* to a single bit we want to encrypt, **C** to be the ciphertext, and **s** to be the secret key, then we have an (insecure) homomorphic encryption scheme to encrypt one bit. (Of course, we assume there is a way to obtain a random ciphertext **C** from a fixed bit m and a fixed secret key **s**.) I illustrate this in figure 15.10 in a Lego kind of way.

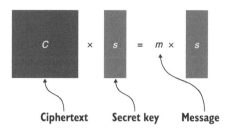

Figure 15.10   **We can produce an insecure homomorphic encryption scheme to encrypt a single bit *m* with a secret vector s by interpreting *m* as an eigenvalue and s as an eigenvector and then finding the associated matrix C, which will be the ciphertext.**

To decrypt a ciphertext, you multiply the matrix with the secret vector **s** and see if you obtain the secret vector back or 0. You can verify that the scheme is fully homomorphic by checking that the decryption of two ciphertexts added together ($\mathbf{C}_1 + \mathbf{C}_2$) results in the associated bits added together:

$$(\mathbf{C}_1 + \mathbf{C}_2)\mathbf{s} = \mathbf{C}_1\mathbf{s} + \mathbf{C}_2\mathbf{s} = b_1\mathbf{s} + b_2\mathbf{s} = (b_1 + b_2)\mathbf{s}$$

Also, the decryption of two ciphertexts multiplied together ($\mathbf{C}_1 \times \mathbf{C}_2$) results in the associated bits multiplied together:

$$(\mathbf{C}_1 \times \mathbf{C}_2)\mathbf{s} = \mathbf{C}_1\,(\mathbf{C}_2\mathbf{s}) = \mathbf{C}_1\,(b_2\mathbf{s}) = b_2\mathbf{C}_1\mathbf{s} = (b_2 \times b_1)\,\mathbf{s}$$

Unfortunately, that scheme is insecure as it is trivial to retrieve the eigenvector (the secret vector **s**) from **C**. What about adding a bit of noise? We can change this equation a bit to make it look like our learning with errors problem:

$$\mathbf{Cs} = m\mathbf{s} + \mathbf{e}$$

This should look more familiar. Again, we can verify that the addition is still homomorphic:

$$(\mathbf{C}_1 + \mathbf{C}_2)\mathbf{s} = \mathbf{C}_1\mathbf{s} + \mathbf{C}_2\mathbf{s} = b_1\mathbf{s} + \mathbf{e}_1 + b_2\mathbf{s} + \mathbf{e}_2 = (b_1 + b_2)\mathbf{s} + (\mathbf{e}_1 + \mathbf{e}_2)$$

Here, notice that the error is growing ($\mathbf{e}_1 + \mathbf{e}_2$), which is what we expected. We can also verify that the multiplication is still working as well:

$$(\mathbf{C}_1 \times \mathbf{C}_2)\mathbf{s} = \mathbf{C}_1\,(\mathbf{C}_2\mathbf{s}) = \mathbf{C}_1\,(b_2\mathbf{s} + \mathbf{e}_2) = b_2\mathbf{C}_1\mathbf{s} + \mathbf{C}_1\mathbf{e}_2 = b_2\,(b_1\mathbf{s} + \mathbf{e}_1) + \mathbf{C}_1\mathbf{e}_2$$
$$= (b_2 \times b_1)\,\mathbf{s} + b_2\mathbf{e}_1 + \mathbf{C}_1\mathbf{e}_2$$

Here, $b_2\mathbf{e}_1$ is small (as it is either $\mathbf{e}_1$ or 0), but $\mathbf{C}_1\mathbf{e}_2$ is potentially large. This is obviously a problem, which I'm going to ignore to avoid digging too much into the details. If you're interested in learning more, make sure to read Shai Halevi's "Homomorphic

Encryption" report (2017), which does an excellent job at explaining all of these things and more.

15.2.5 *Where is it used?*

The most touted use case of FHE has always been the cloud. What if I could continue to store my data in the cloud without having it seen? And, additionally, what if the cloud could provide useful computations on that encrypted data? Indeed, one can think of many applications where FHE could be useful. A few examples include

- A spam detector could scan your emails without looking at those.
- Genetic research could be performed on your DNA without actually having to store and protect your privacy-sensitive human code.
- A database could be stored encrypted and queried on the server side without revealing any data.

Yet Phillip Rogaway, in his seminal 2015 paper on "The Moral Character of Cryptographic Work," notes that "FHE [. . .] have engendered a new wave of exuberance. In grant proposals, media interviews, and talks, leading theorists speak of FHE [. . .] as game-changing indications of where we have come. Nobody seems to emphasize just how speculative it is that any of this will ever have any impact on practice."

While Rogaway is not wrong, FHE is still quite slow, advances in the field have been exciting. At the time of this writing (2021), operations are about one billion times slower than normal operations, yet since 2009, there has been a 10^9 speed-up. We are undoubtedly moving towards a future where FHE will be possible for at least some limited applications.

Furthermore, not every application needs the full-blown primitive; somewhat homomorphic encryption can also be used in a wide range of applications and is much more efficient than FHE. A good indicator that a theoretical cryptography primitive is entering the real world is standardization, and indeed, FHE is no foreigner to that. The https://homomorphicencryption.org standardization effort includes many large companies and universities. It is still unclear exactly when, where, and in what form homomorphic encryption will make its entry into the real world. What's clear is that it will happen, so stay tuned!

15.3 *General-purpose zero-knowledge proofs (ZKPs)*

I talked about zero-knowledge proofs (ZKPs) in chapter 7 on signatures. There, I pointed out that signatures are similar to non-interactive ZKPs of knowledge for discrete logarithms. These kinds of ZKPs were invented in the mid-1980s by Professors Shafi Goldwasser, Silvio Micali, and Charles Rackoff. Shortly after, Goldreich, Micali, and Wigderson found that we could prove much more than just discrete logarithms or other types of hard problems; we could also prove the correct execution of any program even if we removed some of the inputs or outputs (see figure 15.11 for an example). This section focuses on this general-purpose type of ZKP.

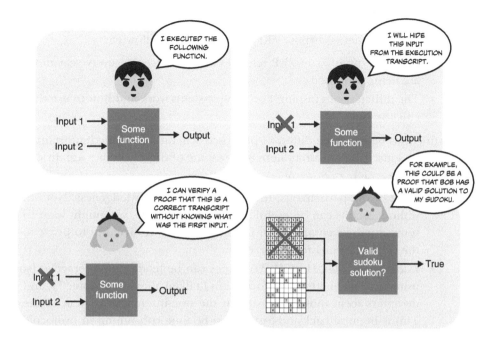

Figure 15.11 General-purpose ZKPs allow a prover to convince a verifier about the integrity of an execution trace (the inputs of a program and the outputs obtained after its execution) while hiding some of the inputs or outputs involved in the computation. An example of this is a prover trying to prove that a sudoku can be solved.

ZKP as a field has grown tremendously since its early years. One major reason for this growth is the cryptocurrency boom and the need to provide more confidentiality to on-chain transactions as well as optimize on space. The field of ZKP is still growing extremely fast as of the time of this writing, and it is quite hard to follow what are all the modern schemes that exist and what types of general-purpose ZKPs there are.

Fortunately for us, this problem was getting large enough that it tripped the *standardization threshold*, an imaginary line that, when reached, almost always ends up motivating some people to work together towards a clarification of the field. In 2018, actors from the industry and academia joined together to form the ZKProof Standardization effort with the goal to "standardize the use of cryptographic zero-knowledge proofs." To this day, it is still an ongoing effort. You can read more about it at https://zkproof.org.

You can use general-purpose ZKPs in quite a lot of different situations, but to my knowledge, they have mostly been used in the cryptocurrency space so far, probably due to the high number of people interested in cryptography and willing to experiment with the bleeding edge stuff. Nonetheless, general-purpose ZKPs have potential applications in a lot of fields: identity management (being able to prove your own age without revealing it), compression (being able to hide most of a computation), confidentiality (being able to hide parts of a protocol), and so on. The biggest blockers for more applications to adopt general-purpose ZKPs seem to be the following:

- The large number of ZKP schemes and the fact that every year more schemes are being proposed.
- The difficulty of grasping how these systems work and how to use them for specific use cases.

Distinctions between the different proposed schemes are quite important. Because it is a great source of confusion, here is how some of these schemes are divided:

- *Zero-knowledge or not*—If some of the information needs to remain secret from some of the participants, then we need zero-knowledgeness. Note that proofs without secrets can be useful as well. For example, you might want to delegate some intensive computation to a service that, in turn, has to prove to you that the result they provide is correct.
- *Interactive or not*—Most ZKP schemes can be made non-interactive (sometimes using the Fiat-Shamir transformation I talked about in chapter 7), and protocol designers seem most interested in the non-interactive version of the scheme. This is because back-and-forth's can be time consuming in protocols, but also because interactivity is sometimes not possible. So-called non-interactive proofs are often referred to as *NIZKs* for *non-interactive ZKPs*.
- *Succinct proofs or not*—Most of the ZKP schemes in the spotlight are often referred to as *zk-SNARKs* for *Zero-Knowledge Succinct Non-Interactive Argument of Knowledge*. While the definition can vary, it focuses on the size of the proofs produced by such systems (usually in the order of hundreds of bytes), and the amount of time needed to verify them (within the range of milliseconds). zk-SNARKs are, thus, short and easy to use to verify ZKPs. Note that a scheme not being a zk-SNARK does not disqualify it for the real world as often different properties might be useful in different use cases.
- *Transparent setup or not*—Like every cryptographic primitive, ZKPs need a setup to agree on a set of parameters and common values. This is called a *common reference string* (CRS). But setups for ZKPs can be much more limiting or dangerous than initially thought. There are three types of setup:
  - *Trusted*—Means that whoever created the CRS also has access to secrets that allow them to forge proofs (hence, it's why these secrets are sometimes called "toxic waste"). This is quite an issue as we are back to having a trusted third party, yet schemes that exhibit this property are often the most efficient and have the shortest proof size. To decrease the risk, MPC can be use to have many participants help create these dangerous parameters. If a single participant is honest and deletes their keys after the ceremony, the toxic waste gets flushed.
  - *Universal*—A trusted setup is said to be universal if you can use it to prove the execution of any circuit (bounded by some size). Otherwise it is specific to a single circuit.

- *Transparent*—Fortunately for us, many schemes also offer transparent setups, meaning that no trusted third party needs to be present to create the parameters of the system. Transparent schemes are by design universal.

- *Quantum-resistant or not*—Some ZKPs make use of public key cryptography and advanced primitives like bilinear pairings (which I'll explain later), while others only rely on symmetric cryptography (like hash functions), which makes them naturally resistant to quantum computers (usually at the expense of much larger proofs).

Because zk-SNARKs are what's up at the time of this writing, let me give you my perception as to how they work.

15.3.1 *How zk-SNARKs work*

First and foremost, there are many, many zk-SNARK schemes—too many of them, really. Most build on this type of construction:

- A proving system, allowing a prover to prove something to a verifier.
- A translation or compilation of a program to something the proving system can prove.

The first part is not too hard to understand, while the second part sort of requires a graduate course in the subject. To begin, let's take a look at the first part.

The main idea of zk-SNARKs is that they are all about proving that you know some polynomial $f(x)$ that has some roots. By roots I mean that the verifier has some values in mind (for example, 1 and 2) and the prover must prove that the secret polynomial they have in mind evaluates to 0 for these values (for example, $f(1) = f(2) = 0$). By the way, a polynomial that has 1 and 2 as roots (as in our example) can be written as $f(x) = (x - 1)(x - 2)h(x)$ for some polynomial $h(x)$. (If you're not convinced, try to evaluate that at $x = 1$ and $x = 2$.) We say that the prover must prove that they know an $f(x)$ and $h(x)$ such that $f(x) = t(x)h(x)$ for some target polynomial $t(x) = (x - 1)(x - 2)$. In this example, 1 and 2 are the roots that the verifier wants to check.

But that's it! That's what zk-SNARKs proving systems usually provide: something to prove that you know some polynomial. I'm repeating this because the first time I learned about that it made no sense to me. How can you prove that you know some secret input to a program if all you can prove is that you know a polynomial? Well, that's why the second part of a zk-SNARK is so difficult. It's about translating a program into a polynomial. But more on that later.

Back to our proving system, how does one prove that they know such a function $f(x)$? They have to prove that they know an $h(x)$ such that you can write $f(x)$ as $f(x) = t(x)h(x)$. Ugh, . . . not so fast here. We're talking about *zero-knowledge* proofs right? How can we prove this without giving out $f(x)$? The answer is in the following three tricks:

- *Homomorphic commitments*—A commitment scheme similar to the ones we used in other ZKPs (covered in chapter 7)

- *Bilinear pairings*—A mathematical construction that has some interesting properties; more on that later
- The fact that *different polynomials evaluate to different values most of the time*

So let's go through each of these, shall we?

15.3.2 *Homomorphic commitments to hide parts of the proof*

The first trick is to use *commitments* to hide the values that we're sending to the prover. But not only do we hide them, we also want to allow the verifier to perform some operations on them so that they can verify the proof. Specifically, they need to verify that if the prover commits on their polynomial $f(x)$ as well as $h(x)$, then we have

$$com(f(x)) = com(t(x))\ com(h(x)) = com(t(x)\,h(x))$$

where the commitment $com(t(x))$ is computed by the verifier as the agreed constraint on the polynomial. These operations are called *homomorphic operations,* and we couldn't have performed them if we had used hash functions as commitment mechanisms (as mentioned in chapter 2). Thanks to these homomorphic commitments, we can "hide values in the exponent" (for example, for a value v, send the commitment $g^v \bmod p$) and perform useful identity checks:

- The equality of commitments—The equality $g^a = g^b$ means that $a = b$
- The addition of commitments—The equality $g^a = g^b g^c$ means that $a = b + c$
- The scaling of commitments—The equality $g^a = (g^b)^c$ means that $a = bc$

Notice that the last check only works if c is a public value and not a commitment (g^c). With homomorphic commitments alone we can't check the multiplication of commitments, which is what we needed. Fortunately, cryptography has another tool to get such equations hidden in the exponent—*bilinear pairings.*

15.3.3 *Bilinear pairings to improve our homomorphic commitments*

Bilinear pairings can be used to unblock us, and this is the *sole reason* why we use bilinear pairings in a zk-SNARK (really, just to be able to multiply the values inside the commitments). I don't want to go too deep into what bilinear pairings are, but just know that it is another tool in our toolkit that allows us to multiply elements that couldn't be multiplied previously by moving them from one group to another.

Using e as the typical way of writing a bilinear pairing, we have $e(g_1, g_2) = h_3$, where g_1, g_2, and h_3 are generators for different groups. Here, we'll use the same generator on the left ($g_1 = g_2$) which makes the pairing symmetric. We can use a bilinear pairing to perform multiplications hidden in the exponent via this equation:

$$e(g^b, g^c) = e(g)^{bc}$$

Again, we use bilinear pairings to make our commitments not only homomorphic for the addition, but also for the multiplication. (Note that this is not a fully homomorphic scheme as multiplication is limited to a single one.) Bilinear pairings are also used in other places in cryptography and are slowly becoming a more common building block. They can be seen in homomorphic encryption schemes and also signatures schemes like BLS (which I mentioned in chapter 8).

15.3.4 Where does the succinctness come from?

Finally, the *succinctness* of zk-SNARKs comes from the fact that two functions that differ evaluate to different points most of the time. What does this mean for us? Let's say that I don't have a polynomial $f(x)$ that really has the roots we've chosen with the verifier, this means that $f(x)$ is not equal to $t(x)h(x)$. Then, evaluating $f(x)$ and $t(x)h(x)$ at a random point r won't return the same result *most of the time*. For almost all r, $f(r) \neq t(r)h(r)$. This is known as the *Schwartz-Zippel lemma*, which I illustrate in figure 15.12.

Schwartz-Zippel lemma

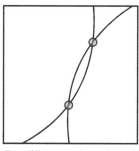

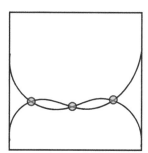

Two different polynomials of degree 1 intersect in at most 1 point.	**Two different polynomials of degree 2 intersect in at most 2 points.**	**Two different polynomials of degree 3 intersect in at most 3 points.**

Figure 15.12 The Schwartz-Zippel lemma says that two different polynomials of degree n can intersect in at most n points. In other words, two different polynomials will differ in most points.

Knowing this, it is enough to prove that $com(f(r)) = com(t(r)h(r))$ for some random point r. This is why zk-SNARK proofs are so small: by comparing points in a group, you end up comparing much larger polynomials. But this is also the reason behind the trusted setup needed in most zk-SNARK constructions. If a prover knows the random point r that will be used to check the equality, then they can forge an invalid polynomial that will still verify the equality. So a trusted setup is about

1. Creating a random value r
2. Committing different exponentiations of r (for example, g, g^r, g^{r^2}, g^{r^3}, . . .) so that these values can be used by the prover to compute their polynomial without knowing the point r
3. Destroying the value r

Does the second point make sense? If my polynomial as the prover is $f(x) = 3x^2 + x + 2$, then all I have to do is compute $(g^{r^2})^3 \, g^r \, g^2$ to obtain a commitment of my polynomial evaluated at that random point r (without knowing r).

15.3.5 *From programs to polynomials*

So far, the constraints on the polynomial that the prover must find is that it needs to have some roots: some values that evaluate to 0 with our polynomial. But how do we translate a more general statement into a polynomial knowledge proof? Typical statements in cryptocurrencies, which are the applications currently making the most use of zk-SNARKs these days, are of the form:

- Prove that a value is in the range $[0, 2^{64}]$ (this is called a range proof)
- Prove that a (secret) value is included in some given (public) Merkle tree
- Prove that the sum of some values is equal to the sum of some other values
- And so on

And herein lies the difficult part. As I said earlier, converting a program execution into the knowledge of a polynomial is really hard. The good news is that I'm not going to tell you all about the details, but I'll tell you enough to give you a sense of how things work. From there, you should be able to understand what are the parts that are missing from my explanation and fill in the gaps as you wish. What is going to happen next is the following:

1 Our program will first get converted into an arithmetic circuit, like the ones we saw in the section on MPC.
2 That arithmetic circuit will be converted into a system of equations that are of a certain form (called a rank-1 constraint system or R1CS).
3 We then use a trick to convert our system of equations into a polynomial.

15.3.6 *Programs are for computers; we need arithmetic circuits instead*

First, let's assume that almost any program can be rewritten more or less easily in math. The reason why we would want to do that should be obvious: we can't prove code, but we can prove math. For example, the following listing provides a function where every input is public except for a, which is our secret input.

Listing 15.1   A simple function

```
fn my_function(w, a, b) {
  if w == true {
    return a * (b + 3);
  } else {
    return a + b;
  }
}
```

In this simple example, if every input and output is public except for a, one can still deduce what a is. This listing also serves as an example of what you shouldn't try to prove in zero-knowledge. Anyway, the program can be rewritten in math with this equation:

$$w \times (a \times (b + 3)) + (1 - w) \times (a + b) = v$$

Where v is the output and w is either 0 (false) or 1 (true). Notice that this equation is not really a program or a circuit, it just looks like a constraint. If you execute the program correctly and then fill in the inputs and outputs obtained in the equation, the equality should be correct. If the equality is not correct, then your inputs and outputs don't correspond to a valid execution of the program.

This is how you have to think about these general-purpose ZKPs. Instead of executing a function in zero-knowledge (which doesn't mean much really), we use zk-SNARKs to prove that some given inputs and outputs correctly match the execution of a program, even when some of the inputs or outputs are omitted.

15.3.7 An arithmetic circuit to a rank-1 constraint system (R1CS)

In any case, we're only one step into the process of converting our execution to something we can prove with zk-SNARKs. The next step is to convert that into a series of constraints, which then can be converted into proving the knowledge of some polynomial. What zk-SNARKs want is a *rank-1 constraint system* (R1CS). An R1CS is really just a series of equations that are of the form $L \times R = O$, where L, R, and O can only be the addition of some variables, thus the only multiplication is between L and R. It really doesn't matter why we need to transform our arithmetic circuit into such a system of equations except that it helps when doing the conversion to the final stuff we can prove. Try to do this with the equation we have and we obtain something like

- $a \times (b + 3) = m$
- $w \times (m - a - b) = v - a - b$

We actually forgot the constraint that w is either 0 or 1, which we can add to our system via a clever trick:

- $a \times (b + 3) = m$
- $w \times (m - a - b) = v - a - b$
- $w \times w = w$

Does that make sense? You should really see this system as a set of constraints: if you give me a set of values that you claim match the inputs and outputs of the execution of my program, then I should be able to validate that the values also correctly verify the equalities. If one of the equalities is wrong, then it must mean that the program does not output the value you gave me for the inputs you gave me. Another way to think about it is that zk-SNARKs allow you to verifiably remove inputs or outputs of the transcript of the correct execution of a program.

15.3.8 *From R1CS to a polynomial*

The question is still: how do we transform this system into a polynomial? We're almost there, and as always the answer is with a series of tricks! Because we have three different equations in our system, the first step is to agree on three roots for our polynomial. We can simply choose 1, 2, 3 as roots, meaning that our polynomial solves $f(x) = 0$ for $x = 1$, $x = 2$, and $x = 3$. Why do that? By doing so, we can make our polynomial represent all the equations in our system simultaneously by representing the first equation when evaluated at 1, and representing the second equation when evaluated at 2, and so on. The prover's job is now to create a polynomial $f(x)$ such that:

- $f(1) = a \times (b + 3) - m$
- $f(2) = w \times (m - a - b) - (v - a - b)$
- $f(3) = w \times w - w$

Notice that all these equations should evaluate to 0 if the values correctly match the execution of our original program. In other words, our polynomial $f(x)$ has roots 1, 2, 3 only if we create it correctly. Remember, this is what zk-SNARKs are all about: we have the protocol to prove that, indeed, our polynomial $f(x)$ has these roots (known by both the prover and the verifier).

It would be too simple if this was the end of my explanation because now the problem is that the prover has too much freedom in choosing their polynomial $f(x)$. They can simply find a polynomial that has roots 1, 2, 3 without caring about the values a, b, m, v, and w. They can do pretty much whatever they want! What we want instead, is a system that locks every part of the polynomial except for the secret values that the verifier must *not* learn about.

15.3.9 *It takes two to evaluate a polynomial hiding in the exponent*

Let's recap, we want a prover that has to correctly execute the program with their secret value a and the public values b and w and obtain the output v that they can publish. The prover then must create a polynomial by only filling the parts that the verifier must not learn about: the values a and m. Thus, in a real zk-SNARK protocol you want the prover to have the least amount of freedom possible when they create their polynomials and then evaluate it to a random point.

To do this, the polynomial is created somewhat dynamically by having the prover only fill in their part, then having the verifier fill in the other parts. For example, let's take the first equation, $f(1) = a \times (b + 3) - m$, and represent it as

$$f_1(x) = aL_1(x) \times (b + 3)R_1(x) - mO_1(x)$$

where $L_1(x)$, $R_1(x)$, $O_1(x)$ are polynomials that evaluate to 1 for $x = 1$ and to 0 for $x = 2$ and $x = 3$. This is necessary so that they only influence our first equation. (Note that it is easy to find such polynomials via algorithms like Lagrange interpolation.) Now, notice two more things:

- We have the inputs, intermediate values, and outputs as coefficients of our polynomials.
- The polynomial $f(x)$ is the sum $f_1(x) + f_2(x) + f_3(x)$, where we can define $f_2(x)$ and $f_3(x)$ to represent equations 2 and 3, similarly to $f_1(x)$.

As you can see, our first equation is still represented at the point $x = 1$:

$$f(1) = f_1(1) + f_2(1) + f_3(1)$$

$$= f_1(1)$$

$$= aL_1(1) \times (b+3)R_1(1) - mO_1(1)$$

$$= a \times (b+3) - m$$

With this new way of representing our equations (which remember, represent the execution of our program), the prover can now evaluate parts of the polynomial that are relevant to them by:

1. Taking the exponentiation of the random point r hidden in the exponent to reconstruct the polynomials $L_1(r)$ and $O_1(r)$
2. Exponentiating $g^{L_1(r)}$ with the secret value a to obtain $(g^{L_1(r)})^a = g^{aL_1(r)}$, which represents $a \times L_1(x)$ that is evaluated at an unknown and random point $x = r$ and hidden in the exponent
3. Exponentiating $g^{O_1(r)}$ with the secret intermediate value m to obtain $(g^{O_1(r)})^m = g^{mO_1(r)}$, which represents the evaluation of $mO_1(x)$ at the random point r and hidden in the exponent

The verifier can then fill in the missing parts by reconstructing $(g^{R_1(r)})^b$ and $(g^{R_0(r)})^3$ for some agreed on value b with the same techniques the prover used. Adding the two together the verifier obtains $g^{bR_1(r)} + g^{3R_1(r)}$, which represents the (hidden) evaluation of $(b+3) \times R_1(x)$ at an unknown and random point $x = r$. Finally, the verifier can reconstruct $f_1(r)$, which is hidden in the exponent, by using a bilinear pairing:

$$e(g^{aL_1(r)}, g^{(b+3)R_1(r)}) - e(g, g^{mO_1(r)}) = e(g, g)^{aL_1(r) \times (b+3)R_1(r) - mO_1(r)}$$

If you extrapolate these techniques to the whole polynomial $f(x)$, you can figure out the final protocol. Of course, this is still a gross simplification of a real zk-SNARK protocol; this still leaves way too much power to the prover.

All the other tricks used in zk-SNARKs are meant to further restrict what the prover can do, ensuring that they correctly and consistently fill in the missing parts as well as optimizing what can be optimized. By the way, the best explanation I've read is the paper, "Why and How zk-SNARK Works: Definitive Explanation" by Maksym Petkus, which goes much more in depth and explains all of the parts that I've overlooked.

And that's it for zk-SNARKs. This is really just an introduction; in practice, zk-SNARKs are much more complicated to understand and use! Not only is the amount of work to convert a program into something that can be proven nontrivial, it sometimes adds new constraints on a cryptography protocol. For example, the mainstream hash functions and signature schemes are often too heavy-duty for general-purpose ZKP systems, which has led many protocol designers to investigate different ZKP-friendly schemes. Furthermore, as I said earlier, there are many different zk-SNARKs constructions, and there are also many different non-zk-SNARKs constructions, which might be more relevant as general-purpose ZKP constructions depending on your use case.

But, unfortunately, no one-size-fits-all ZKP scheme seems to exist (for example, a ZKP scheme with a transparent setup, succinct, universal, and quantum-resistant), and it is not clear which one to use in which cases. The field is still young, and every year new and better schemes are being published. It might be that a few years down the line better standards and easy-to-use libraries will surface, so if you're interested in this space, keep watching!

Summary

- In the last decade, many theoretical cryptographic primitives have made huge progress in terms of efficiency and practicality; some are making their way into the real world.

- Secure multi-party computation (MPC) is a primitive that allows multiple participants to correctly execute a program together, without revealing their respective inputs. Threshold signatures are starting to be adopted in cryptocurrencies, while private set intersection (PSI) protocols are being used in modern and large-scale protocols like Google's Password Checkup.

- Fully homomorphic encryption (FHE) allows one to compute arbitrary functions on encrypted data without decrypting it. It has potential applications in the cloud, where it could prevent access to the data to anyone but the user while still allowing the cloud platform to perform useful computation on the data for the user.

- General-purpose zero-knowledge proofs (ZKPs) have found many use cases, and have had recent breakthroughs with small proofs that are fast to verify. They are mostly used in cryptocurrencies to add privacy to or to compress the size of the blockchain. Their use cases seem broader, though, and as better standards and easier-to-use libraries make their way into the real world, we might see them being used more and more.

When and where cryptography fails

16

Greetings, traveler; you've come a long way. While this is the last chapter, it's all about the journey, not the end. You're now equipped with the gear and skills required to step into the real world of cryptography. What's left is for you to apply what you've learned.

Before parting ways, I'd like to give you a few hints and tools that'll be useful for what follows. The quests you'll face often follow the same pattern: it starts with a challenge, launching you on a pursuit for an existing cryptographic primitive or protocol. From there, you'll look for a standard and a good implementation, and then you'll make use of it in the best way you can. That's if everything goes according to plan. . . .

Before we part

Someone who seeks to bridge the gap between theory and practice will have to slay many dragons. Here's your sword—take it.

16.1 *Finding the right cryptographic primitive or protocol is a boring job*

You're facing unencrypted traffic, or a number of servers that need to authenticate one another, or some secrets that need to be stored without becoming single points of failure. What do you do?

You could use TLS or Noise (mentioned in chapter 9) to encrypt your traffic. You could set up a public key infrastructure (mentioned in chapter 9) to authenticate servers via the signature of some certificate authority, and you could distribute a secret using a threshold scheme (covered in chapter 8) to avoid the compromise of one secret to lead to the compromise of the whole system. These would be fine answers.

If the problem you're facing is a common one to have, chances are that you can simply find an existing cryptographic primitive or protocol that directly solves your use case. This book gives you a good idea of what the standard primitives and common protocols are, so at this point, you should have a good idea of what's at your disposal when faced with a cryptographic problem.

Cryptography is quite an interesting field, going all over the place as new discoveries and primitives are invented and proposed. While you might be tempted to explore exotic cryptography to solve your problem, your responsibility is to remain conservative. The reason is that *complexity is the enemy of security*. Whenever you do something, it is much easier to do it as simply as possible. Too many vulnerabilities have been introduced by trying to be extravagant. This concept has been dubbed *boring cryptography* by Bernstein in 2015, and has been the inspiration behind the naming of Google's TLS library, BoringSSL.

Cryptographic proposals need to withstand many years of careful scrutiny before they become plausible candidates for field use. This is especially when the proposal is based on novel mathematical problems.

—Rivest et al. ("Responses to NIST's proposal," 1992)

What if you can't find a cryptographic primitive or protocol that solves your problem? This is where you must step into the world of *theoretical* cryptography, which is obviously not the subject of this book. I can merely give you recommendations.

The first recommendation I will give you is the free book *A Graduate Course in Applied Cryptography*, written by Dan Boneh and Victor Shoup, and available at https://cryptobook.us. This book provides excellent support that covers everything I've covered in this book but in much more depth. Dan Boneh also has an amazing online course, "Cryptography I," also available for free at https://www.coursera.org/learn/crypto. It is a much more gentle introduction to theoretical cryptography. If you'd like to read something halfway between this book and the world of theoretical cryptography, I can't recommend enough the book, *Serious Cryptography: A Practical Introduction to Modern Encryption* (No Starch Press, 2017) by Jean-Philippe Aumasson.

Now, let's imagine that you *do* have an existing cryptographic primitive or protocol that solves your solution. A cryptographic primitive or protocol is still very much of a theoretical thing. Wouldn't it be great if it had a practical standard that you could use right away?

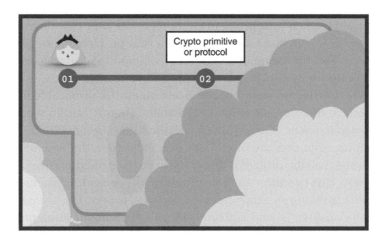

16.2   How do I use a cryptographic primitive or protocol? Polite standards and formal verification

You realize that a solution exists that meets your needs, now does it have a standard? Without a standard, a primitive is often proposed without consideration for its real-world use. Cryptographers often don't think about the different pitfalls of using their primitive or protocol and the details of implementing them. *Polite cryptography* is what

Riad S. Wahby once called standards that care about their implementation and leave little room for implementers to shoot themselves in the foot.

The poor user is given enough rope with which to hang himself—something a standard should not do.

—Rivest et al. ("Responses to NIST's proposal," 1992)

A polite standard is a specification that aims to address all edge cases and potential security issues by providing safe and easy-to-use interfaces to implement, as well as good guidance on how to use the primitive or protocol. In addition, good standards have accompanying test vectors: lists of matching inputs and outputs that you can feed to your implementation to test its correctness.

Unfortunately, not all standards are "polite," and the cryptographic pitfalls they create are what make most of the vulnerabilities I talk about in this book. Sometimes standards are too vague, lack test vectors, or try to do too much at the same time. For example, *cryptography agility* is the term used to specify the flexibility of a protocol in terms of cryptographic algorithms it supports. Supporting different cryptographic algorithms can give a standard an edge because sometimes one algorithm gets broken and deprecated while others don't. In such a situation, an inflexible protocol prevents clients and services from easily moving on. On the other hand, too much agility can also strongly affect the complexity of a standard, sometimes even leading to vulnerabilities, as the many downgrade attacks on TLS can attest.

Unfortunately, more often than cryptographers are willing to admit, you will run into trouble when your problem either meets an edge case that the mainstream primitives or protocols don't address, or when your problem doesn't match a standardized solution. For this reason, it is extremely common to see developers creating their own mini-protocols or mini-standards. This is when trouble starts.

When wrong assumptions are made about the primitive's threat model (what it protects against) or about its composability (how it can be used within a protocol), breakage happens. These context-specific issues are amplified by the fact that cryptographic primitives are often built in a silo, where the designer did not necessarily think about all the problems that could arise once the primitive is used in a number of different ways or within another primitive or protocol. I gave many examples of this: X25519 breaking in edge cases protocols (chapter 11), signatures assumed to be unique (chapter 7), and ambiguity in who is communicating to whom (chapter 10). It's not necessarily your fault! The developers have outsmarted the cryptographers, revealing pitfalls that no one knew existed. That's what happened.

If you ever find yourself in this type of situation, the go-to tool of a cryptographer is pen-and-paper proof. This is not quite helpful for us, the practitioners, as we either don't have the time to do that work (it really takes a lot of time) or even the expertise. We're not helpless, though. We can use computers to facilitate the task of analyzing a mini-protocol. This is called *formal verification*, and it can be a wonderful use of your time.

Formal verification allows you to write your protocol in some intermediate language and test some properties on it. For example, the *Tamarin protocol prover* (see figure 16.1) is a formal verification tool that has been (and is) used in order to find subtle attacks in many different protocols. To learn more about this, see the papers "Prime, Order Please! Revisiting Small Subgroup and Invalid Curve Attacks on Protocols using Diffie-Hellman" (2019) and "Seems Legit: Automated Analysis of Subtle Attacks on Protocols that Use Signatures" (2019).

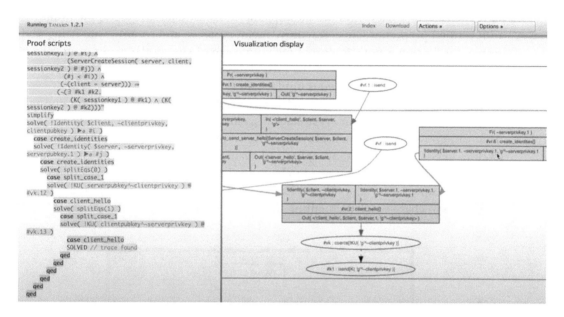

Figure 16.1   The Tamarin protocol prover is a free formal verification tool that you can use to model a cryptographic protocol and find attacks on it.

The other side of the coin is that it is often hard to use formal verification tools. The first step is to understand how to translate a protocol into the language and the concepts used by the tool, which is often not straightforward. After having described a protocol in a formal language, you still need to figure out what you want to prove and how to express it in the formal language.

It is not uncommon to see a proof that actually proved the wrong things, so one can even ask who verifies the formal verification? Some promising research in this area is aimed at making it easier for developers to formally verify their protocols. For example, the tool Verifpal (https://verifpal.com) trades off soundness (being able to find all attacks) for ease of use.

You can also use formal verification to verify a cryptographic primitive's security proofs using formal verification tools like Coq, CryptoVerif, and ProVerif, and even to generate "formally verified" implementations in different languages (see projects like

The KRACK attack

It does happen that critical differences are made when writing a formal description of a protocol as compared to the actual protocol being implemented, which then leads to gaps and real-world attacks. This is what happened in 2017, when the KRACK attack (https://krackattacks.com) broke the Wi-Fi protocol WPA2, even though it had been previously formally verified.

HACL*, Vale, and fiat-crypto, which implement mainstream cryptographic primitives with verified properties like correctness, memory safety, and so on). That being said, formal verification is not a foolproof technique; gaps between the paper protocol and its formal description or between the formal description and the implementation will always exist and appear innocuous until found to be fatal.

Studying how other protocols fail is an excellent way of avoiding the same mistakes. The cryptopals.com or cryptohack.org challenges are a great way to learn about what can go wrong in using and composing cryptographic primitives and protocols. Bottom line—you need to thoroughly understand what you're using! If you are building a mini-protocol, then you need to be careful and either formally verify that protocol or ask experts for help. OK, we have a standard, or something that looks like it, now who's in charge of implementing that?

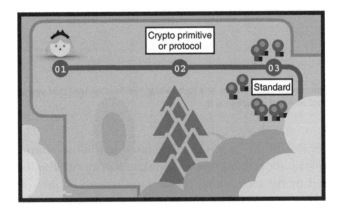

16.3   *Where are the good libraries?*

You're one step closer to solving your problem. You know the primitive or protocol you want to use, and you have a standard for it. At the same time, you're also one step further away from the specification, which means you might create bugs. But first, where's the code?

You look around, and you see that there are many libraries or frameworks available for you to use. That's a good problem to have. But still, which library do you pick? Which is most secure? This is a hard question to answer. Some libraries are well-respected, and I've listed some in this book: Google's Tink, libsodium, cryptography.io, etc.

Sometimes, though, it is hard to find a good library to use. Perhaps the programming language you're using doesn't have that much support for cryptography, or perhaps the primitive or protocol you want to use doesn't have that many implementations. In these situations, it is good to be cautious and ask the cryptography community for advice, look at the authors behind the library, and perhaps even ask experts for a code review. For example, the r/crypto community on Reddit is pretty helpful and welcoming; emailing authors directly sometimes works; asking the audience during open-mic sessions at conferences can also have its effect.

If you're in a desperate situation, you might even have to implement the cryptographic primitive or protocol yourself. There are many issues that can arise at this point, and it is a good idea to check for common issues that arise in cryptographic implementations. Fortunately, if you are following a good standard, then mistakes are less easy to make. But still, implementing cryptography is an art, and it is not something you should get yourself into if you can avoid it.

One interesting way to test a cryptographic implementation is to use *tooling*. While no single tooling can cater to all cryptographic algorithms, Google's Wycheproof deserves a mention. Wycheproof is a suite of test vectors that you can use to look for tricky bugs in common cryptographic algorithms like ECDSA, AES-GCM, and so on. The framework has been used to find an impressive number of bugs in different cryptographic implementations. Next, let's pretend that you did not implement cryptography yourself and found a cryptography library.

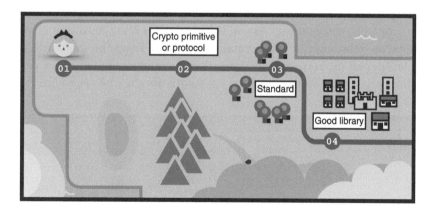

16.4 Misusing cryptography: Developers are the enemy

You found some code you can use, you're one step further, yet you find there are more opportunities to create bugs. This is where most bugs in applied cryptography happen. We've seen examples of misusing cryptography in this book again and again: reusing nonces is bad in algorithms like ECDSA (chapter 7) and AES-GCM (chapter 4), collisions can arise when the misuse of hash functions happen (chapter 2), parties can be impersonated due to lack of origin authentication (chapter 9), and so on.

> *The results show that just 17% of the bugs are in cryptographic libraries (which often have devastating consequences), and the remaining 83% are misuses of cryptographic libraries by individual applications.*

> —David Lazar, Haogang Chen, Xi Wang, and Nickolai Zeldovich
> ("Why does cryptographic software fail? A case study
> and open problems," 2014)

In general, the more a primitive or protocol is abstracted, the safer it is to use. For example, AWS offers a Key Management Service (KMS) to host your keys in HSMs and to perform cryptographic computations on-demand. This way, cryptography is abstracted at the application level. Another example is programming languages that provide cryptography within their standard libraries, which are often more trusted than third-party libraries. For example, Golang's standard library is excellent.

The care given to the usability of a cryptographic library can often be summarized as "treating the developer as the enemy." This is the approach taken by many cryptographic libraries. For example, Google's Tink doesn't let you choose the nonce/IV value in AES-GCM (see chapter 4) in order to avoid accidental nonce reuse. The libsodium library, in order to avoid complexity, only offers a fixed set of primitives without giving you any freedom. Some signature libraries wrap messages within a signature, forcing you to verify the signature before releasing the message, and the list goes on. In this sense, cryptographic protocols and libraries have a responsibility to make their interfaces as misuse resistant as possible.

I've said it before, I'll say it again—make sure you understand the fine print (all of it) for what you're using. As you've seen in this book, misusing cryptographic primitives or protocols can fail in catastrophic ways. Read the standards, read the security considerations, and read the manual and the documentation for your cryptographic library. Is this it? Well, not really. . . . You're not the only user here.

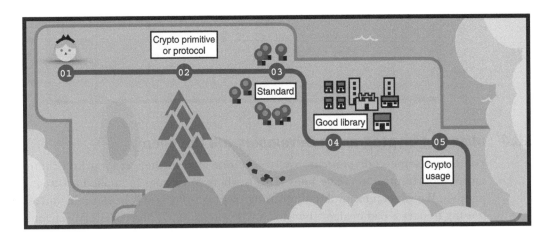

16.5 *You're doing it wrong: Usable security*

Using cryptography solves problems that applications have in often transparent ways but not always! Sometimes, the use of cryptography leaks to the users of the applications.

Usually, education can only help so much. It is, hence, never a good idea to blame the user when something bad happens. The relevant field of research is called *usable security*, in which solutions are sought to make security and cryptography-related features as transparent as possible to users, removing as many opportunities for misuse as possible. One good example is how browsers gradually shifted from simple warnings when SSL/TLS certificates were invalid to making it harder for users to accept the risk.

> *We observed behavior that is consistent with the theory of warning fatigue. In Google Chrome, users click through the most common SSL error faster and more frequently than other errors. [. . .] We also find clickthrough rates as high as 70.2% for Google Chrome SSL warnings, indicating that the user experience of a warning can have a tremendous impact on user behavior.*
>
> —Devdatta Akhawe and Adrienne Porter Felt
> ("Alice in Warningland: A Large-Scale Field Study
> of Browser Security Warning Effectiveness," 2013)

Another good example is how security-sensitive services have moved on from passwords to supporting second-factor authentication (covered in chapter 11). Because it was too hard to force users to use strong per-service passwords, another solution was found to eliminate the risk of password compromise. End-to-end encryption is also a good example because it is always hard for users to understand what it means to have their conversations end-to-end encrypted and how much of the security comes from them actively verifying fingerprints (covered in chapter 10). Whenever cryptography is pushed to users, great effort must be taken to reduce the risk of user mistakes.

> **Story time**
> Years ago I was asked to review the end-to-end encryption proposal of a widely-used messaging application. The proposal included the usual state-of-the-art protocol, the Signal protocol (covered in chapter 10), yet it didn't offer a functionality for users to verify the public keys of (or the session keys with) other users. This meant that while your communications were end-to-end encrypted in the presence of a passive adversary, a rogue employee could have easily updated a user's public key (or some users' session keys), and you would have not been able to detect the man-in-the-middle attack.

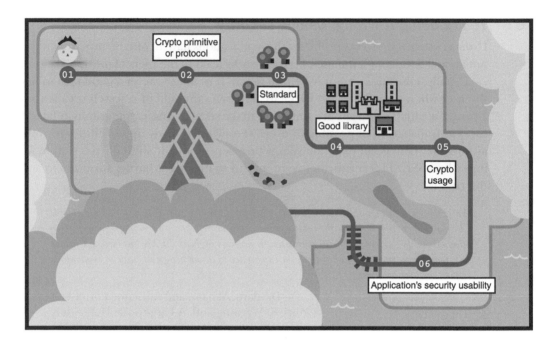

16.6 *Cryptography is not an island*

Cryptography is often used as part of a more complex system that can also have bugs. Actually, most of the bugs live in those parts that have nothing to do with the cryptography itself. An attacker often looks for the weakest link in the chain, the lowest hanging fruit, and it so happens that cryptography often does a good job at raising the bar. Encompassing systems can be much larger and complex and often end up creating more accessible attack vectors. Adi Shamir famously said, "Cryptography is typically bypassed, not penetrated."

While it is good to put some effort into making sure that the cryptography in your system is conservative, well-implemented, and well-tested, it is also beneficial to ensure that the same level of scrutiny is applied to the rest of the system. Otherwise, you might have done all of that for nothing.

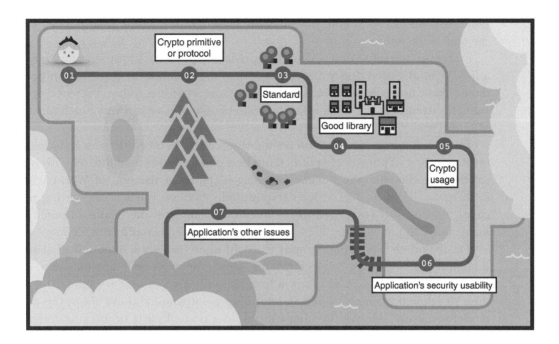

16.7 Your responsibilities as a cryptography practitioner, don't roll your own crypto

That's it, this is the end of the book, you are now free to gallop in the wilderness. But I have to warn you, having read this book gives you no superpowers; it should only give you a sense of fragility. A sense that cryptography can easily be misused and that the simplest mistake can lead to devastating consequences. Proceed with caution!

You now have a big crypto toolset at your belt. You should be able to recognize what type of cryptography is being used around you, perhaps even identify what seems fishy. You should be able to make some design decisions, know how to use cryptography in your application, and understand when you or someone is starting to do something dangerous that might require more attention. Never hesitate to ask for an expert's point of view.

"Don't roll your own crypto" must be the most overused cryptography line in software engineering. Yet, these folks are somewhat right. While you should feel empowered to implement or even create your own cryptographic primitives and protocols, you should not use it in a production environment. Producing cryptography takes years to get right: years of learning about the ins and outs of the field, not only from a design perspective but from a cryptanalysis perspective as well. Even experts who have studied cryptography all their lives build broken cryptosystems. Bruce Schneier once famously said, "Anyone, from the most clueless amateur to the best cryptographer, can create an algorithm that he himself can't break." At this point, it is up to you to continue studying cryptography. These final pages are not the end of the journey.

I want you to realize that you are in a privileged position. Cryptography started as a field behind closed doors, restricted only to members of the government or academics kept under secrecy, and it slowly became what it is today: a science openly studied throughout the world. But for some people, we are still very much in a time of (cold) war.

In 2015, Rogaway drew an interesting comparison between the research fields of cryptography and physics. He pointed out that physics had turned into a highly political field shortly after the nuclear bombing of Japan at the end of World War II. Researchers began to feel a deep responsibility because physics was starting to be clearly and directly correlated to the deaths of many and the deaths of potentially many more. Not much later, the Chernobyl disaster would amplify this feeling.

On the other hand, cryptography is a field where privacy is often talked about as though it were a different subject, making cryptography research apolitical. Yet, decisions that you and I take can have a long-lasting impact on our societies. The next time you design or implement a system using cryptography, think about the threat model you'll use. Are you treating yourself as a trusted party or are you designing things in a way where even you cannot access your users' data or affect their security? How do you empower users through cryptography? What do you encrypt? "We kill people based on metadata," said former NSA chief Michael Hayden (http://mng.bz/PX19).

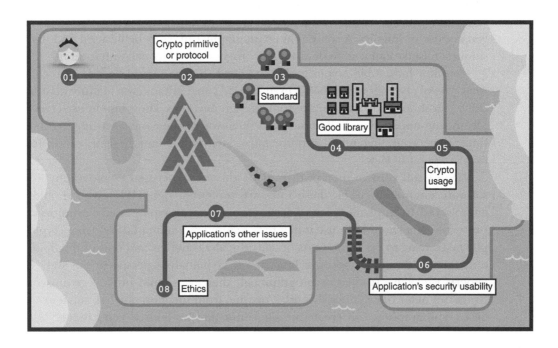

In 2012, near the coast of Santa Barbara, hundreds of cryptographers gathered around Jonathan Zittrain in a dark lecture hall to attend his talk, "The End of Crypto" (https://www.youtube.com/watch?v=3ijjHZHNIbU). This was at Crypto, the most respected cryptography conference in the world. Jonathan played a clip from the television series *Game of Thrones* to the room. In the video, Varys, a eunuch, poses a riddle to the hand of the king, Tyrion. This is the riddle:

> *Three great men sit in a room: a king, a priest, and a rich man. Between them stands a common sellsword. Each great man bids the sellsword kill the other two. Who lives, who dies? Tyrion promptly answers, "Depends on the sellsword," to which the eunuch responds, "If it's the swordsman who rules, why do we pretend kings hold all the power?"*

Jonathan then stopped the clip and pointed to the audience, yelling at them, "You get that you guys are the sellswords, right?"

Summary

- Real-world cryptography tends to fail mostly in how it is applied. We already know good primitives and good protocols to use in most use cases, which leaves their misuse as the source of most bugs.

- A lot of typical use cases are already addressed by cryptographic primitives and protocols. Most of the time, all you'll have to do is find a respected implementation that addresses your problem. Make sure to read the manual and to understand in what cases you can use a primitive or a protocol.

- Real-world protocols are constructed with cryptographic primitives by combining them like Lego. When no well-respected protocols address your problem, you'll have to assemble the pieces yourself. This is extremely dangerous as cryptographic primitives sometimes break when used in specific situations or when combined with other primitives or protocols. In these cases, formal verification is an excellent tool to find issues, although it can be hard to use.

- Implementing cryptography is not just difficult; you also have to think about hard-to-misuse interfaces (in the sense that good cryptographic code leaves little room for the user to shoot themselves in the foot).

- Staying conservative and using tried-and-tested cryptography is a good way to avoid issues down the line. Issues stemming from complexity (for example, supporting too many cryptographic algorithms) is a big topic in the community, and steering away from over-engineered systems has been dubbed "boring cryptography." Be as boring as you can.

- Both cryptographic primitives and standards can be responsible for bugs in implementations due to being to complicated to implement or to vague about what implementers should be wary of. Polite cryptography is the idea of a cryptographic primitive or standard that is hard to badly implement. Be polite.

- The use of cryptography in an application sometimes leaks to the users. Usable security is about making sure that users understand how to handle cryptography and cannot misuse it.
- Cryptography is not an island. If you follow all of the advice this book gives you, chances are that most of your bugs will happen in the noncryptographic parts of your system. Don't overlook these!
- With what you have learned in this book, make sure to be responsible, and think hard about the consequences of your work.

appendix
Answers to exercises

Chapter 2

Can you tell if a hash function provides hiding and binding if used as a commitment scheme?

A hash function is *hiding* thanks to the pre-image resistance property; that is, if your input is random enough so that no one can guess it. To fix that, you can generate a random number and hash it with your input, and later, you can reveal both your input and the random number to *open* your commitment. A hash function is *binding* thanks to the second pre-image resistance property.

By the way, there is no way this string represents 256 bits (32 bytes), right? How is this secure then?

We don't care about collision resistance. We only care about second pre-image resistance. Thus, we can truncate the digest to reduce its size.

Can you guess how the Dread Pirate Roberts (the pseudonym of Silk Road's webmaster) managed to obtain a hash that contains the name of the website?

Dread Pirate Roberts created a lot of keys until one ended up hashing to that cool base32 representation. Facebook did the same and is accessible from facebookcorewwwi.onion (https://facebook.com/notes/protect-the-graph/making-connections-to-facebook-more-secure/1526085754298237). These are called *vanity addresses*.

Chapter 3

Can you figure out how a variable-length counter could possibly allow an attacker to forge an authentication tag?

By observing the following message, where || represents string concatenation, MAC(k, "1" || "1 is my favorite number"), an attacker can forge a valid authentication tag for the eleventh message, MAC(k, "11" | " is my favorite number").

Caution: not all MACs are PRFs. Can you see why?

Imagine that the following function is a valid MAC and PRF: MAC(key, input), then is the following function a valid MAC? NEW_MAC = MAC(key, input) || 0x01? Is it a valid PRF? It is a valid MAC as it prevents forgery, but it's not a valid PRF, as you can easily distinguish the output from a totally random string (because the last byte is always set to 1).

Chapter 6

Using the same shared secret with everyone would be very bad; can you see why?

If I can encrypt messages to you with this shared secret, I can also decrypt messages from other people.

Do you see why you can't use the key exchange output right away?

Remember what you've learned in chapter 5 on key exchanges. In (FF)DH, calculations happen modulo a large prime number *p*. Let's take a small prime number as example, 65,537. In hexadecimal, our *p* is written as 0x010001, and in binary, it is written as 0000 0001 0000 0000 0000 0001. In binary, notice the zeros preceding the first one because we represent our number in bytes (multiple of 8 bits).

If you understand modular arithmetic, you know that numbers modulo this prime *p* will never be larger, meaning that the first 7 bits will always be set to 0. In addition, the eighth bit will most often be set to 0 rather than 1. This is not *uniformly random*. Ideally, every bit should have the same probability of being set to 1 or to 0.

Chapter 7

As you saw in chapter 3, authentication tags produced by MACs must be verified in constant time to avoid timing attacks. Do you think we need to do the same for verifying signatures?

No. This is because the verification of an authentication tag involves a secret key. Verifying a signature only involves a public key and, thus, does not need to be verified in constant time.

Chapter 8

Imagine for a minute that mixing different sources of entropy was done by simply XORing them together. Can you see how this might fail to be contributory?

A backdoored source of entropy could set its output as the XOR of all the other sources of entropy, effectively canceling all entropy to 0.

Signature schemes like BLS (mentioned in figure 8.5 and in chapter 7) produce unique signatures, but this is not true for ECDSA and EdDSA. Do you see why?

In ECDSA, the signer can choose different nonces to produce different signatures for the same key pair and message. While EdDSA is a signature algorithm that deterministically derives the nonce based on the message to be signed, this does not mean that the signer cannot use any nonce if they so choose.

Chapter 9

A compromise of the server's private key at some point in time would be devastating as MITM attackers would then be able to decrypt all previously recorded conversations. Do you understand how this can happen?

The attacker would then be able to rewind history and impersonate the server at the time the handshake was performed. Indeed, the attacker now has the server's private key. All the other information to perform the key exchange and derive the posthandshake symmetric keys is public.

The values `signatureAlgorithm` and `signatureValue` are not contained in the actual certificate, `tbsCertificate`. Do you know why?

The Certificate Authority (CA) needs to sign the certificate, which leads to a paradox: the signature cannot be part of the signature itself. The CA must, thus, append the signature to the certificate. Other standards and protocols might use different techniques. For example, you could include the signature as part of `tbsCertificate` and pretend that it is made of all 0s when you sign or verify the certificate.

Chapter 10

Do you know why the email's content is compressed before it is encrypted and not after?

A ciphertext is indistinguishable from a random string according to the definition of a cipher. Due to this, compression algorithms are incapable of finding patterns to efficiently compress encrypted data. For this reason, compression is always applied before encryption.

Can you think of an unambiguous way of signing a message?

One line: authenticate the context. A way to do this is to include both the sender and the recipient's names and their public keys in the signature and then encrypt that.

Chapter 11

Sometimes applications attempt to fix the issue of the server learning about the user passwords at registration by having the client hash (perhaps with a password hash) the password before sending it to the server. Can you determine if this really works?

Client-side hashing alone does not work as the infamous pass-the-hash attack showed (https://en.wikipedia.org/wiki/Pass_the_hash); if the server stores Alice's hashed password directly, then anyone who steals it can also use it as a password to authenticate as Alice. Some applications perform both client-side hashing and server-side hashing, which, in this case, can perhaps prevent an active attacker from knowing the original password (although an active attacker might be able to disable client-side hashing by updating the code of the client application).

Imagine a protocol where you have to enter the correct 4-digit PIN to securely connect to a device. What are the chances to pick a correct PIN by just guessing?

That's 1 out of 10,000 chances to correctly guess something. You'd be happy if you were playing Lotto with these odds.

index